T0381091

THE COUPLE'S MATCH BOOK

Lighting, Rekindling, or Extinguishing the Flame

Daniel Eckstein, PhD

Order this book online at www.trafford.com
or email orders@trafford.com

Most Trafford titles are also available at major online book retailers.

Printed in the United States of America.

ISBN: 978-1-4269-7198-3 (sc)
ISBN: 978-1-4269-7199-0 (e)

Library of Congress Control Number: 2011909527

Trafford rev. 02/26/2013

 www.trafford.com

North America & international
toll-free: 1 888 232 4444 (USA & Canada)
phone: 250 383 6864 ♦ fax: 812 355 4082

Dedication

To the Goddess, universally known by such names as: Mother Mary, Tara, and Quan Yen. She has been known to me personally as:

- Frances White Eckstein, my mother and original encourager;

- Donna, my beloved "top of the Ferris wheel 4th of July" one and only "sis-ter;"

- Attavia, her young knight in shining armor whose Michelangelo Sistine Chapel finger I never quite touched;

- Judy Gail, my wife for twelve years and now a best friend, the essence of kindness;

- Ammaji, my spiritual teacher;

- Phyliss Cooke, my three decade best friend, colleague, and co-author; and confidant. Phyliss died in 2011.

- Katrina, my Dulcinea.

- To Peggy: Canada blooms . . . . forever

- To Amy: Both my grandmothers died when my parents were 12. You've been that and invaluable in the past decade keeping track of all these contributors. This book would not have been possible had you not been the string that kept my balloon from flying into the clouds. Happy 60th anniversary to both you and Wes—you've lived the wisdom in this book. Amy also died in 2011.

Thanks

My special thanks to: Jon Carlson, for his kind introduction as well as Pat Love, Roy Kern, Frank Walton, and Jeff Zeig; to all the contributors who truly have made this a team effort; and to Amy Zimmerman, Dee Dee Kirk, and Judy Shofner for their invaluable assistance in preparing the manuscript. Ronda Harris has also been an invaluable editor.

Foreword

Many people are surprised to learn that most failed relationships do not suffer from a lack of love. Those who end their marriage frequently love one another very much but just are not satisfied with their relationship with one another. This book will be as good as you care to make it. If you are reading this foreword, the odds are pretty good that you are at least *interested* in repairing relationships. Dan Eckstein and his collaborators have provided the tools necessary to repair couple and family relationships.

Relationship repair is a process. Relationship mechanics (counselors and therapists) provide consumers (families and couples) with the tools. The consumers need to use these tools. The need seems to be very high for these tools; it seems as though couples, however, are willing to live without them or the demand is quite low. Relationships, according to some experts, control the depth of our happiness and maybe our mental health. The problem as to why we are willing to accept poor relationships when tools are available remains a puzzle. Perhaps this is a topic for another book or perhaps families and couples will self-correct once they realize that suffering and relationship are not synonymous terms.

Each of the papers in this collection is a gem. I appreciate their practical nature. I hope that you are moved enough to stop often and put this book down and just relate with others.

Jon Carlson, Psy.D., Ed.D is Distinguished Professor of Psychology and Counseling at Governors State University, University Park. Jon is the author of 40 books, 150 journal articles, and the developer of over 200 DVDs/videotapes.

Dr. Carlson was named one of five "Living Legends in Counseling" in 2004 by the American Counseling Association. Some of Jon's most well known books include: Adlerian Therapy; The Mummy at the Dining Room Table; Bad Therapy; The Client Who Changed Me; American Shaman; Time for a Better Marriage; and Moved by the Spirit: Stories of Spiritual Transformation in the Lives of Leaders.

* * * * * * * * *

It's amazing how this book works. Practical, powerful, and immediately productive. Dr. Eckstein's warmth and wisdom fill these pages; he provides a pathway to love and a guide to good living. Backed by research from the most famous experts in the field, Dr. Eckstein gives us an immediate relationship fix guaranteed to inspire and instruct us in the ways of love. (Pat Love)

Pat Love, Ed.D, is author of *Hot Monogamy, The Truth About Love*, and *How to Improve Your Marriage Without Talking About It*. She has appeared on the Oprah show several times. She is a regular contributor to popular magazines such as *Cosmopolitan, Men's Health, Good Housekeeping, Men's Magazine* and *Woman's World*. Dr. Love is faculty Emeritus, Imago Institute for Relationship Therapy and a recipient of the Smart Marriages Impact Award. She is a Licensed Marriage and Family Therapist, Approved, and a past president of the International Association for Marriage and Family Counseling.

* * * * * * * * * *

The Couple's Match Book:
Lighting, Re-Kindling, or Extinguishing the Flame

Dedication   v

Thanks   vi

Foreword—Jon Carlson, Pat Love   vii

Table of Contents   ix

Preface and Biography—Daniel Eckstein   xv

Chapter I.   Relationship Theory and Research
Introduction

Sections:
1. *The A's and H's of Healthy and Unhealthy Relationships:*   5
    Four Activities for Relationship Renewal (Daniel Eckstein)
    Activity 1: "A" and "H" Relationships
2. *The Seven Methods of Encouragement for Couples*   14
    (Phyliss Cooke and Daniel Eckstein)
    Activity 2: Encouragement Story

Chapter II.   Relationship Inventories and Questionnaires

Sections:
3. *The Noble Eightfold Relationship Matrix* (Phil Ginsburg,   29
    Daniel Eckstein, Yu-Fen Lin, Chi-Sing Li, and Bill Mullener)
    Activity 3: Creating Your Noble Eightfold Relationship Matrix (NERM)
4. *TODAY . . .*   37
5. *Antidotes for Infidelity and Prescriptions for Long Lasting*   38
    Relationships: Four Couples' Activities (Judith A. Nelson,
    Chi-Sing Li, Daniel G. Eckstein, Pedra Ane, and William Mullener)
    Activity 4: Childhood Role Models
    Activity 5: Flexibility and Intimacy
    Activity 6: Assessing Commitment
    Activity 7: Trust and Forgiveness

6. *A Couple's Activity for Understanding Birth Order Effects:*   45
    Introducing the Birth Order Research-Based Questionnaire
    (Daniel Eckstein, Mark A. Sperber, and Kristen Aycock Miller)
    Activity 8: Birth Order Research-Based Questionnaire
    Activity 9: Family of Origin Birth Order Interview Questions

7. *Counseling Is The Answer ... Counseling Is The Answer ...*   56
    But *What Is The Question?* (Daniel Eckstein)
    Activity 10: Twenty-five Questions for Couples and Families
    Activity 11: Further Questions to Ponder

8. *The Cultural Relationship Interview Matrix: Four Activities for*   65
    Couples (Chi-Sing Li, Yu-Fen Lin, Daniel Eckstein)
    Activity 12: Create Your Own Matrix
        My Matrix -- Cultural Relationship Interview Matrix (CRIM)
    Activity 13: Create Your Partner's Matrix (My Partner's Matrix)
        My Prediction/Perception of My Partner's Matrix
    Activity 14: The Cultural Relationship Interview
    Activity 15: Create a Matrix for the Two of You (Our Matrix)
        Our CRIM (Your relationship CRIM as a Couple)

9. *A F.A.M.I.L.Y. Approach to Self-Care: Creating a Healthy*   79
    Balance (Donna Eckstein)
    Activity 16: The F.A.M.I.L.Y. Self-Care Assessment Inventory
    Activity 17: Graphing Your Scores

Chapter III.   Understanding and Respecting Personality Differences

Sections:

10. *The Couple's Personality Preferences Questionnaire (CPPQ)*   99
     (Daniel Eckstein

11. *The "How I Remember My Family" Questionnaire*   108
     Excerpts from Richard E. Watt's "Using Family-of-Origin Recollections in
     Premarital and Marriage Counseling"

12. *The "#1 Priority" Questionnaire For Couples & Families*   111
     (#1 PQ) (Daniel Eckstein)
     Activity 18: #1 PQ

13. *The Pet Relationship Impact Inventory (PRII)* (Daniel Eckstein)   118
     Activity 19: Pet Assessment Questions
     Activity 20: The PRII

14. *Winnie-the-Pooh: A "Honey-Jar" for Me and for You*   131
     (Sharon Kortman and Daniel Eckstein)
     Activity 21: Self and Other Personality Descriptions

        Activity 22: Array Interaction Inventory (Self)

        Activity 23: Array Interaction Inventory (Partner)

15: *The Bushido Matrix for Couple Communication*   149
(Chi-Sing Li, Yu-Fen Lin, Phil Ginsburg, Daniel Eckstein)

        Activity 24: Using the Bushido Matrix Worksheet (BMW)

16. *Creating Respect in Couples: The Couple's Respect Questionnaire (CRQ)*   157
Donna Eckstein, Sarah Eckstein, and Daniel Eckstein

17. *Styles of Conflict Management* (Daniel Eckstein)   171

Chapter IV.   Role Perceptions

Sections:

18. *The Use of Image Exchange in Examining Relationship Role*   177
Perceptions (Daniel Eckstein, Fern Clemmer, and Armando Fierro)

        Activity 25: Image Exchange

        Activity 26: Application to You as a Couple

19. *Relationships as a "Three-Legged Sack Race"* (Daniel Eckstein,   189
Marilyn Leventhal, Sherry Bentley, and Sharon Kelley)

        Activity 27: Your Assessment of Your Relationship

20. *A Dozen Commitment Considerations for Couples* (Amy Kirk,   197
Daniel Eckstein, Sheryl Serres, and Sallie Helms)

        Activity 28: The Couples' Commitment Interview (CCI)

        Activity 29: Integration of Your Interviews

21. *The "Staying Together in Needy Times" (STINT) Couple's*   210
Questionnaire (Daniel Eckstein and Phil Ginsburg)

        Activity 30: The STINT Relationship Checklist

Chapter V.   Role Communication Style

Sections:

22. *The Couple's Gender-Based Questionnaire (CGQ):*   218
Thirty-Three Relationship Considerations (Daniel Eckstein,
Pat Love, Kristen Aycock, and V. Van Wiesner, III)

        Activity 31: The Couple's Gender-Based (CBG) Questionnaire

23. *The Non-Violent Relationship Questionnaire (NVRQ)*   228
(Daniel Eckstein and Lucy La Grassa)

        Activity 32: The NVRQ

        Activity 33: Predication of Your NVRS

24. *A Linguistic "Asking, Promising, Asserting, and Declaring"*   241
Couples' Communication (Daniel Eckstein, Torrey Byles,
and Sherri Bennett)

    Activity 34: Assessing Your Communication as a Couple

    Activity 35: Examples of your Own Four Communication Methods

25. *A Couple's Advance Directives Interview using the Five*   248
     Wishes Questionnaire (Daniel Eckstein and Bill Mullener)

    Activity 36: Five Wishes Questionnaire

Chapter VI.   Problem-Solving Strategies

Sections:

26. *Thirty-three Suggestions for Relationship Renewal*   254
    (Daniel Eckstein and John Jones)

27. *Into the Woods: Introducing the Couples Metaphoric Interview*   260
    Matrices (Sarah Eckstein, Jennifer Straub, Nicole Russo,
    and Daniel Eckstein)

    Activity 37: An Activity for You as a Couple

28. *Walls and Windows: Closing and Opening Behaviors for*   274
    Couples (Daniel Eckstein)

29. *The Angry, The Angrier, and The Angriest Relationships*   276
    (Robert Willhite and Daniel Eckstein)

    Activity 38: The Anger Worksheet

    Activity 39: The Aggression Barometer

    Activity 40: The Anger Expression Inventory (The Anger Scale)

30. *Four Couples' Sleep Satisfaction Interviews:*   290
    Recommendations for Improving your Nights Together
    (Miller "Rocky" Garrison and Daniel Eckstein)

    Activity 41: Sleep Satisfaction Life-line Interview

    Activity 42: Relationship Sleep Metaphors Discussion

31. *"Six-thinking Hats" Problem Solving Model to Couples*   301
    Counseling (Daniel Eckstein, Chi-Sing Li, and Yu-Fen Lin)

32. *Combining Socratic Questions with the ADAPT Problem-solving*   308
    Model Implications for Couples' Conflict Resolution
    (Al Milliren, Mary Milliren and Daniel Eckstein)

    Activity 43: Analyze the Gap

    Activity 44: Develop Resources

    Activity 45: Align Goals

    Activity 46: Planning the Intervention Strategy: go to BED

    Activity 47: Track Implementations

33. *Forgiveness: The Other Relationship "F Word"—A Couple's*   319
    Dialogue (Daniel Eckstein, Shannon McRae, and
    Mark Sperber)

Activity 48: Exploring the Concept of Forgiveness

Activity 49: Dialogue on Religious and Spiritual Relationships

Activity 50: Experiential Activity

34. *Two Couples' Problem Solving Activities:*   333
    The One Hour Conference and A 6-Step Dialectical Method
    (Susan Rosenthal and Daniel Eckstein)

35. *The Process of Early Recollection Reflection (PERR)*   341
    for Couples and Families (Daniel Eckstein, Deborah Vogele Welch
    and Victoria Gamber)

    Activity 51: The PERR Process

    Activity 52: Additional ER Reflection Activity

36. *The Relationship Decision Making Box (RDMB):*   354
    A Questionnaire for Exploring the Decision-Making Process)
    (Nate Larsen, Malcolm Gray, and Daniel Eckstein)

    Activity 53: Scoring your RDMB

Chapter VII.   Closing Comments

Sections:

37. *Cracking the Shell* (Daniel Eckstein)   361
38. *Al Ellis Up Close and Personal* (Al Ellis and Debbie Joffe Ellis)   366
39. *A Dozen Reflections on Writing the "For couples"*   375
    Column in The Family Journal: for the Past 18 Years
    (Daniel Eckstein)

Epilogue   381

Preface

I have chosen the metaphor of a *match book* as the title of this book. There are several meanings for the process of finding and making a match. From a purely biological perspective such a process is necessary for our survival. From an emotional perspective the process of finding, making, maintaining, and even enriching an intimate partnership is one of the most challenging adult development tasks. Forming and maintaining a lasting bond has never been more challenging. Divorce rates continue to rise.

With the increasing impact of the internet in many people's lives around the world, matches have been made through that medium. Many couples have met through Match. Com©, E-Harmony©, or similar on-line services. That's one play on words from the title.

Then there is the match book itself. That's where I've used the development process of fire. "There was a spark" is one way first attractions have been described. The developing process of relationships is then followed with the adjectives of *lighting, re-kindling and extinguishing* the flame which comes from those initial sparks.

For some individuals, the coupling process is fairly straight forward. In many cultures marriages are arranged. In others, the process consists of forging an intimate relationship and maintaining it throughout the adult life cycle literally "until death do us part."

And then there are the rest of us. In the spirit of "you teach best what you most need to learn" concept I have been on both sides of the couples counseling table. I have had two marriages of 13 years each. I lived with another woman in a common law marriage for an additional 3 years.

I have been single the last 15 years. I often say my own relationships are indeed the voyage of the *Titanic.* I both hit and missed some major icebergs along the way. Like my mother used to say in the two decades that passed between my father's death and her own, "I'd rather be alone than wish I was alone." Actually I've focused more on my own Spiritual Path and also in doing what I can in learning from my own personal and professional journey to assist couples in the *lighting, re-kindling,* or *extinguishing* phase of fire in their own relationships.

In my own journey, I've learned to distinguish intimacy from sexuality both with men and with woman. I now cherish deeply caring and cherishing friendships extending three decades or more. A recent friend when I was 15 re-emerged. My high school best friend and teammate remains a special relationship. Three Adlerian psychology friends of 40 years I consider to be adopted brothers. I've also fallen deeply and madly in love with a Spiritual teacher with whom I have studied meditation for 26 years.

As a licensed psychologist for 40 years and a licensed professional counselor-supervisor for 5 years, I've also shared the many roller coaster rides of the coupling and uncoupling process. One of the most challenging situations for me as a therapist has been when a couple comes for counseling and one hopes I can help them save their marriage while the other already has one foot out the door. That often but not always involves a new *flame-filled* intimate relationship. Getting them on the same page often means confronting that discrepancy.

I've also learned the value of *focus* in my times with such couples. One concrete way of changing the frequent focus of blame and anger sounds like this: "Apart from what is going on between the two of you right now, I'd like you to consider the intra-personal consequences of your possible separation. Often underneath the anger between you and your partner, there is an even deeply experienced grief at the *loss of a dream*. There are many dreams you had for both you and your partner in this relationship." The anger often melts into tears of genuine sadness. "Grief is the price of caring," I say. "And in many ways a divorce is more challenging than a death because you partner is still alive."

I am also a university teacher and a researcher. I have both taught marriage and family courses. I continually research proven theories and intervention techniques. Since 1993 I have written a quarterly column called "For Couples" in *The Family Journal: Counseling and Therapy for Couples and Families*. It is the journal of the International Association of Marriage and Family therapists which is a division of the American Counseling Association.

Most of the time I have collaborated with colleagues who are making positive contributions to counseling couples. The column features activities couples can do together or individually for their own relationship development, maintenance, and renewal. Often the extinguishing part of the cycle is best helped by a trusted Religious or Spiritual Teacher, and/ or a psychologist, counselor or social worker.

From those columns I've put together *The Couple's Match* Book: *Lighting, Re-Kindling, or Extinguishing the Flame*. My contributing colleagues and I have attempted to combine relationship theory in practical ways so you as a couple can use that wisdom in your own partnership. One of the consequences of an obsession with work is that often time is not spent nurturing the partnership at home. Five hours a week has been shown by John Gottman and Nan Shivers to significantly improve relationships.

In my column and in this book I have adopted the following four-fold relationship assessment tools proposed by Jay Haley in his book *Uncommon Therapy* (1973/1993):

1. *Understanding and respecting personality differences*
2. *Role Perceptions:* The *job description* each of you has for each other; are you on the same page (goal alignment is how Adlerian therapists call it)
3. *Communication skills:* They are a skill that can be learned, practiced, and improved if each of you is willing
4. *Problem solving skills*: Couples who stay together tend to have no fewer actual challenges than do couples who divorce; what distinguishes them is a problem-solving versus blame and punishment perspective

When working with couples I often ask them in the first session to give their own rating regarding their perceived satisfaction on each of those four variables, one being low and ten being high. I ask each partner to cite examples of that personal rating. A difference of three or more points between partners is most often a source of conflict in relationships. That's often a concrete way of establishing a benchmark of their current relationship. It also provides a shared nomenclature that I can use in later sessions in conceptualizing challenges.

The Couple's Match Book: Lighting, Re-Kindling, or Extinguishing the Flame is organized by first featuring relationship theory and research. Activities are featured for assessment purposes. Four sections follow that focus on personality, role perceptions, communication, and problem-solving as described above. A typical format for each article is to include an introduction to the concept of focus. This is followed by some type of experiential activity by you the couple. It may involve a questionnaire, an interview, or a similar way to have you concretely apply the topic of the article. A brief review of some literature and/or an actual case study is then presented. Implications and applications for you as a couple conclude the activity.

It is expected that couples will pick and choose the particular activities that are most appropriate for you.

The final section of the book is made up of personal stories written by couples themselves. I find them inspiring. This is where real life experiences are shared by individuals and couples who have shown the courage to be transparent with you. One writer initially wanted to withdraw her own story of abuse because of the shame she felt in acknowledging how she allowed this to happen. Thankfully, she changed her mind by telling me "if just one woman finds hope in my story, then it has been worth it."

I am especially pleased that Albert Ellis, one of the giants in the counseling field wrote an intimate piece about a love of his life, Debbie Joffrey Ellis, that he found in his 90s. Their comments on what each means to the other both in life when it was written and later after the death of Al gives me goose bumps each time I write or reflect on that eternal love.

That's in fact one of the encouraging concepts I hope you will consider. The experience of deep and abiding love truly transcends all time and space. The love to and from my mother and my father burn brightly in my heart decades after their death.

Even if your own partner leaves you, remember the love that is in your heart can indeed be an eternal flame. That doesn't mean to stalk or to never let go of the other person. It does mean that your own experience is under your control relative to matters of the heart. This is a book written to you and about you as a couple. If your partner is unwilling or unable to complete the activities with you, it's also a concrete self-assessment for you personally in relation to forming and nurturing a meaningful match in your own life.

The Couple's Match Book: Lighting, Re-Kindling, or Extinguishing the Flame can be useful for couples in the pre-commitment phase, the maintenance and renewal phase, and also as a way of helping conceptualize issues in the ending of a relationship. While written to be an activity for you as a couple, you are invited to complete the activities and/or to discuss your responses with a trusted Religious/ Spiritual/Therapeutic confidant. You can look on my website, www.leadershipbyencouragement.com for all of the activity templates.

Just as the existential question and answer of how a musician gets to Carnegie Hall, hopefully *Match Book* can help provide a concrete way of enhancing your skills by *practice, practice, practice.*

Commit five hours a week to one of the most important and yet far too often taken for granted relationships in your life and I am confident your relationship and you personally will be richly rewarded. I hope you find some useful tools for assisting that commitment within the pages of this book.

It takes a lot of courage to risk being vulnerable by committing to an intimate relationship. Good for you!!

If I and my colleagues can provide just one of two helpful concepts I hope the exchange can be a fair one relative to both your expense and time spent on these *fiery* activities.

* * * * * * * * * *

There is no vow that can create love. And there is no love that can be vowed if it true.

A man will quest a lifetime to learn to love. And love is expressed in happiness, in joy, in what is natural. And to the level of what is natural, love is expressed fully. Love cannot be commanded; it cannot be contrived. Communication cannot occur where it has not already occurred. That which comes in the name of the Father comes without recognition comes without purpose of being, but for the purpose of being which Love is.

The spiritualist seeking wisdom does not know love; the spiritualist seeking love does not know wisdom, yet its wisdom expressed only as love is the wisest.

The encyclopedia of how to enlighten is written well in many great books. Yet no man can write an encyclopedia of love. Love is a quiet thing; it is private intuition; it is outrageous; it is beyond the ability to control. The madness that results from love; the joy that results from only love; the pain that results from love—each is expressed in jubilance.

Swami Paramanda Saraswatti, Workshop
The Foundation for Meditative Studies
Ashland, Oregon, Nov. 17, 2010.

Daniel Eckstein

Biography of Daniel Eckstein

Daniel Eckstein, Ph.D., is an author, psychologist, public speaker, workshop presenter, consultant, and communications specialist. He is a professor of Medical Psychology at Saba University School of Medicine, Saba, National Caribbean, Netherlands. He is also on the staff at the Saba memorial Hospital and is a part-time on-line faculty for Capella University, Minneapolis, Minnesota.

For the past eighteen years, Dr. Eckstein has written a quarterly column "For Couples" in the *Family Journal.* He is author of *Psychological Fingerprints, Leadership by Encouragement, Raising Respectful Kids in a Rude World, Psychological Fingerprints: Life-Style Assessment,* and *Leadership Repair*. He is a former president of the North American Society of Adlerian Psychology and the recipient of the diplomat from the same group.

Dr. Eckstein is a master of teambuilding, group problem solving, strategic planning, and in understanding how one's personality impacts work. He used these skills when he played professional football for two years with the Green Bay Packers and the Hamilton Ontario Tiger-Lats.

Chapter I:
Relationship Theory and Research

An Introduction to
Repairing and Renewing Couples' Relationships

The very joy of intimate relationships is often coupled with profound hurt and wounding. Opening one's heart to love is one of the most courageous and the most vulnerable things to do. Kahlil Gibran, the legendary Lebanese poet, wrote these classic lines about relationships:

When love beckons to you follow him,
Though his ways are hard and steep.
And when his wings enfold you yield to him,
Though the sword hidden among his pinions may wound you.
And when he speaks to you believe in him,
Though his voice may shatter your dreams
    as the north wind lays waste the garden.

For even as love crowns you so shall he crucify you.
Even as he is for your growth so is he for your pruning.
Even as he ascends to your height and caresses your tenderest branches
    that quiver in the sun,
So shall he descend to your roots and shake them in their clinging to the earth . . . .

Love has no other desire but to fulfill itself.
But if you love and must needs have desires, let these be your desires:
To melt and be like a running brook that sings its melody to the night.
To know the pain of too much tenderness.
To be wounded by your own understanding of love;
And to bleed willingly and joyfully.
To wake at dawn with a winged heart and give thanks for another day of loving;
To rest at the noon hour and meditate love's ecstasy;
To return home at eventide with gratitude;
And then to sleep with a prayer for the beloved in your heart and a song of praise
    upon your lips. [1]

The poignant phrase, "For even as love crown you so shall he crucify you" richly captures the approach-avoidant polarity confronting many of us in relationships. Finding the balance between a sense of self while also bonding with others is a major task of adult development.

For many of us, the heart is quite sensitive and easily hurt. For others, if we were wounded early in life, we feel that, in the classic words of a song by Simon and Garfunkel, "I am a rock, I am an island . . . and a rock feels no pain."

Consider the analogy of a raincoat—such a garment helps protect us when it is raining. But later, when the sun comes out, if we are still wearing the raincoat, the very garment that once protected us now insulates and isolates us.

Most of us have been wounded in relationships—this book is meant to help improve relationships, understanding and respecting personality differences, negotiating job descriptions, and improving communication are all problem-solving strategies that are helpful approaches to improving intimacy between couples.

A sad reality in our world is that this book on relationships in general and on wounding in particular is a luxury for more than 80% of the world. Using the wisdom of Abraham Maslow's hierarchy of needs, physiological needs (food, water, warmth, reproduction) are our most basic and fundamental needs. Next come safety—a home and health, which are less fearful needs. For much of the world, these are the primary and fundamental needs. It is only then that the third need, the task of love, can be addressed. Esteem needs and self-actualization complete Maslow's hierarchy. He described physiological and safety issues as *D needs,* meaning deficiency was the primary driving force behind physiological and safety issues. The latter three he called *B needs*—the positive effort to be more happy than sad in the world.

This book addresses the need for relationship, the desire for partnership which goes beyond basic biological procreation by addressing the hunger of the heart. But it is also here that emotional wounding also occurs. There are countless ways in which we can be wounded. This is not a book about how or why this occurs. Rather, this is a book about how to renew, revitalize, and repair such wounding. The activities suggested here are not meant to replace how others (counselors, coaches, religious figures, and even friends) can often be helpful in assisting couples to better hear and understand each other. But an underlying philosophy presented in these articles is that couples who take time to discuss their responses to these worksheets can understand, communicate, and problem-solve with one another.

Psychologists talk often about bonding and attachment issues that occur early in life. During that formative period of life, some of us decided to have secure, loving, constant bonding with the significant others in our lives. Others chose a more anxious, fearful, and doubtful belief that we feel safe forming intimate, lasting relationships. Still others withdrew from pain through a decision of withdrawal, becoming the "island with no bridges to and from it" poignantly described above.

But no matter how early or how long the pattern has been repeated, the theme of existential philosophers is the belief that people can cause change to occur. And sometimes the change happens in an instant.

Many times, the process of change is gradual and imperceptible. And habits are difficult to break. Recovering alcoholics and those recovering from other addictive behaviors vividly recall one instant when a new decision was made.

So too it is with the habits we have learned in relationships. The activities, the psychological theory, and the scientific research behind them are meant to help individuals become more aware of the changing nature of relationships and then to realize that new decisions are possible in the present moment. Tony Robbins likes to say "the past does not equal the future."

So too with relationship challenges. The passage of time can indeed heal all wounds. Other times it happens in a moment of insight, coupled with a commitment to change.

Endnotes

[1] Reprinted from *The Prophet*, by Kahlil Gibran, by permission of Alfred A. Knopf, Inc. Copyright © 1923 by Kahlil Gibran and renewed 1951 by Mary G. Gibran and Administrators C.T.A. of Kahlil Gibran Estate.

Section 1:

The A's and H's of Healthy and Unhealthy Relationships: Four Activities for Relationship Renewal

Daniel Eckstein

Here are five activities couples can do with each other for the purpose of renewing their relationship. Consider the following analogy involving the letters *A* contrasted with the letter *"H."* Tony Reilley, a colleague consulting with the author, described the insights he gained from marital counseling through three significant marital partner relationships like this . . .

He described his first two relationships as being the letter A. Consider the three lines comprising the letter—one straight line on the left, a leaning line on right connected at the top and lastly the cross bar between them. In his first marriage his wife *leaned* heavily against him. The connecting cross bar (their relationship) while strong, bore so much pressure, it eventually collapsed from the shear continuous stress on it. With this weight, the marriage didn't work out. In his second relationship, while he liked rescuing the *wounded bird* (his hurt partner), there was no possibility for long-term growth together.

Tony described his third relationship as being the letter H. This consists of two strong independent lines but the connecting *cross bar* line showed that their interdependence was not as strong. Thus, in their personal strength, there was less power between them due to more upright parallel lines.

Please note: All Activities are numbered sequentially throughout the book. and you can look on my website, www.leadershipbyencouragement.com for all of the activity templates.

Now reflect on this model both for current and past relationships.

Activity 1: "A" and "H" Relationships

Answer these questions individually and then discuss them as a couple, if possible.

1. What are some A type relationships you know now or have known?
2. How about the contrasting letter H relationships? What was (is) different in these relationships?
3. What was (could) be necessary in your current relationship(s) to shift from an A to an H?
4. What might such a shift gain you?

---

5. What might such a change cost you?
6. Or consider another relationship metaphor—consider the images of a balloon and a string. in what ways are you like a balloon in your significant relationships?
7. In what ways are you the string in your significant relationships? One can complement the other if each are mutually appreciated in a relationship. How is that balance in yours?

The "H" metaphor can be restated to mean that each individual in a relationship leading to marriage is to be of equal strength as a foundation of this new family unit. Pillars will not support a building unless they are firmly anchored, placed in parallel positions, and bear equal weight.

The author uses the "Relationship as a Three-legged Sack Race" metaphor as another way of contrasting the following three different attachment styles. Burlap couples' sack race is used to illustrate the various ways of bonding with others attachment styles. "All four legs in the sack" is an example of *enmeshment*, no differentiation between the couple. "No legs in the sack" indicates disengagement, two or more individuals living parallel lives under the same roof. "One leg in the sack and one out" represents an *interdependent* relationship while simultaneously valuing and honoring each individual as just that.[2]

The Healthy Couple: A Brief Sketch

Healthy individuals are usually attracted to other optimally functioning people in their interpersonal transactions. Using the concept of Abraham Maslow's [3] hierarchy of needs, they are seeking to fulfill Being (B) needs, not Deficiency (D) needs for sharing and for enriching their lives in an intimate relationship. They are not clinging in a desperate way because they are empty nor do they fear they will be unable to survive alone. Rollo May richly contrasted the difference as being "I need you because I love you" with the idea "I love you because I need you." [4]

Maslow depicts healthy individuals as being highly evolved and mature. A solid sense of personal identity provides the capacity for true intimacy. As fully integrated people they are much more likely to choose mates who also have a sure sense of their own being and boundaries. Such individuals have the desire and capacity for a reciprocal, constantly evolving, intimate relationship.

Maslow characterized the self-actualizing healthy person as courageous, spontaneous, innovative, integrated, self-accepting, and expressive. Such individuals frequently gravitate toward healthy partners. These become healthy couples who cope well with the usual transitions and reoccurring challenges in everyone's life.

The healthy couple appears to be a multidimensional, complex, non-summative unit. The ten dimensions the Timberlawn group[5] concretely delineated are:

1. What is the *systems orientation* with respect to the external world?
   Healthy couples perceive themselves as a unit in which their relationship to each other is special and precious. Sometimes they choose to be together as a couple, at home or participating in work related social activities, enjoying each other's company.

2. What are the *boundaries* between individuals and between generations? Healthy couples are cognizant of and comfortable with their adult identities; they do not need their children to parent them nor to become symptomatic to bond together. If they have children, they can leave them free to participate in age-appropriate activities and non-family as well as family relationships. The same is true in relation to their own parents. They are respected and cared about but are not allowed to come between the couple and the commitment to privacy with each other.

3. *Boundary* issues also involve the recognition that individuals require privacy, and from such quiet inner alone time, couples can then chart new directions.

4. What kind of *communication* occurs? There are few double-bind communications between the healthy couple. Wishes and expectations are most often clearly conveyed. Each person's verbal and non-verbal message is concordant. The content or message and the intent or metamessage, consistent. Functioning couples creatively seek solutions and communicate in unique and varied ways. They use a broad repertoire of exchanges sent through olfactory, kinesthetic, visual, tactile, and auditory channels of communication. Each person remains an individual; therefore, (s)he does not want to look, act, or sound alike. Paradoxically, the healthy also often like to function in tandem as one unit.

5. What is the distribution of power; who assumes leadership and control? The relationship is likely to be equalitarian and mutually supportive. The parents are often quite equally matched and probably shift in terms of lead-taking on different issues in accordance with who feels most strongly about a given matter. When there are children, power and control are not abdicated to them. Conversation is liberally laced with "I" statements expressing personal ideas and feelings. Children of such a union sense the strong parental alliance and are rarely allowed to *divide and conquer*. Their core images do not become split into viewing one parent as good and one as bad. Each may assertively express his or her viewpoints and needs, yet neither is likely to resort to downgrading, sabotaging or acquiescing.

6. What is the permissible and expressed *affective range*, and to what is this conducive in terms of intimacy and closeness? The healthy couple are in touch with and expresses a wide range of emotions. Laughter, tears, sadness, and joy are shared. Losses can be discussed and mourning is permitted and understood. They frequently

have fun together and believe life should encompass the pursuit of contentment and pleasure. Work and play may be intertwined. Optimism, humor, and a sense of the absurdity of life are apt to be attributes they both possess.

7. Are *autonomy and individuality* encouraged or discouraged? Through their own more self-sufficient and self-determining niche in the family and in the large world, healthy parents encourage their children to pursue their own choices by paradoxically both guiding and concurrently setting them free (roots and wings). They are much less likely to go into severe depression or to experience more than a fleeting empty nest syndrome when their children depart and the couple are in their middle years.

8. Healthy couples have productive ways for coping with and for replacing dysfunctional solutions. They believe their own strength and adaptability and reach out to appropriate people and resources when the need arises if they cannot manage on their own. They do not expect life to be problem free, and they do not become profane when something distressing occurs. Thus, they are reframed until they become stressors for which the couple then seeks the most efficacious course of action.

9. Is there a *problem solving and negotiation* approach to handling disagreements and decision-making? Negotiation is a decidedly different transactional mode than compromise or conciliation. Negotiation is hearing the other's input and trying to resolve stalemates at the highest level by drawing upon everybody's suggestions. To negotiate successfully, each participant needs verbal skills, the ability to engage the issues, and skills for listening to the other's position.

10. Does the couple have a sense of purpose and meaning in life and a *transcendental value system*, or do they feel alienated and adrift in the world? Healthy couples exhibit a clear and shared belief system. They believe their life matters and have a deep and abiding sense of meaning and purpose.

Seven Marriage Principles

John Gottman and Nan Silver have written an excellent book entitled *The Seven Principles for Making Marriage Work*.[6] Based on as little time as a fifteen minute couple's interview, they are able to predict divorce with a better than 90% success rate. Gottman and Silver stress that happily married couples have what they call an *emotionally intelligent marriage*; they are optimistic that it is a skill that can be learned by most couples.

Marriage Statistics

Gottman and Silver note the chance of a first marriage ending in divorce over a 40-year period is now over 67% Half of all divorces will occur in the first 7 years. Other studies find the divorce rate for second marriages to be almost 10% higher than for first marriages.

Research by Lois Verbaugge and James House of the University of Michigan indicates that an unhappy marriage can increase your chances of getting sick by roughly 35% and even shorten your life by an average of 4 years. People who are happily married live longer, healthier lives than either divorced people or those who are unhappily married.

Predicting Divorce

Here are six specific warning signs that have assisted Gottman & Silver in obtaining 90+% accuracy in predicting a couple's divorce in interviews in what they call the *love lab*.

1. Harsh Startup: A counselor can predict the outcome of a conversation based on the *first three minutes* of the fifteen-minute interaction 96% of the time. This is the first divorce warning signal.

2. The Four Horseman: Gottman & Silver have identified what they have creatively called *the Four Horseman of the Apocalypse* These four horsemen clip-clop into the heart of a marriage in the following order: *criticism, contempt, defensiveness and stonewalling."*
   Horseman #1: Criticism—Criticism is finding fault or blaming your partner.
   Horseman #2: Contempt—Contempt, the most destructive of the four horsemen, is poisonous to a relationship because it conveys disgust.
   Horseman #3: Defensiveness is actually a way of blaming your partner by saying, in effect, "The problem isn't *me*, it's you."
   Horseman #4: According to Gottman and Silver, "a *stonewaller* . . . tends to look away or down without uttering a sound. . . . Stonewalling usually arrives later . . . than the other three horsemen. It takes time for the negativity created by the first three horsemen to come overwhelming enough that stonewalling becomes an understandable out."
   It is not the mere presence of these negative signs that dooms the couple to failure. In fact, Gottman and Silver say, "You'll find examples of all four horsemen and even occasional flooding in stable marriages. But when the four horsemen take up *permanent* residence, when either partner begins to feel flooded routinely, the relationship is in serious trouble."

3. *Flooding:* Flooding means that a spouse's negativity is so overwhelming and so sudden, that it leaves the partner in shock. The person then becomes anxious and hyper-vigilant about preparing for the next attack to which he or she feels powerless to defend. Frequently a partner deals with the fear by simply withdrawing emotionally from the relationship.

4. *Body Language:* First, the heart speeds up. Hormonal changes occur including the secretion of adrenaline, resulting in a fight or flight response. Blood pressure also

often increases. Problem-solving skills diminish as a primal fight or flight defensive posture is utilized.

5. *Failed Repair Attempts:* Not only do repair attempts defuse emotional tension between spouses, they also can help rescue relationships by lowering the stress level and by preventing the heart from racing and making one feel flooded.

6. *Bad Memories*: Couples feeling negative toward their spouse frequently re-write and remember their past from a negative rather than a positive perspective. Some couples may seek counseling; others disengage by being and merely living under the same roof as the spouse. Divorce, affairs, or leading parallel lives are some the ways couples revolve the crises of their marriages.

7 Ways of Repairing Marriage

Fortunately, in the immortal words of Yogi Berra "It ain't over till it's over." Here are seven principles Gottman and Shivers suggest for repairing wounded relationships:

Principle 1: Enhance Your Love Maps

Successful couples know each other's world, something Gottman and Silver describe as ". . . having a richly detailed *love map* . . . for that part of your brain where you store all the relevant information about your partner's life . . . those couples have made plenty of cognitive room for their marriage. They remember the major events in each other's history, and they keep updating their information as the facts and feelings of their spouse's world change . . . No wonder the biblical term for sexual love is to 'know'."[7]

Principle 2: Nurture Your Fondness and Admiration

They recommend that by focusing on your past, you can often detect what they call "embers of positive feelings. Couples who put a positive spin on their marriage's history are likely to have a happy future as well. When happy memories are distorted, it's a sign that the marriage needs help."[8]

Principle 3: Turn toward Each Other Instead of Away

Here is another creative metaphor they use relative to having an *emotional bank account.* "Partners who characteristically turn toward each other rather than away are putting money in the bank. They are building up emotional savings that can serve as a cushion when times get rough, when they're faced with a major life stress or conflict."[9]

Principle 4: Let Your Partner Influence You; It is very encouraging to feel you make a positive difference in your partner's life.

Principle 5: Solve Your Solvable Problems

This can best be demonstrated by softening your startup; learning to make and receive repair attempts; soothing yourself and each other; compromising; and being tolerant of each other's faults.

Principle 6: Overcome Gridlock

Gridlock is a good indication that the hopes and dreams of the couple are not being met.

Principle 7: Create Shared Meaning

The more couples speak candidly and respectfully with each other, the more likely there is to be a blending of a shared sense of meaning.

The Seven Principles for Making Marriage Work also contain a number of useful activities and exercises couples can use illustrative of much of Gottman and Silver's seminal couples research. Seligman[10] notes that Gottman and Silver predicted accurately which marriages would improve over the years. Such couples devote an extra five hours per week to their marriage. Here are specific recommendations for how couples can nourish their relationship.

- *Partings.* Before these couples say goodbye every morning, they find out one thing that each is going to do that day (2 minutes x 5 days = 10 minutes).
- *Reunions.* At the end of each workday, these couples have a low-stress reunion conversation (20 minutes x 5 days = 1 hour, 40 minutes).
- *Affection.* Touching, grabbing, holding, and kissing, all laced with tenderness and forgiveness (5 minutes x 7 days = 35 minutes).
- *One weekly date.* Just the two of you in relaxed atmosphere, updating your love (2 hours once a week).
- *Admiration and appreciation.* Every day, genuine affection and appreciation is given at least once (5 minutes x 7 days = 35 minutes). given at least once (5 minutes x 7 days = 35 minutes).

Emotional Alchemy

In *Emotional Alchemy*, Tara Bennett-Goleman[11] relates Buddhist philosophy concepts such as *mindfulness* and the cognitive behavioral term *schemes* in a creative combination. She quotes an acupuncturist who defined alchemy as "accepting everything in the pot without trying to reject or correct it—seeing that even the negative is part of the learning and healing." Such a concept is essential for couples and families who have decided their mission is to change each another. According to Bennett-Goldman, "Mindfulness, refined awareness, is the fire in this inner alchemy . . . Mindfulness entails a new way of paying attention, a way to expand the scope of awareness while refining its precision."

Piaget introduced the term *schemas* to illustrate ways that we are organizing information. Early in life we form board categories based on our childhood and adolescent experiences. The following ten major identified schemas are: *abandonment; deprivation; subjugation; mistrust; unlove-ability; exclusion; vulnerability; failure; perfectionism*; and *entitlement*. Such schemas often result in experiencing these experiences more readily than others, plus minimizing one's belief in being able to problem solve that particular issue.

In order to assist couples in becoming more aware of their schemes, Bennet-Goleman suggests the following five steps.

1. *Acknowledge*—Realize that you are preoccupied, or you're overreacting, or you did or say something in appropriate.
2. *Be open to your feelings*—Schemes have distinctive emotional flavors: abandonment triggers anxiety, mistrust elicits rage; deprivation can foster a deep sadness.
3. *Notice your thoughts*—What are you thinking? What are you telling yourself about what happened, what you did or said?
4. *What does this remind you of?*—Have you had other similar episodes? Does this remind you of any episodes or feelings from your early years?
5. *Look for a pattern*—Can you see some consistency with other times you've had similar reactions?[12]

Summary

In this chapter, four models, questionnaires, and related activities have addressed what noted marriage and family therapists have identified as distinguishing characteristics of happy versus unhappy couples. It has meant to provide an overview to some representative core issues that can be an essential first step for couples in identifying and then repairing their relationship utilizing a problem-solving approach.

Marriage—as its veterans know well—is the continuous process of getting used to things you hadn't expected.

Tom Mullen[13]

Endnotes

[2]
Eckstein, D., Levanthal, M., Bentley, S., & Kelley, S. (1999) Relationships as a "three-legged sack race". *The Family Journal, 7*, 4, 399-405.

[3]
Maslow, A. (1968). *Toward a psychology of being* (2nd Ed.) New York: Van Nostrand

[4]
May, R. (1995). *Love and Will*. New York: Delacorte Press.

[5] Bowers, M.B., Steidl, J. Rabiovitch, D., Brenner, J.W., & Nelson, J.C. "Psychotic illness in midlife" In W.H. Norton & T.J. Scaramella (Eds.) *Mid-life: developmental and clinical issues.* New York: Brunner/Mazel. (1980): 73-84.

[6] Gottman, J.M., & Silver, N. (1999). *The seven principals for making marriage work* New York: Three Rivers Press.

[7] *Ibid.,* p. 48

[8] *Ibid.,* p. 64

[9] *Ibid.,* p. 50

[10] Seligman, M. (2002). *Authentic Happiness.* New York: Simon & Schuster.

[11] Bennett-Goleman, T. (1999). *Emotional alchemy: How the mind can heal the heart* New York: Harmony Books. p. 6

[12] *Ibid.,* p. 86.

[13] Mullen, Tom. As cited in Glenn Van Ekeren (1994) *Speaker's source book II.* New York: Prentice Hall.

Section 2:

The Seven Methods of Encouragement for Couples

Phyliss Cooke and Daniel Eckstein

Introduction

Encouragement is a key skill in couple's understanding and nurturing one another. Dinkmeyer and Eckstein[1] define encouragement as "a process that focuses on the individual's resources and potential in order to enhance self-esteem and self-acceptance. Discouragement is based on lack of belief in one's abilities to find solutions and to make positive movement. Encouragement is strongly correlated with an optimistic philosophy of life, whereas discouragement is too often synonymous with pessimism."[2]

Dinkmeyer and Eckstein summarize their *Leadership by Encouragement* philosophy as follows: "Successful encouragement is an emotional experience that translates into cognitive decisions. To encourage is to realize that although there are negative and positive emotions, ultimately it is one's own perception that makes a profound difference in one's view of, response to, and approach to life. Encouragement is one of the practical building blocks that can help bridge the gap between our potential and our self-imposed limitations."[3]

Adlerian psychiatrist Rudolf Dreikers said, "Humans need encouragement like plants need water." In a previous article in *The Family Journal*, Eckstein, et al. described *The Four Directions of Encouragement*[4] this way: To encourage requires a subtle shift of focus in a world in which people are too often bombarded about shortcomings and the deficiencies of their birth, their parents, their culture, their organization, and, of course, themselves. Those encouraging people have the ability to perceive a spark of divinity in everyone and then to act as a mirror that reflects that goodness to them.

To encourage is to unite such dualities as: labor/management, male/female, Democrat/Republican, black/white. Encouraging persons have *cue ball* personalities—they make things happen as contrasted with an *eight ball* personality that sits passively on the table waiting to be knocked around. Encouragers are trendsetters who help translate dreams into reality.

Some of our most powerful encouraging role models have been such notable spiritual teachers as Jesus Christ in the West and the Buddha in the East. The greatest leaders are the ones who truly inspire us to seek the *more* of life, the ones who help us to remember our dreams, the ones who touch our hearts with a phenomenal ability to see beauty in all things. They inspire us to new heights because of their ability to assist us in seeking, and ultimately believing, that we will indeed find our own personal heaven.

Successful encouragement is a felt emotional experience that translates to cognitive decisions. It is sometimes impossible to put encouragement into words because it is a felt emotional experience that translates to cognitive decisions. The profound simplicity of encouragement is that it is an attitude that inspires and empowers. To encourage is to realize that although there truly is a dark side and a light side, ultimately it is one's own perception of a glass half-full versus half-empty that makes a profound difference in one's approach to life's challenges.

To be in the presence of what has indeed been the darkness while nonetheless seeing the potential goodness-lightness-within all things is a characteristic of our encouraging heroes. Carl Rogers described it as an actualizing tendency, the desire within human beings to be *more*.

A compassionate approach to encouragement from and to the heart's center creates an opportunity for the divinity within each person to rise. During the present political, economic, and spiritual global challenges, there is a brightness that inspires hope and confidence in a belief in a better world. Encouragers can make a difference by using their own unique gifts to inspire others to reach for their dreams.

In this article, couples will be invited to interview each other. A suggested format developed by the co-authors along with John Jones will be introduced below. Following that, the authors will identify seven most re-occurring content themes based on interviews with more than 500 people.

Encouragement Interviews

Instructions: For best results, it is suggested that one partner interview the other and discuss it at a first meeting, if possible. A follow-up interview with the other partner is suggested.

The benefit of such a structure is that the focus ideally stays on the partner describing who was an encourager and how they were encouraged. If separate meetings are not possible, a brief break is suggested between the changes of interviewer/sharer roles. If one's partner is not available, one can interview him or herself by recording personal responses. More than one encouragement story can, of course, be related. Sometimes taking different time periods such as early childhood (1-5); elementary school age (6-11), etc., is another way to focus on encouragement at different lifespan development chronological times.

The source of the encouragement can be a person, a pet, or an inanimate object such as a book, music or simply witnessing an event involving others.

The objective of the interview activity is to help the subject recall a person or an event from which they drew encouragement. After conducting the interview, review the *Seven Methods of Encouragement* identified by the authors in their study, then see if the method of encouragement in your recollection is similar to the seven methods the authors have identified.

Here is the suggested encouragement story interview format the authors have used with more than 1,000 individuals over the past five years.

Activity 2: Encouragement Story

The Recollection	Your Response
The person (or source) of the encouragement was . . .	
If the source was a person, what is your relationship to the person who encouraged you:	
What the person said about you or to you:	
What was the situation in which the encouragement occurred?	
Your age at the time of the event:	
Looking back, how does this encouragement relate to the person you have become?	

The Seven Methods of Encouragement

Co-author Phyliss Cooke conducted a content analysis of the encouragement stories for the most-frequently re-occurring themes. The 1000 person interview sample consisted of approximately 60% women and 40% men. Ages ranged from 18-80; the mean age was 33 years. The geographic distribution of participants in the study was 40% U.S; 30% Canada; 20% Turkey and Turkish Cypriots; 10% other countries (Iran, Australia, and Saudi Arabia).

The seven content analysis categories that emerged are listed from the most frequently occurring story themes to the least occurring themes were:

Role Model
Identifying Strengths and Weaknesses
Consistency of Support over the Long Haul
Seeing the Person as Special
Passionate Inspiration
Supporting a Person's Special Interests
Encouraging Career Choices

Representative encouragement stories for each category follow each of the seven themes. Each participant named signed a form giving permission for his or her story to be quoted.

The Seven Categories of Influencing Through Encouragement

1. **Role Model:** This is based on the principle that "I'd rather *see* a sermon than *hear* one any day." Social learning psychologists stress that modeling and imitation are two primary forms of learning. Fear of consequences seems to be as influential as the anticipation of rewards in adopting a role model.
   Coach to teenager—"I'm going to chew you out and you'd better come back tomorrow for more . . . that's how life is. "That is how I coach now, no excuses!"
   "I learned how to be a lady by watching how she behaved toward others."
   "I learned how to be a man."
   "I was constantly praised and encouraged for small achievements and I learned the importance of token rewards: smiles, hugs, kind words."

Virginia Hoffman's father was a positive role model to her. He said, "Virginia, people can take away you house, your job, take away everything but they can not take away your education." He put $7000 aside for me to go to college. Virginia notes that, "I raised my kids same way my father raised us. He taught me to think for myself."

Zoe Christo credits her grandmother's positive influence on her as a child. Her grandmother told her, "You are 'perfect'—you can do anything you want," "you come from a good family," "you just need to do things right and I will show you how." Her grandmother helped teach Zoe about responsibility. The grandmother's words helped her cope with her own hurt and anger when her parents locked her in the stable with the horses. Today Zoe says her grandmother has helped her to "have great successes. I have developed strong values and a set of standards."

By sharing health challenges his own son had, one teacher modeled through self-disclosure to *Pinor Esendagh*. "You have the power to handle your problems. The problem was about my health. And he said that there could be many people who have worse problems than you have, so he made me feel better. I had this problem for 4 years and it was going to be over, but suddenly it occurred again. And for me, it was so hard to handle it. He gave me high morale with his encouragements. He told me some stories about his son who was having lots of problem about his health. And he has to live with this problem the rest of his life. But maybe one day I will get rid of the problem that I have. So, also this made me feel better. Now, I feel that I am more powerful because of it. I can't lose myself when I have health problems, but I don't be demoralized because I know that there can be worse situations or problems than I have."

2. **Identifying Strengths and Weaknesses:** A wide range of talents, skills, and personal qualities were mentioned.

"My tennis skills . . ."

"I had a high IQ and could accomplish whatever goals I set . . ."

"I had writing talent . . ."

"My first grade teacher gave me better marks than I earned to stimulate me . . . I now try always to do my best as a result."

Mark O'Connell is an executive in an electronics payments/financial services firm. His sixth grade teacher helped Mark reframe his own negative assessment of his math skills. The teacher told him, "You think you are not strong in math but you are an above-average student—you can be the best in the class." He also told Mark that not only did he believe him to have superior academic ability, but that he also had strong leadership potential.

Mark describes this teacher as having been a major turning point in his life, because it really planted the seeds for becoming achievement-oriented and more self-motivated. Mark felt much more self-confident particularly that he could take leadership roles and most importantly, it taught him that the best kind of leader makes people around him/her feel more confident and competent themselves. Mark is not (and dislikes) autocratic bossy leaders and uses a very different management style that has gained him the respect and loyalty of his employees over the years.

Sometimes a person is paradoxically encouraged when someone belittles, humiliates or uses criticism rather than compliments. For example, a teacher once said, "You aren't worth a plug nickel." In retrospect, the receiver of this communication says, "This teacher became that critical voice. But I wouldn't give her the satisfaction of knowing this because she really meant what she said." Such encouragement impacts the person our narrator has become, in that, "I probably wouldn't have gone to army or to school. I probably wouldn't have taken any risks."

Marnie Greenspoon's story concerned how a fifth grade teacher encouraged her to keep a journal of her creative writing. What is noteworthy here is how she was pleasantly surprised when asked to reflect on these acts of kindness in her subsequent life. She says, "I guess I never really thought about that incident too much, especially because I haven't kept up my creative writing over the last few years. But now that I think about it, her encouragement gave me a sense of confidence in my own abilities. When I was in university, I studied psychology; however my love of language continued as almost every one of my elective classes was an English course. I found myself in all these English literature courses surrounded by honors English majors, yet my confidence didn't waiver (at least not too much), as I believed in my abilities. Not only did I make it through those courses, but also I finished either top of my class, or close behind in every single one of them. I don't think I could have persevered and succeeded as I did had Mrs. Bergman not instilled such confidence in me."

Kastelan M. was very nervous because she had been asked to lead a group at an outdoor wilderness facility. Her co-worker group leader said to her, "You have the skills to do this. I've seen you with these boys and you have a good rapport with them. I'm confident that you'll do just fine; just trust yourself." Such a vote of confidence had this positive impact. "It was great. It forced me to develop my own style and through experience I've been able to bring these skills to my other jobs. I know I feel more comfortable and secure with my ability to process with adolescents."

3. **Supporting Over the Long Haul (Consistency):** Mottos to live by and attributing the encouragement from birth or earliest recollections as themes.

   "Courage is not the absence of fear but the ability to carry a task through (to completion)."

   "Numerous positive statements through my formative years are the basis of my self-confidence."

In these cases it was not a single incident that was identified—instead it was statements like "she was always there for me;" or "he was always in my corner."

   "From an early age my mother stressed to me that it's OK to make mistakes—it's only though mistakes that we learn. That was at a time when I was tearing up my entire page of homework when I made a mistake. Through her advice, I relaxed and rewrote my homework. When I made a mistake, I simply corrected it on the paper itself without ripping out the paper."

   "My math teacher said, 'You have a bright mind' . . . my friends said 'You can do an incredible amount of things at the same time and still be friends' . . . my daughter says 'You're my best friend and I can trust you' . . . I feel it's my responsibility to fit their expectations."

   "My mother would tell me, 'If you put forth your best effort, you can make it happen'."

Joy Morassatti credits her children's pre-school teacher in helping her feel more self-confident as a parent. The teacher told her, "You really are getting a lot out of our parent-study groups. You will end up teaching it." The teacher continued to show interest by asking Joy about her progress with having a better relationship with her children. She especially urged her to have greater self-compassion for what she perceived to be some errors of her own parenting style. An improved relationship with both her son and her daughter has been the result.

Moni Kiba had an undergraduate college professor who encouraged her to go to graduate school to become a social researcher. Long after she graduated, her former professor still is considered a primary person to contact when letters of recommendation are needed. Her mentor's encouragement helped her gain the needed self-confidence to explore new career choices.

Peggy Geddes credits her dear friend Lucy La Grassa for being there for her over the past 25 years. "She saw and appreciated the 'essence' of me. She saw how I really was. For example, I had watched a documentary on refugees; I commented to her, "Why do they live in such despair? It seems to me that if you had a big pot and everyone put a little in it there would be enough for everyone."

"She replied to me, 'Peggy, how you live your life and how you really are is so different.' She explained that although I often appeared to not care in my daily life I care deeply for others. That was my nature to be most tender and strong. It was very encouraging for me. What was important was for one person to know my heart. One has to care deeply for someone else to know his or her heart."

Hoda Esifaie's grandmother was there for her—like many comments in the long haul category. She says, "It was no specific situation. It was everything she did and everything about her that make her so great." "It was not what she said, it was the things she did. I was always told actions speak louder than words. My grandmother always put others first. She was happy making others happy and doing things for them. It was like karma. What goes around comes around. She got respect from everyone. At her funeral, half of San Francisco was there and not one person could say, let alone think, one bad or negative thing about her. She told me no matter what I do in my life I'm going to be great."

4. **Seeing the Person as Special:** One person who saw the narrators as special in spite of many others who didn't seems to be what had the most impact.

"My older sister said she was proud just to be seen with me."

"I was always scolded at home but my teacher paid attention to me and complimented and encouraged me."

Rhonda Payne cites her sixth grade teacher as seeing something special in her. "My Art teacher in grade six called me 'Honey Fox.' She asked me to try. Whenever I said I couldn't do that, she asked me to try because I guess she believed in me. She would tell me 'Of course you can do that thing.' My achievements were a surprise to me. I felt special; it was her belief that she and I shared a special bond in the art. We were the artists in that room. I stepped into that room and became an artist. It made me realize that I can do anything and she wasn't even family."

After many years in advertising, Rhonda is a coach today. The lingering impact on her is that, "I could trust her respect because it had to be earned. She certainly had a great influence in my creativity, she taught me how important it is and what a wonderful refuge it is. I can still think of this painting I did of the swan."

Lynn Van Leeuwen says her calculus teacher used a creative baseball metaphor when he called on her to solve a problem no one else had completed. "We are bringing in Sandy Koufax," he would say. When she felt shy and uncomfortable about going to the board even though she knew the answer, her teacher simply winked at her privately as his encouragement. "I think about the incident when I face difficult situations and I remember his confidence in me," Lynn says of that eternal encouraging experience.

Kerby Moore credits his hockey coach for helping him make the team. "He said, 'Never quit, size means nothing.' I was trying to make a high-level hockey team and felt I was too small to play that level. I left try-out camp halfway through. My coach told me not to quit, that my size shouldn't stop me. I made the team. It challenged me, encouraged me to work harder, reminded me I almost quit. I haven't forgotten that it doesn't matter what the obstacles are if you don't give up on yourself you will succeed."

Sabiye Serinay's best friend loaned her a dress to attend a special party. Her friend also introduced her to makeup which really felt good to her.

Ronda had begun to smoke again; she had not had a cigarette for several years. One day while sharing lunch with her best friend, Sue said to her, "I care for you so much and really hate to see you start smoking again." This spoke to Ronda's heart and, yes, she quit. It's now 35 years later, and Ronda still remembers Sue's kindness.

5. **How to Inspire Self and Others (Inspiring Others):** Passionate inspirational encouragement themes in this category, usually during difficult times in the person's life, were the characteristic here.

"I'm in your corner, and I always will be!"

"I was unfairly accused and he stood by me."

"My piano teacher in grade school said I was an inspiration to *her*; two decades later we have become friends despite our 30 year ago difference."

"Although I learned English as a child in China, I was feeling inadequate when I applied for my first job as a teacher in Ontario. In my interview the principal said, 'You are here to teach music—the English will come later'."

"My friend helped me learn how to drive. One day she came by to pick me up in her own car to teach me how to start the engine and run the car. Finally I did . . . she told me I could learn fast and that I would be a good driver."

Colleen Hurst credits her musical director's reframed failure and inspired her by saying, "There are no failures, just less successful outcomes." You make believe and then you believe and you can do it, and do it. He gave me such courage. He still does."

"I still hear his voice and encouragement and we are also still in touch." The context of his comments came as she was preparing for a role she had wanted for a long time. Colleen says, "The audition was heavy and hard and I was pleasantly surprised—I got it! I did it, I did it—the competition was major and I did it." Later her teacher helped her with her solos. "His encouragement allowed me to step into the moment and succeed," she says. "I still recall his words of encouragement to this day. I can still feel those wonderful feelings I felt back then. It's very powerful—*to this day!!!*"

Note how Colleen has internalized and thus made the auditory sound of her encourager timeless in that regard. Long after the chronological moment has passed, she still has the seeds that have been planted which often bear eternal fruit.

Janice Passe's husband ran beside her the final two kilometers of a 10-kilometer race. He ran beside her the whole time talking about other things to keep her mind occupied. He encouraged her to speed up and give it her all at the finish line—which she did. This has helped Janice realize that if she keeps faith in herself she can do more than she sometimes thinks. It also has encouraged her to continue running and possibly attempt to run a half marathon in the future.

Burcu Kurtdereli credits his mother as his inspiration. "She always encouraged me saying, 'You always do good things. You can be successful in all areas. You have a lot of abilities.' She also talks with me very friendly. This is helping me to do things successfully. When I want to do something new she encourages me. 'You can do it. Don't worry,' or when I am anxious about doing something she helps me. Besides these she trusts me." He concludes, "This encouragement affects me in a positive way, because I do something with ambition. Now I have a good self-esteem. I can do anything successfully. I am ambitious and this helps me to do things in a good way or complete the job I take."

6. **Supporting A Person's Special Interests:** As in Role Modeling, the focus here is on the respondent's qualities and/or skills that form the basis for the guidance and support

provided. in contrast to having the encourager's qualities or skills be the focus of their interaction.

"She encouraged me to capitalize on my love for children."

"Life is too short not to enjoy it . . . be your own person."

As a child, **Sherie Benicki's** father told her, "You're cute, you're bright and you've got hair like spun gold; you can be anything you want to be." Although he offered to take her to visit colleges as a high school senior, he honored her selection of a vocational school by giving her $200 towards her tuition. Today her father's support has helped her become what she describes as "the little engine that could get started."

Doug Eckstein describes how his father, who was a minister, originally opposed his possible divorce. "Remember, I married you and you made a vow to God to stay together forever," he told his son. The college student drove his motorcycle from his Tennessee College to Atlanta where his parents lived. But the motorcycle broke down mid-way. Doug had no funds to repair the bike. His father told him to wait where he was and he would come and pick him up.

It was late at night when the father arrived. They rented a motel room. As they sat in their respective beds alone in the dark the father simply said, "Tell me everything, son."

For two straight hours Doug poured out his heart to his father describing various incidents related to the failing marriage.

His father simply listened to his son. When Doug finished his story, he was in tears; after a long pause his father said, "I never thought I'd say this, Doug, but I feel you are in fact making the right choice in seeking a divorce!!!"

7. **Encouraging Career Choices**—themes here emphasize specific career choices made due to the influence of or help from others' input.

"Since she said I had a gift for math and I would do well in the subject, I explored careers with this talent in mind."

"I knew I wanted to be a nurse and she helped me get into a school after I was rejected by the first one."

"They said I was a natural born leader, strong and courageous, qualities needed when one is called to a ministry . . . and I realized that I was a leader, I had been called to a ministry."

It is important to realize that encouragement occurs in many ways other than just with and because of people. Many of us feel a sense of calm and a feeling of wellbeing in such nature spots as the ocean, mountains, garden, mountain streams, the forests, a special tree house, and other magical places. Likewise pets, animals, and plants are all capable of encouragement. One of the authors (Eckstein) was swimming with the dolphins in Key Largo, Florida. One of the owners described an incident where a normally friendly dolphin kept bumping one of the swimmers so hard in the right side that she had to be taken to the hospital. It was only there that undiscovered cancer was discovered. Intervention in the cancer's formative stage prevented what would have been probable death within a month if not detected and treated when it was.

Sometimes encouragement comes in the least expected ways. **Raymond Laffier** has been a concession owner at the fair for the past 33 years. His next-door neighbor provided the inspiration. Raymond says, "I told him I wanted to travel with the fair but others thought that was a bad choice. He told me to follow my own dreams because if I don't I may always wonder 'What if?' I was pleased someone sided with me. I thought, 'Yes, I don't want to wonder 'What if?' I went the next day to the fair and signed up. I was over cutting his lawn after school. There was a fair in town and I was excited. (He) Gave me the courage to try new things and let me know I wasn't a child but a man . . . it has been a wonderful career with no 'What if's'"

Jennifer Laffier honors her ninth grade art teacher for helping her become the art therapist she is today. She says her teacher "suggested I look at Toronto Art Therapy Institute. She felt this career was perfect for me since I loved art and helping people. She saw I was good at this. I was surprised she had noticed this. I did take her advice and look up this career. It made me feel good that someone had noticed these good qualities in me."

"It was during career week at school. She called me in privately to the art room. I originally thought I was in trouble for something. She encouraged me to think of my career choices at an early age, when other kids felt aimless."

George Brotman is a coach and a strategic planning consultant. He credits a significant other for inspiring his career choice. "During our time together I was told I exhibited skills that related to coaching. I was told I was a natural and should really consider and explore the coaching process."

Today he observes that, "Coaching has opened up my world and view especially after experiencing the Foundation Course. Understanding how people think so differently with different thought processes, coupled with their motivations and stumbling blocks are specific skills he has learned.

Salih Aricioqtu credits her career counselor with helping her make a career choice. She explained, "I was graduating from high school and still I couldn't decide which one of two jobs I should choose. Since primary school I was dreaming to become an English teacher because the course I like most was English but, when the time came that I had to give my decision,

I became confused and began to think about also psychological counseling and guidance as an alternative job. I talked about all these dilemmas to the person that encouraged me and she told me to 'Listen to voice of your heart' and she offered me to search in detail about both jobs to know them better and give my decision according to it. I said OK and we did it. She helped me very much and made me recognize what I really want to become." "To sum up, with this person's professional help, I gave my certain decision and chose Psychological Counseling and Guidance as my occupation."

Application

After interviewing your partner on one or more encouragement stories, discuss the various categories of encouragement. Stories can, of course, fit into one or more of the seven content analysis themes.

Then please discuss together the specific role of encouragement by talking about such questions as:

1. What are some specific examples of how we have encouraged one another?
2. Each of you may also want to state how you might appreciate being more encouraged by your partner in the future.

Note: Your *tone* of voice in making this request can be encouraging in and of itself. For example, using this, as an opportunity to dump blame, criticism, and contempt on your partner is certainly not modeling the very thing you are requesting.

Summary

This article suggests a structured interview format for couples to reflect on who has encouraged them and how they have been encouraged. Couples have a responsibility to be a source or encouragement for their spouses and partners.

We believe that by practicing these Seven Methods of Encouragement and providing opportunities for each other to re-experience moments of past encouragement through reflection. a stronger positive bond can be created between you. By committing to being more encouraging with one another and by having follow-up discussions to track your progress, you as a couple can help establish a more favorable emotional climate for you both.

A Tribute to Phyliss

This article is dedicated to the memory of my four decade friend, colleague and co-author Phyliss Cooke, who died July 8, 2011.

Together we learned of this model in workshops with the co-creator. Phyliss provided key background resources and timely examples for this article. True to her own generous spirit, she declined the invitation to be a co-author. She wanted the next generation of recent Masters of Counseling degree recipients Nicole Russo and Jen Straub to take that torch.

Dr. Cooke also created the seven content analysis themes that were the basis of our encouragement article for couples in the journal in which this article was published. She lived her own created themes of encouragement with me, her students, and her colleagues, including:

1. Being a positive role model;
2. Seeing strengths and abilities in others;
3. Support over the long haul (consistency);
4. Seeing people as special;
5. Inspiring others;
6. Supporting what others are interested in, especially in dark times;
7. Helping make a career choice

In my 18 years of writing the "for couples" column the first way of assessing couples has been both an understanding and of respecting of personality differences. In our workshops I was the flamboyant loud exuberant one; Phyliss was the subtle, quite Al Ellis cognitive-behavior trained brilliant one.

I was the balloon; she was the string. We honored, respected, and valued our complementary styles. We were the essence of a "for couples" working team. Working friendships are indeed their own form of intimate partnership. Rather than being critical and offended that I spelled her name Phyllis even after all those years, she just smiled and gave me the auditory anchor of one L and two hissing snake sounds of a double ss to help me.

Phyliss, you encouraged me in my darkest hours. You complemented rather than criticized my short comings. You just smiled when I feigned an entitlement confrontation of your early memory of a teacher giving you an A-. "Can she do that?" you indignantly complained to your mom. Ah, the future makings of a true Mensa member. If you can't be one yourself, at least make a Mensa member a friend and co-author has been my philosophy.

This year you gave me the gold Situational Leadership buttons you got and I did not when we both went through the training; you were asked to be a trainer and not me. You knew I felt rejected by this. I cherish those gold buttons from you Phyliss.

I sadly remove your name as a reference from my résumé. I smile in gratitude for your encouragement to me of taking my present position when I had at first turned it down. We worked together; we wrote together; we laughed together; we lived the planned renegotiation model presented here.

Now I grieve alone.

Thanks for the deep and abiding gift of intimate and enduring male-female friendship Phyliss. This one's for you "my Pal" as you and no one else so affectionately called me. I weep remembering you saying that to me. Thanks for being my Pal for more than 40 years, Phyliss.

My hope for each of you reading this note is that you too will be blessed with such an enduring friendship. If you have one now, let them know how very valued they are in your heart. It is there they are indeed eternal.

Daniel Eckstein

The Cooke-Eckstein collaborative connection:

Cooke, P., & Eckstein, D., (2009). *Encouragement: Improving one's outlook*. In Biech, E., (Ed.).*The 2009 Pfeiffer Annual Handbook: Consulting*. San Francisco, CA: Wiley, 13-22.

Cooke, P., & Eckstein, D. (2009). Assertiveness training. *Encyclopedia of Counseling*. Alexandria, Va. American Counseling Association, p. 32.

Eckstein, D. Cooke, P., & Eckstein, D. (2007). Types and sources of encouragement for coaches, *International Journal of Coaching in Organizations*, 4, 62-71.

Eckstein, D., & Cooke, P. (2005). The seven methods of encouragement for couples. *The Family Journal: Counseling and Therapy for Couples and Families, 13*(3), 342-350.

Endnotes

[1]   Dinkmeyer, D., & Eckstein, D. (1996) Leadership by Encouragement, Boca Raton: Fla.: CR Press.

[2]   Dinkmeyer, et.al., p. 7

[3]   Eckstein, D., Belongia, M., & Elliott-Applegate, G. (2000) The Four Directions of Encouragement Within Families, *The Family Journal*, p. 216.

[4]   Dinkmeyer, et.al., *op.cit.,*. p. 406-415.

Biography

Phyliss Cooke, Ph.D., was a licensed clinical psychologist and consultant in private practice.

From 1978 to 1988, Dr. Cooke was a senior consultant, dean of an intern training program, and dean of a master's degree program in human resource development for University Associates, Inc. (later called Pfeiffer and Company), an internationally known consulting and publishing company based in San Diego, California. She co-authored a variety of articles and created several popular training instruments and structured activities published in the Pfeiffer & Jones *Annuals* for group facilitators and consultants. Dr. Cook died in 2011.

Chapter II:
Relationship Inventories and Questionnaires

Section 3:

The Noble Eightfold Relationship Matrix

Phil Ginsburg, Daniel Eckstein, Yu-Fen Lin,
Chi-Sing Li, and Bill Mullener

There is joy in the simplest of things—a spring flower; a child's laughter; a puppy playfully chasing its tail; a couple holding hands while looking at each other with loving eyes. Just as there is joy, there is also anguish. It takes little effort to see suffering all around us. It seems that we are inundated with reports of economic pressures, racial and political strife, and senseless violence. Many in the West have traditionally found comfort in the roots of Judeo-Christian religious doctrine. In the East, many have relied on ancient Buddhist ideology to put into perspective disparate experiences of joy and suffering.

The purpose of this article is to introduce the wisdom of the Buddhist Noble Eightfold Path (Figure 1) for relationship enrichment. The article will be organized as follows: following a brief summary of the history, the eight aspects of the Buddhist principles will be defined and illustrated. You as a couple will then be invited to fill out what we are calling the Noble Eightfold Relationship Matrix. Also featured will be three couple's responses describing how the concepts are utilized in their own marriage. While the concepts presented in the article are derived from Buddhist philosophy, the authors have found that the concepts have been useful to those who may hold a diverse set of beliefs. Although none of the authors themselves are practicing Buddhists, the concepts themselves have been found to be helpful in their work with couples regardless of their religious, spiritual, and/or philosophical beliefs.

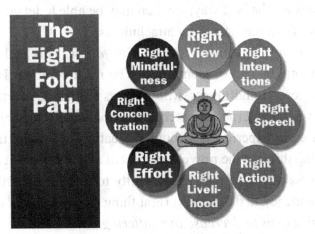

Figure 1. The Noble Eightfold Path

History

Buddhism can be traced as far back as 500 BCE. The founder was Siddartha Gautama, who, later in life, transformed into what we now call the Buddha. Buddha is often misunderstood as the name of an historical figure from India; but this is not the case. Buddha is a principle, not a person. Buddha actually means "awake." When asked, "Are you a god?" Gautama . . . replied "No." "Then what are you?" the man asked again. Gautama's answer was, "I am awake" (Tea Alchemy, n.d.) The authors feel it is important to clarify how Gautama himself developed his own belief system and tried to communicate the importance of becoming aware of one's own set of principles.

Cantwell and Kawanami (2002) note that in his teaching of the Four Noble Truths, Buddha felt that everything is conditioned and subject to change, but people, ignorant of this reality, become attached to impermanent things. He proposed that the only cure is the Noble Eightfold Path. It consists of a set of methods encompassing morality, meditation and wisdom. The ultimate goal is enlightenment (nirvana), freedom from the cycle of conditioned existence.

The Four Noble Truths

According to the Buddha, *suffering* is an integral part of the human experience. It refers to a basic unsatisfactoriness running through our lives, the lives of all but the enlightened. Sometimes this unsatisfactoriness erupts into the open as sorrow, grief, disappointment, or despair; but usually it hovers at the edge of our awareness as a vague unlocalized sense that things are never quite perfect, never fully adequate to our expectations of what they should be. (Bodhi, B., 1999, p.6) The fact that suffering is a central theme in people's lives is the first of four noble truths.

The second noble truth is that much of our suffering comes from the stubborn *belief that we MUST have certain things*. These things can be material in nature, or they may be relationships that we feel we cannot be whole without. Many times we are attached to certain ideas and insist that our way is the only way.

A realization of hope is the third noble truth. By accepting that our idea of what should be is not necessarily always the best way, we then may be able to let go of the people, places and things to which we form our unhealthy attachments.

The fourth noble truth is *that there is a path to follow*. This path is characterized by cultivating wisdom, morality, and concentration. The most common Buddhist practice for cultivating these qualities is mindfulness. Mindfulness (Sanskrit, smirti) is nonattached yet fully engaged witnessing of internal or external phenomena. Being mindful involves fully attending to what arises in experience without evaluating or interpreting it cognitively or emotionally, as if seeing through the proverbial eyes of a child. (Gehart & McCollum, 2007, p. 217) Children possess a type of purity and ability to see things as they are. In a child's innocence there is a tendency to do the next right thing. *Being mindful of retaining our own childlike qualities can help us to decrease our suffering.*

The decision to write this article came about as the authors discussed how the eightfold path could be used by you, the couple, to minimize the suffering that you may experience in your relationship. Bodhi (1999) notes that:

> To sum up, we find three requirements for a teaching proposing to offer a true path to the end of suffering: first, it has to set forth a full and accurate picture of the range of suffering; second, it must present a correct analysis of the causes of suffering; and third, it must give us the means to eradicate the causes of suffering. (p.5)

In other words, it is important that we be rigorously honest with ourselves about our situation. To the best of our ability we need to know the source of our suffering (does it come from within or is it caused externally). It is important that we be willing to ask ourselves, again with rigorous honesty, can the path we are about to choose take us where we want/need to go? Will following this path make things better and reduce suffering? The path we choose may not be easy.

Albert Ellis, the renowned originator of Rational Emotive Behavior Therapy, felt that much of the suffering that people experience is self induced. Unless they are willing to let go of the *musts*, *shoulds*, and *oughts* that are part of their belief system, they will likely continue to experience suffering and not be able to fully enjoy the present (Heery, 2000).

Ellis encouraged people to view things as they really are. This is similar to what the Buddhist describes as being *Right View*. It is the first of eight principles or aspects along the eightfold path. The eight principles are **Right View, Right Intention, Right Speech, Right Action, Right Livelihood, Right Effort, Right Mindfulness,** and **Right Concentration**. "The eight aspects of the path are not to be understood as a sequence of single steps, instead they are highly interdependent principles that have to be seen in relationship with each other." (Thebigview, n.d.).

Definitions

In the following section we have defined the principles of the *noble eightfold path* in such a way as to make it easier for you to draw parallels to situations and events in your own life. Although each virtue is preceded with the adjective *right*, the authors have found it useful to suggest that there is not one and only one *right* way of being in a relationship; that can be especially challenging if one member of the relationship arrogantly believes that his or her beliefs are superior. While teaching in a medical school, co-author Eckstein heard the term *high yield*, in the context of students getting the maximum payoff for the minimal amount of time spent studying for their many exams. Consider *high yield* results as another way of thinking about what you as a couple might achieve by utilizing the following eight virtues in your relationship.

1. *Right View* is seeing things as they really are without fear or expectations.
2. *Right Intention* naturally follows from *Right View* and involves giving up the need for controlling and manipulating other people, places, and things.
3. *Right Speech* allows us to be genuine, to speak without a filter. We have no ulterior motives. We talk not just to be understood; rather we communicate truth without expectation as to what the outcome of our sharing may be. We speak authentically from our hearts.
4. *Right Discipline* involves letting go of activities that can complicate our lives. We eat what we need, we get the material things that we need, but we make a conscious choice to keep our lives uncomplicated. We learn to understand the difference between wants and needs.
5. *Right Livelihood* implies that whatever it is we are given to do, that we do so with a full heart and an eye to excellence. We make a conscious effort to ensure that what we do for our livelihood does not negatively impact the rights of other living things. Our livelihood ideally makes a contribution to the common good in some manner.
6. *Right Effort*: If we are truly following the path when we deal with challenges as they come, there is no struggle as we interact with others and experience ourselves. When we are involved in *Right Effort,* we experience maximum impact for minimal energy.
7. *Right Mindfulness* is the part of the path that allows us to be conscious of how we are performing the other steps on the path. We notice our physical selves, our breathing, our touch, and how our bodies experience the five senses. We have awareness of our feelings and emotions; we are aware of our state of mind and our reactions to what we encounter.
8. *Right Concentration* allows us to be more fully focused in the moment. We are not day dreaming about *what ifs*, but allow ourselves to be immersed in the *now*. We are acutely aware of our views, intentions, speech, discipline, livelihood, effort and mindfulness. We are aware of what we perceive and in turn how we are perceived.

The Elephant in the Room

O how they cling and wrangle, some who claim
For preacher and monk the honored name!
For, quarreling, each to his view they cling.
Such folk see only one side of a thing.
(Wang, n.d.)

Keown in (2006) wrote of a story that the Buddha once told of a King who assembled the blind men in his village to gather around an elephant. The King split the blind men into several separate groups.

Each group was then taken to an elephant and introduced to a different part of the animal—the head, trunk, legs, tail, and so forth. Afterwards, the king asked each group to describe the nature of the beast. Those who had made contact with the head described an elephant as a water-pot; those familiar with the ears likened the animal to a winnowing basket; those who had touched a leg said an elephant was like a post, and those who had felt a tusk insisted an elephant was shaped like a peg. The groups then fell to arguing amongst themselves each insisting its definition was correct and all the others were wrong.

There are many occasions in marriage where each partner can perceive the very same thing quite differently. Often couples choose to leave things unspoken like an elephant in the room that no one dares talk about until resentments build up, unintended words are spoken and emotions boil over. Hurt and suffering are often the result for the couple, and their loved ones.

Activity 3: Creating Your Matrix

The authors have found it can be helpful for couples to fill in a matrix as an exercise that can be done together. The matrix, created by Daniel Eckstein, can be used as a visual tool for how you are applying the virtues both individually and together in your relationship. The concepts are meant to be a starting point for stimulating your own creative discussion.

There are several ways to use the matrix. Each of you individually can fill in your responses. It is not expected you will have a response for each cell; rather, look over the matrix and respond to the items that are most relevant to you. You could then meet with your partner and discuss your responses.

A second option is for you to go through the matrix together and to jointly relate your own associations and illustrations. A third variation is for you to interview each other.

The eight virtues are listed on the vertical dimension of the matrix. The horizontal axis features the following five reflective questions:

1. How was this modeled for you as a child and/or adolescent? Who modeled this for you?
2. What are some examples of this in your adult life for you personally?
3. Cite examples of when you believe your partner demonstrated this virtue.
4. With respect to you as a couple together, what are some positive examples of this virtue in your relationship?
5. Which of the eight virtues is underutilized and/or undervalued in your current relationship? In what way? List some possible suggestions for improvement if you have them

Noble EightFold Relationship Matrix (NERM)		Who and how was this modeled to you as a child and/or adolescent?	What are some examples of this in your adult life for you personally?	Cite examples of when you believe your partner demonstrated this virtue.	With respect to you as a couple together, what are some positive examples of this virtue in your relationship?	Which of the eight virtues is underutilized and/or undervalued in your current relationship? In what way? List some possible suggestions for improvement if you have them.
Wisdom	Right View					
	Right Intention					
Ethical Conduct	Right Speech					
	Right Action					
	Right Livelihood					
Mental Development	Right Effort					
	Right Mindfulness					
	Right Concentration					

Your Own Action Plan

After completing your own matrix and reading the case studies, here are suggested ways for you both to summarize and to consider your own application for relationship enhancement. Although the matrix is meant to be an activity you can complete alone or as a couple, you may find it helpful to discuss your responses with someone such as a counselor, a spiritual or religious person or a trusted friend. Here are some "next-step" considerations:

1. In completing the matrix were there any significant *ah-ha's* of new awareness or insight?

2. Which of the eight virtues seemed to be most positively demonstrated in your relationship?

3. Which ones were under-utilized?

4. In reading the three couples responses, which responses were most relevant to you? In what way?

5. What would be an agreed upon action plan for you to better utilize any of the principles for improving your own relationship?

Summary

The purpose of the article has been to introduce the Noble Eightfold Relationship Matrix as a creative way for couples to view their relationship. A similar matrix with a specific focus on the role of culture in your relationship can be found in Li, Lin, and Eckstein (2007).

It is the hope of the authors that by using the principles of the Noble Eightfold Path, you may find a way to live in closer harmony together. By utilizing these ancient precepts we feel that you both may gain deeper insight into yourselves as individuals, how you live in concert with one another and what you project as a couple both within the relationship and to others whose paths you will cross in your journeys.

References

Blind Men and the Elephant. Retrieved June 21, 2010 from

Bodhi, B. (1999). *The noble eightfold path: The way to the end of suffering*. Kandy, Sri Lanka: Buddhist Publication Society.

Cantwell, C. & Kawanami, H. (2002) Buddhism. In Linda Woodhead, Paul Fletcher, Hiroko Kwanami & David Smith (Eds.), *Religions in the Modern World: Traditions and Transformations*. London: Routledge.

Gehart, D., & McCollum, E. (2007). Engaging Suffering: Towards a Mindful Re-Visioning of Family Therapy Practice. *Journal of Marital & Family Therapy, 33*(2), 214-226.

Heery, M. An Interview with Albert Ellis, PhD (2000). *Psychotherapy.net* Retrieved May 30, 2010 from http://www.psychotherapy.net/interview/ Albert_Ellis

Keown, D. (1996). In *Buddhism: A very short introduction*. New York: Oxford University Press.

Li, C., Lin, Y., & Eckstein, D. (2007). The Cultural Relationship Interview Matrix: Four Activities for Couples. *The Family Journal*, 15,2,143-151.

Tea Alchemy. (n.d.). *What does "buddha" mean?* Retrieved May 30, 2010 from http://www.tealchemy.org/ where/buddha/index/html

Thebigview. (n.d.) *About Buddhism.* Retrieved May 30, 2010 from

Biographies

Phil Ginsburg is in the last semester pursuing his masters degree in counseling and marriage and family therapy at Sam Houston State University. He graduated with a degree in Community and Public Service from the University of Massachusetts Boston. Prior returning to school for his Master's degree he worked as a chemical dependency counselor with women and children in a long term residential treatment facility. Earlier in Phil's career he was President of an international semiconductor distribution company. Phil was responsible for locations around the US as well as in China and London. He enjoys writing music and poetry in his spare time. He is married to Joy Ginsburg. They have four children ages 7-11, Henry, Bobby, Ethel, and Evan.

Chi-Sing Li, Ph.D., Chi-Sing Li is an Associate Professor of Sam Houston State University in Huntsville, Texas. He is also a Licensed Professional Counselor-Supervisor and Licensed Marriage and Family Therapist Approved Supervisor in Texas. His research interest includes Counseling with Asian American, International Students and Clinical Supervision. He is an editorial reviewer for Professional Issues in Counseling.

Yu-Fen Lin, M.Div., Ph.D., Yu-Fen Lin is an Assistant Professor of University of North Texas at Dallas. She is also a Licensed Professional Counselor-Supervisor in Texas. Her specialty and research interest center around gender sensitive individual/group therapy, multicultural counseling, and supervision. She is served as editorial reviewers in different prestigious journal such as Counseling and Values and Professional Issues in Counseling.

Bill Mullener, MA, LPC, LCDC, NCC, is a counselor and psychotherapist with the Champions Christian Counseling Center in Tomball, TX. He attended Texas A&M University and Sam Houston State University, and retired from both the United States Air Force and Delta Airlines after serving in both the Vietnam and Persian Gulf conflicts. His areas of specialization include substance abuse, marriage and family therapy, co-occurring disorders, and Veterans issues. He is currently enrolled in the Doctor of Ministry program at the Graduate Theological Foundation. Bill and his wife reside in Plantersville, TX.

Section 4

Today . . .

Mend a quarrel. Search out a forgotten friend. Dismiss suspicion, and replace it with trust. Write a love letter. Share some treasure. Give a soft answer. Encourage youth. Manifest your loyalty in a word or deed. Keep a promise. Find the time. Forego a grudge. Forgive an enemy. Listen. Apologize if you were wrong. Examine your demand on others. Think first of someone else. Appreciate, be kind, be gentle. Laugh a little more. Deserve confidence. Take up arms against malice. Decry complacency. Express your gratitude. Worship your God. Gladden the heart of a child. Take pleasure in the beauty and wonder of the earth. Speak your love. Speak it again. Speak it still again. Speak it still once again.

"On This Day." 1999. Shakthi. 5, 4, pg. 18

Section 5:

Antidotes for Infidelity and Prescriptions for Long Lasting Relationships: Four Couples' Activities

Judith A. Nelson, Chi-Sing Li, Daniel G. Eckstein,
Pedra Ane, and William Mullener

The use of medical metaphors can help clients express the strong emotional content of experiences of unfaithfulness. The metaphors such as antidote, antibody, immunity, prescription, vaccine, and booster shots are appropriate for couples wishing to guard against unfaithful behaviors. In this article, we introduce four activities for couples to use with to create their own metaphors as they investigate their perceptions and early experiences of commitment and faithfulness. The authors also use the medical metaphors of injury, trauma, and immunodeficiency to describe the intense emotional content of infidelity to the couples who may be questioning their ability to remain faithful to each other or who are experiencing jealousy or suspicion regarding their partners' relationships with others.

Defining Infidelity and Trauma

The word infidelity means the breaking of trust. According to Lusterman, such an expectation of mutual trust is the foundation of commitment to each other. The author states:

> One significant element of this trust is the unspoken vow that the couple will remain sexually exclusive. Another is that there is a certain level of emotional intimacy that is reserved for the couple, not to be shared with others. Having pledged faithfulness, it is not surprising that the discoverer experiences such shock on finding that a mate has violated it. Infidelity occurs when one partner in a relationship continues to believe that the agreement to be faithful is still in force, while the other partner is secretly violating it. [1]

Sex and intimacy are critical aspects of a successful relationship. Unfortunately, these two critical factors do not necessarily occur together contributing to the occurrence of sexual frustration, loss of emotional intimacy, engagement in sexual and intimate relationships, and eventual relationship separations and terminations. Whether or not a couple adopts a monogamous or non-monogamous relationship, a couple's success does not often occur in the absence of attention to those factors that challenge a committed relationship.

The novelty of new passionate relationships often obscures attention to the challenges that most couples will face.[2] Subotnik and Harris cited the most common reasons for affairs as being transitional anxiety, unfulfilled expectations, unrealistic ideas about love and marriage, a need for attention, boredom, an unavailable spouse, lack of sexual desire, and the exit affair. "Based on many years of leading divorce recovery groups, we have found that the most troubling issues fall into the categories relating to survival, self-esteem, and the social world."[3] Glass pointed out that "A happy marriage is not a vaccine against infidelity."[4]

Building Immunity

Just as getting a vaccine is a way of helping prevent diseases, there are many ways for each individual in the partnership to develop a tolerance against the normal biological attraction to others. Such emotional and psychological vaccines help form a protective boundary and establish a built-in resistance insulating partners when temptation arises as it inevitably will. The following activities can be assigned to help couples build their immunity against infidelity.

Childhood Role Models

The best predictor of a person's future marital satisfaction is one's own perception of the happiness of his or her parents. Eckstein and Cooke[5] interviewed more than 1,000 individuals relative to who encouraged them and how. They found that parents were the most often cited source of encouragement, and the most frequent method of encouragement was *walking the talk* by being positive role models. Teachers, coaches, and religious leaders were the next most frequently cited sources of encouragement. Talk with your partner about the childhood role models you remember, using the following questions as a guie:

Activity 4: Childhood Role Models

1. What are some of your earliest memories growing up with respect to both commitment and infidelity?
2. Who were some of your role models who were in committed relationships?
3. What characterized the commitment of those role models?
4. What were some positive and negative messages you heard about relationships as you were growing up?
5. Did any of your original family members ever have an affair that you knew about? If so, how was it resolved?
6. Can you relate any incident(s) in which trust was originally broken and then restored? If so, what helped reestablish trust?

Flexibility and Intimacy

Love and Stousy[6] talked about the concept of changing needs. A different type of stimulation does not apply just in bed; it can be applied across the board through all activities a couple enjoys together. Staying flexible and willing to change over the years will keep a couple together when nothing else will. Separating sex and intimacy as couples age can offer the best intimacy of a lifetime. Gottman and Silver[7] discussed the concept of "turning toward your partner." When circumstances change, times get tough, or the unexpected happens, couples may withdraw from each other rather than turning to each other for support. Turning toward each other invites intimacy. Your partner should be the one person you look to when you feel sad, depressed, or overwhelmed. Talk with your partner about your perceptions of intimacy and how it might change over time

---

Activity 5: Flexibility and Intimacy

1. Describe an intimate moment or time with your partner that did not involve sex. What circumstances or events made that moment possible? How did you feel toward your partner at the time?
2. What are the specific areas in your relationship where trust is strong resulting in a closer, more intimate connection to your partner?
3. What are the specific areas in your relationship where trust is weak resulting in a less intimate connection to your partner?

Assessing Commitment

Using another metaphor, the authors propose that commitment is the string that securely tethers the balloon of infidelity. In a recent survey,[8] individuals were asked to describe their perceptions of commitment in romantic relationships. Findings indicated that participants rated commitment as foundational to fidelity, and for more than 50% of the participants, spirituality was tied closely to their perceptions of commitment.

Because spirituality appears to be central to commitment, it is important for couples to consider what role spirituality and religion will play in their relationship as a couple. For example, couples should consider how their individual and collective ideas guide their commitment in the relationship; how much responsibility they feel to each other, to their own value systems, or to a higher power to make the relationship work; and whether their individual or collective ideas about spirituality offer any support or sense of comfort and help for the difficulties in the relationship.

Talk to each other about your perceptions of the notion of commitment in marriage. The following questions help you both make each partner's own perception of commitment more concrete. Not only is the content of each question important but also the very process of couples taking the time for relationship building is an excellent preventative measure to infidelity in and of itself.

Activity 6: Assessing Commitment

1. What do you most want to understand about your partner with respect to the idea of commitment?

2. What do you most want your partner to understand about you with respect to the idea of commitment?

3. What were some early messages you received about the concept of commitment when you were growing up?

4. With respect to previous relationships, cite specific examples of both high and low commitment.

5. What do you most want to understand about your partner with respect to the idea of commitment?

6. What do you most want your partner to understand about you with respect to the idea of commitment?

7. What were some early messages you received about the concept of commitment when you were growing up?

8. With respect to previous relationships, cite specific examples of both high and low commitment.

9. In other areas of your life, besides your current relationship, cite some specific examples of when your sense of commitment was strong.

10. Contrast that with times when you did not feel as committed.

11. How do you define commitment in your own marriage or relationship?

12. With regard to your present relationship to whom or to what do you feel most committed (i.e., spouse? God? children? your principles?)

Trust and Forgiveness

Breaking of one's agreements is one of the most common ways for trust to be broken in relationships. If there is going to be trust between the couple, forgiveness is one of the core prescriptive salves that can help heal many emotional wounds. Ortega and Fleming stressed that forgiveness is not given because it is deserved. It cannot be earned. It is given by faith. The motivation does not come from the character qualities of the offender.

Forgiveness is not a feeling. It is a decision. Feelings follow as the healing process is worked out. Forgiveness is not a process; healing is a process. Once forgiveness has been declared, it has taken place. It does not need to be repeated. When the angry or hurt feelings reoccur, they do not indicate a lack of forgiveness. They indicate that further healing still needs to take place. Part of the healing process is reminding oneself that these infractions have been forgiven. Answering the pain with a reminder will lessen the pain and eventually it will be gone.[9]

Activity 7: Trust and Forgiveness

1. Cite some specific areas in your relationship in which your trust is strong.
2. Cite some specific areas in your relationship in which trust is weaker.
3. On a 1 to 10 scale, 1 being low and 10 high, how would you rate your own jealousy? Give an explanation of your rating.
4. Cite some examples of when and under what circumstance you have forgiven someone?
5. Has anyone ever said "I forgive you" to you personally? If so, how did you react?
6. Have you ever known another couple that survived infidelity on the part of one or both partners? Is so, how did they resolve the hurt?
7. What is your personal history with infidelity?
8. What are some of your own suggestions for both you and your partner for building immunity to infidelity?
9. What has been your history together of talking about attractions to others outside of your relationship?

Booster Shots

The following are additional preventative ways that can help couples avoid infidelity. Planned renegotiation is a problem-solving method in which couples regularly plan time to review and renew their relationship. One simple process is to ask each other, "What would you like more of? less of?" and "What are you getting the right amount of in our relationship?"[10]

Glass suggested the following seven tips for preventing infidelity.

1. Maintain appropriate walls and windows. Keep the windows open at home. Put up privacy walls with others who could threaten your marriage.
2. Recognize that work can be a danger zone. Don't lunch or take private coffee breaks with the same person all the time. When you travel with a coworker, meet in public rooms not in a room with a bed.
3. Avoid emotional intimacy with attractive alternatives to your committed relationship.

4. Protect your marriage by discussing relationship issues at home. If you do need to talk to someone else about your marriage, be sure that person is a friend of the marriage.

5. Keep old flames from reigniting. If a former lover is coming to the class reunion, invite your partner to come along.

6. Don't go over the line when you're online with Internet friends. Discuss your online friendships with your partner and show his or her e-mail if he or she is interested. Don't exchange sexual fantasies online.

7. Make sure your social network is supportive of your marriage. Surround yourself with friends who are happily married and who don't believe in fooling around.[11]

Concluding Remarks

In this article, the authors have used medical metaphors describing some of the ways that couples both catch the virus of infidelity as well as some antidotes that can help build immunity against it. Commitment is one of the best ways of preventing infidelity. Four activities have been described for couples to use in talking to each other about their own experiences, feelings, insecurities, and past behaviors relating to infidelity.

Biographies

Pedra Ane was born and has lived the majority of her life in Texas. After teaching public elementary school for 18 years, she made a career shift that fulfilled a lifelong dream. Pedra Ane is a Licensed Professional Counselor Supervisor and Certified School Counselor in the state of Texas. She is currently in private practice in The Woodlands, Texas working with young children, adolescents, individuals, couples, and families.

Judith A. Nelson, Department of Educational Leadership and Counseling, Sam Houston State University, Huntsville, Texas.

Endnotes

[1] Lusterman, D. (1998). *Infidelity: A survival guide.* Oakland, CA: New Harbinger, p. 3.

[2] Rasmussen, P., & Kilborne, K. (2007). Sex in intimate relationships: Variations and challenges. In P. Peluso (Ed.), *Infidelity: A practioner's guide to working with couples in crisis* (pp. 27-28). New York: Taylor & Francis.

[3] Subotnik, R., & Harris, G. (2005). *Surviving infidelity.* Avon, MA: Adams Media, p. 175.

[4] Glass, S. (2003). "Not Just Friends"—Rebuilding trust and recovering your sanity after infidelity. New York: Free Press, p. 380.

[5] Eckstein, D., & Cooke, P. (2005). The seven methods of encouragement for couples. *The Family Journal: Counseling and Therapy for Couples and Families, 13,* 342-350.

[6] Love, P., & Stousy, J. (2007). How to improve your marriage without talking about it. New York: Doubleday.

[7] Gottman, J., & Silver, N. (1999). The seven principles for making marriage work: A practical guide from the country's foremost relationship expert. New York: Three Rivers Press.

[8] Nelson, J., Eckstein, D., Kirk, A., & Serres, S. (2007). *The couples' commitment interviews.* Retrieved August 1, 2007, from http://freeonlinesurveys.com/

[9] Ortega, A., & Fleming, M. (2005). *The dance of restoration.* Chattanooga, TN: Living Ink, pp 120-121.

[10] Sherwood, J., & Glidwell, J. (1973). Planned renegotiation: A norm setting OD intervention. In J. Jones & J.Pheiffer (Eds.), *The 1973 annual handbook for group facilitators* (pp. 195-202). La Jolla, CA: University Associates.

[11] Glass, *loc. cit.* p. 381.

Section 6:

A Couple's Activity for Understanding Birth Order Effects: Introducing the Birth Order Research-Based Questionnaire[1]

Daniel Eckstein, Mark A. Sperber, and Kristen Aycock Miller

The role of birth order on one's personality and romantic relationship is the focus of this article for you as a couple. The premise is that exploring and understanding your birth order history, you might gain understanding of your present relationship. Future implications and a continued commitment to relationship renewal are the belief underlying this activity.

The article is organized as follows: there will be a brief introduction to the importance of family of origin and birth order. You as a couple will then individually take and score what the authors have created for this article called Birth Order Research-Based Questionnaire (BORQ). The questionnaire is a didactic experience that explores your awareness of common personality traits related to birth order and is based on the authors' review of statistically significant birth order research studies. The next step is to interview each other about your experiences growing up. The article concludes with a review of some pertinent literature regarding the effects of birth order on personality. The article concludes with an experiential couple's activity where you can consider the implications birth order on your relationship and how you might apply insights that you may have gained.

Birth Order Effect on Your Personality

Sigmund Freud and Alfred Adler, two of the founders of Western psychology, exemplify birth order strife. Freud is often considered Western psychology's firstborn son and somewhere in the background Adler likely fits as the second. The strong beliefs of Freud and Adler in the effects of birth order on a person's core personality eventually influenced their initial choices of patients and the iconic theories that they both developed based on this clinical evidence (Ansbacher & Ansbacher, 1956). Freud, his mother's undisputed favorite and a typical firstborn, was conscious of his social status and valued authority and power over his peers.

Adler's early memories include references to how his older brother was stronger and more athletic and in Adler's opinion his parents' favorite. One of Adler's early memories as reported by Mosak and Kopp (1973) consisted of the following,

> I remember sitting on a bench bandaged up on account of rickets, with my healthy elder brother sitting opposite me. He could run, jump, and move about quite effortlessly, while for me, movement of any sort was a strain and an effort. Everyone

went to great pains to help me and my mother and father did all that was in their power to do. (p. 158)

As a second son both biologically and of modern psychology, Adler disagreed with Freud's "firstborn" notion of the Oedipus complex (with its overemphasis on parent-child relations). In elaborating on the psychological significance of birth order, Adler saw his patients as individuals struggling for power and a sense of competence (the fate of many younger siblings). Truth is sometimes greater than fiction. Alfred Adler not only resided in the professional shadow of Sigmund Freud in his early career, but his biological older brother was named . . . you got it, SIGMUND. During his lifetime, Adler seemed to constantly have an older brother named Sigmund and even today in many theories books the chapter on Adler is often listed under the "neo-Freudian" analytic models.

Review of Related Literature

The sheer volume of research on birth order can be overwhelming. Miley (1969), Forer (1977), Watkins (1986), and Stewart and Stewart (1995) compiled bibliographies on birth order research. Stewart and Stewart found 1,065 items published about birth order from 1976 to 1993. Eckstein (2000) cited 154 statistically significant birth order studies and compiled the differences in an attempt to make sense of the broad amount of information. The next question is "so what?" and "how can we apply this information?" The authors believe that these results should be generalized to helping you as a couple.

The alchemy of family dynamics often produces siblings that are often as different in their personalities as individuals from different families. In *Born to Rebel*, Sulloway (1996) argued that birth order explains why siblings often are quite different. Siblings use physical advantages in size and strength to gain a competitive edge. Sulloway asserted that, over time, strategies perfected by firstborns spawn counterstrategies by later-borns. The result is what Sulloway called an "evolutionary arms race" (p. 15) played out within the family.

> Childhood and the family are central to the story of human behavior because they provide the immediate causal context for these developmental scenarios. Childhood is about the search for a family niche. The first rule of the sibling road is to be different from one's brothers and sisters, especially if one happens to be a later-born. Sibling diversity is testimony to the powerful role that the environment plays in personality development. Although evolutionary principles guide this process, the story is one of seamless interactions between genetic potentials and environmental opportunities. (Sulloway, p. 118)

Sulloway (1996) applied personality factors related to the firstborn and later-born birth order positions. Sulloway asserted that firstborns are typically more achievement oriented, antagonistic, anxious, assertive, conforming, extraverted, fearful, identified with parents, jealous, neurotic, organized, planful, responsible, self-confident, and traditional. They also tend to affiliate under stress and are more likely than later-borns to assume leadership roles. Conversely, Sulloway found later-borns are generally more adventurous, altruistic, cooperative, easygoing, empathetic, open to experience, popular, rebellious, risk-taking, sociable, and unconventional.

One of the most comprehensive articles on birth order the authors found was a contribution by Herrera, Zajonc, Wieczorkowska, and Cichomski (2003). In the introduction preceding their four research studies, Herrera et al. (2003) noted that while birth order studies number in the thousands, beliefs about birth order are strikingly scarce. They cited Alfred Adler as an important contributor to such research. Herrera et al. (2003) stress such studies are important because

> they reflect some reality about the correlates of birth order and may well influence the actual role of birth order in society. Important decisions in interpersonal interactions, mating, appointments, promotions, awards, and distinctions might well be made with birth order entering, often unconsciously, as an important consideration. (p. 142)

After combining samples from the United States and in Poland, the following is a summary of some of the four studies conducted by Herrera et al. (2003). They found that their 196 participants believed that

    (a)   firstborns are the most intelligent, responsible, obedient, stable, the least emotional, and quite clearly the least creative,

    (b)   only children are the most disagreeable, (c) middle-borns are the most envious and the least bold and talkative, and

    (d)   last-borns are the most creative, emotional, extraverted, disobedient, irresponsible, and talkative. (p. 144)

There also seemed to be no self-esteem problems for any of the birth order groups. They rated their own respective birth order positions highest for the characteristics of agreeableness, intelligence, obedience, responsibility, and stability.

Herrera et al. (2003) also found birth order differences relative to career stereotypes. In both a Wisconsin-focused study and a Stanford University California-based study, they found that firstborns were more likely to work as accountants, lawyers, astronauts (interestingly, the first 16 astronauts were oldest or firstborn males), architects, police officers, surgeons, or college professors. Conversely, later-borns were stereotyped in such occupations as firefighter, high school teacher, musician, photographer, social worker, and stunt man. The authors found that the average prestige of occupations attributed to firstborns was significantly higher than last-borns. Similar trends were found in a fourth study comparing actual occupational prestige and academic attainment of the various birth ranks. Herrera et al. (2003) concluded their commentary on birth order by noting:

> People's beliefs in such differences show strong and consistent patterns, replicable over diverse populations . . . It is entirely possible that people's beliefs about birth order rank differences may induce differences in parents' expectations for their own children and about other people in general. They may also induce differences in the attributions about their children's abilities and behavior. As a result people may react differently to firstborn and later-born children . . . That behavior, in turn, might strengthen their beliefs. (p. 150)

A core Adlerian premise is that the same lifestyle carries one to the heights of success is the lifestyle that leads to our greatest challenges (Ansbacher & Ansbacher, 1956), so too there are advantages and disadvantages to each birth order position. One hypothesis of second born advantage is that second-borns benefit from observing the mistakes of the older sibling.

An example of the down side of the focus on sibling rivalry and competition in life is the first author's own vivid experience one day of running single file through lush tropical foliage in Maui, Hawaii. This author obliviously passed beside majestic waterfalls and beautiful vistas. Thirteen miles into the run, the author realized he had indeed missed all such exquisite scenery because he had been fixated on staying behind and indeed in watching the butt of the other runner who was leading the way through the forests. It is a powerful example of how many individuals spend much of their life in such a limiting focus on that butt ahead of them while missing the forests and waterfalls that are all around them.

The reader might consider Alfred Adler who brought birth order to prominence (Ansbacher & Ansbacher, 1956) who also stressed that the golden rule of Individual Psychology is that everything can be different. Similarly, birth order personality implications are not "one size fits all." Instead they are an important tool such as gender, family values, ethnicity, community values, and related variables that are important aspects of personality.

Kevin Leman is the author of 25 books on marriage- and family-related topics. Some specific books on birth order include: *The New Birth Order* (1998), *Birth Order Book* (2007), *The Perfect Match* (2004), and *Firstborn Advantage* (2008). In *The Birth Order Connection* (2001), he stresses that birth order is often overlooked when choosing a mate despite it being a vitally important variable to consider. While none of his content seems to reflect any research base, it is included here to acknowledge birth order in the popular press. Leman (year) defines birth order in the broad terms of "the totality of your family's influence on your own personality" (p.67). Consistent with the authors own comments on the topic, he stresses that chronological birth order is impacted by such factors as spacing; sibling gender, physical, mental, or emotional differences; sibling deaths, adoptions, illness, blended families; parental birth order; and critical parents. Here is what he considers "best birth order blends."

Only-Youngest
Firstborn-Youngest
Middle-Youngest

He writes that "If you want the absolute best match, it's a female only (or firstborn) marrying a male youngest child who has older sisters." (p. 69) Conversely, Leman's "worst birth order blends" are

Only-only
First-First
Youngest-Youngest
Early Middle-Early Middle
Late Middle-Late Middle

Leman (2001) uses the following medical metaphor in further elaborating on his personal birth order opinions:

A romantic relationship between two people of the same birth order can be a lot like taking an overdose of medicine . . . most medicines have some side unpleasant side effects. If you take more of a particular medicine than has been prescribed, it won't increase the benefits of the medicine, but it will increase the side effects. (p. 70-71)

For those of you who in fact are of the above "worst" birth order combination, perhaps before filling for a divorce, you can take comfort in Adler's comment regarding the fundamental principles of Adlerian psychology, that being that "everything can be different."

Based on 154 studies cited in Eckstein (2000) and 185 studies in Eckstein, Sperber, Wiesner, McDonald, Aycock, and Watts (manuscript in preparation), here is a summary of statistically significant research findings on birth order: They are listed in the rank order of most number of research studies for each respective birth order empirical studies.

Birth Order Research-Based Questionnaire (BORQ)
By Daniel Eckstein, Mark A. Sperber, and Kristen J. Aycock

Instructions: The following birth order characteristics are based on a review of over 200 statistically significant research articles as reported in Eckstein (2000) and Eckstein, Sperber, Wiesner, McDonald, Aycock, and Watts (manuscript in preparation). It is important to note that these characteristics are not true of ALL people in each birth order category (and may not be true for you), but are found to be common.

You are invited to take this questionnaire. Before scoring, you may want to compare your answers with your partner's and see whether you can come to a consensus collaboratively on

DANIEL ECKSTEIN, PhD

what you believe is the correct answer for each question. Additionally, you will name the five characteristics (e.g., most popular) that are most like you regarding your family and that the five that are least like you. Finally, score the questionnaire and discuss how well you were able to identify the correct birth order attributes and how well you fit one of the birth order typologies (e.g., firstborn).

Activity 8:
Birth Order Research-Based Questionnaire (BORQ)

Please choose one of the following birth order categories for each of the statements (1-30). (a) oldest (b) only (c) middle (d) youngest (e) no significant differences noted

1) Highest social interest/agreeableness _____
2) Greatest feelings of not belonging in the family _____
3) Highest academic success _____
4) Most need for achievement _____
5) Most sociable family member _____
6) Most likely to seek support under stress _____
7) Most empathic _____
8) Least likely to get into trouble _____
9) Most likely to go to college _____
10) Most likely to be stated as parents' favorite _____
11) Most likely to succeed in team sports _____
12) Most likely to be an alcoholic _____
13) Most likely to have behavior problems _____
14) Most likely to conform to parental values _____
15) Most rebellious _____
16) Most likely to have a negative view of childhood _____
17) Most often felt they were the parent's favorite _____
18) Fearful in new situations _____
19) Most cooperative _____
20) More artistic, less scientific _____
21) Most resilient _____
22) More likely to be selfish _____
23) Most popular _____

50

24) More dependent on others' approval _____
25) Most likely a finalist in American Idol _____ 26) Most cautious _____
27) Strongest gender identity _____
28) Most likely to be a swimmer _____

Step 1. *Predicting your birth order characteristics.*

1. Name five characteristics you feel are most accurate in describing you? For what reason?
2. Name five characteristics you feel you will be the least accurate in describing you? For what reason?

In the boxes below check the items you correctly answered.

A-Oldest	B-Only	C-Middle	D-Youngest	E-No significant differences
_____ 3	_____ 4	_____ 2	_____ 1	_____ 10
_____ 6	_____ 9	_____ 5	_____ 7	_____ 17
_____ 14	_____ 13	_____ 8	_____ 12	_____ 21
_____ 18	_____ 19	_____ 11	_____ 15	_____ 25
_____ 24	_____ 22	_____ 16	_____ 20	_____ 28
_____ 29	_____ 27	_____ 26	_____ 23	_____ 30

(For supporting research, please reference Appendix)

Step 2. Rubric:

Scores 24-30—Superior!!!—You knocked the cover off the baseball!
Scores 18-23—Good work! More homers than strike-outs
Scores 12-17—Questionable . . . more misses than hits
Scores 0-11—Subpar: a big swing, but nothing but wind.

Step 3.

Write a paragraph in your own words summarizing the implications of your results. For example, you might consider the five characteristics that were most like you and how well these characteristics fit a particular birth order position? Did the five characteristics that were least like you fit with a particular birth order position? Consider the same questions for both partners. Finally, how you did you do at correctly identifying birth order characteristics?

Activity 9:
Family of Origin (or Equivalent) Birth Order Interview Questions

The following questions are based on family of origin explorations described by Eckstein (2003) in his Eckstein Life Style Inventory. Ideally each of you will interview each other using the suggested questions below. If that is not possible complete your own responses to the questions and share with your partner at a later time.

Here are some suggested questions for you to ask each other pertaining to your childhoods.

A. Describe yourself and your siblings from the perspective of when you were six or seven years of age. Write the name and age of each sibling (including you) in descending order beginning with the oldest. Include any deceased siblings, siblings separated from the family, or siblings living elsewhere. Also note any other known pregnancies terminated by abortion, miscarriage, or still-birth, entering the appropriate in the ordinal positions. Include any step-siblings and note when they entered the family.

Using your age as a baseline, note the differences in years of age, plus or minus, between each sibling and yourself. Describe each sibling again including you.

Sibling 1:
Name:
Age:
Description

Sibling 2:
Name:
Age:
Description
**Continue this description of each sibling, step-siblings, etc., as noted in the directions.

B. Further sibling descriptions: Please respond to the following questions as you would have responded when you were a young child of six to seven years of age. If there were only two of you, answer each question in relation to your sibling. If you are a single child, answer the questions from the perspective of comparing yourself to children in general.
   1. Who was most different from you? How?
   2. Who was most like you? How?
   3. Who fought and argued? What was your role in the disagreements and how did you respond to conflict?

4. Who played together?

5. Who took care of whom?

C. Sibling ratings: Look over the following descriptions. Note three to five of the most characteristic descriptors for you as a child by circling them. Also, note three to five descriptors that were least characteristic of you as a child by putting a box around them.

If you are an only child, rate yourself in comparison to the peer group you associated with as a child or with children in general. Focus your rating on your personal opinion of your family situation during the first seven years of your life as much as possible.

1. Intelligent	14. Sense of humor
2. Hardest worker	15. Idealistic
3. Best grades in school	16. Materialistic
4. Helped around the house	17. Standards of accomplishment
5. Conforming	18. Athletic
6. Rebellious	19. Physically strong
7. A pleaser	20. Emotionally strong
8. Critical of others	21. Attractive
9. Considerate	22. Spoiled
10. Selfishness	23. Punished
11. Getting one's way	24. Spontaneous
12. Sensitive, easily hurt	25. Any other descriptive
13. Temper tantrums	objectives

D. Additional childhood and adolescent developmental considerations
   a) How would you describe your own birth order in the family? For example, while you may have been chronologically the third-born you may have felt you were more like a firstborn by virtue of being the firstborn male or because you grew up in a blended family. Do you feel more like a firstborn or a later-born?
   b) What are some of the defining characteristics in your opinion about these placements in families (or family equivalents)
      1. Oldest
      2. Only
      3. Second-born
      4. Middle-child
      5. Youngest

Relationship Application

Here is a one way of summarizing the implications of the study for your respective birth order personality.

1. What are some major traits you feel are characteristic of you?
2. Name some specific behavioral examples of how have these been demonstrated in your current relationship?
3. What do you feel are some important traits that are characteristic of your partner?
4. Give some specific examples of how your partner has demonstrated this in your relationship.
5. Brainstorm together—think of some suggestions to enable the two of you to collaboratively understand and mutually respect each other's personality characteristics. For example, what would each of you like to change within yourself to improve the relationship? How can an awareness and appreciation of different styles help you be more considerate of each other in your partnership?

Summary

The purpose of the article has been for readers as a couple to explore the relationship implications of your respective family of origin birth-order dynamics. While the activity was designed to be an interview between the couple, you may also find it helpful to discuss your responses with a counselor or trusted spiritual advisor. The authors have introduced the Birth Order Research-Based Questionnaire (BORQ) to test your content knowledge of statistically significant research studies. Supplemental interview questions for exploring your respective family of origin (or equivalent) experiences have also been introduced. A summary of implications and next steps for you as a couple concluded the article.

References

Ansbacher, H. L., & Ansbacher, R. R. (Eds.). (1956). The individual psychology of Alfred Adler. New York: Basic Books.

Eckstein, D. (2000). Empirical studies indicating significant birth-order-related personality difference. Journal of Individual Psychology, 56, 481-494.

Eckstein, D. (2003). Footprints and fingerprints of my 30-year journey in lifestyle assessment. Journal of Individual Psychology, 59, 410-420.

Eckstein, D., Sperber, M. A., McDonald, J., Wiesner, V. V., Aycock, K. J., & Watts, R. E. One hundred eighty-five statistically significant studies on birth order: Researching personality and family dynamics. Unpublished manuscript.

Forer, L. K. (1977). Bibliography of birth order literature in the '70s. Journal of Individual Psychology, 33, 122-141.

Herrera, N. C., Zajonc, R. B., Wieczorkowska, G., & Cichomski, B. (2003). Beliefs about birth rank and their reflection in reality. Journal of Personality and Social Psychology, 85, 142-150.

Leman, K. (1998). The new birth order. Grand Rapids, MI: Fleming Revell.

Leman, K. (2001). The birth order connection. Grand Rapids, MI: Fleming Revell.

Leman, K. (2004). The perfectmatch.GrandRapids, MI: FlemingRevell. Leman, K. (2007). The new birth order. Grand Rapids, MI: Fleming Revell.

Leman, K. (2008). Firstborn advantage. Grand Rapids, MI: Fleming Revell.

Miley, C. H. (1969). Birth order research 1963-1967. Bibliography and index. Journal of Individual Psychology, 25, 64-70.

Mosak, H., & Kopp, R. (1973). The early recollections of Freud, Jung, & Adler. Journal of Individual Psychology, 29, 117-135.

Stewart, A. E., & Stewart, E. A. (1995). Trends in birth-order research: 1976-1993. Journal of Individual Psychology, 51, 21-36.

Sulloway, F. J. (1996). Born to rebel. New York: Pantheon Books. Watkins, C. E. (1986). A research bibliography on Adlerian psychological theory. Individual Psychology, 42, 123-132.

---

[1] Eckstein, D., Miller, K., Sperber, M., McDonald, J., Wiesner, V., Watts, R., and Ginsburg, P. (2010). A review of 200 birth order studies: Lifestyle studies, *Journal of Individual Psychology*, 66.4. (in press)

Biographies

Kristen J. Aycock Miller is in the Department of Counseling and Psychological Services at Georgia State University.

Mark Sperber, M.A. is in private practice in Houston Texas.

Section 7:

Counseling Is The Answer . . . Counseling Is The Answer . . . But What Is The Question? 25 Questions for Couples and Families

Daniel Eckstein

The title for this article was inspired by a Charles Schultz "Peanuts" comic strip. For three frames Charlie Brown waves a placard proclaiming "Christ is the answer, Christ is the answer, Christ is the answer." The final frame shows Snoopy's replying placard "But what is the question?"

A premise of this column is that families and couples can often obtain insights simply through the process of self-assessment or interviewing and then by relating to the partner's responses to a series of personal and relationship oriented questions. Part I provides 25 such questions. After discussing Part 1 answers, the couple/family members then are invited to do Part 2 together. Couples and families can take and discuss the responses to the questions together. Later, if desired, the issues can be discussed with a counselor.

Part 1

Answer the questions from the perspective of either (a) your partner; (b) another family member; and/or (c) yourself. The suggested sequence is similar to the process used in couple's renewal seminars called "Marriage Encounter."

Here are the questions—feel free to pass on any item if so desired. First answer the questions alone. Then share your responses with your partner or family member(s) with either one person going through his or her responses to all the questions. The roles should then be reversed with the other person(s) sharing responses to all the questions. A second option is to give the answers to each separate question, each person alternating going first or second in the order of sharing. Whichever method is used, the third step suggested is that a time of discussion follow the responses. Surprises, new learnings, reminders of previous learnings, and lastly the implications for you personally, then your relationship and/or family relationship can be identified and discussed. The maximum benefit will be gained by answering the questions specifically about your partner or one other family member. You can, of course, complete several versions of the questionnaire for each family member.

Procedure

An American Indian koan that can be viewed as one way of describing empathy is "If you want to understand my world, walk a mile in my moccasins."

What follows are a series of 25 questions which the author has used personally, based on his own counseling. Also included are questions plus the writings from various marriage and family therapy books and journals and particular contributions of solution-focused therapy.

Activity 10: Twenty-Five Relationship Questions

1. On a scale of 1-10, rate your current level of satisfaction with your relationship. Elaborate on the specific reason(s) for giving this numeric value.
2. What are some activities in which you currently experience joy, fun, and/or happiness between you and _____?
3. What (if anything) do you do primarily with or for yourself alone that brings you happiness?
4. What was the high of the last year for you personally? . . . and now for you as a couple or family?
5. Can you remember a time recently when you pleasantly surprised yourself or did something out of character that pleased you?
6. How about the same question for you as a couple? (Or family?)
7. Can you recall a time when you thought you had a problem in your relationship but instead you did not? . . . What changed it from being a problem to not being a problem?
8. What amount of the time do you feel you are aligned or in harmony in your relationship? Cite specific examples of how you feel both aligned and unaligned with your partner.
9. How do you think your friends would describe your relationship between you and _____?
10. Cite some examples of how your partner (family member[s]) has encouraged you in the past month.
11. Cite some examples of how your partner (family member[s]) has discouraged you in the past month.
12. What do you think your responses to #9, #10, and #11 say about *your* wants, needs, motivators, and values?
13. When you and your partner are (a) happy together contrasted with being (b) in conflict with each other, what would actually be seen and/or heard if it had been videotaped on those times?
14. What do you have as a right to expect from your partner? (family member?)
15. What does your partner (family member) have a right to expect from you?
16. Consider the following three different ways of describing the attachment between you and your partner. In what ways would you describe your relationship as:
    a) Secure (cite examples)
    b) Anxious or ambivalent (cite examples)
    c) Avoidant (cite examples)

17. What specifically would it (a) look like; (b) feel like; (c) sound like, and/or even (d) smell like when you and your partner are really connected with each other?

18. Contrast the above concrete ways of describing your relationship when you are feeling alienated and/or distant from your partner?

19. Using the analogy of flags used at a race track, what would you define as (a) green flags—indicators that say go forward, positive indictors in your relationship? (b) yellow flags—what are the caution signals in your relationship that have or may be slowing down the relationship race? (c) red flags—what has stopped the race in past relationships or what could end it in the future?

20. When you and your partner (family member) have challenges, how do you typically resolve them?

21. Give (an) example(s) of when your problems in the relationship are not occurring.

22. How do you prevent the problem from getting worse?

23. If you were to wake up tomorrow and a miracle has occurred in your relationship with the result that all the challenges between you and your partner and/or family were resolved, how would your life be different? Assume that the miracle occurred during the night when you were asleep—what small differences would you be able to identify the next morning that would indicate that indeed a miracle had occurred?

24. What needs to be different in your relationship to make your life happier?

25. How would others around you be able to know your relationship had changed in a positive manner?

Part 2

Complete your answers to the following questions as well as the suggested activities together as a couple or as a family.

Activity 11: Further Questions to Ponder

A. Consider a challenging situation in your relationship.
   1. If you were to have a dream or symbolic form for you and your partner, what would it be?
   2. How would these two symbolic forms relate to each other?
   3. Where would this take place?
   4. What if it never changed, if it went on forever, how would that be for you?
   5. Now, together actually act it out—*be* your story.

B.   Process your experience
1.   Were either of you surprised by each other's story?\
2.   What characters, values, or beliefs of your two stories were in conflict?
3.   What part(s) of your story was(were) in harmony?
C.   Now create a *new story* which combines your two individual stories. What alternative attitudes, and/or behaviors would be necessary to creatively combine these separate stories into one complimentary "once upon a time . . . ?"
D.   Discussion:
1.   What parallels can you draw between your stories and your actual relationship?
2.   Cite examples of complimentary and conflicting challenges in your relationship.
3.   What problem-solving strategies did you utilize in creating your new combined couples story?
E.   Implications/Applications
1.   How can you apply any of the insights from this activity for improved personal strategies in your relationship?
2.   What would be some suggested problem-solving strategies you might utilize to make the stories better?
3.   How can you plan to have more fun in the future, both for yourself personally as well as for your partnership and/or family unit?

Review of Literature

In Solution Focused Brief Therapy, Berg[1] believes that instead of trying to get rid of the problem, a better focus for couples is to identify and strengthen the already existing solution. It is an optimistic premise that the solution exists and is merely waiting to be remembered or rediscovered. The key ingredient is to listen to your partner and not pay too much attention to the problem that you two may describe. Two primary techniques are asking the Miracle Question (#23), and by using Scaling Techniques (#1) and (#8).

Pat Love[2] believes the following phases are characteristic of primary love relationships. Love postulates that attraction is the first stage of the primary love relationship. Stages of primary love relationship are as follows:

1.   **Attraction stage**: She believes we are more attracted to some individuals and not to others because humans exude a chemical called pheromones. Thus, it is often our chemicals and our hormones that are leading us. We are often attracted to people who represent unfinished business and who can complete our lives. Nature has two drives, those being: *procreation*, to keep our species alive, and *diversity*—the more diverse we are, the better

we are able to survive. The attraction stage is about getting together, not necessary about staying together. She says attraction is a purely chemical response to nature's attempt to procreate the species. Because attraction decreases the more often it is experienced, many individuals participate in dangerous, risk-taking behaviors in order to get the euphoria of the chemical high of attraction by choosing a partner who is dangerous, unavailable, or with whom a relationship must be secretive.

2. **Infatuation stage** (*limerance*): This is an altered state of consciousness that makes us feel euphoric. It leaves us longing for more, as if we are walking three feet off the ground; limerance is chemically induced. We are also under the influence of dopamine, and norepinephrine. By using a provocative phrase called "Hot Monogamy," she contends that staying with one partner is a choice; it is about our intentions. Our partner thus becomes the catalyst of this euphoric feeling—we feel open, zestful, we feel/show love, and we are undefended too. When we believe we are falling in love, and in our culture, we too often equate infatuation with love. Much of our music reinforces this notion. Danger, fear, and risk all enhance the limerance experience. When the amphetamine high starts to wane, couples will up the ante by engaging in behaviors which their family/ friends would not approve of, such as having a secret relationship with someone who is not approved of by family/friends. Pat Love contends that because amphetamines are activated by the presence of the partner, sexual energy has more to do with biology than the relationship itself. For example, a high-testosterone person falls for a low-testosterone person. The "low T" person's sexual energy spikes. The "high T" people feels like they have died and gone to heaven, because they believe they have found someone who will fulfill them sexually. Three to six months later, the body develops a tolerance and the amphetamine high begins to wane; it is a time-limited experience. Other cultures recognize limerance but do not value it as our culture does. It is usually not a rationale for a long-term relationship in other cultures. In the limerance phase the intensity of desire is misinterpreted during attraction and infatuation as depth of emotion. In reality it is time limited, usually decreasing in three to six months.

3. **Attachment stage**: In this phase partners value each other, and they practice caring behaviors. They are under the influence of endorphins, resulting in feelings of peace, calm, and safety. Love reports that many people lack the ability to attach because we only know what we were taught in childhood. She believes the ultimate leap is to realize that couples can be in a relationship while still being who they are without being abandoned or being swallowed up by the other person. She stresses that it is not the level of desire that makes "hot monogamy;" rather it is the profoundness of connectedness between the individuals. Love has developed the following equation to define love: **nature** + **choice** + **history** + **psychodynamics** = **love**.

Other Attachment Theories

Other attachment theories are presented below:

- The ways in which adult behavior in romantic relationships reflect the attachment relationships identified in early caregiver relationships. Hazan and Shaver[3],[4] used a three-category measure of adult attachment based on the typology of Ainsworth et al.[5] and discovered that adults could be classified the same way (secure, anxious/ambivalent, and avoidant) in their romantic relationships. Secure lovers show high levels of relationship trust, commitment, acceptance and relationship longevity. Anxious/ambivalent lovers demonstrate more jealousy and obsession about their lovers than secure lovers do. Avoidant lovers fear intimacy and commitment.

- Young and Acitelli[6] explored the relationship between attachment style, the degree of public commitment to the relationship, and the perception of a partner. They found that securely attached individuals' perceptions of their partners were not affected by their marital status, indicating that securely attached people do not need overt indicators of commitment to feel positively about their partners. For insecurely attached individuals, the researchers found that perception of one's partner was heavily influenced by overt displays of commitment between the partners.

  Individuals who describe their attachment style as anxious/ambivalent often view marriage as an indicator that they are worthy of love; conversely, for avoidant individuals, marriage may indicate to them that their partners are not committed and thus are not to be trusted.

  Marital status has also found to be important to anxious/ambivalently attached individuals. Married men with this particular attachment style have significantly less positive perceptions of their partners than married men with other attachment styles or unmarried men with the same attachment style. Of the three attachment types, anxious/ambivalent individuals are more likely to view their partners as worthy and able while doubting their own worth and ability.

- Differing attachment styles affect how a person reacts emotionally to the termination of a romantic relationship. How a person reacts emotionally to the termination of a romantic relationship is strongly related to his/her attachment style. For example, avoidant subjects have demonstrated the least amount of emotional distress, while anxious/ambivalent subjects exhibited the most emotional distress. After the relationship has been terminated, anxious/ambivalent subjects are the most likely to report that they are still in love. Insecure attachment (more specially, avoidant attachment) predates relationship instability.

Boundary Issues

Attachment disorders are evident in Pia Melody's[7] addictive cycle in codependent addicted relationships, more commonly referred to as the Love Addict/Love Avoidant Cycle. She says that for a "Love Addict," the greatest fear is that of abandonment with an underlying fear of intimacy. Other characteristics include:

- Being responsive to the avoidant's seductiveness and entering the relationship in a haze of fantasy
- Getting high from the fantasy
- Denying how walled in the avoidant really is
- Experiencing an event that shatters the denial
- Experiences of intense emotional withdrawal follows the denial
- Obsessive planning then occurs, often leading to addictions (food, drugs, alcohol, sex, nicotine, love)
- The person then returns to the fantasy or moves on to a new relationship

Conversely, for what Melody defines as a "Love Avoidant," the greatest fear is that of intimacy with an underlying fear of abandonment. Here are some of the characteristic phases:

- The person enters the relationship because he/she can't say no
- There is a wall of seduction that impedes intimacy; the person goes behind a wall of seduction making the love addict feel special
- It is a wall of anger that justifies abandonment by becoming overwhelmed by enmeshment and/or neediness of love addict and by protecting oneself by being critical of the love addict
- The person then abandons the relationship in some way
- This usually cycles into an addiction process; (i.e. sex, love, alcohol, drugs, work, gambling, etc.)
- The person may return to the relationship out of guilt or of fears of abandonment, or he/she moves on to connect with another partner

Encouragement

As Watts and Pietrzak[8] observe, Adlerian psychology stresses that encouragement skills include demonstrating concern for each other through active listening and empathy; communicating respect for, and confidence in one's partner; focusing on each other's strengths, assets, and resources; seeing the humor in life experiences. Solution Focused Brief Therapy (SFBT) stresses that couples are not sick and thus are not identified or labeled by their diagnosis. Goals of SFBT are to help couples change their behaviors and attitudes from a problem/failure focus to a focus on solutions/successes and to discover and develop latent assets, resources, and strengths that may have been overlooked as the couple focuses primarily on problems and limitations.

William O'Hanlon[9] has identified the following ten types of questions and statements in solution-based therapy.

1. *Scaling Questions* are designed to get continual assessment and feedback from the person/family and get them to realize changes or gray areas in the problem situation.

2. *Difference Questions* are designed to highlight differences and get the person to compare and contrast things about the problem, exceptions or solutions.

3. *Accomplishment Questions* attempt to get the person or family to recognize that something positive happened as a result of their efforts.

4. *Goal Questions* assist the person or the family to identify what they are interested in accomplishing or setting the end point for therapy or problem resolution.

5. *Compliments/Praise* encourages the acknowledgment for accomplishments, good intentions, or level of functioning.

6. *Atypical Experiences in Regard to the Problem (Exceptions)* help to elicit descriptions of times when things went differently from the usual problem situation.

7. *Description Questions* ask the person or the family to describe the problem or solution situation in observable terms.

8. *Smaller Step Questions/Comments* are designed to get couples to scale back grand ideas about their goals or progress into achievable ends or progress.

9. *Highlighting Change/New Stores* help couples notice or acknowledge changes or differences in their perceptions of themselves or other people's views of them.

10. *Motivation Questions* explore the motivation to change and to determine whether you have a "customer" for change.

Part 3—Summary

Having answered the questions, completed the exercise together and reading the material, answer some concluding questions such as:

1. What are some of your major learnings or relearnings about yourself?

2. What were some major learnings or relearnings about your partner (family member[s])? bring you closer together as a couple or a family?

Endnotes

1   Berg, I. K., & Dolan, Y. (2000). Tales of solutions: A collection of hope inspiring stories. New York: Norton.

2   Love, P. (1994). Hot monogamy [Audiotape]. New York: Sounds True.

3   Hazan, C., & Shaver, P. (1987). Romantic love conceptualized as an attachment process. Journal of Personality and Social Psychology, 52(3), 511-524.

4   Hazan, C., & Shaver, P. (1990). Love and work: An attachment theoretical perspective. Journal of Personality and Social Psychology, 59,270-280.

5   Ainsworth, M.D.S., Blehar, M., Walters, E., & Wall, S. (1978). Patterns of attachment: A psychological study of the strange situation. Hillsdale, NJ: Lawrence Eribaum.

6   Young, A. M., & Acitelli, L. K. (1998). The role of attachment style and relationship status of the perceiver in the perceptions of the romantic partner. Journal of Social and Personal Relationships, 75(2), 161-173.

7   Melody, P. (1992). Facing love addiction. San Francisco: Harper.

8   Watts, R. E., & Pietrzak, D. (2000). Adierian "encouragement" and the therapeutic process of solution-focused brief therapy. Journal of Counseling & Development, 78(3), 442-445.

9   O'Hanlon, W. (2000). Do one thing right: Ten simple ways to change your life. New York: Quill.

Section 8:

The Cultural Relationship Interview Matrix:
Four Activities for Couples

Chi-Sing Li, Yu-Fen Lin, Daniel Eckstein

Abstract

An understanding of one's own and his/her partner's cultural heritage is essential aspect to enhancing the relationship. In this article, the authors introduced the Cultural Relationship Interview Matrix (CRIM). It is a form for couples to complete individually and then to interview each other. The purpose is for bringing awareness to their respective cultural heritage and for enhancing their communication. Four activities and seven matrixes are included in the suggested exercises.

Introduction

We are currently living in a pluralistic, multicultural world. We encounter and establish relationships with people of other "cultures" almost daily. Race, ethnicity and culture are powerful variables that have tremendous influence on people's thought process, decision-making ability, behaviors and perception of their world.[1] Recent data from the U.S. Census Bureau[2] indicate a disbursal of new immigrants to part of the Southeast and Midwest that have not experienced such growth trends in the past. For example, the international born population in South Carolina grew 48% from 2000 to 2005. Similar gains were noted in Indiana (30%) and Nebraska (34%).[3]

The share of the U.S. population that is white but not Hispanic is also declining as minority groups grow more rapidly. Immigrants to the U.S. from other countries now make up 12.4% of the U.S. population; that is an increase from the 11.2% in the 2000 Census.[4]

Culture impacts personality differences, role perceptions, communication and problem solving in couple relationship. When couples are able to share their culture(s) with each other, it can enhance their relationship and bring their communication and connection to a different level. As Satir said, "Communication is the largest factor determining what kinds of relationships one makes with others and what happened to him in the world about him."[5]

A Brief Review of the Literature
Cultural Considerations for Couples

Here are some of the following issues that are most important for couples relative to their cultural heritage:

- What is the suggested age for marriage and why?
- What are some of the expectations of both men and woman in your culture?
- Is there a history of arranged marriages? If so, who and how are they arranged?
- What are some of the most important considerations in your culture for mate selection?
- What are the roles of each of your families of origin in your current marriage?[6]
- What are some cultural expectations of the division of responsibilities between you?
- What are some issues of power and influence relative to such issues as gender from your cultural perspective?
- What is the role of religion in your culture? Is there a predominate religion in your culture? Is so, did you and do you currently practice that religion?
- If your partner is from another religious background how does that impact your current relationship?
- How do the two of you manage your finances? Is there agreement in this area?

Advantages and Disadvantages of Intercultural Marriages

Representative advantages include: more through preparation for marriage, greater degree of commitment; more self-other differentiation, tolerance, respect and tolerance and more accepting of differences.

Noteworthy disadvantages of intercultural marriages include: less common ground in the relationship; learning and growth can be inhibited by conflicting backgrounds; social stigma and non-acceptance by others; and institutional racism. There are both the advantages and disadvantages of intercultural marriages.[7]

Monogamy, Male Dominance and Female Attractiveness

Lucas, et.al.[8] researched marital satisfaction in more than 2,000 couples of the U.S. U.K, China, and Turkey. They focused on the following three re-occurring characteristics in all four cultures: *Homogamy* (the tendency to select mates that are similar to oneself), *male dominance*, and *female attractiveness*. There are basic differences in the more individualistic western orientation compared to a come collectivistic Eastern tendency. Marriages in Eastern cultures generally reflect such collectivistic values as harmony and benefits to the extended family.

In their research for the above-mentioned four cultures, Lucas et al propose that "it is likely that cultural values may have shaped the criteria utilized to define marital satisfaction. For example, while wives from America and China both preferred husband ascendancy on income, the reason for this preference may have differed. American wives may have preferred a higher earning husband because this leads to personal satisfaction with the marriage. Chinese wives, on the other hand, may have preferred the same ascendancy not because it leads to personal satisfaction, but rather because a providing husband more really services many of the familial obligation and instrumental concerns that characterize marriage within that culture"[9]

Marriage in Malta

Abela, Frosh, and Dowling[10] explored the low incidence of marriage breakdown in the Mediterranean island of Malta. They particularly focused on the role of culture in relationships. While as many as one in three marriages in the U.S. and the U.K. end in divorce, only 3.7% of the couples in Malta ever separate.[11] Key variable that were discovered included a much stricter sense of morality than other European countries. Faithfulness, respect, discussing problems, and spending time together were all positive factors in couples staying together.

Broke-back Mountain, Same Sex Commentary

Rose and Urchel[12] analyzed the complexity of love as portrayed in the movie adaptation of Annie Proulx's[13] short story. Both the author and Roger Ebert[14] viewed the relationship between Del Mar and Jack Twist as a bond founded on love. Others however use the terms *obsession* and *sexual predator.* Rose and Urchel concluded that "it is not only the heterosexist macho culture of 1960's America but also the lack of an empathetic and nurturing upbringing, especially that fostered by fathers as role models, that preclude the development of a healthy openly public partnership between two men in love. Both characters suffered from emotional repression stemming from the lack of close familial relationships in childhood and from trauma and abuse their fathers inflict upon them."[15]

The Purpose of this Article

Since culture is such a significant aspect of one self and in couple relationships, this article has been designed for helping couples in exploring the role of culture in their lives through interviewing one another. Just as Watts and Pietrzak[16] stressed the importance of encouragement in relationships, it is our hope that you as a couple will be encouraging each other in this interview.

Couple communication is for those who want to take charge of their lives by developing more fulfilling ways of being together. Sharing with each other is crucial to individual and relationship growth.[17]

The authors have created the Cultural Relationship Interview Matrix (CRIM) as a tool to facilitate the couple communication process. The CRIM has been drawn from the group cultural variables of Sue and Sue[18] and the development model of Erik Erikson[19] to form an 11 x 5 matrix.

Sue and Sue[20] suggested the following eleven cultural reference groups to which people may belong, *age, culture, ability/disability, ethnicity, gender, geographic location, marital status, race, religious preference, sexual orientation,* and *socioeconomic status*. They further inferred that some group identities may be more salience than other but they may change over time.

Erikson[21] identified eight developmental stages of psychosocial development for each individual. Each stage of the development presents itself with conflict/challenge. Successful adjustment to the conflict/challenge at one stage positively influences the way of coping in the next stage. The process of resolving conflicts plays a significant role in the development of one's personality. We have borrowed ideas from Erikson's model to create the following five stages of development in our matrix. They are *childhood, adolescence, single adult, adult coupled,* and *coupled with children* (if applicable.)

Organization of the Interview

The interview process will be organized in the following manner. First, you as a couple will be invited to share your cultural experience with your partner in a structured format. You and your partner will then be asked to create your own cultural matrix (My Matrix) separately with the help of a list of questions and the CRIM. After each of you has completed your own cultural matrix, you will be invited to outline a cultural matrix of your partner (My Partner's Matrix) based on your prediction/perception and experience with your partner. Next, you will be encouraged to sit face-to-face sharing with each other the matrixes you created. The final activity is to work with your partner together in creating the matrix for the two of you (Our Matrix).

Tips for Being a Good Interviewer

Egan[22] summarized key nonverbal skills as guidelines for interviewers to visibly tune in with the interviewee in the acronym SOLER. They are facing the person *squarely*, adopting an *open* posture, remembering that it is possible at times to *lean toward* the other, maintaining good *eye contact* and trying to be relatively *relaxed* or natural in these behaviors. These nonverbal guidelines, when being applied, provide an inviting, trusting and safe environment for communication.

Here are six suggested ways you and your partner can be encouraging to one another:

1. Demonstrating concern through active listening and empathy;
2. Communicating respect for and confidence in the other person;
3. Focusing on each other strengths, assets and resources;
4. Helping each other generate perceptual alternatives for discouraging fictional beliefs;
5. Focusing on efforts and progress, and
6. Helping each other see the humor in life experiences.[23]

Activity 12: Create Your Own Matrix (My Matrix)

The objective of this activity is to explore the role and the effect of culture when you were growing up as a child and in the relationship with your partner right now. You are invited to spend as much time as needed to create your own cultural matrix. Choose any of the following three to five cultural factors listed on the CRIM which are most important to you right now. Feel free to add any other cultural factor(s) that are not on the list but are significant to you.

The following questions will serve as guidelines to stimulate your thoughts and feelings as how the cultural factors may have influenced you. To assist you in creating your own matrix, you can fill any of the cultural factors in the blank below.

A. The role of culture in your *childhood*
   • What did you hear about _____ from your family or family equivalent?
   • What was your first memory that you have about _____?
   • What did you hear about _____ from the media?
   • What did you hear about _____ from your friends and your school?
   • What did you hear about _____ from your religion?
   • Do you remember a significant experience about _____?

B. The role of culture in your *adolescence*
   • In contrast to your childhood, what were some changes if any that occurred for you about _____ as an adolescent?
   • How were you similar and/or different in your attitudes about _____?
   • As an adolescent, what were some significant messages about _____ that you learn from the family or family equivalent?
   • Do you remember a significant decision or conclusion that you made about _____?

C. The role of culture in your *adulthood* when you were *single*
   • Do you remember a significant decision or conclusion that you made about _____?

- What are the significant messages about _____ you got from family? How do you deal with these messages? (Agree? Disagree? Covertly? Overtly?)
- What were the significant messages about _____ you got from media?
- What were the significant messages about _____ you got from friends?
- What were some things about _____ that you said to yourself?
- In contrast to your childhood, what were some significant changes (if any) that occurred with you regarding _____ as a single adult?
- How did _____ affect you in pursuing a relationship?
- What would be important for your partner to know about you regarding _____?

D. The role of culture in your adulthood when you were/are *coupled*
- How does my belief about _____ impact my current or past relationship(s) with my partner(s)?
- How does (did) my partner's belief about _____ impact my life?
- How does (did) my family's belief(s) about _____ impact our relationship?
- How does (did) the belief of my partner's family about _____ impact our relationship?

E. The role of culture in your adulthood when you were/are *coupled with child(ren)* (if applicable)
- How has my belief about _____ changed or stay the same after having children?
- How has my belief about _____ changed or stay the same after my children have become adolescents?
- How has my belief about _____ changed or stay the same after my children have become adults?
- How has my belief about _____ changed or stay the same after having grandchildren?

F. Transcending questions based on your total life
- If you are first or second generation in the country that you currently reside, what are (were) some significant messages you got about _____ that you haven't discussed so far and it is important for your partner to know?
- What else is important that you haven't explored that you think it is important for your partner to know?
- What is your belief and experiences about any of these eleven categories that you would like to share with your partner?
- What are some cultural activities in which you currently participate with your partner?
- Can you remember a time recently when you made a decision based on your culture that pleased you or/and your partner?

My Matrix: Cultural Relationship Interview Matrix (CRIM)

Now, complete your own matrix here:

	Childhood	Adolescent	Adult Single	Adult Coupled	Coupled with Child(ren)
Age					
Culture					
Disability/ Ability					
Ethnicity					
Gender					
Geographic Location					
Marital Status					
Race					

Religious Preference					
Sexual Orientation					
Socioeconomic Status					

Activity 13: Create Your Partner's Matrix (My Partner's Matrix)

The objective of this activity is to process your understanding of your partner's culture through your prediction/perception and experience of your partner by means of the CRIM. You are encouraged to add any other significant cultural factors to the list. Again, you and your partner are invited to choose three to five factors out of the CRIM list that speak to you most and begin describing your partners with those factors. Also, you can make use of the questions in Activity A to help complete this activity. You are encouraged to take as much time as needed to complete this activity.

Using both the above example as a sample of illustration and the same questions from Activity A that you use in your own matrix, now create your prediction/perception of your partner's CRIM in my partner's CRIM #5.

II. My partner's CRIM (My prediction/perception of my partner's profile)

	Childhood	Adolescent	Adult Single	Adult Coupled	Coupled with Child(ren)
Age					
Culture					

Disability/ Ability				
Ethnicity				
Gender				
Geographic Location				
Marital Status				
Race				
Religious Preference				
Sexual Orientation				

Activity 14: The Cultural Relationship Interview

After you and your partner have completed your own matrix and your partner's matrix, it is time to sit down together and share the results. Find an environment that is quiet, relaxed and reasonably free from distractions. Take turns to share the matrixes starting with "My Matrix" and then "My Partner's Matrix."

The objective is to communicate your findings with each other by active listening. You and your partner are asked to listen to each other by simply restating what each other has said without giving any of your comments. You are encouraged to use the transcending questions from Activity A for exploring further with your partner when you see appropriate. This is one of the most important activities in this interview process. You and your partner may want to take more time to process with each other. At the end of the interview, summarize and conclude what you hear from each other. The following questions may be of help in your reflection:

1. What are some of the major cultural themes you hear from yourself/your partner?
2. What new understanding have you gained and old knowledge you've confirmed about your/your partner's culture through this interview?
3. How does this interview impact you/ your partner in an intellectual/emotional level?
4. What stands out the most to you/your partner during the interview?
5. How do you and your partner's cultural matrixes impact your relationship?

Here are 15 additional general questions you can ask yourself as a couple. Pick any 3-5 of them that you feel are useful to your discussion.

1. What are some activities in which you currently experience joy, fun, and/or happiness between you and your partner?
2. What (if anything) do you do primarily with or for yourself alone that bring you happiness?
3. What was the high point of the last year for you personally? And now for you as a couple or family?
4. Can you remember a time recently when you pleasantly surprised yourself or did something out of character that pleased you?
5. How about the same question for you as a couple? (Or family?)
6. Can you recall a time when you thought you had a problem in your relationship but you did not? What changed it from being a problem to not being a problem?
7. Cite some examples of how your partner has encouraged you in the past month.
8. When you and your partner are (a) happy together, contrasted with being (b) in conflict with each other, what would actually be seen and/or heard if it had been videotaped on those times?
9. What do you have a right to expect from your partner?
10. What does your partner have a right to expect from you?
11. What would it specifically (a) look like, (b) feel like, (c) sound like, and/or even (d) smell like when you and your partner are really connected with each other?
12. Contrast the above concrete ways of describing your relationship when you are feeling alienated and/or distant from your partner.

13. When you and your partner (family member) have challenges, how do you typically resolve them?
14. What needs to be different in your relationship to make your life happier?
15. How would others around you be able to know your relationship had changed in a positive manner?[24]

Activity 15: Create a matrix for the two of you (Our Matrix)

The objective of this activity is to determine the compatible nature as well as the potentially conflictual and/or complimentary nature of the cultural matrixes of the two of you. When you and your partner have completed the interview (Activity C), hopefully you have gained a greater understanding of each other. You may also have become more aware as how the matrixes impact your relationship "for better or for worse."

You are now ready to create your couple CRIM #3. In the space below identify three to five factors, which have surfaced in your discussions. These cultural factors represent the most salient issues for you as a couple right now. Ideally you will do this by consensus; however, the authors suggest that "agreeing to disagree" is a paradoxically creative problem-solving strategy for approaching this activity. It is the hope of the authors that this activity can serve as "an integrating snap" shot of the cultural identity of your relationship.

Our CRIM (Your relationship CRIM as a couple)

	Compatibility	**Differences or Potential Conflicts**
Age		
Culture		
Disability/ Ability		
Ethnicity		

Gender		
Geographic Location		
Marital Status		
Race		
Religious Preference		
Sexual Orientation		
Socioeconomic Status		
Other Culture Relevant to Both of You		

Here are 15 of a total of 33 general suggestions for relationship renewal as proposed by Eckstein & Jones.[25] They can help integrate the specific focus of the CRIM into an ongoing commitment for you as a couple in constantly better understanding and thereby constantly improving your own relationship.

1. *Fantasy.* Each of you tells the other what you can imagine about the other.
2. *I-you-we.* Each of you takes a turn making three statements: One begins with *I*, one with *you*, and one with *we*.

3. *More/less/right amount.* Each of you makes the following requests: What I need more of from you, what I need less of from you, and what I am getting the right amount of from you.

4. *Hopes, dreams.* Each of you shares your best-case scenarios, the dream-come-true, if your relationship went to a higher level of mutual enjoyment.

5. *Predictions.* Each of you attempts to predict the other's response to the activity: "In the next few minutes, I would guess that you would . . ."

6. *Puzzlements.* Each of you makes the statement, "What puzzles me about you is . . ."

7. *Role reversal.* Each of you plays the other for a few minutes as a form of feedback. Tell each other how well each of you did as the other partner.

8. *Self-disclosure.* Each of you tells the other important facts about yourself. See if you can be creative and relate something to your partner that he or she may never have heard you say before.

9. *Tell me more.* Each of you interviews the other for a set period of time, repeatedly making the request, "Tell me more." Then, change roles of interviewer/sharer.

10. *Testing consensus.* Each of you summarizes next-step action planning, observing within the other nonverbal and verbal indicators of commitments to the solution.

11. *Three yeses.* Each of you interviews the other until each of you gets an answer of "yes" three times in a row.

12. *The time I knew I was in love with you.* Each of you relates to the other again, although you may have said it countless times, the moment/event that convinced you of love for each other. See if you can recall something different or relate it to somewhat differently than before.

13. *Metaphor exchange.* Create a metaphor for each other as well as for the relationship. For example, "Our relationship is like a comfortable set of slippers."

14. *Early recollections.* Each of you shares two or three formative early memories from your childhood. Together, discuss how the memories may be played out or reenacted in the marriage now.

15. *Share peak experiences and times alone and/or together when magic happened.*

Summary

This article explored the impact of culture in couple relationships. The authors designed the CRIM to initiate a unique communication process for couples to heighten their awareness of selves and their partners and to help couples to formulate a snap shot of their own cultural identity. It is the hope of the authors that the readers can utilize the CRIM as a tool to stimulate an intellectual/emotional conversation with each other and to further enriches their couple relationship.

Endnotes

[1] Sue, D.W. & Sue D. (2003). *Counseling the culturally diverse: Theory and practice*. 4th edition. Hoboken, NJ: John Wiley & Sons.

[2] U.S. Census Bureau, 2006

[3] El Nasser, H. (2006, Aug.16). Census: Newest arrivals Fan Out, USA Today, A1,4.

[4] Rodriquez, L. (2006, Aug 16). Houston's Hispanics at opposite ends of the age spectrum, Huston Chronicle, A1,4.

[5] Satir, V. (1972). *Peoplemaking*. Science and Behavior Books, Inc., Palo Alto, California., p. 30.

[6] Bhugra, D., & DeSilva, P. (2000). Couple therapy across cultures. *Sexual and Relationship therapy, 15*, 183-192.

[7] *Ibid. pg. 189.*

[8] Lucas, T., Wendorf, C., Imamoglu, E., Shen, J., Parkhill, M., Waitsfield, C., et.al. (2004). Marital satisfaction in four cultures as a function of homogamy, male dominance and female attractiveness, *Sexualities, Evolution and Gender, 6*, 97-130.

[9] *Ibid. p. 122.*

[10] Abela, A., Frosh, S. & Dowling, E. (2005). Uncovering beliefs embedded in the culture and its implication for practice: The case of Maltese married couples. *Journal of Family therapy, 27*, 3-23.

[11] National Statistics Offices. (2003). *Labor Force Survey*. Malta: NSO.

[12] Rose, J., & Urshel, J. (2006). Understanding the complexity of love in Brokeback Mountain. *The Journal of Men's Studies, 14* (2), 247-251.

[13] Prouix, A. (1997). *Brokeback mountain*. New York: Scribner.

[14] Ebert, R. (2006, January 13). All-embracing tragedy. (Review of the motion picture *Brokeback Mountain. South Bend Tribune*, p. D4.

[15] Rose & Urshel, *loc. cit.* p.248.

[16] Watts, R.E., & Pietrzak, D. (2000). Adlerian "encouragement" and the therapeutic process of solution-focused brief therapy. *Journal of Counseling & Development, 78* (3), 442-445.

[17] Miller, S., Nummally, E., & Wackman, D. (1986). *Couple communication I: Talking together*. Interpersonal Communication Programs, Littleton, Colorado.

[18] Sue & Sue, *loc. cit.*

[19] Erikson, E. H. (1963). *Childhood and society*. New York: W.W. Norton.

[20] Sue & Sue, *loc. cit.*

[21] Erikson, *loc. cit.*

[22] Egan, G. (2007). *The skilled helper*. (8th ed.). Thomson, CA: Brooks/Cole.

[23] Watts & Pietrzak, *loc. cit.* pp. 442-443.

[24] Eckstein, D. (2001). Counseling is the answer...but what is the question?: 25 Questions for couples and families. *The Family Journal: Counseling and Therapy for Couple and Families, 9* (4), 463-464.

[25] Eckstein, D. & Jones, J. (1998). Thirty-three suggestions for relationship renewal. *The Family Journal: Counseling and Therapy for Couple and Families, 6*, (4), 335.

Section 9:

F.A.M.I.L.Y. Approaches to Self-Care: Creating a Healthy Balance

Donna Eckstein, Ph.D.

Health is a question of balance. The purpose of this article is to assist the reader to understand and individualize concepts of health. Basic human needs and problem-solving skills are presented to assist with identifying goals. Questions are used to help the reader develop his or her own personal plan of action for self-care. A self-care assessment inventory is included to identify your current level of balance with self-care. The assessments can be taken individually or in the context of a supportive relationship. This may include a partner, friend, family member, or a professional.

Support can make a difference. Stress can play a major role in undermining your self-care. Unrealistic expectations can increase stress and challenge health. It is easy to withdraw, isolate, and restrict supportive interactions when feeling stressed. This article focuses on the role of supportive relationships and social support in helping to identify sources of stress and resistance to self-care. The benefits of supportive relationships and social support systems are presented as tools for success in developing and maintaining a balance with your self-care.

F.A.M.I.L.Y. Approaches to Self-Care was developed by the author as a systematic model focusing on health factors in your self-care. The use of supportive relationships and social support has been encouraged to help with your success in self-care behavior. Social support has been identified as a powerful factor in helping to make behavioral changes. The acronym *F.A.M.I.L.Y.* represents additional factors of health that have been included in this model of self-care. Health factors include:

F - Fitness
A - Adaptability
M - Moving Through Loss
I - Independence
L - Longevity
Y - Your Motivation

The F.A.M.I.L.Y. Self-Care Assessment Inventory is a tool used to assess the level of balance in your self-care behavior. It focuses on five different dimensions of the self: physical, mental, spiritual, emotional, and social. The goal is to create a comprehensive self-assessment of self-care behaviors and to assist in developing a concrete plan of action for the self-improvement of your health care.

You are encouraged to utilize this article to identify your bottomline in healthcare. What does health mean to you? What is *most important* to you for improving your self-care? Who and/or what *supports* your ability and your success at this time in your life? What *action* could you take that would support you to be more successful in creating a healthy balance in your life?

Review of the Literature

Concepts of Health

Basic principles of health found in many of the ancient philosophies include the belief in the importance of balance for creating and maintaining health. The roles of the physical, mental, spiritual, social, and emotional parts of oneself have been emphasized in the development of a balance of health.

The Greek philosopher, Pythagoras, identified harmony, equilibrium, and balance of energies as the goal of Pythagorean life. Hippocrates believed that health was based on a state of balance in the body. He focused on the patient's participation in creating, maintaining, and restoring health. The Greek concept embraced a strong mind and a strong body.[1]

Eastern philosophies focus on principles of harmony and balance for creating and maintain one's health. In China and Japan, martial arts are essentially a system of practical and technical methods for training mind, body, and spirit to maintain health.[2] The attitude of flow, movement, balance, and harmony was emphasized and reflected through disciplines such as Tai Chi Chuan and Aikido. A Chinese doctor summarized his belief that there was only one illness: a disturbance of the balanced way. In India, a basic tenet of Yoga is that the balance of the body, mind, and spirit is essential to a person's continuum of existence.[3]

Western psychological theory also identified the criterion of balance as a definer of health. Sigmund Freud,[4] who declared himself a "psychophysical parallelist," believed that psychic processes cannot occur in the absence of physiological processes, and that the latter must precede the former.

Jung[5] identified the individual's psychophysiological constitution. He believed that people might experience themselves as being prisoners of their own body's and psyches' needs, and they must determine how they would deal with this psychophysiological constitution. People could live in defiance of the demands of their bodies and ruin their health; the same could be done in regard to the psyche. Jung explained that a person who wanted to live would develop ways to refrain from these tricks and, at times, would inquire into the needs of the body and psyche.

Psychological theories by Perls,[6] Maslow,[7] and Adler[8] described human nature as including a basic postulate that the person contains within him or herself the social potential for healthy and creative growth. Themes interrelated with health have included factors such as (a) the concept of holism, (b) the development of self-esteem, and (c) the ability to be present-oriented.[9] Perl's Gestalt psychology uses the concept of holism. It can be summed up in the Gestalt saying, "The whole is greater than the sum of its parts." Maslow believed that, in order to understand the individual fully, you must approach him or her as a unit or whole, striving toward self-actualization, growth, and excellence. Maslow's Hierarchy of Needs ranged from basic needs to higher needs beginning with biological, safety, belongingness, esteem and self-actualization. Adler noted, "It is always necessary to look for . . . reciprocal actions of the mind on the body, for both of them are parts of the whole with which we should be concerned." These theorists believed that negative influences could be overcome as an individual accepted responsibility for his or her life.[10]

Sport psychologists Sonstroem and Morgan[11] defined self-esteem as "an empirically supported exercise outcome." Their research focused on the effects of physical exercise for improving one's self esteem. Self-acceptance, self-love, and personal competence were used to define dimensions of favorable self-esteem. They defined personal competence as the feeling of capability to master and control oneself and aspects of the environment.

Both contemporary and ancient philosophies focused on the principle of being present, in the here and now. Brenner[12] wrote, "The degree that one focuses backward or forward is the degree that one suffers." He explained, "Man's past, when analyzed, points to the future but is only viewed in balance by being in the present." Philosopher George Leonard[13] believed techniques borrowed from a martial art could be applied to intimate relationships as "there is no greater service that you can do for another person than to be really present for them."

The ancient concept of holism developed by the Greeks has increasingly been reflected in modern medicine. Physician Sherwin Nolan's[14] article has described American medicine as being in the midst of a tremendous change; sometimes getting sick may require more than just a pill to get well. Hippocrates suggested that sickness reflected a disruption in the health-giving balance of the body: nutrition, personal habits, even thoughts and experience. Sheally and Bressler (as cited in Oyle[15]) purported that the next great advance in health will not come from labs or hospitals, but from what people can learn to do for themselves. Sheally has written that the role of medicine is to teach people good habits and the principles of self-response.

Calming the Critic: Overcoming Perfectionism and Stress

Positive emotional states may promote healthy perception, beliefs, and even physical well-being. To explore potential mechanisms linking pleasant feelings and good health, Salovey et al.[16] considered several lines of research. They included (a) direct positive effect on physiology, especially the immune system; (b) the informational value of emotional experiences; (c) the psychological resources engendered by positive feeling states; (d) the ways in which mood can motivate health-relevant behaviors; and (e) the elicitation of social support.

Positive thoughts, hardiness, generalized self-efficacy, and optimism were strongly correlated with health and resistance to stress. Disease was seen, not only as suffering, but also as a fight to maintain the homeostatic balance of our tissues, despite damage. Stress, as the engineers speak of stress and strain in connection with the interaction of force and resistance, was described as a form of pressure caused by negative feeling and inaccurate perceptions.

Behavior and moods are affected by the way one thinks. By changing the way one thinks, one can alter one's behavior and moods. Cognitive Therapy, based on Beck's theory, has explained that (1) moods are created by "cognitions" or thoughts, which are defined as "the way you look at things—your perception, mental attitudes, and beliefs;" (2) thoughts are dominated by pervasive negativity when feeling depressed, and (3) negative thoughts cause emotional turmoil and often contain gross distortions.[17]

Adler wrote that a person's internal beliefs and private logic guide both the feelings and the behaviors of the individual. People who have realistic beliefs are able to accept themselves as imperfect. People have a tendency to put pressure on themselves and disturb themselves by the perpetuation of their irrational beliefs. Major beliefs described by Ellis[18] include

- I must be loved or approved by everyone.
- I must be perfectly competent and productive.
- It is a catastrophe when things go other than the way I might wish.
- Life must be absolutely fair.
- It is better to avoid life's difficulties than to take responsibility for changing them.

Accurate appraisals of the self and the environment are essential to maintaining positive mental health and the ability to create a healthy balance with one's thoughts, feelings, behaviors, social interactions, and spiritual connections. Beck[19] believed the greater the discrepancy between one's private logic and reality, the greater the potential for unhealthy behaviors in response to life events. He wrote, "Once you have learned how to perceive life more realistically, you will experience an enhanced emotional life with a greater appreciation for genuine sadness—which lacks distortion—as well as joy."

Depression is the world's number one public health problem, reported Beck.[20] He found that depressed patients see themselves as deficient in many of the qualities they value highly: intelligence, achievement, popularity, attractiveness, health, and strength. Beck characterized a depressed self-image using four Ds. "You feel *Defeated*, *Defective*, *Deserted*, and *Deprived*." He further explained that negative emotional reactions often inflict their damage because of low self-esteem, which he described as a lack of true support from within. He concluded that the use of cognitive therapy provided superior results to antidepressant therapy alone.

Perfectionism has been described by Beck as "man's ultimate illusion." Learning to recognize perfectionist, distorted, and unrealistic expectations of oneself and of others can help prevent negative thoughts and feelings that sabotage and undermine one's physical, mental, social, emotional, and spiritual health. Perfectionism can interfere with your ability to create and follow-through with self-care. It becomes more difficult to see yourself as being healthy, to identify how to create a healthy balance, or to follow through with the identified plan for self-care. Beck has written that these individuals quickly feel defeated after some short-term gains; they begin to isolate from others, and they revert to their previous unhealthy behaviors.

Over the past decades, the research on mindfulness techniques has shown the effectiveness of these approaches in populations that struggle with emotional regulation. Recent research by Williams and Zylowska noted that those who studied the effects of mindfulness meditation with emotional regulation have been encouraging.[21]

The mindful experiencing of emotion, with the title Mindful Emotional Management, was described by D. A. Eckstein.[22] In addition to core concepts of mindfulness in daily life, he teaches and devotes time to experimenting with three basic affective mindfulness techniques:

- Mindful Experiencing of Emotions
- Mindful Releasing of Emotions
- Mindful Connections of Emotions—"Strengthening Core Relationships"

Mindful Experiencing of Emotion, as explained by D. A. Eckstein, is when "one first recognizes the emergence of the physical and cognitive aspects of the feelings, then acknowledges whatever judgments and resistances are triggered, and finally 'takes a step back' from them, softening and detaching, until an attitude of curiosity and openness is attained. Participants will be encouraged to experiment in this setting with neutral or slightly positive emotion both to ensure success and to eliminate the risk of emotional flooding."

Mindful Releasing of Emotions involves a simple, four-step emotional release technique; whereas, *Mindful Connections* focuses on the importance of the concept of "Strengthening Core Relationships." In his private practice as a counselor, he does individual, couples, and family sessions to strengthen core relationships as he considers connection as an important need. He realized the importance of strengthening core relationships when a participant at a conference was sharing that he never understood about his problems until his kids broke down and told him how his behaviors affected them. Eckstein realized no amount of pressure on the father would have broken through the father's denial without that bond with his kids. He ended by asking, "Why would we want to 'manage emotions' if no one cares about us, and we don't care about anyone either?"

Family and Social Support

In his book *Ties That Stress . . . The New Family Imbalance*, Elkind[23] focused on changes from the nuclear to permeable boundaries within families. He explained that the nuclear family provided clear-cut, often rigid, boundaries between the public and private lives in families, between the home and the workplace, and between children and adults. Dividing lines within the permeable family, however, are reported to be more blurred and difficult to discern. His belief was that the postmodern family is more fluid, more flexible, and more vulnerable to pressures from outside. This was described as the new postmodern family imbalance. Effects of stress and the rapid social change make it hard for the family to keep pace, resulting in dislocations and a decline with balance in families.

Postmodern young people were described[24] as being left without the social envelope of security and protection that shielded earlier generations. Children and teenagers face new demands for independence and maturity. They cope using their own resourcefulness. However, this can encourage parents and society to provide even less security and direction than they have done in the past. Elkind[25] described the family pattern, *the vital family*, which must balance the needs of children and youth with the needs of parents and other adults. This pattern has the best of nuclear and permeable family.

Wayne and May Sotile[26] described the *supercouple syndrome* in their book *Beat Stress Together*, which outlines how couples can recognize stress reactions, alleviate tension, and find time to relax together. The first chapter begins with "Two Incomes, No Sex." The authors explained that a very high percentage of couples evidence at least one high-powered coping habit that allows them to endure despite exceptional stress and strain. They identified these coping strategies as:

> The ability to relentlessly work hard, the tendency to control others, perfectionism, chronic hurry sickness (the tendency to rush, even when there is no objective need to do so), the talent of doing and/or thinking about more than one thing at once, burning competitiveness, and stamina in facing the demands of home and work.[27]

Sotile and Sotile wrote about managing our "Big Life," which includes the capacity to go numb when stressed and pushed to keep going. They described "the new superhero" as being a generation of people facing unprecedented changes and lofty expectations for fulfillment in three major arenas—family, work, and self—as they push and challenge each to get it all: success, health, and happiness. They reported that they have seldom met a couple who reported a comfortable balance across their collective roles. They explained their belief that balance has become the 1990s version of the Beaver Cleaver family myth. They questioned how a comfortable balance of roles can exist when fewer than 15% of American households are blessed with the luxury of an at-home spouse. They further questioned how couples can face the combination of roles when workweeks of 85 to 110 hours a week have been normalized. Couples are not described as living in balance but as living the Big Life. Their research and counseling with more than 5,000 couples resulted in the Beating Stress Together (BEST) Program, which was designed to help "today's chronically crazed, super achieving couples." The nine components of BEST are

- recognizing stress reactions,
- learning to handle change,

- de-stressing your environment,
- building a life in harmony with your values,
- resolving role conflicts,
- finding (or making) time,
- overcoming hurry sickness,
- changing fantasies into action plans, and
- renegotiating relationships to keep intimacy alive.[28]

The stress management process was described in a relationship context. For example, in resolving role conflicts, Sotile and Sotile focused on "calling it what it is, going for good enough, and asking your partner for feedback."[29] They identified the goal as being a "reasonable balance across arenas over a long period of time." They explained that perfect balance was neither possible nor necessary. Couples and families were encouraged to beware of long-term, extreme neglect in one or more areas. "Even during stages of life that preoccupy you with the demands coming from one arena, it is important to at least periodically make it a priority to attend to the neglected arenas."[30] Feedback from a partner was encouraged, as it is difficult to accurately observe one self. Feedback can clarify what and how one needs to change to live in more healthy balance. Sotile and Sotile explained that "if you pair your request for input with a sincerely expressed desire to do what you can to improve your overall teamwork; you are much more likely to receive helpful, caring feedback."[31]

Social supports are a powerful factor in helping make behavioral health changes such as weight loss. Ornish[32] believed that people are most successful when they also address the emotional and spiritual dimensions that most influence what one chooses to do or not to do. He explained that people in this country one hundred years ago had a greater sense of community and connection than they experience now. Such social networks helped protect people from isolation, illness, and premature death. He reported that people who felt socially isolated had 2-5 times the incidence of disease and premature death, due to all causes, than those who had felt a sense of community and connections. People have often tried to heal their isolations by filling the void with temporary relief (cigarettes, food, spending, etc.). Unfortunately, however, behaviors such as overeating and being overweight have often created more negative thoughts and feelings leading to increased isolation.

Human beings can be proactive and engaged or passive and alienated, largely as a function of the social conditions in which they develop. Research guided by Self-Determination Theory has focused on the social-contextual conditions that facilitate the natural processes of self-motivation and healthy psychological development

Factors that enhance intrinsic motivation, self-regulation, and well-being were identified to be three innate psychological needs and processes: competence, autonomy, and relatedness. When satisfied, these factors yield enhanced self-motivation and positive mental health. A lack of these factors leads to diminished motivation and well-being.[33]

Development of Questionnaire
The F.A.M.I.L.Y. Self-Care Assessment Inventory

F.A.M.I.L.Y. Approaches to Self-Care is a result of the author's research for her dissertation,[34] focused on ancient and modern principles of health as applied to fitness training. It evolved into a model for self-care based on feedback from individuals, groups, and classes with seniors in the author's professional work.

This approach to self-care identified basic human needs and problem-solving skills for self-care behaviors and strategies to meet those needs. The model for self-care behavior focused on the need for integration and balance in five different dimensions of self (physical, mental, spiritual, emotional, and social).

Creating a Healthy Balance was developed to assist the reader with integrating the information and identifying a plan of action to improve health. Unfortunately, people often implement a plan to improve their health, adding a level of stress that offsets any gains. The book, "Health Is a Question of Balance"[35] provided the definition for health used in developing this model focused on health, balance, and self-care behavior.

The F.A.M.I.L.Y. Self-Care Assessment Inventory was designed specifically to describe how factors of health are present in each of the different dimensions of self. The profile of one's scores is used to illustrate the results of one's self-report of their current behavior.

This inventory was written for the purpose of examining, improving, and maintaining one's health. The focus is on assessing the level of self-care behaviors (*balance*), determining how they move together as a whole unit (*integration*), and exploring how they play together at the same time (*harmony*).

The goal of this model and inventory was to develop a comprehensive assessment of self-care behaviors to assist in creating a plan of action for self-improvement with one's health. Principles of health are used as a guide to your assessment of a healthy balance, which honors and respects all the different aspects of your health and how they work together throughout the course of your life. What is considered a healthy balance in your twenties is different in your fifties and eighties. A healthy balance for a parent with one child may be different for that same parent with three children.

The inventory was designed to provide a comprehensive assessment of factors of health for self-care. It can also be used to assess health factors of specific interest to you (i.e., Fitness, Adaptability, Your Motivation, etc.). The inventory can be used by an individual, alone or with someone who provides social support, for creating success in one's self-care behavior.

These assessments can be used individually. Professionals can also give these assessments separately to their clients to complete. The results could be discussed and clarified in the context of a supportive relationship. An objective view may provide good feedback and new insights. Problems such as addictive behaviors, chemical imbalances, or personality disorders could be discussed with a supportive health professional.

Fitness strategies evolved while the author worked with athletes and trainers who wanted concrete, how-to guidelines to enhance their health, performance, and team chemistry. Problem-solving skills focused on creating a healthy balance and increasing the ability to manage stress, *stress fitness*. Fitness strategies focus on needs and areas to be strengthened:

Physical:	*Fitness & "Fuel for Fitness"*—Healthy habits of sleep, diet, exercise, water, vitamins, etc.	
Mental:	*Focus & Follow-Through*—Planning, prioritizing, and organizing effectively	
Social:	*Family/Friends, Funds, for Fun (Life)*	
Emotional:	*Feelings*—Mindful Management of emotions (anxiety, grief, sadness, etc.)	
Spiritual:	*Faith*—Reliance and commitment based upon one's belief's and source of trust	

Adaptability developed while working with seniors and with patients who had been hospitalized due to a mental illness. They were struggling to develop skills to help cope with the difficulties and challenges of learning about decreased ability, disability, and critical need for adaptability. The ability to adapt to the demands of their environment, their bodies, and their minds was often painful, causing feelings of hopelessness. One senior stated that she felt like her body had become the enemy. Depression and anxiety centered on difficulties with adjusting to the changes in life. These changes included decreased alertness to their environment, decreased physical activity, as well as decreased social support and spiritual connection. Also included in these changes were increased passivity and isolation. Slipping into a rut and becoming isolated were deadly traps. The seniors focused on staying active—the best that they could. Problem-solving skills focused on increasing the ability to adapt to the changes in their lives by

Physical:	*Active*—Staying physically active	
Mental:	*Alert*—Mindfulness of changes in environment, others, and self	
Social:	*Inter-Active*—Socially connected with supportive relationships	
Emotional:	*Assertive*—Expressing feelings needs/wants, and beliefs	
Spiritual:	*Aware*—Connections to power greater than self to guide and positively cope with life	

Moving Through—Loss and Change began with seniors, clients, and patients talking about their problems in Grief and Loss Groups. They shared the losses they had experienced: physical mobility, emotional support from their mates, social structures of family and work, sources of money, memory, and their sense of meaning. Many of the seniors identified the loss of their ability to drive as one of the biggest losses in their lives. The author calls this the *"Loss of the 5 Ms."*

Physical:	*Mobility*—Maintain and improve the ability to walk, drive, etc.
Mental:	*Memory*—Short and long-term memory for quality of living
Social:	*Money*—Income to meet one's needs and wants
Emotional:	*Mates*—Loving relationships
Spiritual:	*Meaning*—Life based on what is important and meaningful

Independence was derived from individuals and families working through their problems. Problem-solving skills included accessing resources and help, developing independence, or maintaining independence to the best of their ability. Getting needs met was in the context of individual and family pressures and stress. Problem-solving skills also focused on their independence by strengthening the ability to develop and maintain

Physical:	*Initiative*—Proactive versus reactive behavior
Mental:	*Insight*—Perceptive and intuitive awareness & understanding of self and others.
Social:	*Intimacy*—Connections with supportive and loving relationships
Emotional:	*Identification*—Identification and management of emotions; Includes feelings related to self-image and self-esteem.
Spiritual:	*Inter-connections*—Spiritual connections and beliefs.

Longevity focused on an awareness and recognition of basic human needs and skills to care for yourself, increasing your ability to live potentiality more effectively and longer. It was adapted from a model used by Steven Covey in *The 7 Habits of Highly Effective People.*[36] Basic human needs in caring for self include the ability to

Physical:	*Live*—Health and well-being
Mental:	*Learn*—Education throughout life
Social:	*Laugh*—Enjoying life
Emotional:	*Love*—Comfort with loving and being loved
Spiritual:	*Listen*—Able to listen to what's important to you and others with empathy

Your Motivation can be seen in identifying why one would want to create a healthy balance. This is the driving force behind your behavior. The author's focus on the identification of one's motivation came from working with the University of California-San Diego California Cancer Prevention Program, a statewide telephone-counseling program for smoking cessation. Their motto was *Motivation + Preparation = Success*. Identifying your specific motivation, your bottom line for self-care may be the most important step you take to benefit from this assessment.

Priorities with Self-Care

It is recommended that you take *The F.A.M.I.L.Y. Self-Care Assessment Inventory* for a comprehensive assessment of your health and self-care behaviors. A profile of your scores can be charted on a graph. The questionnaire, *Creating a Healthy Balance*, can be utilized to develop a plan of action for self-care. *The Circle of Life* is a model for integration with self-care behavior physically, mentally, socially, emotionally, and spiritually. *Health—A Balancing Act* illustrates the value of identifying behaviors that support your efforts to create a healthy balance, defining your positive outcomes, and recognizing early signals of imbalance. *Caring for Self* identifies behaviors that support the different aspects of the self, working together.

The following questions are also presented to provide different levels of assessment, based on one's individual needs and interests. These questions can be used to identify priorities and assist in creating a plan of action for self-care. The questions can be answered separately or as a follow-up to the previous questions.

- In what areas do you feel competent about your self-care?
- What is it that you do to create a healthy balance in your life?
- What are your challenges in creating a healthy balance?
- Who and/or what supports you in creating your success with self-care?
- Take a moment to identify what is most important to you about your health, your "bottomline?" Limit your response to a few words. Examples may include more energy, feel better, live longer, etc. Keep it simple!

Integrating the Plan of Actions

Take a few minutes to identify what you would like to do to create a plan of action for your self-care. This article focuses on the value of

- Reviewing the literature, focusing on concepts of health.
- Assessing your strengths, challenges, and balance of your self-care.
- Identifying significant sources of social support in your life.

What have you determined is most important in improving your health? Write a self-care behavior, for each of the five dimensions, which you could do to create a healthy balance. For example, if *more energy* was identified as being what is most important in improving your health, then what behaviors could you do physically, mentally, socially, emotionally, and spiritually to create more energy in your life? *The Circle of Life* can be used as a model to illustrate your integration with *Creating a Healthy Balance*.

What one behavior would have the most positive impact for creating a healthy balance for you? For example, exercise. What would be one action step you could do with that behavior? For example, you could walk four mornings a week. Keeping this action step simple may be an important factor toward your success.

What would be one source of support in your successful plan to create a healthy balance? For example, would walking with a friend on Saturday morning be helpful? Write this below the triangle *Health—A Balancing Act*, to illustrate a behavior that supports you while creating and maintaining a healthy balance in your life. Identify the warning signs that indicate you may be getting out of balance with your self-care. Examples could come from a lack of self-care behaviors such as skipping meals, not exercising, not getting enough sleep, over-committing yourself, over-spending, and/or over-eating. Recognizing your warning signs faster and earlier is an important step in maintaining a healthy balance throughout your life.

In summary, identify what helps you to integrate, respect, and honor all aspects of yourself, the good and the bad, the healthy and unhealthy, so they can work together in *Caring for Self*. What behavior supports the different aspects of self to work together in harmony and joy? Examples could be journaling, spiritual reading, or talking to a partner, family member, or professional. This may be your greatest support.

- The behavior that would have the most positive impact on creating health is . . .
- The action step that supports maintaining this behavior is . . .

Here's to the clarity of your bottom line, your health, and your ability to create a healthy balance in caring for self.

The F.A.M.I.L.Y. Self-Care Assessment Inventory

This inventory can be used by completing individual sections or by completing the entire inventory to assess your strengths, challenges, and level of balance for your self-care. The number of health factors you choose to assess is an individual decision based on how comprehensive you would like the assessment of self-care behavior to be.

The F.A.M.I.L.Y. Self-Care Assessment Inventory can be completed in 1 to 5 steps:

1. *Complete the assessment.* Identify your current level of balance in your physical, mental, social, emotional, and spiritual self-care behaviors. Write your own ratings on the line marked *rating* in each square in a row, either across or down. Focus on how you subjectively view your current level of self-care behaviors.

To make it easier, you could score your behavior using only vertical and/or horizontal columns. For example, you may choose to score the vertical column based on strategies limited to your "physical" health. Alternatively, you may choose to score only the horizontal row related to "Fitness." This is an easier way to start and a choice that many make. Add the scores vertically (if you complete a column) or horizontally (if you completed a row). Write the total of the scores either at the bottom of each column or on the side of each row. Divide the total of each column or row by 5 to get an average score. If easier, divide by 10 and then divide it in half.

2. *Identify strengths and areas for improvement* in current self-care. *Self-Care Behavior Inventory & Graph.* Plot the scores of your responses for the assessment You may choose to discuss your results with a supportive person to help you to develop a self-care plan and routine that could be maintained. Rate your "zone" for self-care behavior using the following scale:

1-2 = Below Range   3-8 = Healthy Balance   9-10 = Above Range

3. *Identify your motivation, values, and goals*. *Circle of Life.* This is the last health factor in the column at the bottom of the assessment inventory. It can be used to identify your motivation for self-care in each of the five dimensions of self. Naming your motivation and values for health can be an important step in changing behavior.

4. *Identify specific self-care behaviors and social support*. *Health is a Balancing Act.* Identify self-care behaviors and social support that would have the greatest impact in meeting your goals to create and maintain a healthy balance in your self-care behavior.

5. *Create a simple plan of action* using 5 Steps for Creating a Healthy Balance. *Caring for Self.*

1. F.A.M.I.L.Y. Approaches to Self-Care

Health Factors	Descriptions
Fitness	The ability to stay fit and healthy.
Adaptability	The ability to adapt to the demands of your environment throughout life.
Moving Through	Recognizing and moving through loss and change.
Independence	The ability to function independently, moving from dependence to independence to inter-dependence.
Longevity	Meeting basic human needs & living longer.
Your Motivation	Identifying your motivation and commitment to improve your health.

Activity 16:
The F.A.M.I.L.Y. Self-Care Assessment
Health Factors in the 5 Dimensions of Self

		Physical	_Mental_	_Social_	_Emotional_	_Spiritual_	_Total_	_Avg._
Fitness Strategies	Developing skills, habits, and strategies to create and maintain health	_**Fitness & Fuel for Fitness**_ Healthy habits of sleep, diet, exercise, water, vitamins, etc. Rating:____	_**Focus & Follow-Through**_ Planning, prioritizing, and organizing effectively. Rating: ____	_**Family, Friends, Funds for Fun**_ Encouraging & supportive relationships, work, and enjoyable activities. Rating: ____	_**Feelings**_ Mindful Management of emotion and stress feelings (anxiety, grief, sadness, etc.) Rating: ____	_**Faith**_ Reliance and commitment based upon one's belief's and source of trust. Rating: ____	____	
Adaptability	Adapting to the demands of your environment	_**Active**_ Staying physically active. Rating: ____	_**Alert**_ Mindfulness of changes in the environment, others, and self. Rating: ____	_**Inter-Active**_ Socially connected with supportive relationships. Rating: ____	_**Assertive:**_ Expressing feelings needs/ wants, and beliefs. Rating: ____	_**Aware:**_ Connections to power greater than self to guide and positively cope with life. Rating: ____	____	
Moving Through	Recognizing and moving through loss and change	_**Mobility**_ Maintain and improve the ability to walk, drive, etc. Rating: ____	_**Memory**_ Short and long term memory for quality of living. Rating: ____	_**Money**_ Income to meet one's needs and wants. Rating: ____	_**Mates**_ Quality relationships. Rating: ____	_**Meaning**_ A life based on what is important and meaningful. Rating: ____	____	
Independence	Maintaining Independence	_**Independence**_ Proactive versus reactive behavior. Rating: ____	_**Insight**_ Perceptive and intuitive awareness & understanding of self and others. Rating: ____	_**Intimacy**_ Connections with supportive relationships. Rating: ____	_**Identification**_ Identification and management of emotions. Include feelings of self-image & esteem. Rating: ____	_**Inter-Connections**_ Spiritual connections and beliefs. Rating: ____		
Longevity	Improving basic human needs	_**Living Longer**_ Health and well-being. Rating: ____	_**Learning**_ Education throughout life. Rating: ____	_**Laughter**_ Enjoying life. Rating: ____	_**Loving**_ Comfort in loving and being loved. Rating: ____	_**Listening**_ Able to listen to what's important to you and others with empathy. Rating: ____		
Total:		____	____	____	____	____		
Average:		____	____	____	____	____		

Identify Your Motivation

Review titles in the vertical columns above. <u>Circle </u>the one(s) that represents what you value most.

You!	Your Motivation	*Physical* (Ex: Fitness)	*Mental* (Ex: Learning)	Social (Ex: Family, Fds.)	*Emotional* (Ex: Loving)	*Spiritual* (Ex: Meaning)

Identify Strengths and Challenges
Self-Care Behavior Inventory & Graph

How does your behavior create balance, or imbalance, in your health at this time in your life? The profile can be used to illustrate strengths and areas for improvement in your current self-care behaviors and to identify your current level of balance. With this model, a <u>score of 3-8 </u>may be viewed as a range in the <u>zone of of healthy balance</u> in self-care. Extremely high or low scores may be considered risk factors for imbalances in your health. Watch for scores illustrating deficiency or excess in your self-care behavior.

Instructions: Write the average scores from the Assessment Inventory at the bottom of the columns completed. Write an X for number you scored in each column. Create an graph by connecting the X's with lines. Identify a <u>primary</u> strength and area for improvement in the columns completed and write it in the bottom section of this page.

Activity 17:
Health Factors with Coping Skills

	Fitness	**A**daptability	**M**oving Through	**I**ndependent Living	**L**ongevity
10					
9					
8					
7					
6					
5					
4					
3					
2					
1					
Score	___	___	___	___	___

Five Dimensions of Self

	Physical	Mental	Social	Emotional	Spiritual
10					
9					
8					
7					
6					
5					
4					
3					
2					
1					
Score	___	___	___	___	___

	Strengths	Areas for Improvement
Health Factors with Coping Skils		
Five Dimensions of Self		

Identify Your Motivation, Values, & Goals

Circle of Life

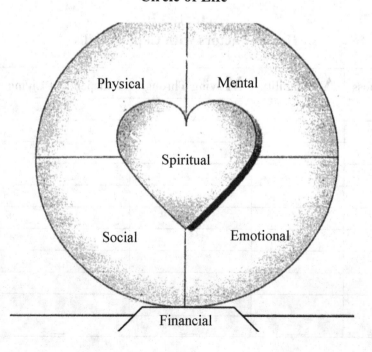

The *Circle of Life* can be used to illustrate the inter-connections between your values and motivation to Create a Healthy Balance in your self-care behaviors. What have you been told or learned about the value of creating a healthy balance in your life? What is it that you want and value in self-care at this time in your life vs. what you think you should be doing?

1. Review the motivating areas of self-care within each of the five dimensions of self that you identified at the bottom of the assessment.

2. Identify the value you associate with that motivation. Identifying what is valued with self-care can be an important part of this inventory. For example

Sample Values = Health, Happiness, and Love.

Dimension of Self	Motivation	Value
Physical	Fitness	Health
Mental	Insight	Responsible & Successful
Social-Financial	Family, Fds, Funds for Fun (& Life)	Loving Connections-Enjoying Life
Emotional	Love	Happiness-Loving & Being Loved
Spiritual	Meaning	Trust & Inner Guidance

Your motivation and value with self-care

Dimension of Self	Motivation	Value
Physical		
Mental		
Social-Financial		
Emotional		
Spiritual		

3. Based on what you have listed as your motivation above, identify a goal for 3 or 4 areas that you would like to improve to create a healthy balance in your self-care behavior.

4. Outside each of the five dimensions of self, write your motivating health factors (identified on the assessment inventory), current self-care behaviors, and goals for self-care.

5. Inside the circle, write a value that you think supports your motivation and goals.

4. Identify Specific Goals
Health—A Balancing Act

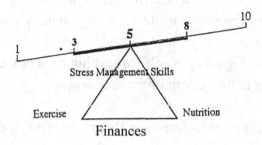

What self-care behavior, social support, and action steps would have the greatest impact in creating and maintaining a healthy balance for your self-care behavior?

_____

_____

_____

_____

Create A Simple Plan of Action—Caring for Self

Creating a Healthy Balance—What does it look and feel like for you?
- What's most important to you for your health now and over the course of your life?
- What are the positive outcomes with creating a healthy balance focusing on these behaviors?

Self-Care Behaviors—Be Specific.
- Use the triangle above to illustrate self-care behaviors in your plan of action. Exercise, nutrition, and stress management are three areas of self-care.
- Is there a specific self-care behavior in one or all of these areas within your plan of action to create a healthy balance and caring for you?

Getting Support—When you double your stress, double your support!
- Health is a balancing Act. What supports you with creating a healthy balance and caring for yourself? Again, use the triangle to show exercise, nutrition, and stress management areas.
- What social support could also help with your success? If walking is a behavior you want to increase, would walking with a friend support your success in maintaining your self-care?

Taking Action—Keep it Simple!
- What action step would have the greatest impact in creating a healthy balance within your self-care behavior?
- What is it that you can do that day?

Maintaining Self-Care: Recognize when you are getting out of balance . . . faster and earlier!
- What behaviors let you know that you are in balance with your self-care?
- Identify behaviors that signal an imbalance in your self-care.
- What are the early warning signs that you are creating an imbalance in yourself?

Biography

Donna Eckstein, Ph.D.(*A F.A.M.I.L.Y. Approach to Self-Care: Creating healthy Balance*) is presently working as an associate professor with the Community College Continuing Education Emeritus Program in San Diego, California. She has over 30 years of counseling, education, community, and clinical experience working at the San Diego Pain Treatment Center, Sharp Mesa Vista Hospital, Alvarado Family & Sports Medicine Center, Southern Caregiver Resource Center, University of California-San Diego (UCSD) Cancer Prevention Program, San Diego Community College, and Capella University.

Endnotes

[1] Nieman, D. (1989). Exercise and the Mind. *Woman's Sports and Fitness,* September 54-57.

[2] Yuasa, Y. (1978). *The Body: Toward an Eastern Mind-body Theory.* Albany, NY: State University of New York Press.

[3] Jackson, D. (1975). *Yoga and The Athlete.* New York: World Publication.

[4] Jones, E. (1953). *The Life and Work of Sigmund Freud.* Vol. 1. New York: Basic Books.

[5] Jung, C. G. (1975). *The Collected Worlds of C. G. Jung.* Vol. 8. New York: Princeton University Press.

[6] Perls, F. (1992). *Gestalt therapy verbatim.* Gouldsboro, ME: Gestalt Journal Press.

[7] Maslow, A. (1966). *The Psychology of Science: A Reconnaissance.* Chicago, IL: Henry Regency.

[8] Adler, A. (1958). *What Life Should Mean To You.* New York: Capricorn.

[9] Tageson, W. C. (1982). *Humanistic Psychology: A Synthesis.* Chicago, IL: Dorsey Press.

[10] Hall, C. S., & Lindsey, G. (1957). *Theories of Personality.* New York: John Wiley & Sons.

[11] Sonstroem. R. J., & Morgan W. P. (1989). Exercise and self-esteem: Rationale and model. *Medicine and Science in Sports and Exercise,* 21, n3 328-337.

[12] Brenner, P. (1978). *Health Is A Question of Balance.* Marina Del Rey, CA: De Vorss & Co.

[13] Leonard, G. (1990). *The Ultimate Athlete.* Berkley, CA: North Atlantic Books.

14 Nolan, S. B. (1989). Medicine's next step: Complete healing. *Self*, March, 140-142.

15 Oyle, I. (1979). *The New American Medicine Show.* Santa Cruz, CA: Unity Press.

16 Salovery, P., Rothman, A. J., Detweiler, J. B., Steward, W. T. (2000). Emotional states and physical health. *The American Psychologist*, v55, i1 p. 110.

17 Beck, A. (1979). *Cognitive Therapy and the Emotion Disorders.* New York: New American Library Trade.

18 Ellis, A. (1998). *A Guide to Rational Living.* New York: Wilshire.

19 Beck, *loc. cit.*

20 Beck, *loc. cit.*

21 Williams, J. C., Zylowska, L. (2009). Mindfulness Bibliography. *Mindful Awareness Research Center, UCLA Semel Institute*, 2009. Web. 3 Jan. 2010.

22 Eckstein, D. Personal communication. 31 Jan. 2010.

23 Elkind, D. (1995). *Ties that stress...the new family imbalance.* Cambridge, MA: Harvard University Press.

24 Elkind, *loc.cit*

25 *Ibid.*

26 Sotile, W.M., & Sotile, M.O. (1998). *Best stress together.* New York: John Wiley.

27 *Ibid.* pg. 9.

28 *Ibid.* pg. 123.

29 *Ibid.* pg. 123.

30 *Ibid.* pg. 123.

31 *Ibid.* pg. 123.

32 Ornish, D. (1993). *Eat More: Weigh Less.* New York: Harper Collins

33 Ryan, R. M., & Deci, E. L. (2000). Self-determination theory and the facilitation of intrinsic motivation, social development, and well-being. *The American Psychologist*, v55 i1 p. 68.

34 Eckstein, D. (1990). Psychological effects of an aerobic bodymind fitness training program. Doctoral dissertation, United States International University.

35 Brenner, P. (1978). Health is a question of balance. Marina del Ray, CA: DeVorss & Co.

36 Covey, S. R. (1989). The 7 habits of highly effective people. New York: Simon & Schuster.

Chapter III:
Understanding and Respecting Personality Differences

Section 10:

The Couple's Personality Preferences Questionnaire (CPPQ)

Daniel Eckstein

Eckstein and Kern (2009) use the metaphor of "psychological fingerprints" to describe one's characteristic style or personality. During the nineteen years the author has written the "for couples" column for *The Family Journal*, he has used the relationship assessment methodology proposed by Haley (1973). Understanding and respecting personality differences is the focus of this article. The other three methods include: role perceptions, communication, and problem-solving skills.

As a way for each of you understanding some basic consistent and defining personality descriptors, five animals will be used as a metaphor for basic lifestyles. After selecting which of the five is most like you and in what way you focus your relationship, you will also predict the same for your partner. After completing the Couples Personality Preferences Questionnaire (CPPQ), each of you will individually score and profile your results. After writing your response to some reflective questions, each of you will discuss both your own profile plus your predictions. Implications and next step applications for you, plus additional personality tools, conclude the article.

In order to introduce the idea of personality differences as reflected in style, the author has developed the following self-scoring questionnaire.

1. The first step is for you to consider the following five animals:

Tiger   Chameleon   Turtle   Eagle   Salmon

2. With respect to your present relationship, which one of these animals would you say is most like your own personality?

   _____

3. Give a brief description of an actual example of how you acted this way with or toward your partner

_____

_____

4. In your partnership, how are the other four animals like or unlike you?
   a) _____
   b) _____
   c) _____
   d) _____

5. Which of the five animals would you say is most like your partner?
   a) _____
   b) Write a brief description of an actual example

   _____

   _____

   _____

6. Which of the five animals do you feel your partner will say is most like you?
   a) _____
   b) describe a time you feel he or she use to identify you with this trait

B. After answering these 5 questions, independently takes the Couple's Personality Preferences Questionnaire (CPPQ)

Instructions: Read each of the following statements and assign points according to these guidelines:

Always	**5 points**
Usually	**4 points**
Sometimes	**3 points**
Seldom	**2 points**
Almost never	**1 point**

1. I persist at a task until it is finished.

2. When faced with a challenge, I would describe myself as being a persistent problem-solver who does not give up easily.

3. I am the kind of person who "sticks my neck out" to take a lot of chances in our relationship.

4. I am constantly seeking a better way of doing things in our home.

5. When we have a disagreement, I would describe myself as being forceful in stating my own opinion.

6. I am often recognized by my partner as an expert or an authority in one or more areas.

7. My partner can count on me to keep my agreements.

8. I prefer to be alone or with just one or two friends than in a large group.

9. I can anticipate problems before they arise.

10. I protest issues of injustice, unfairness, or hypocrisy when they arise between us.

11. I am interested in time management, planning the most efficient use of my day.

12. I consider myself as someone who follows the rules.

13. I think before I act.

14. I like having my own space in certain places in our home.

15. My partner has described me as being rebellious.

16. I set goals for myself and work hard to attain them.

17. I withhold my true feelings with him or her just to keep the peace.

18. I am "set" in my ways, my habits, and my opinions.

19. When we are in a conflict, I am confident that I have the ability to "rise above it" and thereby gain a better perspective.

20. I believe most couples compromise their true feelings just to conform to the status quo.

21. When we are riding in a car together, I'd prefer to be the driver.

22. I have a stubborn streak in me on certain things.

23. Compared with others, I feel I am more private and sensitive than they are.

24. I will stick to my own opinion or beliefs even when someone disagrees with me.

25. I believe that creating a better relationship will require me to change old habits, thoughts, and patterns.

26. I go after what I want.

27. I focus so much on the feelings of my partner that expressing my own emotions makes me uncomfortable.

28. With respect to our finances, I would describe myself as being conservative.

29. I am confident as long as I am free to follow my dreams.

30. My personal truth to me is more important than the social graces that my in-laws sometimes expect of me.

C. Now you can predict your results by actually scoring the list of statements you just read. After scoring, you will be asked to reflect and compare these results to your own initial assessment of your personality or lifestyle.

The Relationship Couple's Personality Preferences Questionnaire.
Daniel Eckstein

Instructions

- Transfer the points you assigned each item on the questionnaire into the appropriate box
- Add the number of points in each column. This is your raw score for the column
- Record the total in the large box at the bottom of the column

Column 1 Item 1	Column 11 Item 2	Column 111 Item 3	Column 1V Item 4	ColumnV Item 5
6 _____	7 _____	8 _____	9 _____	10 _____
11 _____	12 _____	13 _____	14 _____	15 _____
16 _____	17 _____	18 _____	19 _____	20 _____
21 _____	22 _____	23 _____	24 _____	25 _____
26 _____	27 _____	28 _____	29 _____	30 _____

According to Adler (1930) our characteristic reactions to life (lifestyle) are formulated before the age of five. Once this framework (or template) has been selected, all new experiences tend to be subjectively interpreted or filtered through that original framework. Although each of us has our own unique and creative style, early formative experiences help establish a "pre-formed working hypothesis" through which later preferences, values, and beliefs are evaluated and formulated. Through the use of factor-analysis research, Thorne (1975) identified the following five trait descriptive categories: aggressive, conforming, defensive, individualistic, or resistive. In order to avoid possible negative stereotyping and to identify the strengths of these more clinically oriented personality descriptions, the five lifestyle categories are given representative animal labels: tiger, chameleon, turtle, eagle, and salmon.

 **Tigers** are generally considered to be aggressive. They enjoy exercising authority, like to be the center of attention, and may insist on having their own way. Tigers usually were childhood leaders and continue in this role as adults. They are also enterprising, vigorous, and ambitious.

 **Chameleons** are generally seen as conforming. They are flexible, and are more likely to face problems directly. Chameleons frequently move up rapidly in business as they are dependable, hard-working, and honest. They are cooperative, social, warm helpful and practical.

 Turtles are generally thought to be defensive. They are earnest and resourceful and lead self-controlled, stable lives. Turtles are frequently loners with one or two close relationships. They are intuitive and sensitive and have some trouble admitting fallibility. Others may consider turtles to be stubborn because they have no interest in changing the status quo.

 Eagles tend to be seen as individualistic. They are not concerned with public opinion and may be egotistic and infringe on the rights of others to get their own way. Eagles are capable, industrious, assertive, and adventurous and idealize progress. They are found in any field that values independence and are frequently entrepreneurial.

 Salmon usually are considered resistive. They prefer to swim against the current rather than support establishment values. Salmon may take up causes against oppression and demand that they be heard. They are vigorous, progressive, and rebellious and dislike what they consider to be false social niceties.

Typology considerations

Adler (1929) was careful to caution against reifying typologies and was clear about their usefulness. "Do not consider human beings as types, because every person has an individual style of life. If we speak of types, therefore it is only as intellectual devise to make more understandable the similarities of individuals." (p. 102)

Boldt and Mosak (1998) stress that "Each person has a unique story of my life that a personality typology cannot portray. In addition, no one is pure type . . . . Indeed, as one gets closer to another's story one finds more, not less." (p. 496) Barzun (1960) further states: "To believe that one can capture so mysterious an entity as a complex human being in a diagnostic [word] or phrase deluding and invalidates the assertion that psychological investigation is a quest for the truth: all too often, it is a gathering of evidence to reaffirm what someone already believes about a particular set of behaviors." (p. 7)

D. Predicting Your Score

First, circle the adjectives you feel are most characteristic of you in your part nership at the present time.

Tiger	Chameleon	Turtle	Eagle	Salmon
Aggressive	cooperative	stable	capable	persuasive

confident	sociable	self-controlled	industrious	independent
persistent	warm	placid	strong	vigorous
persuasive	helpful	earnest	forceful	demanding
self-reliant	diligent	defensive	foresighted	rebellious
independent	persistent	stubborn	clear thinking	protecting
initiator	gentle	apologetic	independent	forceful
ambitious	honest	insecure	intelligent	competitive
potential leader	sincere	resourceful	spontaneous	progressive

Based on the adjectives you have circled and your answers in the questionnaire, prioritize which of the above animals you feel represents you:

1. _____

2. _____

3. _____

4. _____

5. _____

E. CPPO Profile

You will next find out how you scored. Note that all five animal types are presented sequentially throughout the questionnaire. Simply transfer your scores horizontally across the answer sheet and then add the total column vertically for each animal type.

Transfer each of your total scores for each of the five typologies onto the following graph and connect the dots to form a continuous line in the form of a graph.

—30	—29	—28	—27	—26
—29	—28	—27	—26	—25
—28	—27	—26	—25	—24
—27	—26	—25	—24	—23
—26	—25	—24	—23	—22
------------	------------	------------	------------	------------
—25	—24	—23	—22	—21
—24	—23	—22	—21	—20
—23	—22	—21	—20	—19
—22	—21	—20	—19	—18
—21	—20	—19	—18	—17
------------	------------	------------	------------	------------

−20	−19	−18	−17	−16
−19	−18	−17	−16	−15
−18	−17	−16	−15	−14
−17	−16	−15	−14	−13
−16	−15	−14	−13	−12
−15	−14	−13	−12	−11
−14	−13	−12	−11	−10
−13	−12	−11	−10	−9
−12	−11	−10	−9	−8
I **Tiger**	**II** **Chameleon**	**III** **Turtle**	**IV** **Eagle**	**V** **Salmon**

F. Now rejoin your partner and interview each other on the following questions.

1. How did your predictions compare with your final scores, as well as with your original animal selection?

   _____
   _____
   _____

2. Were there any surprise? If so, what were they? Do you agree with your scores?

   _____
   _____
   _____

3. Partner one, ask this of partner two.
   a) What do you predict your partner chose as the animal most like your?

      _____
   b) For what reason? _____
   c) Partner one, now share with him or her what you actually predicted and why.
   d) Discuss any surprises you two have in your respective predictions

4. Reverse roles and partner two ask the same questions of partner one.

G. Implications and Applications

Discuss your understanding of each of your styles. Then focus on how each of you could better respect each of your personality differences.

H. Additional Personality Resources

For more information on understanding and respecting relationship personality considerations, check the following eight resources:

1. Eckstein, D. (2001b). The #1 Priority Questionnaire (#1 PQ) for couples & families. *The Family Journal: Counseling and Therapy for Couples and Families*, 10, 439-442.

2. Eckstein, D., & Ford, R. (2000). The role of temperament in understanding couple's personality preferences. *The Family Journal: Counseling and Therapy for Couples and Families*, 7, 298-301.

3. Eckstein, D. (2002a). The Couples Enneagram Questionnaire (CEQ). *The Family Journal: Counseling and Therapy for Couples and Families,* 10, 101-108.

4. Eckstein, D. (2000b). The pet relationship impact inventory (PR II). *The Family Journal: Counseling and Therapy for Couples and Families*, 8, 192-198.

5. Kortman, S., & Eckstein, D. (2004). Winnie-the-Pooh: A "honey jar" for me and you. *The Family Journal: Counseling and Therapy for Couples and Families*, 12, 67-77.

6. Eckstein, D., & Shapiro, S. (2004). The Guiding Self-Ideal Questionnaire (GSIQ): *Relationship implications. The Family Journal: Counseling and Therapy for Couples and Families*, 12, 11-20.

7. Page, L., & Eckstein, D. (2003). Full Resource Partnering Questionnaire (FRPQ). *The Family Journal: Counseling and Therapy for Couples and Families*, 11, 413-419.

8. Eckstein, D., Sperber, M., & Miller, K. (2009). A couples activity for understanding birth order effects: Introducing the Birth-Order Research Questionnaire (BOIQ). *The Family Journal: Counseling and Therapy for Couples and Families,* 17, 342-349.

References:

Adler, A.(1930). Nochmals-die Einheit der Neurosen. *International Journal Psychology*, 8 2001-216.

Barzon, B.(1960) *Permanent Partners*. New York: Penguin, 6-7.

Boldt, R.M., and Mosak, H.(1998) Understanding the Storyteller's Story: Implications for Therapy. *The Journal of Individual Psychology* 64, no. 4 406.

Eckstein, D., & Kern, R. (2009). *Psychological fingerprints* (6th ed.). Dubuque, IA: Kendall Hunt.

Eckstein, D., Sperber, M., & Miller, K. (2009). A couples activity for understanding birth order effects: Introducing the Birth-Order Research Questionnaire (BOIQ). *The Family Journal: Counseling and Therapy for Couples and Families,* 17, 342-349.

Eckstein, D., & Shapiro, S. (2004). The Guiding Self-Ideal Questionnaire (GSIQ): *Relationship implications. The Family Journal: Counseling and Therapy for Couples and Families,* 12, 11-20.

Eckstein, D. (2000b). The pet relationship impact inventory (PR II). *The Family Journal: Counseling and Therapy for Couples and Families,* 8, 192-198.

Eckstein, D. (2002a). The Couples Enneagram Questionnaire (CEQ). *The Family Journal: Counseling and Therapy for Couples and Families,* 10, 101-108.

Eckstein, D., & Ford, R. (2000). The role of temperament in understanding couple's personality preferences. *The Family Journal: Counseling and Therapy for Couples and Families,* 7, 298-301.

Eckstein, D. (2001b). The #1 Priority Questionnaire (#1 PQ) for couples & families. *The Family Journal: Counseling and Therapy for Couples and Families,* 10, 439-442.

Haley, J. (1973). Uncommon therapy. New York, NY: Norton.

Kortman, S., & Eckstein, D. (2004). Winnie-the-Pooh: A "honey jar" for me and you. *The Family Journal: Counseling and Therapy for Couples and Families,* 12, 67-77.

Page, L., & Eckstein, D. (2003). Full Resource Partnering Questionnaire (FRPQ). *The Family Journal: Counseling and Therapy for Couples and Families,* 11, 413-419.

Shulman, B.(1973) *A Comparison of Allport's and the Adlerian Concept of Lifestyle.* Chicago: Alfred Adler Institue,

Thorne, F.(1929) *The Science of Living.*New York: Greenberg, 102.

Section 11:

The "How I Remember My Family" Questionnaire

Excerpts from Richard E. Watt's
"Using Family-of-Origin Recollections in Premarital and Marriage Counseling"

Please answer the following questions based on your childhood memories of your family. Please do not write on this sheet.

My Father

1. How would you describe your father? How would you describe his personality style?

2. How would you describe your relationship to him?

3. In what ways are you similar to your father? In what ways are you different?

My Mother

1. How would you describe your mother? How would you describe her personality style?

2. How would you describe your relationship to her?

3. In what ways are you similar to your mother? In what ways are you different?

My Parents' Marriage

1. How would you describe your parents' views of their roles and responsibilities as husband and wife? Was one partner more dominant, or was it a fairly equal relationship? What is your overall impression of their relationship?

2. What was the decision-making process? That is, how were decisions made, and who usually made them?

3. How would you describe the communication between your parents in their marital relationship?

4.   How was marital conflict handled?

5.   How did your parents manage finances?

6.   What was the division of labor in managing the home, possessions, social life, vacations, and the like?

7.   How did your parents relate to extended family members (in-laws, other relatives, and close family friends)?

8.   How did your parents view human sexuality? How was intimacy and sexuality understood and expressed in their relationship?

9.   How did your parents address the subject of religion?

10. What impact did your father's and mother's vocations have on their marital relationship?

11. What aspects of your parents' marriage do you want to incorporate into your marriage? Why? (Be sure to check your responses to questions 1-8 above.)

12. What aspects of your parents' marriage do you want to avoid? Why? (Be sure to check your responses to questions 1-8 above.)

Your Parents as Parents

1.   How did your parents feel about having children? Do you want children? Why or why not? How is your perspective of children similar and/or different to that of your parents?

2.   Describe your parents' *parenting* style. That is, describe your parents as parents. Were they in agreement on how the children should be reared? Please explain your answer.

3.   What aspects of their parenting style do you want to incorporate into your family? Why?

4.   What aspects of their parenting style do you want to avoid? Why?

Your Siblings

1. How many brothers and sisters do you have? In what order were they born?

2. How would you describe your brother(s) when you were children? How would you describe him/them now?

3. How would you describe your sister(s) when you were children? How would you describe her/them now?

4. Which of your siblings are you most like? Please explain.

5. Which of your siblings are you most unlike? Please explain.

Endnotes

1 Watts, Richard E. "Using Family-of-Origin Recollections in Premarital and Marriage Counseling." *The Journal of Individual Psychology*. 53, n. 4 (1997):429-434.

Section 12:

The "#1 Priority" Questionnaire
For Couples and Families (#1 PQ)

Daniel Eckstein

The following activity is meant to help couples and families in identifying and hopefully in appreciating different personality wants and needs based on early formulative decisions in each person's life. Answer the following questions, focusing primarily on your interactions with your partner (and/or your family), using the following scale:

       1 - Almost never true of me
       2 - Usually never true of me
       3 - Sometimes true of me
       4 - Often true of me
       5 - Almost always true of me

Activity 18: The "#1 Priority" Questionnaire
For Couples and Families (#1 PQ)
My Rating

1. I would typically describe myself as being an easy going person.
2. I would describe myself as being a considerate person.
3. There are actors and there are re-actors; I describe myself as and action-oriented actor rather than a more passive re-actor.
4. I consider myself to be quite knowledgeable in many areas of my life.
5. It is important for me to avoid stress whenever possible.
6. I often volunteer for projects.
7. I have often been described as a back-seat driver.
8. I frequently feel overwhelmed, over-responsible, and/or over-involved in various activities in our home.
9. I "play it safe" rather than taking risks when the outcome is in doubt.
10. I get anxious when I feel others do not approve of my actions.
11. I have good organizational skills.
12. Feeling unappreciated and unvalued are sources of stress for me.
13. I seldom volunteer for a new project.

---

14. I often withhold my true feelings if I think other people would disapprove of me.
15. avoid being humiliated whenever possible.
16. Being viewed as competent is important to me.
17. I mind my own business.
18. I am good at knowing what other people want and need.
19. I am more of a planner than as a spontaneous person.
20. I like being the winner in various games I play.

Theory Input

The number-one priority is determined on the basis of the person's answers to the question "What is most important in my quest for belonging?" A related question involves "What must I avoid at all costs?" Kefir[1] originally defined four number-one priorities: **comfort, pleasing, control and superiority**. Kefir & Corsini[2] later refined these concepts. Dewey[3] also credits Rudolf Dreikurs and William Pew with the same four priorities. She notes that although it is often difficult for an individual to determine his or her own life-style, the relative order of priorities is generally recognizable.

The following chart (in *Psychologist Fingerprints: Lifestyle Assessment & Intervention*, 2002[4]) compares the four priorities with what is to be avoided at all costs:

Number-one priorities:	*To be avoided at all costs:*
Comfort	Stress
Pleasing	Rejection
Control	Humiliation
Superiority	Meaninglessness

Although people seldom give up their number-one priority, it is possible to become more aware through insight and to "catch oneself" being over-involved in each priority. A quick assessment of each couple's life-style and core convictions could be accomplished by an investigation of the person's number-one priority. The priorities are further defined as follows:

Comfort

Self-indulgence and immediate gratification characterize the comfort priority. The price for pleasure is often in diminished productivity, since such individuals will not risk frustration and do not want responsibility. Being able to delay immediate gratification is necessary for such vocational fields as medicine and graduate school, as they require many years of training prior to completion. Some stress is also helpful in providing a positive motivator. For example, it is a grain of sand which motivates an oyster to form a pearl. Undue comfort is often correlated with lethargy and diminished risk-taking.

Pleasing

Pleasers often are challenging in respecting themselves or in receiving respect from others. The price the pleaser pays is often stunted growth, alienation and retribution. Pleasers are good at tuning in to what others want and need. Pleasers are characterized by an "external locus of control" using Rotter's[5] term where one's happiness is in someone else's hands. Pleasers frequently have difficulties in the political arena because there is always someone who disapproves of their actions. Pleasers often choose perfectionist role models with whom they vainly jump through countless hoops, almost always in vain, as the "Good Housekeeping Seal of Approval" simply will never be granted.

Control

There are two sub-types of control: control of others and control of self. By striving for, and perhaps even attaining control, the negative consequence is that feelings of challenge and resistance in those around them are often evoked. Control of self is characterized by being on edge, uptight, and hyper. Diminished spontaneity, creativity, flexibility and an inability to go with the flow are additional emotional costs for over-control.

Superiority

Being competent, being right, being useful, being a victim, or being a martyr are some of the specific manifestations of superiority. First-borns often expect to be number-one and are subjected to a feeling of meaninglessness when dethroned. Such strivings also lead to undo competitive behavior. There is a profound parable relative to getting to the top described in Trina Paulus' *Hope For the Flower*.[6] It is a story of an aggressive caterpillar who literally steps on top of others in his single-minded quest to get to the top of a *caterpillar pillar*. His own awakening occurs when his former partner appears to him as a brilliant yellow butterfly. He then leaves the vertical pillar to begin his own metamorphosis by being willing to let go of his former self, or die, to enter a cocoon for his own transformation.

The price paid for superiority is over-involvement, over-responsibility, fatigue, stress, psychosomatic illnesses, and uncertainty about one's relationships with others. The #1 priority is determined by the following chart.

Problems:	Someone Can Be A Friend To You By:	What I Really Want Is:
Invite revenge cycles & others to feel rejected. Feel resentful and ignored. Get in trouble for trying to look good while doing bad. Not having things the way you want them. Reduction in personal growth. Lots of sense of self and what pleases self.	Telling you how much they love you. Teaching you a lot. Showing approval. Showing appreciation. Letting you know you won't be in trouble if you say how you really feel.	To do what I want while others clap. For others to like me, accept me, and be flexible. For others to take care of me and make hassles go away.
Lack spontaneity. Social and emotional distance Want to keep others from finding weak spots. Invite power struggles. End up sick. Avoid dealing with issues when you feel criticized. Get defensive instead of open. Sometimes wait for permission. Critical and fault finding.	Saying "OK." Giving you choices. Letting you lead. Asking how you feel. Giving you time and space to sort out your feelings.	To be in control even though others can be better, smarter. To get respect, cooperation and loyalty. For others to have faith in me and give me permission to do what I want. To have choices and go at my own pace.
Overwhelmed, overburdened. Invite others to feel incapable and insignificant. Seen as a know-it-all or rude & insulting and don't know it's a problem. Never happy because you could have done more or better. Have to put up with so many imperfect people around you. Sometimes you don't do anything.	Telling you how significant you are. Thanking you for your contributions. Helping you get started with a small step. Telling you you're right.	To do it best. To get appreciation and recognition from others and a spiritual connection. To be told I'm right.

Problems:	Someone Can Be A Friend To You By:	What I Really Want Is:
Suffer boredom. Lazy, lack of productivity. Hard to motivate. Don't do your share. Invite special attention and service. Worry a lot but no one knows how scared you are. Lose out on the contact of sharing. Juggle uncomfortable situations rather than confront them. Wait to be taken care of instead of becoming independent. Invite others to feel stressed.	Not interrupting. Inviting your comments. Listening quietly. Leaving room for you. Showing faith. Encouraging small steps.	For things to be as easy as they look. To be left alone. To have my own space and pace. I don't want to argue.

Adapted from Eckstein, Daniel, & Kern, Roy (2002). *Psychological Fingerprints: Lifestyle Assessment & Intervention*. Dubuque, IA: Kendall/Hunt

Prediction of Your Score

1. Based on the above presented theory, predict what you feel would be your #1 priority.
2. Now predict what you feel will be your partners (and other family members if applicable) #1 priority.

Scoring—#1 Priority (#1 PQ)

Create and score your questionnaire like the one shown below. First, transfer your scores into the columns. Then add each of the numbers in each column to get a total score. Your highest score is your #1 priority.

1. _____   2. _____   3. _____   4. _____
5. _____   6. _____   7. _____   8. _____
9. _____   10. _____   11. _____   12. _____
13. _____   14. _____   15. _____   16. _____

17. _____   18. _____   19. _____   20. _____

Total Score:

Comfort _____   Pleasing _____   Control _____   Superiority _____

Reflection

Reflection of your and your partner's (and family members, if applicable) scores.
1. Do you agree with your own score? (Describe why or why not.)
2. Site specific behavioral examples of how you actually do this in your home with your partner and/or other family members.
3. Were you accurate in your predictions of your partner and/or other family members? (Describe why or why not.)
4. Cite specific behavioral examples of how each family member actually behaviorally demonstrates the #1 priority *now*.

Implications for You, Your Partner, and/or Family

See if you can identify how you might or actually have had arguments between your respective #1 priorities. For example, you may be more of a pleaser and your partner more into comfort. You would take pleasure in making him or her happy.

1. How have or might you and your partner have conflicts between your respective #1 priorities. For example, both of you are controllers or both of you want to be superior.
2. What are some problem-solving strategies that you might employ relative to resolving such differences described in #2?

Summary

An understanding of each person's personal preferences is an important part of appreciating both the benefits and costs of one's own personality preferences. It also is a key ingredient in the crucial attitude of mutual respect with couple and family relationships. The author has developed the #1 priority questionnaire as a way of introducing a way of assessing them of discussing the issues of personality differences within relationships.

Endnotes

[1] Kefir, N. (1972) "Priorities." Unpublished manuscript.

[2] Kefir, N., and Corsini, J. (1974) Dispositional sets: A contribution to typology. *Journal of Individual Psychology, 30*, 163-187.

[3] Dewey, E. (1978). *Basic Applications of Adlerian Psychology*. Coral Springs, FL: MTI Press.

[4] Eckstein, D., & Kern, R. (2002). *Psychological Fingerprints: Lifestyle Assessment & Intervention* Dubuque, IA: Kendall/Hunt.

[5] Rotter, J. (1980/1973/1954). *Social Learning and Clinical Psychology*. New York: Johnson.

[6] Paulus, T. (1972) *Hope for the Flowers*. New York: Paulist Press.

Section 13:

The Pet Relationship Impact Inventory (PRII)

Daniel Eckstein

Introduction

It has been said that there are two types of people in the world—those who believe there are two types and those who do not. With respect to the roles of pets with couples and families, the polarities might be described as "those who love and adore pets as regular members of the family" and "those who do not." This article begins on a personal note; I recently held my beloved fourteen-year companion as the vet injected morphine into the veins of a critically ill dog. Between the tears of sadness and of joy at such a long-term attachment, I held Anuenue (Hawaiian for "rainbow") as her soul left her body and, from my point of view, went to "doggy heaven" where a great celebration in her honor began. "No dog was ever more loved" the vet gently exclaimed as she touched my arm draped around the now lifeless body that a moment earlier had housed the elusive breath of life. "And no one has loved me more" I thought to myself as I carried Anuenue's body back into the clinic for her cremation.

For many children, it was a beloved family pet where they learned the deep bond of attachment that comes from loving and being loved. Grief and loss are also resulting lessons when death or separation from one's pet occurs. Of course adults also form deep bonds with their pets. "Man's best friend" is the phrase associated with the unique relationship between men and dogs. It has been said that "money can buy a dog, but only love can make him wag his tail." And management consultant Ken Blanchard[1] describes his personal aspiration as "wanting to be the kind of person my dog thinks I am." Inclusion in the family photo is further testimonial of the integral parts pets play in many households.

There are many other important lessons to be resolved relative to the issue of family pets. A big one is the issue of control. Many adults still remember and harbor the resentment when one or both parents said "no" to adopting a stray animal that appeared on their doorstep. And the author vividly remembers a couple's counseling session involving a woman fiercely loyal to her cat who had been asked to marry a man who was allergic to the cat. "It's either the cat or me," the male suitor demanded. "See ya," she replied as she walked out of the session.

The purpose of this article is to explore the role of pets in your family of origin as well as your current relationship and/or family issues relative to the impact of pets on the home. A series of self-reflective questions will help identify such pet relationships. To explore different personality variables, a questionnaire will then be presented. Following a theoretical input, the questionnaire will be scored and interpreted by you, the respondent and also, if possible, by your partner or other family member(s). The theory of pets' impact on couples and families will then be briefly presented.

Activity 19: Pet Self-assessment Questions

You and your partner (if applicable) and/or your children are invited to respond *individually* to the following questions. Later you are encouraged to discuss your respective responses to the items. Respond to each question in the following sequence:

a)   from your family of origin or family equivalent;

b)   from one or more previous significant relationships and/or marriages (if applicable) and; from your current significant relationships, marriage and/or family.

For each question, put "N/A" if it is not applicable to you personally.

1.   What were(are) the name(s) of some of your special pets?
2.   When you think about your special pet(s), what were(are) some special rituals or repetitive activities that you shared together?
3.   What were(are) some of the family issues surrounding the role of pets in your household? (i.e. who wanted/did not want a particular pet, etc.)
4.   How were(are) the issues/differences resolved?
5.   How did(does) your current beliefs about the role of pets in your family fit (or not) with your partner's and/or children?
6.   What problem-solving strategies were(are) employed relative to the care and upkeep of pets in your home?
7.   How did(do) you feel the issue of pets in your home positively and/or negatively impacted(s) your past and present family/ families/relationship(s)?

Activity 20: The Pet Relationship Impact Inventory (PRII)

Questionnaire: The PRII has been created by the author by adapting the personality theory of Will Schutz in his Fundamental Orientation Relationship Inventory/Behavior (FIRO/B) Questionnaire.

For each item, give yourself a numerical rating using the following criteria:

1 - Almost never true of me
2 - Usually never true of me
3 - Sometimes true of me
4 - Often true of me
5 - Almost always true of me

Note: The past and present tense are noted for completing your answers first from the perspective of your family of origin and then from your current family or relationship.

1. At special holidays, special gifts for my pet were(are) bought.
2. When I came(come) home, it was(is) important for me to be "greeted" or in some way recognized by my pet.
3. I attempt(ed) to influence the behaviors of my pet.
4. I let my pet decide what (s)he wanted to do. (i.e. what and when to eat, etc.)
5. I had(have) a very close personal relationship with my pet(s).
6. I like(d) my pet being warm and friendly towards me.
7. Pets appear in many of my family photos.
8. I want(ed) my pet to desire being close to me.
9. I like(d) feeling in charge of care of my pet.
10. My pet strongly influenced(s) my behavior.
11. I felt(feel) intimate attachment with my pet(s)
12. My pet(s) is(are) very nurturing to me.
13. If I were(am) going for a ride or walk, whenever possible, I prefer(ed) to take my pet(s) with me.
14. When I (would) leave the house or place where my pet was(is) housed, it was(is) important for me that my pet acknowledges I was leaving.
15. I want(ed) my pet to do things the way I want(ed) them done.
16. My pet strongly affect(ed)(s) how I spent my week.
17. I engage(d) in activities involving my pet(s).
18. "Doggie sugar" (licks, etc.) was(is) very important to me.
19. I like(d) physical contact with my pet (petting, preening, etc.).
20. Whenever possible, I want(ed) pets to go on family outings and holidays.
21. I strongly attempt(ed) to influence my pet's behavior.
22. I humorously view(ed) myself as the type of person who the dog "takes for a walk".
23. My pet(s) slept(sleep) in bed or close besides me in my home.
24. I genuinely miss(ed) my pet when apart from him/her.
25. I consider(ed) my pet to be a regular member of the family.
26. I like(d) the feeling that my pet wanted to be a part of my family.
27. I view(ed) myself as being in charge of my pet.
28. It might be said that my pet "adopted me".
29. I felt(feel) warm and close to my pet.
30. The loss or death of my pet(s) did(would) profoundly affect(ed)

Theoretical Input

Will Schutz[2] identified three basic interpersonal issues; those being that of *inclusion*, *control*, and *affection*. Although he later changed the term affection to openness, the author has kept the original term affection with respect to pet relationships. Each of the three issues of inclusion, control, and affection have two sub-scales; those being how much I *express(ed) towards my pet(s)* and conversely *how much I want(ed) being* express(ed) towards me by my pet(s). Thus the desired expression by me towards my pet(s) is the former scale, while the wanted expression towards me from my pet(s) is the later dimension. Here is a visual description of the pet-related personality styles.

	I = Inclusion	C = Control	A = Affection
E-Expressed Toward My Pet(s)	I had(have) pets and I include(d) pets as part of my family.	I took(take) charge of my pet(s). I influence(d) my pet(s) behavior.	I was(am) emotionally close (attached) to my pet(s).
W-Wanted From My Pet(s)	I want(ed) a pet(s) to be a part of my family.	I want(ed) my pet(s) to influence my behavior.	I want(ed) my pet(s) to be close to me.

Predicted Scores for You and Other Member(s) of Your Family

Given the above theory, predict your score by circling High, Medium, or Low on each of the six dimensions. After doing your own self-assessment and labeling that as a #1 below, do the same for a spouse or significant relationship (#2), a child (or children) #3, #4, etc., and other significant home relationships (i.e. grandparent(s)). Also, predict your total Pet Interaction Index (PII), overall measure of how important pets are to you and to other family members.

* The total of all three expressions (PAL)/wanted levels (PNL) respectively.

** The total of all six scales and is a global measure of how much of a commitment and of important a pet(s) is/are (were) in your life.

	I Inclusion	C Control	A Affection	*Total PAL Pet Activity Level (PAL)
E—Expressed				H=
Toward My Pet(s)				M=
				L=
	H, M, L	H, M, L	H, M, L	* Total PAL

				Pet Need Level (PNL)
W-Wanted				H=
From	H, M, L	H, M, L	H, M, L	M=
My Pet(s)				L=
				* Total PAL

	Total Inclusion: H=	Total Inclusion: H=	Total Inclusion: H=	GRAND TOTAL
	M=	M=	M=	** Pet Interaction
	L=	L=	L=	Index (PII)

Scoring

Now you will actually score your inventory in the following manner. Every six items responds to the six personality variables of *expressed inclusion, wanted inclusion, expressed control, wanted control, expressed affection,* and *wanted affection,* respectfully. Transfer your scores to the boxes below. Then total your scores for the item. The total of your three expressions scores is your *Pet Activity Level* (PAL); The total of your three wanted scales is your overall *Pet Need Level* (PNL); The sum of the six scales is your combined *Pet Interaction Index* (PII).

From You to Your Pet

I Expressed Inclusion	C Expressed Control	A Expressed Affection	Total Pet Activity Level (PAL)
1._____	3._____	5._____	
7._____	9._____	11._____	
13._____	15._____	17._____	
19._____	21._____	23._____	
25._____	27._____	29._____	
Sub Total _____	Sub Total _____	Sub Total _____	Sub-Total _____
Inclusion Total Score _____	Control Total Score _____	Affection Total Score _____	**Grand Total PAL** _____
Wanted Inclusion 2,8, etc.	Wanted Control 4, 9, etc.	Wanted Affection 6, 12, etc.	Total Pet Need Level (PNL)

From Your Pet to You

I Wanted Inclusion	C Wanted Control	A Wanted Affection	Total Pet Activity Need Level (PNL)
2. _____	4. _____	6. _____	
8. _____	10. _____	12. _____	
14. _____	16. _____	18. _____	
20. _____	22. _____	24. _____	
26. _____	28. _____	30. _____	Pet Need Level
Sub Total _____	Sub Total _____	Sub Total _____	
	_____		(PNL) Total _____
			Grand Total **Pet Interaction**
Inclusion Total Score _____	Control Total Score _____	Affection Total Score _____	**Index (PII)** _____
Wanted Inclusion 2,8, etc.	Wanted Control 4, 10, etc.	Wanted Affection 6, 12, etc.	

Your scores on each of the six sub-scales are translated as being *high* (23-30), *medium* (13-22), or *low* (5-12), respectively. Your scores of the *combined* sub-scale of expressed and wanted two inclusions, control, affection scores are *high* (21-25), *medium* (16-20), or *low* (10-15), respectively. Your combined *Pet Interaction Index* (PII) is defined as being *high* (112-150), *medium* (71-111), or *low* (30-70), respectively.

Your Self-Assessment of Your Scores

Now write one-two paragraphs describing what you feel is the meaning of the scores above. You may want to compare your predicted vs. actual scores (any surprises?), and your past vs. your present pet scores. Cite behavior examples of the various scales whenever possible. Also, compare your scores to other family members.

Comparison of Your Scores with
Other Significant Family Relationships

Next, compare your scores with other members of your family or with a significant relationship in your life. For example, consider one person high in wanted inclusion, s/he probably would enjoy the dog inside the house, maybe even in the bedroom. Conversely, a low wanted inclusion partner would not want such an arrangement. Discuss such issues as:

1. In what areas are your similar?
2. In what scales are you different?
3. How do you resolve those differences in your family (relationship)?

Theory Input

What follows is a brief overview to some of the theory involving the impact of pets on relationships.

In *Chicken Soup for the Pet Lover's Soul*,[3] there are many stories illustrating the vital role pets play in many families. Here are some examples.

A woman grieving the recent death of her husband is surprised by the delivery of a golden Labrador retriever puppy. In an accompanying letter written by her husband three weeks earlier, he explained how the puppy was meant to be her companion until the two of them would be reunited.

A three-year old child who consistently makes up stories about "pretend pets" in the absence of real pet one day befriends a wounded wolf. The wolf then becomes a fourteen-year companion of the Arizona-based family. One day the wolf is discovered dead from two gunshot wounds. However; beneath his paws was a motherless wolf-pup needing a home.

The "Puppy Express"

A family 1,500 miles from home in Wyoming had to sell everything just to purchase bus tickets back to their original home in Fort Wayne, Indiana. But the bus would not allow the elderly 17-year old dog ride along. A local vet agreed to keep this senior citizen until they could get enough funds to ship the dog home. Back in Fort Wayne six weeks later, the family was unable to pay the shipping cost of the seventeen-year old dog. Then an ingenious idea was born: "The Puppy Express". Various volunteer riders carried the dogs in their own vehicles connecting to other volunteers who took a week driving across five states and 1,500 miles to reunite the dog with his family. Consider what a "bargain" pets are for humans.

Roger Caras says it this way: "Dog have given us their absolute all. We are the center of their universe. We are the focus of their love and faith, and trust. They serve us in return for scraps. It is without a doubt the best deal man has ever made."[4]

Cynthia Rylant's *Dog Heaven*[5] is a humorous depiction, which children and adults can enjoy as a supplement to grief and loss of a dog. She describes how when dogs go to heaven, God doesn't give them wings; instead they are given fields made just for running, lakes filled with geese for dogs to tease, angel children everywhere with whom they can play with, biscuits in the shapes of cats, squirrels, and ham sandwich biscuits, fluffy clouds for sleeping and special bowls with the dog's name on them, plus plenty of petting from old and new friends for such "angel" dogs.

Other Research

Additional clinical research will be briefly described here. Pets are an essential aspect of early bonding and attachment by children. In addition to assisting in children's verbal and non-verbal communication, they also provide love, security, and emotional support to family members. Pets are often viewed as positive contribution to family morale [6,7]. Children of dog owners report more visits from their friends than non-dog owned families; higher levels of attachment to dogs are positively correlated with confidence and negatively associated with tearfulness and weepiness.[8]

Other studies describe a positive relationship between self-esteem and pet-ownership; the use of pets as a means of stress reduction; the comfort pets provide and pets reduce feelings of adversity or transitional issues such as divorce or bereavement [9,10,11] A strong supportive relationship between pets and several abuse survivors is also noted with pets often being the most significant childhood relationship for such individuals. The loss of a pet can also have a significant source of grief in a family and can lead to disorganization in family functioning. In such cases, counseling may be helpful to the family interactions in processing the impact of the loss on the family.

Mertens[12] observed interactions between 51 families and the 72 cats they owned. She found that the interaction behavior of both partners in the human-cat dyad increased as the duration of human presence at home increased. Women-cat dyads had the best and juvenile-cat dyads had the worst relationship. She also discovered that attachments to pet animals begins as early as 18 months and that from infancy on, 98% of children and adolescents studied indicated that they loved their pets.

Some children who could not have family pets sought out animal companionship. Where housing regulations restrict pet ownership, children discovered ways to have interaction with animals by sharing other people's pets. Some children without pets also developed imaginary animal companions or temporarily nurtured strays or street animals as substitutes. Unfortunately, most of these children had less knowledge about and place less value on animal life than children who owned pets.

Family size, family structure, and mother's employment status influences the presence or absence of a household pet as well as the children's attitudes towards pets. Two-parent families, families with working mothers, and small families with only one or two children are more likely to have pets than one-parent families, families with mothers who remain at home, or large families with three or more children. Children without siblings are also more likely to play with pets and that older children took more care of pets than do younger children.

The Role of Pets in Children's Emotional Development

Most humans have an innate, biologically based need for social interaction; this interaction becomes increasingly focused towards specific figures. Behaviors such as following, smiling towards, holding, and touching are evident in the reciprocal relationship between child and attachment figure. Attachment behaviors are indicative of a lasting emotional bond between the individual and the object of attachment. Pets are often the first "not me" possessions; the term "transitional object" has been used to describe objects such as blankets and cuddly toys to which young children developed strong attachments. Transitional objects help children bridge between themselves and the outside world, and these objects can represent a life "good enough" other, one who adapts to the child's needs.

Such transitional objects often serve compensatory functions such as reducing anxiety, soothing and calming children, promoting exploration and play and facilitating separation from parents. Pets often serve as transitional objects for children. Pet, also known as companion animals, reduce fear and loneliness, can help minimize anxiety during times of stress, promote good mental and physical health for both children and adults as well as provide non-contingent, unconditional love and opportunities for affections. The emotional bond and desire for proximity between children and pets is congruent with attachment behavior towards humans, yet the relationship between child and pet is considered simpler and less conflicted than human relationships.

Pets have been described as serving the function of a living security blanket for children. Some young adolescents use their pets in ways similar to those described for inanimate, transitional objects. Pets may serve as a more mature and socially acceptable type of attachment object rather than blankets or teddy bears, particularly among older preschooler and school age children.[13]

Animal Assisted Activities (AAA)

Animals also have been used as part of therapy for individuals. Animal-assisted *activities* consist of such activities involving pets visiting people as:

- A group of volunteers take their dogs and cats to a nursing home once a month to visit.
- An individual brings her dog to a children's long-term care facility to play" with residents.
- A dog obedience club gives an obedience demonstration at a residential facility for teenagers with delinquent behavior.

Diane Reed founded the Whispering Hope Ranch in Payson, Arizona in the belief that sick or abused animals and sick or abused children will help each other heal. Since she opened the ranch in 1998 Diane has been inviting children and adults who are developmentally disabled, autistic, depressed, handicapped or spiritually disabled to come to a place which offers serenity, the unconditional love, and acceptance that animals are uniquely capable of giving. (whr@ whisperinghoperanch.org.)

Bruce Merrill, director of media research programs at Arizona State University, describes one example as follows:

> The two of them eyed each other suspiciously. The turkey with a badly deformed leg stood her ground in the dusty riding areas not knowing what to make of the six year old, autistic girl standing about 20 feet away. The turkey had just been brought to live at the ranch and had reason to be suspicious of people. Her mangled leg would always be a testimony to how cruel people can be to animals.

> The girl, Jill, in a world only she knew, seemed both afraid of the turkey but in a strong way, drawn to her. It was warm in the summer sun yet the two stayed locked in an almost supernatural embrace. Then Jill, who had never spoken a work in her six years of life, made an unintelligible sound, held out her hand, and began to move slowly toward the turkey. No one knows why the turkey didn't run away when the young girl approached. For the next several minutes the two were involved in a mystical dance; the girl gently petting the turkey while the turkey leaned against the girl as if to say "I need you too." What happened next some say is a miracle. The girls turned and walked to her mother who was nervously watching from the corral gate, held out her arms, and spoke the first word she ever uttered—Mommy! [14]

Information obtained from the AAA web-page (1999) describe the benefits of animal-assisted therapy as greater empathy, an outward focus to help children focus on their environment, nurturing, rapport, acceptance, entertainment, socialization, mental simulation, and physical contact (touch). Physiological benefits for many people include less stress and lower blood pressure. For example, just watching fish in an aquarium can be relaxing as many doctors and dentists have learned by putting them in their offices.

Children's Interview Questions

Here are some questions adapted from Triebenbacher[15] that teachers, parents, and/or counselors can ask children about their pets. This is also an excellent way to develop more rapport and/or understanding of your child's world.

1. What kind of pet(s) do you have at home? What are their names?
2. Which pet is your most special/important?
3. Do you think (Pet's name) is an important part of the family? In what way?
4. Is your pet(s) a special friend to you? How?

5. What do you like about (pet's name)?
6. Tell me the things you do with your pet. How do you show love to your pet?
7. Does (pet's name) liked to be hugged, kissed, and rubbed? What does your pet do to let you know he/she like to be hugged, kissed, rubbed?
8. Do you talk to your pet?
9. Does your pet seem to understand what you say? How does he/she?
10. When you are sick, sad, or upset, does your pet know?
11. How does your pet help you feel better?
12. Do you think your pet thinks about things? What kind of things does your pet think about?
13. Do you think your pet has feeling? What feeling do you think he/she has?
14. If your pet could talk, what do you think he/she would say?
15. How does your pet protect/take care of you?

Non-pet owners can be asked:

1. If you could have any pet at home, what would it be?
2. If you had a pet, what kind of things would you do with your pet?
3. Do you have friends who have pets?
4. If so, do you play with their pets?
5. Do you have a favorite pet that you read about or saw on TV? Or do you have a "pretend pet" that is your own special friend?

Summary/Applications

As you consider all of your responses on the list, think about how all of this impacts your world now relative to your wants, needs, and values as compared with other significant relationships in your life.

> I love my master;
> Thus I perfume myself with
> This long-rotten squirrel.

> I lie belly-up
> In the sunshine, happier than
> You will ever be.

> Today I sniffed many
> Doggy derrieres-and I celebrate
> By kissing your face.

I sound the alarm
Paperboy-come to kill us all-
Look! Look! Look! Look!

I lift my leg and
Anoint a bush, Hello, Spot-
Sniff this and weep.

My human is home!
I am so ecstatic I
Have made a puddle.
Behold my choke chain-
Look, world, they strangle me!
Ack! Ack! Ack! Ack!

Sleeping here, my chin
On your foot-no greater bliss-
Well, maybe catching rats . . .

Dig under the fence-why?
Because it's there.
Because it's there. Because it's there.

My owner's mood is
Romantic-I lie near their
Feet, expelling much gas.

How I love thee?
The ways are numberless as
My hairs on the rug.

I am your best friend,
Now, always, and especially
When you are eating.
Look in my eyes and
Deny it. No human could
Love you so much.

                    Author Unknown[16]

Endnotes

[1] Blanchard, Ken (1999) Leadership from the ground up, teleconference, Dallas, TX November 17th

[2] Schultz, *loc.cit*

[3] Canfield, J., et al., (1998). <u>Chicken Soup for the Pet Lover's Soul.</u> Deerfield Beach, FL: Health Communications, Inc.

[4] Caras, R. (1998), <u>Chicken Soup for the Pet Lover's Soul</u>. Deerfield Beach, FL: Health Communications, Inc. p. 41.

[5] Rylant, C. (I 995). <u>Dog Heaven</u>. New York: Blue Sky Press

[6] Triebenbacher, S. (1998). "Pets as Transitional Objects". <u>Psychological Reports.</u> 82,1, 191-200.

[7] Albert, A. & Anderson, M. (I 996). "Dogs, Cats, and Morale Maintenance". <u>Anthrozooes,</u> 10,2-3, 121-123.

[8] Paul, E. & Serpell, J. (1996). "Obtaining a New Pet", 47 (1-2): 17-29. Applied Animal-Behavior Science.

[9] Covert, A., et al., (1985). <u>Marriage & Family Review.</u> 8 (3-4): 95-108.

[10] Kidd, A. & Kidd, R. (1990). "Factors in Children's Attitudes Towards Pets". Psychological Reports. 66,3, 775-786.

[11] Sable, P. (1995). "Pets, Attachment & Well-Being across the Life Cycle". 341.

[12] Mertens, C. (1991). "Human/Cat Interactions in the Home Setting". <u>Anthrozooes.</u> 4 (4): 214-231.

[13] Triebenbacher, *loc. cit.*

[14] Merrill, Bruce. 1999. "Whispering Hope Ranch—Uncovering A Spiritual Treasure"—unpublished manuscript.

[15] Triebenbacher, *loc. cit.*

[16] McLellan, V. (2006). *The complete book of wacky wit.* Carol Spring, Ill.: Tyndale House

Section 14:

Winnie-the-Pooh: A "Honey-Jar" for Me and For You

Sharon A. Kortman and Daniel Eckstein

Introduction

Winnie-the-Pooh is one of the most beloved of the Walt Disney stories. The present article utilizes tales of four of the forest animals. It is hoped that couples and families can appreciate both the strengths and potential blind spots the Disney characters portray for better appreciating and respecting the different ways people relate to each other.

Many philosophers, spiritual teachers, and other leaders have learned the power of stories in their presentations. Best-selling author Ken Blanchard has used various animal stories in over sixty of his various written presentations. A paradox is that in the innocence of children's stories come some of our most profound truths. Walt Disney literally created a "magic kingdom" that can help us all rediscover the joys of childhood. In *Leadership by Encouragement*,[1] Dinkmeyer and Eckstein end their book by quoting a classic Disney phrase "If you can dream it, you can do it . . . remember this whole thing was started by a mouse."

In *Uncommon Therapy*,[2] Jay Haley proposes the following four ways of accessing couple and family interactions: *personality differences, role perceptions, communication skills*, and *problem solving strategies*. Since 1993, the second author of the *Experiential Activities For Couples and* Families column here has used such a model in *The Family Journal*. This article addresses another creative way to consider personality differences relative to a greater awareness of how different ways of operating within the world are possible by people living under the same roof. (For other ways to access personality in relationships, see Eckstein & Ford,[3]; Eckstein, [4] [pet]; Eckstein, [5] [enneagram]; Eckstein, [6] [#1 priority]; and Page and Eckstein. [7])

An American Indian koan is "if you want to understand my world, walk a mile in my moccasins." Empathy between couples and among family members is enhanced by valuing different personality preferences. Animal typologies are one practical metaphoric way of identifying different ways of behaving. The Hopi medicine wheel uses the qualities of various animals as desired attributes in humans. Respect between couples and families are enhanced when such differences are not judged as better or worse than each other. Dreikurs[8] called this the vertical plane of interpersonal relationships. Contrast that with the horizontal plane where differences are just that—*different*. Just as an apple is not better than an orange or worse (just different) so too the following four animal characteristics can provide both a fun and informative way of characterizing personality differences between couples and family members.

Activity 21: Self and Other Personality Descriptions

If you are familiar with the Winnie-the-Pooh story consider the following memorable four characters in the story . . . *Winnie-the-Pooh*, *Rabbit*, *Tigger*, and *Eeyore*. (If you do not know or do not remember the specific characters, you may want to review some of the descriptions which follow later in the article.)

Answer these questions:
1. Which of these animals is most characteristic of you? In what way?
2. Which is least characteristic of you? How?
3. Which of the four is most and least characteristic of your partner (and/or other family members)? In what ways?

The Array Interaction Model

The Array Interaction Model [9] identifies a Cooperative or Reluctant framework within four Personal Objectives. Although Personal Objectives are much like personality or temperament types, they are more adaptable depending on specific situations. Before we look into the analogies of Winnie-the-Pooh, Rabbit, Tigger, and Eeyore, take a moment to fill out the following short survey.

Activity 22: *Array Interaction Inventory (Self)*

The purpose of the following survey is to assist you in identifying your primary and secondary personal objectives; these are the most natural ways you typically respond to the world.

Directions:
For each of the following seven sentences stems, complete the statement in the following manner.

Rank order the responses in rows below on a scale from 1 to 4 with 1 being "least like me" to 4 being "most like me" by placing your score in the box to the right of the description.

1. I would most describe myself as being:			
Nurturing Sensitive Caring	Logical Systematic Organized	Spontaneous Creative Playful	Quiet Insightful Reflective

2. I value:						
Harmony Relationships are important		Work Time schedules are important		Stimulation Having fun is important i		Reflection Having some time alone is important

3. I am usually:						
Authentic Compassionate Harmonious		Traditional Responsible Parental		Active Opportunistic Spontaneous		Inventive Competent Seeking

4. I could best be described as:						
Empathetic Communicative Devoted		Practical Competitive Loyal		Impetuous Impactful Daring		Conceptual Knowledgeable Composed

5. I approach most tasks in a(n) _____ manner.						
Affectionate Inspirational Vivacious		Conventional Orderly Concerned		Courageous Adventurous Impulsive		Rational Philosophical Complex

6. When things don't "go my way," I would probably . . .						
Say "I'm sorry" Make mistakes Feel badly		Over-control Become critical Take charge		"It's not my fault" fault" Manipulate Act out		Withdraw Don't talk Become indecisive

7. When I've "had-a-bad-day," I would most likely . . .						
Over-please Cry Feel depressed		Be perfectionistic Verbally attack Overwork		Become physical Be irresponsible Demand attention attention		Disengage Delay Daydream
Add score:						

© Kortman, 2003, 1997

Activity 23: Array Interaction Inventory (Partner)

For other family members make a separate rating for each person on this form; answer the questions from the perspective of *your opinion* of your partner (and/or other family members). © Kortman, 2003

1. I would characterize him or her as being:							
Nurturing Sensitive Caring		Logical Systematic Organized		Spontaneous Creative Playful		Quiet Insightful Reflective	
2. (S)he values:							
Harmony Relationships are important		Work Time schedules are important		Stimulation Having fun is important		Reflection Having some time alone is important	
3. (S)he is usually:							
Authentic Compassionate Harmonious		Traditional Responsible Parental		Active Opportunistic Spontaneous		Inventive Competent Seeking	
4. (S)he could best be described as:							
Empathetic Communicative Devoted		Practical Competitive Loyal		Impetuous Impactful Daring		Conceptual Knowledgeable Composed	
5. (S)he approaches most tasks in a(n) _____ manner.							
Affectionate Inspirational Vivacious		Conventional Orderly Concerned		Courageous Adventurous Impulsive		Rational Philosophical Complex	
6. When things don't go his or her way, the most probable action would be to . . .							
Say "I'm sorry" Make mistakes Feel badly		Over-control Become critical Take charge		"It's not my fault" Manipulate Act out		Withdraw Don't talk Become indecisive	
7. When (s)he has "had-a-bad-day," the most probable action would be to . . .							
Over-please Cry Feel depressed		Be perfectionistic Verbally attack Overwork		Become physical Be irresponsible Demand attention		Disengage Delay Daydream	
Add score:							

Four Personality Descriptions

What follows are four personality descriptions using Disney characters as examples. It is important to note that no individual is any pure type; however, we all have more characteristic personality patterns which the Disney characters help identify. It is very possible that you relate to more than one of the animal analogies described as Personal Objectives in the Array Model. One is probably very natural for you; others motivational and maybe one or two you would only go to in your own behavior if the situation demanded it and if you had enough positive energy. Describing behaviors as "like Winnie, Rabbit, Tigger, or Eeyore" also provides a common nomenclature framework from which personality characteristics emerge. Here is a brief description of each style.

Harmony (Winnie-The-Pooh)

A person who is strong in the Personal Objective of Harmony is feeling oriented, very much like Pooh bear. He wants to please others. He enjoys such sensory experiences as his comfort food of honey. Relationships are critical in his world. In fact, he is continually wanting a party just to get the friends together in community. Individuals identifying with Pooh bear in their own personality profile are *sensitive, caring, warm*, and *giving*.

In *Pooh's Grand Adventure*,[10] Christopher Robin comes up to Pooh bear and says, "Pooh, there's something I have to tell you." Pooh bear says, "Is it something nice?" to which the reply comes, "Not exactly." "Then it can wait," says Pooh.

"For how long?"

"Forever and ever . . ."

The two friends then begin singing a friendship song about *forever* and go off into an entire day of play and just being together, never truly coming back to the information that needed to be shared. The koan "feedback is the breakfast of Champions" is *not* a Pooh-like attitude.

A Harmony person engaged in a stress response may react with: "Can we just pretend there is no problem? I'll even say 'I'm sorry', if everything can just be 'all right' again. Can we just have harmony, enjoy each other and be happy?" They tend to *over-adapt, over-please* and become *self-defeating* in their negative behavior. For Winnie the Pooh, he may sigh and say that he really is not that brave or not all that smart either.

Production (Rabbit)

Rabbit's world is characterized by straight rows of carrots in his perfectly manicured garden. He has a precise schedule for harvesting. He has a plan for just about everything; he is the organizer in the group. He says things like, "A thought is not a thing until it's written in ink."[11] People having a primary Personal Objective of Production are *logical, systematic,* and *organized*. They think first in a new situation. They like to have a plan and to be working toward goals or outcomes. They like to see the work accomplished before setting time aside for play.

When people respond in Reluctant behavior from a Production framework, they can become *bossy*, *demanding*, and *perfectionistic*. When Rabbit moves into his Reluctant behavior, he goes from designing a productive structure for work to becoming overly demanding of himself and others. His eyebrows come together with an irritated disposition. Just when Tigger is bouncing along with energy and enthusiasm onto Eeyore's thistle pile, Rabbit confronts him with a critical parent communication of "Tigger! Look what you've done! . . . Do you always have to jump on everything?" [12]

Or, when Tigger comes bouncing through Rabbit's garden: "'Tigger, just look at what you've done to my beautiful garden? . . . You've ruined it, Tigger. It's your doing. You and your confounded bouncing! Oh, why don't you ever stop bouncing?"[13] If you can relate to Rabbit's stress responses, you may also share a tendency to take charge and/or to express anger to others by utilizing sarcastic verbal attacks.

Connection (Tigger)

Depending on your perspective in the moment of his play, Tigger is the character that is the most delightful and/or the most annoying, If he were in a classroom, most teachers would be urging parents to consider medications like Ritalin for his obvious hyperactivity. His report cards would be checked with an *Unsatisfactory* mark for conduct control. In the Array Interaction Model, the Personal Objective of Connection describes a person who is *spontaneous*, *playful*, *energetic*, *witty*, and *fun*. This person enjoys being the center of attention and he or she loves group dynamics. The primary way of viewing the world is through "action". Consider Tigger, with all his gusto, singing, "Bouncy, trouncy, flouncy, pouncy! Full of fun, fun, fun! The most wonderful thing about Tiggers is—I'm the only one!"[14] He loves being unique, one of a kind, center stage, and just matter of factly states that, "Bouncing is what tiggers do best"[15] He adds joy to a room, a smile to Roo, who is his smaller counterpart, and energy into the middle of an ordinary day. In fact, even the most overwhelming of tasks can be accomplished by Tigger when he makes a game out of it. For example, he cleans up Roo's mud pie covered messy room from a rainy day inside play by calling the clean up job a "Tiggerific party."[16]

Individuals strong in Connection typically relate to Tigger's boundless energy and to the typical ways that Tigger moves into Reluctant stress behavior response. In such a mode, he typically *blames others* for his irresponsibility, *makes excuses* or *becomes disruptive*. When he bounces and spills Pooh's honey pots, bounces through Kanga's hanging laundry, he simply says things like, "Ta-ta for now", "Tally-hoo", or "Oops" and when confronted by an angry Rabbit who asks, "Do you always have to jump on everything?" he replies with "Tiggers don't jump—they bounce!" [17] Partners of Tigger-like behaviors are often angry because their stated concerns are "made light of" through fun and laughter. At such times the last song they want to hear is the "don't worry—be happy" with Tigger bouncing merrily along in a disruptive manner.

Status Quo (Eeyore)

Eeyore provides an analogy to the Personal Objective of Status Quo. Such individuals' primary way of viewing the world is through observation first. They *enjoy being alone;* they like *independent* activities; they are very good at *routine* tasks; and they are *insightful* and *reflective*. Although persons strong in Status Quo are often quiet, when they do speak, it is often profound as it is characterized by a synthesis of learning and insight. Consider Eeyore, quietly going about his business, gathering twigs and branches and building himself a new home. He clicks off his tasks, almost without being noticed. When he is with a group of friends, he is "going along with the flow." He says things like, "Thanks for noticing," "Easy come. Easy go."[18] And at the end of *Pooh's Grand Adventure*,[19] they all discover something about themselves through their search for Christopher Robin. Piglet discovers that he is "brave enough," Tigger that he is "strong enough," and Rabbit that he is "smart enough." Eeyore concludes the talk of their discoveries by saying, "Didn't have to come clear out here to find it. Had it inside all along."

When Eeyore responds out of a stress response, he *withdraws*. For example, when Tigger bounces down, destroying his newly made abode, he stoically says, "I didn't think . . . that a pile of thistles that nice could last long."[20] Because he is so often quiet, his stress responses look very much like his positive responses. He is often the most *misunderstood* and *complex* to "figure out" by others in his world.

If you are strong in Status Quo yourself, you may relate as someone who thinks very deeply, analyzing people and situations, but without the need to display that insight to the world. You may sometimes get blamed for not caring when you withdraw in a stressful situation. But what you may need is additional time to process the information, feelings and situation before talking it out or creating a solution to a challenge.

Scoring

Before actually scoring the questionnaire, take a moment to reflect on the following questions using the additional information based upon above descriptions.

1. Which of these characters do you predict will be <u>most</u> like you on the questionnaire? In what ways? For example, what do you do or say that is similar in both Cooperative and Reluctant behaviors?
2. Which of the characters do you predict will be *least* like you? In what ways?

3. For each member of your family, write down how they are *alike* and how they are *unlike* the characters in both positive behavior and in stress responses.

Harmony (Winnie-the-Pooh)	Production (Rabbit)	Connection (Tigger)	Status Quo (Eeyore)

Now, taking the scores from Activities 36 and 37, graph your scores along with your partners. Use one symbol (i.e., an "x" for yours and another "o" to profile for your partner). For other family members use different colors or other symbols, or simply put the names in the grid. When possible, have each family member complete their own inventory to use as a framework for personal reflection and for discussion.

28						
27						
26						
25						
24						
23						
22						
21						
20						
19						
18						
17						
16						
15						
14						
13						
12						
11						
10						
9						
8						
7						

Theory Input

One of the most definitive books on the story itself is by A. A. Milne entitled *The Complete Tales & Poems of Winnie-the-Pooh.*[21] In the following section all quotes from the story-line itself will be from Milne's book. The Disney Group features videos on the topic (see for example Walt Disney Company[22,23]). The vast popularity of the series is illustrated by the fact that a search on www.google.com on the topic of "Winnie-the-Pooh" yielded more than 530,000 references!! For the purpose of our article, three classic books will be cited here.

The Tao of Pooh

One of the best known of the Pooh commentators is Benjamin Hoff[24] and his classic *The Tao of Pooh.* He applies Eastern wisdom to Pooh's tales. In true Taoist terms, Hoff describes the essence of Pooh's philosophy by introducing the concept of the "Uncarved Block," which he defines as "things in their original simplicity contain their own natural power, power that is easily spoiled and lost when that simplicity is changed."[25] Hoff further notes that

> When you discard arrogance, complexity, . . . sooner or later you will discover that simple, childlike, and mysterious secret known to those of the Uncarved Block: Life is Fun . . . From the state of the Uncarved Block comes the ability to enjoy the simple and the quiet, the natural and the plain. Along with that comes the ability to do things spontaneously and have them work . . . As Piglet put it . . . Pooh hasn't much Brain, but he never comes to any harm. He does silly things and they turn out right.[26]

Wu Wei (what Hoff renames as simply "the Pooh way") literally means

> without doing, causing, or making . . . means without meddlesome, combative, or egotistical effort . . . the character Wei developed from the symbols for a clawing hand and a monkey, since the term *Wu Wei* means not going against the nature of things . . . no Monkeying Around . . . The efficiency of *Wu Wei* is like that of water flowing over and around the rocks in its path—not the mechanical, straight-line approach that usually ends up short-circuiting natural laws, but one that evolves from an inner sensitivity to the natural rhythm of things.[27]

It could also be described as Pooh's profoundly simple philosophy of "do without doing." Hoff elaborates the *Wu Wei* principal that characterizes much of Pooh's way of being by illustrating the act of

> striking at a piece of cork floating in water. The harder you hit it, the more it yields; the more it yields, the harder it bounces back. Without expending energy, the cork

can easily wear you out. So, *Wu Wei* overcomes force by neutralizing its power, rather than by adding to the conflict. With other approaches, you may fight fire with fire, but with *Wu Wei*, you fight fire with water.[28]

The *empty mind* is what Taoists call the *great nothing*. Such an attitude helped Pooh discover that the mystery of Eeyore's missing tail was solved when he found that Owl was using the tail as a bell-rope beneath his door knocker. Hoff continues, observing that

> an Empty sort of mind is valuable . . . because it can see what's in front of it. An Overstuffed mind is unable to . . . Knowledge and Cleverness tend to concern themselves with the wrong sorts of things, and a mind confused by Knowledge, Cleverness, and Abstract Ideas tends to go chasing off after things that don't matter, or that don't even exist, instead of seeing, appreciating, and making use of what is right in front of it.[29]

Pooh the Philosopher

In *Pooh & the Philosophers*[30] John Williams sub-titles his humorous yet most scholarly work as "in which it is shown that all Western philosophy is merely a preamble to Winnie-the-Pooh and philosophy" since Winnie-the-Pooh merely consists of what Williams notes as "footnotes to *that* sort of Bear."[31] Particularly noteworthy from the present authors' perspective, but beyond the scope of the present article, is his commentary on Pooh and essentialism.[32] In addition to Pooh being an astute philosopher, Williams believes that "Eeyore clearly represents the Stoic tradition . . . Piglet is rich in allusions to moral philosophy. Owl is . . . a lively satire on . . . academic philosophy that prides itself on its detachment from everyday life. Tigger's search for breakfast demonstrates the importance of secondary motives in Utilitarianism.[33]

Pooh the Psychologist

John Williams has also written an insightful book titled *Pooh & The Psychologists*,[34] subtitled "In Which It Is Proven that Pooh Bear Is A Brilliant Psychotherapist." In the introduction, Williams boldly states his hypothesis that Pooh himself was indeed the major driving force behind the profound personality changes taking place within his friends. Consider for example, how "The timid and overdependent Piglet is transformed into the hero who rescues Wol and even Pooh himself. Rabbit becomes less bossy and drops his original xenophobic prejudice against newcomers like Kanga and Tigger. The once-solitary and depressive Eeyore becomes actively helpful and ends up living a more social life."[35] Also, Williams believes that "Pooh, as 'a Stout and Helpful Bear,' is a lasting reminder that mental and bodily health can go together with a pleasing, through never an excessive, plumpness."[36]

Rabbit

While Rabbit is described by Milne[37] as being excessively "captainish" or bossy, he also receives warm praise; he has frequent visits from Pooh. Williams' own analysis of Rabbit's personality includes a combination of an Adlerian inferiority complex; an authoritative personality is the classic critical parent. From the communication model of transactional analysis, Rabbit is characterized by excessive judgments of others (i.e., When Pooh gets wedged in his home from overeating honey, he sarcastically notes that "It all comes of eating too much . . . I knew one of us was eating too much and it wasn't me"). He initially rejects Kanga and Baby Roo as intruders to a well-established "in" group ("Here we are—you, Pooh, and you, Piglet, and Me—and suddenly—"). Although he even went so far as to suggest kidnapping Roo, there is later the description that Rabbit was playing with Baby Roo in his own house. After that Roo spent every Tuesday with his now "great friend Rabbit."

Rabbit also displayed criticism of his other forest dwellers noting that "In his judgment, Pooh, Piglet, and Eeyore are brainless; Owl's ability to spell 'Tuesday' is often irrelevant; Kanga is too preoccupied with Roo; Roo is too young; Tigger too bouncy. "So there's really nobody but Me, when you come to look at it." [38]

One of the classic stories is called "The House At Pooh Corner," subtitled "In Which Tigger Is Unbounced." Here is an excerpt of William's commentary contrasting the therapeutic approaches of Rabbit and Winnie-the-Pooh.

> Here Rabbit's bossiness and his distaste for Tigger's superabundant vitality join in his attempt to unbounce Tigger by taking him on 'a long exploration' and losing him till the next morning. By that time, Rabbit predicts, 'he'll be a Humble Tigger' . . . Rabbit tries to cure Tigger's bounciness by associating it with the unpleasant experience of being alone and lost in the Forest mist . . . Rabbit's attempt misfires because Rabbit himself gets lost and is eventually rescued by his intended subject, Tigger . . . And the Small and Sorry Rabbit rushed through the mist at the noise, and it suddenly turned into Tigger; a Friendly Tigger, a Grand Tigger, a Large and Helpful Tigger, a Tigger who bounced, if he bounced at all, in a beautiful way a Tigger ought to bounce.[39]

Contrast that with what Williams believes is Pooh's therapeutic approach. Rabbit failed because he was primarily concerned to impose his own standards of behavior on Tigger. Over and over again we notice how careful Pooh is to avoid this dictatorial approach to psychotherapy. His aim always is to help his clients to help themselves and to achieve psychic health in their own way. Though rejecting Rabbit's 'Captainish' attitude, he welcomes his desire to help his friends.[40]

Williams summarizes that Pooh was a masterful therapist with Rabbit in that

> His diagnosis of Rabbit's inferiority complex was Adlerian. The treatment was straight-forwardly behavioral. The painful experience of being lost and alone in the misty Forest stimulated a desire to avoid repetition. The rescue by Tigger not only gave overwhelming relief and pleasure but associated these feelings with Tigger. This in turn led to a cognitive change in his perception of Tigger. He now saw Tigger as a friendly rescuer instead of as an overbouncy menace . . . Pooh saw that Rabbit's 'Captainishness' was by no means wholly bad. A better balanced Rabbit had indeed much to offer the Forest community.[41]

Tigger

A classic case of ADD (Attention Deficient Disorder) from the perspective of Rabbit and in his actual words, Tigger was characterized by "bounciness." But Winnie was wise on his first midnight encounter with Tigger.

> His natural kindliness enforces his professional therapeutic approach when he invites Tigger to stay the night and share tomorrow's breakfast with him. He then tells Tigger that it's the middle of the night, which is a good time for going to sleep . . . It reminds Tigger that he is part of the real world, which contains much more than his psychological difficulties. This soupçon of cognitive therapy continues in Pooh's reminder that the middle of the night is a good time for going to sleep. Sleep is not only especially needed for the hyperactive Tigger, but is one of those natural rhythms to which he should return after his apparently sleepless night.[42]

Tigger is the free or natural child using transactional analysis models of communication identification.

Eeyore

Eeyore makes a great transformation as is noted from his original response to Pooh's "And how are you?" question leading to Eeyore's reply, "Not very *how*. I don't seem to have felt at all how for a long time." Pooh uses cognitive therapy to confront Eeyore's false statement (negative attribution) that his tail was missing because "someone must have taken it" . . . "How like them," he laments. Although Pooh wanted to say something insightful and helpful, he decides instead to act by doing something helpful, namely finding the missing tail.

When Eeyore is sad because it is his birthday and no one has remembered it, Pooh again takes action. He commends Piglet for his idea of getting a balloon; Eeyore's false perceptions of having no friends are indeed changed to his having what Owl inscribed on a cake with a truly "HAPPY BRUTHDTH."

Eeyore was the first to respond when Baby Roo fell into a river while searching for the North Pole by swinging his tail into the water. Williams concludes his thesis of Pooh as a great therapist by noting that

> Pooh solves Owl's problem of communication. He leads the once-timid Piglet to a proper self-esteem which finally enables him to display outstanding courage and generosity. He makes Tigger's bounciness socially acceptable without destroying his admirable vitality. He channels Rabbit's bossiness into the helpful role of a lay counselor. If Pooh had not cured the irrational fear of bears (Arktophobia), the Pooh sage could never have even begun. [43]

The Array Interaction Model

Research has consistently shown that people learn more effectively and that they interact more productively when personal and psychological needs are met.[44] In the midst of complex family dynamics, an understanding of personality needs and interaction styles can help you proactively provide for varying needs and effectively resolve behavioral challenges. The Array Interaction Model[45] and the Array Management Model[46] provide a way for you to orchestrate the management of your own positive behavior and for you to learn about the motivating factors in others' behavior patterns. Such knowledge can help you provide a home environment and community for equipping each person to self-manage in positive ways.

The Array Model is highly correlated to characteristics described in every personality typing classification[47] and is based on insights from models including the Enneagram,[48] Reclaiming Youth at Risk,[49] Myers-Briggs[50] and Process Communication.[51] The Array Model has been designed in a system that differentiates positive and negative responses in a situational model that applies to the processing of relationships and behaviors on a daily basis.

Interaction Styles—Positive or Negative?

The three most common interaction styles include Cooperative, Marginal and Reluctant. A person acting in Cooperative interactions is *positive, agreeable, helpful and collaborative*. The Marginal style of interaction describes a person who is *neutral in attitudes and disengaged in interactions*. The Reluctant mode of interaction describes a person who is *involved, but in a negative way*. The following chart lists common behaviors observed when people are responding within either Cooperative or Reluctant behaviors.

Cooperative Behaviors	Reluctant Behaviors
Asks questions	Gets angry, verbally attacks
Works toward goals	Demands perfection
Initiates areas of responsibility	Feels inadequate, is self-defeating
Cares about others	Over-adapts
Is enthusiastic	Draws negative attention to self
Interacts well with others	Blames
Is attentive	Is disruptive
Positively contributes	Withdraws

Personal Objectives/Personality Components

The following figure presents Array Model descriptors; it offers specific Cooperative and Reluctant behavior examples from each Personal Objective, and addresses needs associated with each. You may recognize qualities of your own personality for both primary and secondary Personal Objectives. Because this is a situational model, responses may vary depending both on the situation and expectations from yourself or others.

	Personal Objectives/Personality Component			
	Harmony (Winnie-the-Pooh)	Production (Rabbit)	Connection (Tigger)	Status Quo (Eeyore)
Cooperative: Positive Behavior	Caring Sensitive Nurturing Harmonizing Feeling oriented	Logical Structured Organized Systematic Thinking oriented	Spontaneous Creative Playful Enthusiastic Action oriented	Quiet Imaginative Insightful Reflective Inaction oriented
Reluctant: Negative Behavior	Overadaptive Overpleasing Makes mistakes Cries or giggles Self-defeating	Overcritical Overworks Perfectionist Verbally attacks Demanding	Disruptive Blames Irresponsible Demands attention Defiant	Disengaging Withdrawn Delays Despondent Daydreams

Psychological Needs	Friendships Sensory Experiences	Task completion Time schedule	Contact with people Fun activities Fun activities	Alone time Stability
Ways to Meet Needs	Value feelings Comfortable work place Pleasing learning environment Cozy corner Cooperative work	Value ideas Incentives Rewards Leadership positions Schedules To-do lists	Value activity Hands-on- activities Group interaction Games Change in routine	Value privacy Alone time Independent activities Specific directions Computer activities Routine tasks

Adapted from Kortman/Honaker, 2002.

Relationship Application

Compare your scores from the questionnaire to the chart above. Identify specific examples when you and your partner (and/or family members) illustrated both the Cooperative and Reluctant behaviors described in the chart. Use this process to generate dialogue regarding natural areas of strengths and differences. Capitalize on the positive interactions within the family. Also discuss how you can be encouragers to Cooperative behavior when family members respond within their stress responses, remembering that Cooperative behavior encourages more Cooperative behavior. Next discuss with your partner and other family members how an understanding and appreciation of different personality styles can be an important part of understanding yourself and others. Contemplate "are we better able to 'walk a mile in each other's moccasins' using the Pooh story characters as examples?"

Implications

When you understand the behaviors and needs that drive each personality type, you can provide a variety of choices in your life or in community for allowing these needs to be met. People who are in Cooperative behavior encourage positive behavior from others in their environment. The more Cooperative behavior from multiple people, even those that are very different from one another, the more the environment is positive, productive and enjoyable.

By providing a variety of interaction strategies and expectations throughout the day, your family members will more likely stay in cooperative, positive behaviors. When your feedback is aligned to a person's individual priorities in thinking and behaving, it becomes more motivational to continue in Cooperative behavior.

Benjamin Hoff [52] concludes his own "proudly simple" explanation of Pooh's philosophy to living in this way.

> The masters of life know the Way, for they listen to the voice within them, the voice of wisdom and simplicity, the voice that reasons beyond Cleverness and knows beyond Knowledge. That voice is not just the power and property of a few, but has been given to everyone. Those who pay attention to it are too often treated as exceptions to a rule, rather than as examples of the rule in operation, a rule that can apply to anyone who makes use of it.

Within each of us there is diversity and our natural tendencies. Within each of us an ability to reflect on who we are, make decisions about capitalizing on our strengths and growing in areas of character and positive behaviors. May we apply our insights to the way we also view others, value and encourage them, and find ways to live together in community . . . much like our friends in the Hundred Acre Woods.

Summary

The present article has presented four different personality types using Disney's Winnie-the-Pooh animals as representative examples. Since the style that carries us to the "heights of success" is the same one that carries us to the "depths of despair," an appreciation of both the strengths and blind-spots of each representative animal can be helpful in understanding oneself and others.

Biography

Sharon A. Kortman, Ed.D.(*Winnie-the-Pooh: A "Honey-Jar" for Me and for You*, with Daniel Eckstein) is Lecturer in the College of Education at Arizona State University. She is the Director of the Beginning Educator Support Team (BEST), a partnership between university and school districts providing comprehensive support, training and resources in the areas of teacher induction, mentoring and preparation for aligning practice to the teaching standards. She has served in various teaching and administrative capacities at all educational levels. She is co-author and co-editor of *the BEST Beginning Teacher Experience: Program Facilitator Guide; the BEST Mentoring Experience: Program Facilitator Guide; the BEST Beginning Teacher Experience: A Framework for Professional Development; the BEST Mentoring Experience: A Framework for Professional Development; Trade Secrets for Primary and Elementary Teachers;* and *Trade Secrets for Middle and Secondary Teachers.* She is also co-author and co-editor of all BEST Standards in Teaching and Visitation Coaching curriculum. Her current research emphasis is in the areas of attracting and retaining quality teachers and strengthening effective teaching practices. Dr. Kortman also does writing and consulting in the areas of personality and interaction styles, which along with support to the education profession and personal interactions, positively affects student achievement and family dynamics.

Endnotes

[1]   Dinkmeyer, D. & Eckstein, D. (1996). *Leadership by encouragement.* Boca Raton, FL: St. Lucie Press

[2]   Haley, J. (1980). *Uncommon therapy.* New York: W. W. Norton

[3]   Eckstein, D., & Ford, R. (1999) "The Role of Temperament in Understanding Couple's Personality Preferences," *The Family Journal*, July

[4]   Eckstein, D. (2000). "The Pet Relationship Impact Inventory(PR II)," *The Family Journal*, April

[5]   Eckstein, D. (2002). "The Couples Enneagram Questionnaire (CEQ)" *The Family Journal*, January

[6]   Eckstein, D. (2002). "The #1 Priority Questionnaire (#1 PQ) For Couples & Families" *The Family Journal*, October

[7]   Page, L., & Eckstein, D. (2003) "Full Resource Partnering Questionnaire (FRPQ)" *The Family Journal*, October

[8]   Dreikurs, R. (1973) *Psychodynamics, psychotherapy & counseling.* Alfred Alder Institute

[9]   Knaupp, J. (1997). *Array model.* Unpublished document.

[10] Geurs, Karl (Director). (1997). *Pooh's grand adventure: The search for Christopher Robin.* United States: Disney. (Video).

[11] Geurs, *loc. cit.*

[12] Fremont, E. (1996). *Pooh: Just be nice...and not too rough!* Illus. Darrell Baker. NY: Western. (Disney Enterprises Inc. based on the Pooh stories by A.A. Milne. Copyright The Pooh Properties Trust).

[13] The Walt Disney Company. (1994). *Walt Disney's Winnie the Pooh,* United States of America.

[14] The Walt Disney Company. (1975). *Walt Disney's Winnie the Pooh and Tigger too.* New York: Random House, Inc.

[15] The Walt Disney Company, *loc. cit.*

[16] Birney, B. (1992). Oh, bother! Someone's messy! Illus. Nancy Stevenson. Racine, WI: Western.

[17] Fremont, *loc. cit.*

[18] Geurs, *loc. cit.*

[19] Geurs, *loc. cit.*

[20] Fremont, *loc. cit.*

[21] Milne, A. (2001). The complete tales & poems of Winnie-the-Pooh. New York: Dutton.

[22] The Walt Disney Company, (1975) *loc. cit.*

[23] The Walt Disney Company, (1994) *loc. cit.*

24 Hoff, B. (1982). *The Tao of Pooh*. New York: Penquin.

25 Hoff, pg. 10, *loc. cit*

26 Hoff, pgs. 20-21, *loc. cit.*

27 Hoff, pg. 68, *loc. cit.*

28 Hoff, pg. 88, *loc. cit.*

29 Hoff, pgs. 146-147, *loc cit.*

30 Williams, J. (1995). *Pooh and the philosophers*. New York: Dutton

31 Williams, pg. 1, *loc. cit.*

32 Williams, pgs.167-209, *loc. cit.*

33 Williams, pg. 4, *loc. cit.*

34 Williams, J. (2000). *Pooh and the psychologists*. New York: Dutton

35 Williams (2000), pg. 4, *loc. cit.*

36 Williams (2000), pg. 9, *loc. cit.*

37 Milne, *loc. cit.*

38 Williams (2000), pg. 99, *loc. cit.*

39 Williams (2000), pgs. 100-101, *loc. cit*

40 Williams (2000), pg. 101, *loc. cit*

41 Williams (2000), pgs. 110-111, *loc. cit*

42 Williams (2000), pgs. 68-69, *loc. cit*

43 Williams (2000), pgs. 186-189, *loc. cit*

44 Kortman, S. & Honaker, C. (2002). *The BEST beginning teacher experience: A framework for professional development*. Dubuque, IA: Kendall/Hunt Publishing.

45 Knaupp, *loc. cit.*

46 Kortman & Honaker, *loc. cit.*

47 Knaupp, *loc cit.*

48 Rohr & Ebert, A. (1994). *Discovering the enneagram*. North Blackburn, VIC: Collins Dove.

49 Brendtro, L. K., Brokenleg, M., & Van Bockern, S. (1990). *Reclaiming youth at risk: Our hope for the future*. Bloomington, IN: National Educational Service.

50 Briggs, K.C., & Myers, I.B. (1987). *Myers-Briggs Type Indicator*. Palo Alto: Consulting Psychologists Press, Inc.

51 Kahler, T. (1989). *Process communication model*. Little Rock, AR: Taibi Kahler Associates

52 Hoff, *loc. cit.*

Section 15:

The Bushido Matrix for Couple Communication

Chi-Sing Li, Yu-Fen Lin, Phil Ginsburg, Daniel Eckstein

Values are not only important in any relationship; but our ability to define and stay true to a set of values contributes greatly to how we feel about ourselves.

When a person makes a decision to marry, there are many factors to consider. Of course most people choose someone who is physically attractive to them at some level. In addition to the physical attributes that a person may find attractive, it is quite important that we find a person who is compatible with our set of values, standards, and the way in which we conduct ourselves. In every long term relationship, there are times when turmoil will occur. Over the years it is the common values that are more likely to sustain us through difficult times than anything else.

When each of us is young, at some point we look into to the mirror and imagine what kind of person we will be when we are an adult. As adults there can be times we may find that we are comfortable with whom we have become, but quite often there can be occasions when we find we are quite far away from the person we imagined we would be when we looked into that mirror during our childhood so long ago.

When we are out of touch with our basic core set of values, it can affect all facets of our life including our work, our choices as to how we spend our leisure time, our finances, our spirituality, our parenting and how we treat our spouses as well as ourselves. This can cause discomfort and a dissonance or feeling of being stuck.

Quite often we get so busy that we forget to take the time to define what our value system actually consists of or we may find that even though we do have values that we proclaim are important to us, that we have gotten far away from those basic principles and values. We may find that our words and our actions do not match. When our values and actions are incongruent with one another, it can be a source of great personal discomfort and adversely affect our relationships with our significant others.

In ancient days as early as the 9th century, Samurai warriors developed the Bushido code. This code was a set of values that guided the behavior and decisions of the samurai who served the Japanese emperor. This set of values to a large extent became their way of life. The values that the Samurai held most dear were to be trustworthy and honest. Living a life filled with honor and pride in one's own conduct rather than the pursuit of material riches was the reward the Samurai sought most. In this article we will explore how couples can use the ancient values espoused in the code of the Bushido, the way of the samurai, to enhance and strengthen their marriage and commitment to one another.

Bushido and the Samurai

Bushido comes from a combination of two words. "Bushi" means "Warrior" and "Do" means "way"; to simplify it, the word means "the Way of the Warrior" (Gaskin & Hawkins, 1994; Peterson, 2003). It is a way of preserving peace through the use of force. From the 9th till 12th centuries in Japan, the warrior class was known as samurai or bushi. Samurai were part of the Japanese feudal system, similar to the knights in Europe of the Middle Age. Samurai lived frugal lives with no interest in riches and material things, but rather in honor, respect, and pride. Through carrying out of their virtues, the samurai was able to keep his reputation. The loyalty to the emperor and his feudal lord was unsurpassed. Samurai had no fear of death and would enter any battle against all odds. To die in battle would only bring honor to a samurai's family and to his emperor or lord. Samurai emerged from the provinces of Japan and became the noble ruling class until their decline and abolition in the late 19th century. These warriors were men who lived by Bushido, their way of life (Gaskin & Hawkins; Peterson).

Seven Samurai

The concept and ideology of Bushido and the Samurai were introduced to the U.S. through various epic drama films. *Seven Samurai* and *the Last Samurai* were two of the most popular ones. Winner of the 1954 Venice Film Festival's Silver Lion and having two Oscar nominations, *Seven Samurai* was acknowledged as Kurosawa's and indeed Japan's and World cinema's greatest film (Crogan, 2000). *Seven Samurai* depicted a story about a poor farming village community in the sixteen century. Without a feudal landlord, the village was repeatedly raided by a band of outlaws. The villagers decided to hire samurai to protect themselves from the bandits by offering only board and three meals a day as their payment. The first part of the film depicted the villagers' difficulty searching for samurai who were willing to stoop to working for their social inferior. The latter part of the story was about how the seven samurai won the trust of the villagers and led them for the battle with the bandits. Four of the seven samurai sacrificed their lives in the bloody war but the villagers finally got rid of the bandits and saved their village (Crogan). *Seven Samurai* illustrated the seven core virtues of the Bushido. To fight for justice, to protect the weak and the poor, and to die with honor were values that captured the accent of the film.

The Last Samurai

The *Last Samurai* was a more recent American epic drama directed by Edward Zwick in 2003, with Tom Cruise as Nathan Algren, the main character (la point, n.d.). Set in Japan during the 1870s, the *Last Samurai* told the tale of Captain Nathan Algren, a cynical veteran of the American Civil war, who was hired by the Emperor of Japan to train the imperial army in the art of modern warfare. The Emperor's advisors planned to eradicate a group of rebellious traditionalist Samurai warriors in preparation for more Westernized and trade-friendly government policies. During the battle with the samurai, Algren was captured by the samurai but was later awakened through the learning and the practice of the Samurai's traditions and code of honor. At the end, Algren gave up supporting the new Westernized Japanese government and joined the last samurai in battle in preserving the old Bushido Samurai way of life. The story placed Algren in the struggle between two eras in Japan and two worlds with only his own conscious and his innate sense of honor being his guide (la point).

The Seven Virtues of Bushido

Bushido, the way of the samurai, was not written down until the 19th century and was based on certain "house codes" of various feudal lords (Gaskin & Hawkins, 1994; Peterson, 2000). Bushido described a unique Japanese code of conduct adhered to by the samurai. Bushido emphasized virtues such as loyalty, respect, and self-sacrifice. The actual code of Bushido was passed on verbally from one generation of samurai to another, but over time, seven or eight chief virtues emerged, and became the written form of Bushido (Nitobe, 2005; Nitobe & Lucas,1979). In this article, we put our emphasis on seven core virtues; they were Justice (義 *gi*), Courage (勇 *yū*), Benevolence (仁 *jin*), Politeness (礼 *rei*), Honesty (誠 *makoto*), Honor (名誉 *meiyo*), and Loyalty (忠義 *chūgi*) (Nitobe, 2005; Oriental Outpost, n.d.). This was the set of virtues that the Samurai of Japan and the ancient warriors in Asia had to live and die by. The following gives definitions and descriptions of these virtues:

Justice/ Rectitude/Right Decision (義 *gi*)

This character also means righteousness, morality and the right conduct (Oriental Outpost, n.d.) This is the most essential teaching and principle of the Samurai (Nitobe, 2005; Nitobe & Lucas,1979). It expects all samurai to strictly follow the ethical principle by doing the right thing. A famous samurai defined it as a power of declaration: "Rectitude is the power of deciding upon a certain course of conduct in accordance with reason, without wavering—to die when it is right to die, to strike when to strike is right" (Nitobe, 2005, p. 14). Doing the right thing or making the right decision sometimes is not an easy thing to practice since there seems to be more and more grey area in life. On the other hand, no matter the outcome or result, one does not lose face if they withhold proper justice. This character also means loyalty to friends or groups you belong to. In other words, you will make the right decision and be fair to those you are loyal to. This first virtue for the Samurai is to follow what is ethically or morally correct. It is a challenge in society where people tend to let loose of their responsibilities.

Courage/Bravery (勇 *yū*)

This character can be translated as bravery, fearlessness, or daring in Chinese, Japanese and Korean cultures (Oriental Outpost, n.d.). It challenges samurai to act courageously despite the circumstances. To be brave also means that the samurai has to practice his perseverance and, at the same time, that the samurai is expected to be physically and emotionally strong (Nitobe, 2005; Nitobe & Lucas,1979). Courage is not worthy to be counted unless it is exercised in the cause of righteousness. True courage, according to Bushido, is to live when it is right to live and to die when it is right to die. In other words, courage is doing what is right and appropriate and often times, it takes a lot of courage to act on what is right.

Benevolence (仁 *jin*)

A samurai is not solely a warrior depending on his military strength. A samurai should also possess the virtues of forgiveness, love, empathy and mercy, and affection for others (Nitobe, 2005; Nitobe & Lucas,1979). This character means being kind and loving to those who are close to you and honoring those who are of your senior. This concept also expands to include caring for people in general. Benevolence is believed to come out of our empathy and mercy for others. An old Chinese example for benevolence is the feelings and response one experiences when he sees someone fall into a well. The human nature to offer immediate care and empathy is brought out from this situation. Benevolence has to combine with politeness in order to see the actual effect (Nitobe; Nitobe & Lucas).

Politeness/Respect (礼 *rei*)

This character can also be translated as good manners, rite, worship or an expression of gratitude (Oriental Outpost, n.d.). The gallant manner of a samurai and being courteous and respectful with others in different situations and occasions are part of this virtue. Treating others with dignity and honoring the rules of family as well as the laws of the nation can also be an expression of politeness (Nitobe, 2005; Nitobe & Lucas,1979). More importantly, the emphasis is on being sensitive and caring to others. In other words, the emphasis is on respecting others so that you will be respected. It should be implemented in everything in society or everyday action. It is not something casual but has to be reviewed heavily since politeness affects people and the morale of society. Politeness is not on a superficial level but on a deeper level, being kind and being respectful to others so as to maintain harmony in relationships (Nitobe; Nitobe & Lucas).

Honesty/Sincerity (誠 *makoto*)

This character means truth, faith, fidelity, sincerity, trust and confidence (Oriental Outpost, n.d.). A samurai is expected to be honest and sincere at all times despite their circumstances. At the same time, a samurai is asked to flee from any temptations from businessmen plotting deceptive schemes (Nitobe, 2005; Nitobe & Lucas,1979). Honesty and sincerity are the beginning and the end of all things and honesty and sincerity give meaning to everything. The sincere word coming from the mouth of the samurai carries such weight that it becomes a promise that will be fulfilled without a written pledge. Honesty and sincerity create relationships that are trustworthy.

Honor (名誉 *meiyo*)

This virtue stresses on human dignity and the awareness of one's values and principles. A samurai can sacrifice everything in exchange of honor (Nitobe, 2005; Nitobe & Lucas,1979). Honor is believed to be closely bound up with strong family consciousness and even pre-natal influence. Honor, the opposite of shame, is what a samurai strives for and he refuses to compromise his character by any slight humiliation. This virtue also includes the characteristics of discernment and patience and meekness. This is about having or earning the respect of others and about having a reputation. It is more the status of being worthy of honor and it is not to be confused with doing honorable things.

Loyalty/Faithfulness/Devoted (忠義 *chūgi*)

These characters also contain the ideas of being faithful, devoted, true and obedient (Oriental Outpost, n.d.). This virtue is the utmost important of all. It describes the relationships among samurai and others in various situations (Nitobe, 2005; Nitobe & Lucas,1979). Being loyal to one's mission and one's master is the ultimate creed for a samurai to follow. The economic crisis has brought us to a new reality. There is very minimal organizational loyalty in Corporate America and even in our government. However, strict loyalty to one's master or feudal lord is the code to every samurai. "Till death do us part" can precisely depict the loyalty of a samurai to his emperor.

Activity 24: Using the Bushido Matrix Worksheet (BMW)

The authors have created the Bushido Matrix Worksheet (BMW) for self reflection and couple communication (see Appendix). It can also be utilized in any group setting for couples to generate opportunities for self disclosure and sharing. The BMW acts as a visual aid for readers to examine these seven virtues and how each of these virtues actually applies in our daily living and relationship building. The authors believes that practicing these Bushido virtues can ultimately enhance intra and inter-personal relationship, beginning with personal awareness and extending to couple awareness.

The seven Bushido virtues are listed on the vertical dimension of the matrix of the BMW whereas the horizontal axis features the following five reflective questions:

1. How was this virtue modeled for you as a child/adolescence and who modeled for you?
2. On a scale of 1-10, one being low and ten being high, rate yourself on any three of the virtues you consider as most significant in your life. When/how in your life, apart from your current relationship, have you demonstrated some of these virtues?
3. In previous significant relationships, cite two or three examples of when any of these virtues were violated and/or compromised? (Write the actual number of the experience after given the examples.)

4. Give examples of when/how you and your partner demonstrate this virtues in your relationship?

5. Choose two or three of these virtues you consider important for improving your current relationship. How are you going to do it?

There are various ways to utilize the BMW; the authors suggest one practical model here. First, you are invited to look over these seven Bushido virtues and gain a good understanding of them. Survey the questions on the BMW and spend as much time as needed to answer the questions independently without the presence of your partner. When you and your partner are both ready, you are asked to share your findings with each other. Practice active listening while doing this exercise and record the communication exercise if it deems appropriate for later reference.

Summary

Communication seems to be a vital part of couple relationships based on the feedback of the couple in this study and others with whom we interviewed. It is somewhat like the nervous system in a human body in which the brain sends a message to a corresponding body part for it to function accordingly. Without clear communication, the message would be misinterpreted thus leaving the body malfunctioned; good communication provides vital energy for couple relationships. The authors created BMW as a tool for couples to explore their value system and to enhance their communication at a deeper level. There are also other similar matrixes created by the authors for edifying couple relationships. The matrixes can be found in the articles of Li, Lin, and Eckstein (2007) and Ginsburg, Eckstein, Lin, Li, and Mullener (2010). Each matrix provides a completely different model for developing awareness and understanding for couples. It is the hope of the authors that relationship challenges can be overcome through open, non-judgmental and trusting communication.

Appendix

The Bushido Matrix Worksheet (BMW)

7 Virtues/ 5 Questions	1. How was this virtue modeled for you as a child or adolescence and who modeled for you?	2. On a scale of 1-10, one being low and ten being high, rate yourself on any three of the virtues you consider as most significant in your life. When/how in your life, apart from your current relationship, have you demonstrated some of these virtues?	3. In previous significant relationships, cite two or three examples of when any of these virtues were violated and/or compromised?	4. Give examples of when/ how you and your partner demonstrate this virtues in your relationship?	5. Choose two or three of these virtues you consider important for improving your current relationship. How are you going to do it?
Justice (義 gi)					
Courage (勇 yū)					
Benevolence (仁 jin)					
Politeness (礼 rei)					
Honesty (誠 makoto)					
Honor (名誉 meiyo)					
Loyalty (忠義 chūgi)					

References

Crogan, P. (2000, September 12). *Seven Samurai. Senses of Cinema.* Retrieved from http://www.sensesofcinema.com/2000/cteq/seven/

Gaskin, C. & Hawkins, V. (1994). *The ways of the samurai.* New York: Byron Press Visual Publications.

Ginsburg, P., Eckstein, D., Lin, Y., Li, C., & Mullener, B. (2010). The Noble Eightfold Relationship Matrix. *The Family Journal: Counseling and Therapy for Couples and Families, 18*(4), 427-437.

La point (n.d.). *The Last Samurai.* Retrieved January 4, 2012, from http://www.imdb.com/title/tt0325710/plotsummary

Li, C., Lin, Y. & Eckstein, D. (2007). The cultural relationship interview matrix: Four activities for couples. *The Family Journal: Counseling and Therapy for Couples and Families, 15*(2), 143-151.

Nitobe, I. (2005). *Bushido: The spirit of the samurai.* Boston, Massachusetts: Shambhala Publications, Inc.

Nitobe, I. & Lucas, C. (1979). *Bushido: The warrior's code.* Santa Clara, California: Ohara Publications.

Oriental Outpost (n.d.). *The Way of the Samurai.* Retrieved January 4, 2012, from http://www.orientaloutpost.com/bushido-code-of-the-samurai.php

Peterson, S. (2007, November 17). *Japanese Bushido.* Retrieved from http://www. japanesebushido.org/

Section 16:

Creating Respect in Couples: The Couples Respect Questionnaire (CRQ)

Donna Eckstein, Sarah Eckstein, Daniel Eckstein,

For the past 20 years the column focusing on couples in the Family Journal has been organized around Haley's (1973) four ways of accessing couples. The four ways include understanding and respecting personality differences, role perceptions, communication, and problem-solving skills.

The purpose of the present respect-focused article is for you, as a couple, to explore your own understanding of respecting personality differences. More than 30 years ago, the seeds of the present article were planted when coauthor Daniel Eckstein was counseling a couple. As they bickered back and forth, he had an epiphany: basic respect for one another was what was lacking in their relationship. With that came the realization that, without the foundation of respect, there was no basis for the couple to have a meaningful relationship. Indeed, the couple eventually ended their marriage.

This respect-focused article is organized as follows: Following a brief overview of respect, you will be invited to consider differences in your behaviors, thoughts, and feelings of respect compared to those of your partner. Donna and Sarah Eckstein have created the Couple's Respect Questionnaire (CRQ), identifying several core components contributing to a healthy partnership (see Appendix A).

Answer the questionnaire based on your rating of yourself and/or your partner. The theory behind the questionnaire comes after it. If interested, each of you individually may choose to predict your scores based on the authors' model. The next step in the CRQ is to score, profile, reflect on, and discuss your respective scores. Implications and "next steps" application will conclude the article.

If your partner is unable and/or unwilling to complete the questionnaire, you can limit your reflection and assessment of respectful behavior to yourself, or you may choose to complete the form from the perspective of your partner.

If you are not currently in a committed relationship, you can complete the activity alone from the perspective of past or even possible future significant relationships. While the article is written for you as a couple, you may find it useful to discuss your own responses, based on your assessment of yourself and your partner, with someone you trust. This may include a friend, family member, counselor, psychologist, social worker, or spiritual mentor.

Once you have completed and discussed the CRQ, a brief review of some pertinent literature about the importance of four specific factors contributing to a healthy, respectful partnership is available. Additional activities from previous couples' arti—cles, focusing on understanding and respecting personality and behavioral differences, will conclude the article.

From an Adlerian perspective, some form of inferiority and/ or superiority is at the heart of disrespectful couples' relationships. Dreikurs (1999) contrasted the vertical and the horizontal plane as a concrete way of perceiving yourself in relationship to others. The vertical plane is defined by a "better than/worse than" pecking order, a "top down" approach. Conversely, the horizontal plane stresses "different from," as in "an apple is different from an orange," rather than being somehow "better than or worse than" an apple.

There were four basic ego states proposed by Harris (1967) in his classic book "I'm OK-You're OK." He described a basic superiority position of "I'm OK-You're Not OK" compared to the inferiority belief of "I'm Not OK-You're OK." The most discouraged position is "I'm Not OK-You're Not OK," while the ideal interpersonal orientation is described in the book title. In the present article, the authors encourage partners to attempt to adopt the lens of "I'm OK-You're OK" as much as possible. Methods of abstaining from negative judgment are outlined using the four Rs.

Literature Review

Given that a healthy partnership is a broad concept, there is an equally broad approach to achieving this desired state. Respecting differences, responsibility, a willingness to review, a willingness to release, and many other relationship factors are significant in contributing to a healthy partnership (Bertoni & Bodenmann, 2010; Carlson, 1997; Gottman, Gottman, & DeClaire, 2006; Worthington, Lerner, & Sharp, 2005). Here is some basic information on how to construct the strongest relationship possible.

Respect (Respect for Differences)

One aspect of respect is the way in which a person handles differences between people. Even though numerous findings have revealed that people are romantically more attracted to people who are highly similar to them (Bo¨hm, Schu¨tz, Rentzsch, Ko¨rner, & Funke, 2010; O'Rourke, Claxton, Chou, Smith, & Hadjistavropoulos, 2011), further literature demonstrated that there are many ways to maintain a healthy partnership despite the partner's impactful differences. Differences can include differences in personality, behavior, lifestyle, gender, age, culture, and unique preferences.

Carlson (1997) advised people to seek to understand, over and above seeking to be understood. A need to be right can often compromise your ability to really listen and understand your partner's feelings. Seeing the gray areas where neither partner is perfectly "right" nor "wrong," but just different, can be a very challenging but helpful habit to develop when communicating. Pausing for a moment to understand your and your partner's separate realities is highly recommended (Carlson, 1997). Compromises are often one of the best tools couples can employ to work respectfully together (Bertoni & Bodenmann, 2010).

Vassar (2011) identified a dozen behaviors, not just to talk about respect, but to actually demonstrate it. You can commit to being more respectful to both your partner and, indeed, to all others

- Face the person with whom you are speaking.
- Make and keep eye contact, unless this is considered disrespectful, as in some cultures or situations.
- Use friendly facial expressions and subtly mirror the other person's postures.
- Display open body language and use accepting behaviors: smiling, nodding, etc.
- Stand and or sit with your spine erect.
- Give time to the other person to express his/her thoughts, feelings, needs, values, concerns, beliefs, or perspectives.
- Use "I" messages instead of "You" messages for sharing your opinion.
- When disagreeing with your partner, state it as a personal opinion rather than as a fact.
- Agree to disagree.
- Speak firmly, slowly, and clearly and commit to a calm voice whenever possible.
- Avoid interrupting your partner.
- Practice basic manners by being polite, thankful, appreciative, and sensitive to your partner's opinions and needs. (Retrieved on July 16, 2012, and adapted from http://lakesideconnect.com/anger-and-violence/respect-one-antidote-for-shame/?gclid=CMzj94Ckn 7ECFQW0nQod2ll1Wg)

Responsibility

Responsibility (or response-ability) has two facets: the ability to respond respectfully to your partner, and the ability to accept personal responsibility for your behavior (accountable, trustworthy, and reliable). The ability to respond respectfully during a conflict of differences is an important factor in a healthy partnership (Worthington et al., 2005). There is, however, an array of approaches to respectful partner inter-actions: direct and detailed verbal communication, more passive suggestions of feelings and needs, passionate eruptions of material from both parties at once, etc. (Gottman & Silver, 1999). Johnson and Lebow (2000) highlighted this by stating that in the past decade there had been "a greater recognition that different cultures hold differing expectations for relationships and that one-size-fits-all interventions have intrinsic limits" (p. 32). Identifying yourself and your partner's unique methods of effective communication is vitally important because all couples communicate with each other differently. There is no "cookie cutter" to show all couples exactly how they should communicate in order to achieve the healthiest relationship possible (Gottman & Silver, 1999).

Demonstrate Responsibility

So what can a couple do to demonstrate their responsibility (and "response-ability") when a conflict arises? Many authors advise you to tell your partner how you truly feel and what you need, even though this may cause tension temporarily (Gottman et al., 2006). Bring up the problem with as little criticism and shaming as possible (Garcia, 2012), accept personal responsibility for your portion of the problem immediately (Fincham, Hall, & Beach, 2005), and refrain from interrupting your partner or interpreting the messages before he or she has finished speaking (Gottman et al., 2006). Due to the rich variety of methods by which couples can demonstrate responsibility (response ability), there is a list of relevant articles, books, and other resources at the end of this article for additional information on this fundamental topic.

Review

A willingness to review includes the desire to reflect and communicate with awareness and understanding (reconsider, examine, change, and improve).

Research supports communicating your feelings and/or needs to your partner frequently, even though it may stir up resentment or anger (Gottman & Silver, 1999), This includes your willingness, and ability, to choose your battles wisely. Be sensitive to raising a conflict; is this the appropriate time and place, and is the argument a necessity (Carlson, 1997; Gott-man & Silver, 1999). Carlson (1997) instructed couples to examine a list of the most frequent arguments they have and ask themselves if they were willing to permanently let go of re-engaging any of cyclical conflicts. To facilitate increased prioritizing and perspective, he invented the "time warp game," in which an individual reviews or considers an issue and asks him or herself if this issue is important enough to matter in a year. If it is, it is likely worthy of a serious conversation with your partner. If not, it may be time to let that issue go (Carlson, 1997).

Demonstrate Review

When reviewing arguments or conversations with your partner or just within your own mind, Garcia (2012) encouraged individuals to set their intention on learning from the past. Examine unexplored angles. Identify changes you would make if you could go back and redo that interaction. Then make a personal commitment to try to make those changes, if possible, in the future to the best of your ability (Garcia, 2012). As you go through this sometimes-humbling process of reviewing, try to be patient with yourself and your partner; this is designed to be a learning experience that highlights both your strengths and your areas needing improvement (Carlson, 1997).

Release

Release is the willingness to let go of negative emotions. Conflicts, arguments, and/or abuse; to forgive; to work toward a relationship based on creating respect for differences between you and your partner; the willingness to relinquish or extinguish an unhealthy relationship when appropriate. If a couple is ready to let go of a conflict, how do they do this? Forgiveness is a primary factor in this answer as can be seen in the renowned author Brown's (n.d.) famous witty quote: "One of the keys to happiness is a bad memory."

Worthington, Lerner, and Sharp (2005) noted that couples who can interrupt the cycle of criticism and conflict quickly are significantly happier than those who allow a conflict to be painfully repeated many times. Increased forgiveness is so important, in fact, that it has been shown to significantly reduce a stress hormone, cortisol, in the brain (Kiecolt-Glaser, Bane, Glaser, & Malarkey, 2003). A second benefit of increased forgiveness is it seems to predict a reduced frequency of divorce; a couple is at least 50% less likely to divorce if they can forgive each other (Kiecolt-Glaser et al., 2003). Forgiveness and releasing emotions, however, can be extremely challenging. Couples are encouraged to practice respectful communications by reviewing past arguments, taking responsibility for their behavior, releasing emotions surrounding the conflict, and communicating their forgiveness to each other (Worthington et al., 2005). Practice forgiving your partner for smaller issues first, and focus on expressing empathy and support for your partner (Worthington et al., 2005). Expressing empathy while forgiving your partner can be done by verbally reflecting, repeating back to your partner what you heard, in a thoughtful manner that says you understood what was said about feelings, meanings, and needs (Elliott, Bohart, Watson, & Greenberg, 2011).

Demonstrate Release

The willingness to release emotions and let go of conflicts within yourself as well as with your partner is considered to be crucial by many professionals in the field of psychology (Fennell, 1993; Fincham et al., 2005; Garcia, 2012). An unwillingness or inability to release emotions and let go of conflicts may lead to the need to end the relationship. In the case of a breakup, Garcia (2012) advised individuals to "identify and accept that which cannot be changed and to let go, grieve, and grow from the experience." Letting go of partners can be extremely challenging; however, literature reveals that this process facilitates a healthy forward movement toward a more centered you and better future relationships (Garcia, 2012).

Conclusion

Because each individual is so different, disappointments and disagreements are inevitable in a committed relationship. Finding ways to respectfully communicate negative feelings, to ask for your expectations to be met, review past behaviors, and release resentments that do not serve you are incredibly helpful skills that take time and perseverance to achieve (Fincham et al., 2005). These tactics, however, have been documented as viable means by which healthy, respectful, long lasting, and mutually enriching romantic relationships can be established and maintained for many happy years

Summary

The purpose of the present article has been to focus on the critical role of creating respect in couples using a model that one of the authors, Donna Eckstein, calls The four Rs. A review of the literature on the qualities of healthy relationships has shown that factors involved in creating respect in couples include the abilities to show respect for differences, accepting personal responsibility (response ability), a willingness to review and talk about strengths and conflicts, as well as a willingness to release negative emotions, conflicts, arguments, and/or abuse and to forgive yourself and your partner. It is the belief of these authors that creating respect in couples is a daily commitment to use the four Rs to work toward a healthy and loving relationship.

The CRQ was created by family members Donna and Sarah Eckstein as an introspective and interactive exercise for individuals and couples. The information derived from the CRQ is best supported by an ongoing commitment to working toward a healthy relationship based on creating and improving respect for differences within oneself and one's partner. This may also include the willingness to relinquish or extinguish an unhealthy relationship, when appropriate.

`Appendix B lists additional Family Journal columns for couples, addressing relationship personality differences. All 20 years of Haley's four ways of accessing couples can be found in Eckstein (2012).

Appendix A
Couple's Respect Questionnaire (CRQ)

The CRQ is designed to assist with your awareness, measurement, and reflection of your perceptions. It can be used as a self-assessment of your behavior and/or the behavior of a partner. "Couple" and "partner" are used to describe two people in a relationship. This can include any significant person in your life that you would like to review.

Instructions: To the left of each question, rate your self—assessment for each behavior. If you choose to review and assess your partner (or another significant relationship in your life), you will need two copies of the questionnaire. On the second copy of the CRQ, repeat this process by rating your experience of your partner's behavior. At the end of each section, total and average the scores.

Measure your responses on a scale from 1 to 5 to reflect the degree that you agree or disagree with each statement.

Strongly Disagree	Slightly Disagree	Neither	Slightly Agree	Strongly Agree
1	2	3	4	5

The behaviors are organized and assessed based on the "4 Rs" listed below. The first R is respect. The following three Rs include behaviors that can support and build on respect.

Respect
Responsibility
Review
Release

Section A: The Couples Respect Questionnaire (CRQ)

Respect—Showing respect for differences. (Key words: consideration, acknowledgement, value, courtesy, and love vs. thoughtless, disregard, devalue, rude, and hate)

_____ 1 I do not communicate in a condescending manner.

_____ 2 I assert my needs instead of being non-assertive to avoid upsetting my partner.

_____ 3 I do not take it personally when my partner has a different opinion.

_____ 4 I show love for my partner by avoiding criticism and other negative personal interactions.

_____ 5 I can be aware of my partner's and my own moods and wait until we are both calm to convey a serious message.

_____ 6 I can be different and allow my partner to be different instead of needing to decide who is "right" or "wrong."

_____ 7 I consider my partner's needs and the ways my partner likes to receive messages

_____ 8 I build and maintain self-respect by developing my own interest, goals, and strengths.

_____ 9 I resist the urge to overly blame and judge by turning my criticism, and possible contempt, into a respect for differences.

_____ 10 It is important to me that my partner cares about my feelings and shows sensitivity for my feelings.

Total: _____ *(divide by 10 to get)* **Average:** _____

Responsibility—'Response-ability:' The ability to respond to your partner respectfully and to accept personal responsibility for your behavior. (Key words: accountable, trustworthy, reliable, answerable, and responsible vs. unaccountable, untrustworthy, unreliable, unexplainable, and irresponsible)

_____ 1 I uphold commitments that I make to my partner vs. making excuses.

_____ 2 I refrain from interrupting my partner's messages before my partner has finished speaking.

_____ 3 I respond respectfully during a disagreement or argument with my partner.

_____ 4 I make it known when I need to communicate something serious to my partner.

_____ 5 I respectfully respond to my partner's different style of communication.

_____ 6 I am not aggressive or abusive physically, verbally, or emotionally.

_____ 7 I compliment my partner when he or she does something well.

_____ 8 I respond respectfully when there are cultural and/or sexual differences and expectations about my partner.

_____ 9 I accept responsibility for my own behaviors that create a problem with my partner.

_____ 10 I consider the time and place, as well as my and my partner's behaviors, when bringing up a problem (i.e., not as my partner is walking out the door or just waking up).

Total: _____   **Average:** _____

Review—(Willingness to review)—The ability to reflect and communicate with awareness and understanding. (Key words: reflect, reconsider, examine, change, and improve vs. deflect, inconsideration, overlook, unchanged, and worsen)

_____ 1 I believe that relationships are designed to be a learning experience that highlights both strengths and challenges.

_____ 2 I am committed to self-improvement and relationship improvement.

_____ 3 I'm aware of the hot topics in our relationship that often trigger arguments.

_____ 4 I listen so I can understand what is being said as I interact with my partner.

_____ 5 I am able to assert my needs when appropriate instead of making the needs of my partner more important.

_____ 6 I refrain from jumping to conclusions about my partner's intentions.

_____ 7 I am able to apologize when I think I am wrong.

_____ 8 I review a conversation with my partner to gain further insight, not just to reiterate the points.

_____ 9 I am able to reflect on my needs and effectively communicate them to my partner.

_____ 10 I am willing to work on being patient with myself and with my partner as I go through the process of reflection and review.

Total: _____ **Average:** _____

Release—Willingness to release. (Key words: forgive, let-go, encourage, relief, relinquish, and self-respect vs. blame, restraint, discourage, burden/oppress, extinguish, and self-abandonment)

_____ 1 I have the skills to forgive myself.

_____ 2 I have the skills to forgive my partner, and to say that I have forgiven my partner when appropriate.

_____ 3 I am able to walk away from arguments which I think aren't important in the long run.

_____ 4 I would rather be connected, respectful, and happy with my partner than right.

_____ 5 I am learning to interrupt the cycle of criticism and conflict faster vs. allowing a conflict to be painfully repeated on multiple occasions.

_____ 6 I am able to compromise when differences cause conflict.

_____ 7 I am able to learn from past arguments and/or conflicts (i.e., sex, money, chores, past relationships, etc.).

_____ 8 I am willing to end a relationship that no longer meets or respects my needs.

_____ 9 I refrain from bringing up irrelevant mistakes or poor choices that my partner has made in the past.

_____ 10 I can put myself in my partner's shoes to understand his/her perspective or reasoning in order to let-go and be more willing to change my mind and behaviors when appropriate.

Total: _____ **Average:** _____

Section B: Profile

Plot the average of the totals for each section on the graph provided. You may want to compare the scores from your perception of yourself to the scores of your perception of your partner. For example, mark your score using an "X" or a colored pen to identify your self-rating average score for each section. Connect the marks to form a graph. Use an O or a different color pen to mark your rating of your partner.

Respect

| 1 | 2 | 3 | 4 | 5 |

Responsibility

| 1 | 2 | 3 | 4 | 5 |

Reflect

| 1 | 2 | 3 | 4 | 5 |

Release

| 1 | 2 | 3 | 4 | 5 |

Section C: Reflection: Exploring the Four Rs
Respect, Responsibility, Review, Release

Summary of question content: The questions you just answered were organized by four topics: respecting differences, response ability, review, and release.

- Respect for differences: An awareness of your and your partner's individual patterns of behaviors and lifestyles and your ability to work collaboratively.

- Responsibility (response ability): An ability to respond to your partner respectfully and a willingness to accept responsibility for your own actions.

- Willingness to review: An openness to effectively reflect, understand, and communicate about your and your partner's behaviors and the patterns that emerge.

- Willingness to Release: The willingness to release negative emotions, conflicts, arguments, and/or abuse. It is the ability to forgive yourself and your partner. It is a daily commitment to work toward a relationship based on creating respect for differences between you and your partner. This may include the willingness to relinquish or extinguish an unhealthy relationship when appropriate.

To what extent do you agree or disagree with this profile? Were any parts of your results surprising to you?

After reviewing your profile, what do you consider your areas of strengths?

What do you consider your challenges, conflicts, and/or areas of need for improvement?

After reviewing your profile, what do you consider your partner's areas of strengths?

Based on your findings, what do you consider your partner's challenges, conflicts, and/or areas of need for improvement?

Section D. Discuss Self-Assessment

Write and/or share your experience *with someone you trust* (friend, family member, therapist, etc.) about what you have done with this questionnaire.

Section E: Discussion with Your Partner

Share your experience of the above information with your partner. After sharing your experience with your partner, can you and your partner identify any other steps you would like to take to improve the level of respect for differences that is currently being practiced in your relationship? If so, take this time to design an action plan together that will lead to an increased level of respect for each other's differences in the future.

What is the first step you and your partner would like to take with creating more respect for differences? Is that something that you and your partner are willing to do individually and together?

Congratulations on completing this questionnaire and review. We wish you much success with your commitment to create more respect for differences with yourself and your partner. After completing this, you may be ready for an additional "R"

*R**elax—The Willingness to Relax!*

Humor can be very healthy and healing. After completing the CRQ, one couple who has been married for 44 years added some music and humor by singing some songs about the 4 R's. One of the songs that they sang was "Respect" by Aretha Franklin.

Are there any songs that come to mind for you . . . and your partner?

Appendix B

Articles Addressing Relationship Personality Differences

Duffey, T., Somody, C., & Eckstein, D. (2009). Musical relationship metaphors: Using a Musical Chronology and the Emerging Life Song with couples. The Family Journal: Counseling and Therapy for Couples and Families, 17, 151-155.

Eckstein, D. (2000). The four directions of encouragement. The Family Journal: Counseling and Therapy for Couples and Families, 8, 406-415.

Eckstein, D. (2001a). Counseling is the answer . . . but what is the question? The Family Journal: Counseling and Therapy for Couples and Families, 9, 459-463.

Eckstein, D. (2001b). The #1 Priority Questionnaire (#1 PQ) for couples & families. The Family Journal: Counseling and Therapy for Couples and Families, 10, 439-442.

Eckstein, D. (2004). The "A's and H's" of healthy relationships. The Family Journal: Counseling and Therapy for Couples and Families, 12, 414-418.

Eckstein, D., & Cohen, L. (1998). The couple's relationship satisfaction inventory (CRSI): 21 points to help enhance and build a winning relationship. The Family Journal: Counseling and Therapy for Couples and Families, 6, 155-158.

Eckstein, D., & Cooke, P. (2005). The seven methods of encouragement for couples. The Family Journal: Counseling and Therapy for Couples and Families, 13, 342-350.

Eckstein, D., Juarez-Torres, R., & Perez-Gabriel, A. (2006). The Language Relationship Questionnaire, (LRQ). The Family Journal: Counseling and Therapy for Couples and Families, 14, 408-411.

Eckstein, D., Junkins, E., & McBrien, R. (2003). Ha, ha, ha: Improving couple and family healthy humor quotient (HHQ). The Family Journal: Counseling and Therapy for Couples and Families, 11, 301-305.

Ginsburg, P., Eckstein, D., Lin, Y., Li, C., & Mullener, B.(2010). The noble eightfold relationship matrix (NERM). The Family Journal: Counseling and Therapy for Couples and Families, 18, 427-437.

Holt, M., Devlin, J., Brande Flamez, B., & Eckstein, D. (2009). Using the Holt Relationship Intimacy Questionnaire (HRIQ): What intimacy means to you and your partner. The Family Journal: Counseling and Therapy for Couples and Families, 17, 139-145.

Lessin, A., Lessin, J., Eckstein, D., & Kaufman, J. (2005). Five ways of assessing couple's relationships. The Family Journal: Counseling and Therapy for Couples and Families, 13, 491-495.

Li, C., Len, Y., & Eckstein, D. (2007). The cultural relationship matrix (CRIM): Four activities for couples. The Family Journal, 15, 143-151.

Mansager, E., & Eckstein, D. (2002). The Transformative Experience Questionnaire (TEQ): Spirituality in a couple's context. The Family Journal: Counseling and Therapy for Couples and Families, 10, 227-233.

Page, L., Nisan, L., Eckstein, D., & Ane, P. (2008). The intimacy task inventory: Taking a relationship snapshot. The Family Journal: Counseling and Therapy for Couples and Families, 16, 83-86.

References

Bertoni, A., & Bodenmann, G. (2010). Satisfied and dissatisfied couples: Positive and negative dimensions, conflict styles, and relationships with family of origin. European Psychologist, 15, 175 184.

Böhm, R., Schütz, A., Rentzsch, K., Körner, A., & Funke, F. (2010). Are we looking for positivity or similarity in a partner's outlook on life? Similarity predicts perceptions of social attractiveness and relationship quality. The Journal of Positive Psychology, 5, 431 438. doi: 10.1080/17439760.2010.534105

Brown, R. M. (n.d.). [Quotation]. Retrieved on September 5, 2012, from http://womenshistory. about.com/od/quotes/a/rita_mae _brown.htm

Carlson, R. (1997). Don't sweat the small stuff . . . and it's all small stuff: Simple ways to keep the little things from taking over your life. New York, NY: Hyperion.

Dreikurs, R. (1999). The challenge of marriage. Philadelphia, PA.: Accelerated Development.

Eckstein, D. (2012). The couple's match book: Activities for lighting, re-kindling, or extinguishing the flame. Bloomington, IN: Trafford.

Elliott, R., Bohart, A. C., Watson, J. C., & Greenberg, L. S. (2011). Empathy. Psychotherapy, 48, 43 49.

Fennell, D. L. (1993). Characteristics of long-term first marriages. Journal of Mental Health Counseling, 15, 446-460.

Fincham, F. D., Hall, J. H., & Beach, S. R. H. (2005). 'Til lack of forgiveness doth us part: Forgiveness and marriage. In E. L. Worthington, Jr. (Ed.), Handbook of forgiveness (pp. 207-226). New York, NY: Routledge.

Garcia, F. (2012). Healing good-byes and healthy hellos: Learning and growing from painful endings and transitions. Transactional Analysis Journal, 42, 53-61.

Gottman, J. M. (1993). A theory of marital dissolution and stability. Journal of Family Psychology, 7, 57 75. doi: 10.1037/0893-3200.7.1.57

Gottman, J. M., Gottman, J. S., & DeClaire, J. (2006). Ten lessons to transform your marriage: America's love lab experts share their strategies for strengthening your relationship. New York, NY: Random House.

Gottman, J. M., & Silver, N. (1999). The seven principles for making marriage work: A practical guide from the country's foremost relationship expert. New York, NY: Crown.

Haley, J. (1973). Uncommon therapy. New York, NY: Norton.

Haley, J. (1980), How to be a marriage therapist without knowing practically anything. Journal of Marital and Family Therapy 6, 385-391. doi: 10.1111/j.1752-0606.1980.tb01330.x

Harris, T. A. (1967). I'm OK-you're OK. New York, NY: Harper & Row.

Johnson, S., & Lebow, J. (2000). The 'coming of age' of couple therapy: A decade review. Journal of Marital & Family Therapy, 26, 23-38. doi: 10.1111/j.1752-0606.2000.tb00273.x

Kiecolt-Glaser, J. K., Bane, C., Glaser, R., & Malarkey, W. B. (2003). LoveAging & Mental Health, 15, 344-353. doi: 10.1080/13607863.2010.519324

Vassar, G. (2012). 15 ways to demonstrate relationship respect (retrieved and adopted from Haley, J. (1980), How to be a marriage therapist without knowing practically anything. Journal of Marital and Family Therapy 6, 385-391. DOI: 10.1111/j.1752-0606.1980.tb01330.x

Worthington, Jr., E. L., Lerner, A. J., & Sharp, C. B. (2005). Repairing the emotional bond: Marriage research from 1997 through early 2005. Journal of Psychology and Christianity, 24(3), 259 262.

Biography

Sarah Eckstein graduated from the University of Oregon in 2010 with a Bachelor's degree in Psychology. She graduated with Latin honors and departmental honors due to the completion of her undergraduate honors thesis: *Severe Delinquency and Late Entry into Foster Care: An Ecological Perspective.* She is currently a student in a Masters in Mental Health Counseling program in Ashland, Oregon at Southern Oregon University. As she journeys through her academics, internships, and publications, she remains hungry for knowledge and continues to throw herself through open doors as they materialize.

Section 17

Styles of Conflict Management

Daniel Eckstein

This article features a questionnaire exploring different ways that couples approach conflict. Five animals—shark, owl, fox, turtle, and teddy bear—are used to represent different conflict management styles characterized by a combination of high (or low) personal goals and high (or low) relationship goals. The advantages and disadvantages of each style are also presented, as well as examples of when each pure typology is most appropriate. The article concludes with a series of integrating reflective "next-step" questions for couples.

Each of us has a characteristic personality. Such a style reflects our unique wants, needs, and values. In conflicts, there are specific global patterns that can be identified reflective of how individuals deal with such challenges. The purpose of the following article is to identify several typologies relative to conflict management. No one style is inherently better than the other, and no one is a pure typology. An awareness of one's own style, including the strengths and weaknesses of that style is one objective. A second is a singular understanding of a partner's conflict management style, an important aspect of empathy. Finally, some suggestions on when each style is best utilized can help expand one's own repertoire of responses to conflict management. Couples who stay successfully married report no fewer problems or challenges than those who divorce. What is different is a problem-solving approach to challenges. It is hoped that the present article can assist in awareness and an increased ability to use different strategies/styles relative to resolving inevitable conflicts that arise in all interpersonal relationships.

Personal Reflection

As a way of exploring your style of dealing with conflict between you and your partner, please indicate your responses to the following questions below:

1.   When I am in conflict with my partner I typically:
2.   When my partner is in conflict with me, s(he) typically:
3.   Which of the following animals most closely resembles your usual style of coping with the conflict between you and your partner? (circle one)
     (a) Shark (b) Owl (c) Fox (d) Turtle (e) Teddy Bear
     Briefly describe why you selected this animal.
4.   Which of the following animals most closely resembles what you believe is your partner's usual conflict style? (circle one)
     (a) Shark (b) Owl (c) Fox (d) Turtle (e) Teddy Bear
     Explanation

Theory Input

Everyone has a characteristic style or manner in which we approach conflict resolution with our partners. It is formulated early in our life. Although no one is purely one style (or representative animal), each of us demonstrates tendencies or preferences based on our personality. There are strengths and weaknesses to each approach to conflict resolution. An awareness of one's own style, including the pluses, or assets, and the minuses, or blind spots, is the first step to understanding your own personal approach to conflict resolution. An awareness of how your partner approaches conflict can further assist your understanding of how you each view conflict in your own personal way.

Gerald Dwerks[1] has summarized conflict management research by the Grace Contrino Peace Foundation of Miami, Florida. The present author has adapted that information for this article.

The animals can be represented by considering two variables on a scale of 1 to 9 (with 1 a low rating and 9 a high rating). The vertical axis is based on a 9-to-1 (high to low) concern for personal goals. The horizontal axis is similarly rated on a high-to-low concern for the relationship itself. Based on the two variables of concern for personal goals and concern for the relationship, the characteristic conflict management can be represented as illustrated in Figure 1.

Your personal representative "theory in practice" example:

Consider an actual, recent conflict between you and your partner and answer the following questions:

    a.   Which animal most characterizes your approach to the conflict?
    b.   Which animal most characterizes your partner's approach to the same conflict?
    c.   What were the results? Do you think the conflict was successfully resolved?

There are advantages and disadvantages of each style. Just as in all personality traits, the same style that carries us to the "heights of success" when overused or used exclusively can also carry us to the "depths of despair." Each pure style has its own characteristic assets and liabilities (Figure 2).

Summary

Abraham Maslow[2] said that "if the only tool you have is a hammer, you tend to see each problem as a nail. Likewise, if you have only one predominant conflict resolution style, there are inherent limitations or blind spots.

The present article seeks to increase awareness of your own and your partner's predominant conflict resolution style. "Situational style" is a concept to help expand your own habitual conflict style by introducing other styles and approaches. Representative animals also give you and your partner a common language from which to discuss conflict styles. Again, it should be emphasized that few people are purely one style. Animals have been selected to typify the typologies because, in a manner similar to the American Indian tradition represented in the culture, various personality traits can be represented in a more balanced strong weaknesses manner.

Personal Integration Application

Consider the "new what are the future ramifications to me and my partner in terms of effective conflict resolution?" issue by considering:

1. How do I characterize my own predominant conflict resolution style; what are the major strengths and weaknesses of that style?
2. How would I characterize my partner's style, including strengths and weaknesses?
3. If the above specific, recent conflict (presented in the "theory in practice" example) is still unresolved, how might either or both of us utilize a different style or approach to assist our problem-solving skills?

Figure 1. Styles of Conflict Management

COMPETING: SHARK 9/1	High Concern Personal Goals	COLLABORATING: OWL 9/9
Win/Lose set * Do it my way or not at all" Strategies: * compete, control, outwit, coerce Prefers others who: * avoid or accommodate Leadership Characteristics: * authoritarian * reacts to crisis * power in position	9 8 7 6 5	Win/Win set * My preference is__ "What's your choice?" Strategies: *gather information, look for alternatives, * dialogue openly, welcome disagreement Prefers others who: * Collaborate or Compromise Leadership Characteristics: * big on process, dialogue * planning, discussion to prevent crisis * energized by controversy * examines all options, quick to delegate * power in skill, trust, gifts

(Continued)

Low Concern	COMPROMISING:	High Concern
Relationship		Relationship

COMPROMISING:

FOX   5/5
Win some/Lose some set
 "I'll back off if you do the same"

Strategies:
   * bargain, split the difference
   * a little something for everyone

Prefers others who:
   * compromise or accommodate

Leadership Characteristics
   * anxious but open
   * urges others not to
     be to outspoken

Low Concern Relationship: 5 4 3 2 1

High Concern Relationship: 9 8 7 6

AVOIDING:

TURTLE   1/1

Lose/Lose set
 "Conflict/ What conflict?"

Strategies:
   *like, deny, ignore,
   withdraw, delay, hope

Prefers others who:
   *avoid

Leadership Characteristics:
   *passive, timid
   *inclined to moralize
   *discussions and group
   *Live seems chaotic unfocused,

4
3
2
1

Low
Concern
Personal
Goals

ACCOMMODATING:

TEDDY BEAR   1/9

Lose/Win set
 "Whatever you say"

Strategies:
   *agree, appease, flatter

Prefers others who:
   *focus

Leadership Characteristics:
   *ineffective in groups
   * wishy-washy, easily swayed
   *needs to please all
   *energized by controversy
   *examines all options, quick to delegate

Figure 2: Conflict Styles: When to Use Which Style?

Competing

Often Appropriate When:
  * An emergency looms
  * You're sure you're right, and
    being right matters more than
    preserving relationships

Often Inappropriate When:
  * Collaboration has not yet been
    attempted.
  * Cooperation from others is
    important
  * Self-respect of others is diminished
    needlessly.

Collaborating

Often Appropriate When:
  * The issues and relationship
    are both significant
  * Cooperation is important
  * Reasonable hope exists to address
    all concerns.

Often Inappropriate When:
  * Time is short
  * You're overloaded
  * The goals of the other person
    certainly are wrong.

COMPROMISING:

Often Appropriate When:
  * Cooperation is important but time
    and resources are limited
  * When efforts to collaborate will be
     misunderstood

Often Inappropriate When:
  * Finding the most creative
    solutions possible is essential.
  * When you can't live with the
    consequence

(Continued)

AVOIDING:

Often Appropriate When:
* The issue is trivial.
* The relationship is significant.
* You have little power to block
 the other person.

Often Inappropriate When:
* You care about both the
 relationship and the issues involved

* Used habitually for most issues
* Negative feelings may linger
*Other would benefit from
 caring confrontation

ACCOMMODATING:

Often Appropriate When:
* You really don't care about the
 issue.
* When you realize you are wrong.

Often Inappropriate When:
* You are likely to harbor resentment
* Used habitually to gain
 acceptance (Outcome:
 depression, and lack of
 of self-respect).

Endnotes

[1] Dwerks, G. (1997). Conflict resolution strategies. Paper presented at the Southeast Convention of the North American Society for Adlerian Psychology, Orlando, FL., February 21.

[2] Maslow, A. (1982). Toward a psychology of being (p. 55). Princeton, NJ: Van Nordstrand.

Chapter IV:
Role Perceptions

Section 18:

The Use of Image Exchange in Examining Relationship Role Perceptions

Daniel Eckstein, Fern Clemmer, and Armando Fierro

Introduction

Page and Eckstein[1] note that each of us has a perceived **role perception** that is like an actual job description. That is, our closest relationships can be seen as analogous to jobs that require certain behaviors. Similarly, we have expectations of our partners and/or family members.

Personality differences affect one's desire to even seek the partner's perception. High self-view individuals seek more feedback from significant others than do individuals with low self-view.[2]

Couples' roles in marriage and the communication between them are determining factors in marriage satisfaction. Adler[3] proposed that feedback from significant others forms an early basis for individuals' self-appraisals, prospective roles and communication styles. This article explores the comparison of self—and spouse role perceptions within the context of social and demographic change. Shared role perceptions provide opportunities for couples to better understand each other's opinions. They are instructive and provide a general framework as individuals negotiate and evaluate their interactions and relationships.

This article explores couples' mutual examination of partnership role discrepancies. Based upon subjective self-reports of couples' perceptions of their own and their partner's perceived relationship roles, and the image exchange highlights the benefits of communicated role perceptions and examines what, if any, normative expectations marital partners have of the other and of themselves. It also considers how the presence or absence of behavioral role perceptions guides interactions

The following activity is based on a model originally taught to the first author by his mentor John Jones.[4] The process has been adopted by Dinkmeyer and Eckstein[5] for use in organizations. Here is the process of "image exchange" applied to you as acouple.

Activity 25: Image Exchange

1. Each of you begin the process with three large sheets of paper (poster board or flip chart paper is the preferred size if possible).

2. On the top of the three papers write the following headings . . .
    a. How I see myself in our partnership;
    b. How I see my partner in our relationship;
    c. How I think my partner sees me in our relationship

3. Now each of you go to a separate place and complete your own descriptive adjectives on these three topics. Take as much time as you need. Signal each other when you are both finished with your three postings. Use additional pages if needed for any or all of your independent individual responses.

4. When you come together keep your papers face down initially; flip a coin to determine who is "person A and who is B" in the process.

5. You will then have two rounds in which three postings will be compared side by side. Round one consists of the following sequence:
    a. Partner A post and share your responses to item a. (How I see myself in the relationship); (Partner B ask for clarification of any terms only at this point)
    b. Partner A post and read your responses to item c. (How I think my partner sees me in the relationship—Person B again ask for clarification of terms only at this point—this is not a "point-counterpoint debate."
    c. Partner B post your replies to your own #2b request above (How I see my partner in our partnership)

6. Now the two of you look at the three lists side by side. Answer these questions together . . .
    a. Some of the terms in which we agreed in all three charts were the following . . .
    b. Some of the adjectives in which there was a "disconnect" or a disagreement in the three postings were . . .
    c. Discuss your own reactions to the first part of the "image exchange" process—confront yourselves on the tendency to judge these differences as one of you being superior or inferior in your own "accurate perception" of the "real truth" of the matter.

7. Now reverse the same process with Partner B by:
    a. Person B share your first posting to item 2a. (How I see myself in our relationship);
    b. Person B share your second responses to item 2c (How I think my partner sees me in our relationship in our relationship)
    c. Now partner A share your content from poster #2b (How I see my partner in our relationship)

8. Repeat the same processing steps as noted in step #6 above.

9. Each of you independently write 1-2 paragraphs summarizing your own view some of the significant implications for your perceptions of your own and your partners respective relationship "job descriptions."
10. Then meet again as a couple and compare your respective responses.
11. Although there are no "right" (better than . . .) or "wrong" (worse than . . .) perceptions by either of you, the greater the "gap" between your respective responses the more you may want to consider discussing this with a respected spiritual leader and/or with a marriage and family therapist

Theory of Relationship Role Perceptions

In contrast to traditional husband/wife job descriptions there are currently many contemporary definitions of partnerships, traditional social and value systems that once defined individuals' lives have lost much of their traditional meanings and determinism. As individuals are freed from the constraints of tradition, new possibilities exist for shaping individual lives and relationships. Relative to the past, men and women have greater freedom to explore new lifestyle options. This freedom is particularly apparent in the lives of younger generations. Beck[6] calls this "biographization of youth" which denotes that younger generations define their identities and lifestyles, actively designing lives of their own. Beck[7] suggests that the loosening of tradition is transpiring in a Western context where "the ethic of individual self-fulfillment and achievement"[8] has become a powerful force.

The theory of individualization also highlights the fact that individuals' lives are socially embedded and involved in such institutions as family, labor markets, education, and later, often concerned with the welfare of the larger community.[9] [10] Rights, entitlements and responsibilities currently associated with these institutions are designed more for individuals rather than for the family. Such "institutionalized individualism" can create contradictions and tensions for individuals as they attempt to balance familial roles with other roles and responsibilities in their lives.

With the loosening of tradition, a growing emphasis on self-fulfillment and the challenges posed by institutionalized individualism, the question of how couples negotiate their relationships and roles becomes of increasing interest. Each generation improvises roles as they go along, with little guidance from established norms or expectations.

Ambivalence

Both the positive and negative dimensions of marriage and the contradictions and tensions inherent in family relationships need to be considered. Connidis & McMullin[11,12] emphasize the structurally created contradictions and tensions that individuals encounter as they negotiate their relationships. They define social structure as "sets of social relations based on class, age, gender, race and ethnicity that produce lasting inequality in society."[13] As Adler[14] stated and Connidis and McMullin concur, these sets of unequal social relationships are unfortunate but socially and lastingly embedded. Consequently, they influence the norms and expectations shaping the distribution of responsibility within families. Given couples' differing gender identities and traditions in the social structure, the potential for marital ambivalence exists.

Role Theory and Gender Roles

Sex role identity, often viewed as a stable personality characteristic, can be seen as a social-psychological factor that may be environmentally affected. Role conceptions may be influenced by life situations at different times or even by counseling intervention, especially intervention in the form of encouraged communication concerning gender and family roles. Role theory is concerned with the social context of roles.

The phenomenon of role ambivalence was examined from a role theory perspective by Rossi,[15] who stated that social roles always evoke ambivalence. He posited that when a role is optional or achieved, negative feelings about it are socially acceptable; but if traditional roles (for example, wife and mother) are required or ascribed, ambivalence toward them has been socially unaccepted and sanctioned, creating guilt and other problems for families. If an individual is unable to resolve a role conflict, role performance is impaired.[16,17]

In a growing body of literature on *psychological androgyny*, there is increasing evidence that the stereotypically sex-typed individual has a narrower range of functioning than the androgynous individual. Sex-typed individuals have been found to rank lower in self-esteem and higher in anxiety, and to become physically ill more often than their androgynous counterparts.[18,19,20]

Role strain occurs when an individual anticipates inability to fulfill a role as well as desired. Role conflict occurs with discrepancy between values and role expectations or with two roles (for example, wife and business woman) that cannot both be fulfilled (perhaps because of time constraints) to the satisfaction of the individual juggling the two roles. Women in higher-level positions, face particular conflicts between traditional role expectations and the role of the working person.[21, 22, 23, 24] This is more of a problem for married women with a more traditional sex-based role and division of labor in the household.[25] For women who hold a traditional view of women's roles, any expectations or needs that conflict with the traditional maternal role may be stressful.

Perceptions of Partner's Specific Qualities

Lisa Neff and Benjamin Karney[26] investigating the accuracy of perception of partner's specific qualities found that spouses varied significantly in their perceptions of their partners' specific qualities. For wives, more accurate specific perceptions were associated with their supportive behaviors, feelings of control in the marriage, and whether or not the marriage ended in divorce. They concluded that, "love grounded in specific accuracy appears to be stronger than love absent accuracy."[27]

Individuals who avoid closeness and/or devalue spouses are perceived as unresponsive to spouses' vulnerability.[28] This perception increases the spouse's attachment insecurity and depressive symptoms. Pollock et al.[29] looked at the influence of roles (on a continuum from traditional to extremely egalitarian) on communication. They found that very egalitarian individuals tended to be married to spouses who shared their views. Individuals who were effective in their communication practices tended to be paired, as were individuals whose communication practices were less effective. The more egalitarian couples also communicated more accurately than did the less egalitarian couples.

Flora[30] explored the basic correlation between one's own and others' assessment of himself or herself. The following nine observations included:

1. **It comes down to what you think about yourself**
"Our self-concept is fundamentally shaped by one person in particular: Mama. How your mother (or primary caregiver) responded to our first cries and gestures heavily influences how we expect to be seen by others . . . people with negative self-concepts goad others to evaluate then harshly, especially if they suspect the person likes them—they would rather be right than be admired."[31] ***You probably do know what people think of you.***

2. **Context is the key**

3. **What type of person can handle feedback?**
Some people actively seek feedback from such significant others as one's partner while others do not. Openness and an active curiosity about how you are perceived by your partner can help reduce the gap between your perception of you and that of your partner's opinion of you. Just as many companies conduct exit interviews when an employee leaves a company, relationship "exit-interviews" are similarly potentially useful. This was humorously portrayed in the movie *High Fidelity* in which John Cusack did just that. He listed his top 10 lovers and then went back and asked them what went wrong.[32]

4. **What kind of person rejects feedback?**
Narcissism is one major barrier to blocking feedback. In transactional analysis terms it reflects a basic "I'm ok; you're not ok" form of self-perceived superiority. Why seek feedback from a partner "beneath you" relative to being able to accurately perceive you?

5. **Shyness: a double whammy**

Flora notes that "Shy people convey unflattering impressions of themselves . . . People don't see then as lacking in smarts, wit, or attractiveness but as haughty and detached. When you're anxious, you fail to ask others about themselves or put them at ease in any way, which can be seen as rude and self-centered." [33]

But in some ways excessively shy partners *are* in fact self-absorbed by virtue of what Elkind[34] calls an imaginary audience. In high school this was the self-absorption that everyone is watching your every move. Superiority complex oriented individuals perceive them to being in awe of them ("you're so vain, you probably think this song's about you.") Conversely just the opposite is true of individuals have more for a perceived inferiority relative to others. If the former is truer of you in your present partnership, you will be more dismissing of your partner; if the latter is true you will tend to be more anxious regarding your partners perception of you in the relationship.

6. **Don't worry—you're not see-through**

"The traits others judge us on fall roughly into two categories—visible and invisible . . . others notice our visible traits more than we ourselves do. You would rate yourself higher on the characteristic of daydreams than others would—simply because they cannot easily discern whether or not you're a daydreamer . . . the good news, however, is that on a scale of physical attractiveness, others always rate you about one point higher than you rate yourself. This applies to charm too.

Invisible traits aren't entirely invisible . . . people agree more on your positive attributes than on your negative ones. That's because we are usually less honest about our negative traits in our partnership." [35]

7. **Self-awareness: a blessing and a curse**

The two-edged sword of self-awareness is both a desire for but also often a preoccupation and over concern for how your partner perceives you to be in the relationship.

8. **Do you really want to know how you come off?**

There is also the risk of both giving and receiving your respective perceptions of each other in this way . . . "There's always a trade-off between how good you want to feel and what you want to know."[36]

Downs[37] found a positive correlation between family commitment and role clarity. Dreikurs[38] advocated what he called "horizontal egalitarian mutually respectful relationships." Mast[39] also created what she calls an "Interpersonal hierarchy expectation (INE). She found that individuals who perceive relationships to be in a hierarchy what Dreikurs [40] called the vertical up-down plane of relationships tended to view themselves that way.

In a creative exploration of the positive correlation between positive self-esteem and self-evaluations Brown, Dutton, & Cook[41] identify the following three specific self-statements:

1. If it's an important trait to have, I have it
2. If I have it, it's important to have
3. If it's desirable to possess, I possess it

They note that "high self-esteem people; (a) claim to possess an important trait; and (b) inflate the importance of traits they possess."[42] They also

arrange their self-perceptions to promote positive feelings of self-worth. Interestingly, they did so not by inflating the self-descriptiveness of desirable traits but by minimizing the self-descriptiveness of undesirable traits . . . self-protection may be a more important consideration to high self-esteem people than is self-protection. High self esteem people may simply have found it easier to restore feelings of self-worth by denying they possess these negative traits than by claiming to possess these positive traits.[43]

Individuals also possess self-serving definitions of social traits and categories. When a trait is positive, people emphasize their own attributes in their definition of the trait. When the trait is negative, they de-emphasize self-attributes. High self-esteem individuals typically alter their views of other individuals in maintaining cherished beliefs about themselves. Such individuals often employ self-serving standards of performance when judging the accomplishments of others.[44]

When investigating low self-esteem individuals Beauregard & Dunning found that they still articulate trait definitions that are self-serving as those articulated by their high self-esteem counterparts. Low self-esteem individuals were also balanced. Low self-esteem participants harbored trait definitions that were much less self-serving. They conclude that:

The social judgments people make of others seem to consist of a complex dance between social information, self-behavior, and views about the self. What one person makes of another depends on whether the person sees himself or herself as a competent person or not. As such, the relation of self to social judgment may be a complicated one, but one that may ultimately be explicabe. [45]

Activity 26: Application to You as a Couple

The final suggestion by the authors is for you to discuss the following integrating activity.

Consider your responses in this section to be moving from "now what?" to the "so what?" aspect of your relationship. (What are some concrete "next steps" in both honoring your areas of agreement and in problem solving the "gap" between your respective perceptions of both yourself and your partner in your relationship together.

List some "next steps."

Summary

Since 1993 the first author has used Jay Haley's[46] four ways of accessing couples. Here is a summary of the four methods with corresponding activities in the following articles that can provide you and your partner ways of systematically reviewing your relationship. They include: *personality differences, role perceptions, interpersonal communication skills, and problem solving skills.*

Personality and Cultural Differences

1. *The "A's and H's" of Healthy & Unhealthy Relationships[47]*
2. *The Seven Methods of Encouragement for Couples[48]*

Role Perceptions

1. *The Couple's Relationship Satisfaction Inventory (CRSI): 21 Points to Help Enhance and Build a Winning Relationship[49]*
2. *Couple Rating Scale[50]*
3. *Five Ways of Assessing Relationship Satisfaction[51]*
4. *F.A.M.I.L.Y. Approach[52]*
5. *Assessing Interactive Creativity in Couples[53]*
6. *The Transformative Experience Questionnaire (TEQ): Spirituality in a Couples Context[54]*

Communication Style

1. *The Process of Early Recollection Reflection (PERR) for Couples and Families[55]*
2. *The #1 Priority Couples and Family Questionnaire[56]*

3. *The Role of Temperament in Understanding Couple's Personality Preferences*[57]
4. *The Couples Enneagram Questionnaire (CEQ)*[58]
5. *The Pet Relationship Impact Inventory*[59]
6. *Winnie-the-Pooh: A "Honey-Jar" for Me and For You*[60]
7. *The Guiding Self-Ideal Questionnaire (GSIQ): Twelve Personality Relationship Implications*[61]
8. *Exploring Different Expressions of Love*[62]
9. *Relationships as a "Three-Legged Sack Race"*[63]
10. *Loving and Being Loved: Commitment Implications*[64]
11. *A Couple's Gender-Based Communication Questionnaire*[65]
12. *Games Married Couples Play: Two Theoretical Perspectives*[66]
13. *The Non-Violent Relationship Questionnaire (NVRQ)*[67]

Problem Solving

1. *Styles of Conflict Management*[68]
2. *Thirty-three Suggestions for Relationship Renewal*[69]
3. *Force-field Analysis as an Aid in Decision Making by Couples*[70]
4. *Planned Renegotiation: A Preventative Model for Marriage and Family Counseling*[71]

Endnotes

[1] Page, L. J., & Eckstein, D. (2003). The Full Resource Partnering Questionnaire (FRPQ). *Family Journal, 11*(4), 413-419.

[2] Rankin, K. P., Baldwin, E., Pace-Savitsky, C., Kramer, J. H., & Miller, B. L. (2005). Self awareness and personality change in dementia. *Journal of Neurology, Neurosurgery, & Psychiatry, 76*(5), 632-640.

[3] Adler, A. (1970). Fundamentals of individual psychology. *The Journal of Individual Psychology*, 26, 36-49.

[4] Pfeiffer, J. W., & Jones, John. E. (Eds.). (1974). *A handbook of structured experiences for human relations training*. La Jolla, Ca: International Authors BV.

[5] Dinkmeyer, D. and Eckstein, D. (1996). Leadership by encouragement. Boca Raton, Fla.: CRC Press

[6] Beck, U. (1998). *Democracy Without Enemies*, Translated by M. Ritter. Cambridge: Polity Press.

[7] Beck, U. (1999). *World Risk Society*. Maiden, MA: Blackwell Publishers.

[8] Beck, *op. cit.* p. 9.

[9] Adler, A. (1938). *Social Interest: A challenge to mankind*. London: Faber & Faber, Ltd.

[10] Erickson, E. (1963). *Childhood and Society*, NY: Norton.

[11] Connidis, I. A., & McMullin, J. A. (2002a). Ambivalence, family ties and doing sociology. *Journal of Marriage and the Family.* 64(3), 594-601.

[12] Connidis, I. A. & McMullin, J. A. (2002b). Sociological ambivalence and family ties: A critical perspective. *Journal of Marriage and the Family.* 64(3), 558-567.

[13] Connidis & McMullin, *op. cit.* p. 600.

[14] *Loc. cit.* Adler, 1970.

[15] Rossi, A. S. (1972). The roots of ambivalence in American women. In J. M. Bardwick (ed.), *Readings on the psychology of women.* NY: Harper & Row.

[16] Jackson, E. F. (1962). Status consistency and symptoms of stress. *American Sociological Review.* 27, 469-480.

[17] Sarbin, T. R., & Allen, V. L. (1968). Role theory. In G. Lindzey & E. Aronson (Eds.), *The handbook of social psychology* (2nd ed, Vol. 1) Reading, Mass: Addison-Wesley Publishing Company.

[18] Bem, S. L. (1975). Sex-role adaptability. One consequence of psychological androgyny. *Journal of Personality and Social Psychology,* 31, 634-643.

[19] Bem, S. L., Martyna, W., & Watson, C. (1976). Sex typing and androgyny: Further explorations of the expressive domain. *Journal of Personality and Social Psychology,* 34, 1016-1023.

[20] Deaux, K. (1976). *The behavior of women and men.* Monterey, CA: Brook/Cole.

[21] Bass, B. M., Krusell, J., & Alexander, R. A. (1972). Male managers' attitudes toward working women. *American Behavioral Scientist,* 15, 221-236.

[22] Epstein, C. F. (1970). *Woman's place: Options and limits in professional careers.* Berkeley: University of California Press.

[23] Gordon, R. E., & Hall, D. T. (1974). Self-image and stereotypes of femininity: Their relationship to women's role conflicts and coping. *Journal of Applied Psychology,* 59, 241-243.

[24] Hall, D. T., & Gordon, F. E. (1973). Career choices of married women: Effects on conflict, role behavior and satisfaction. *Journal of Applied Psychology,* 58, 42-48.

[25] Markus, M. (1970). Women and work: Feminine emancipation at an impasse. *Impact of Science of Society,* 20, 61-72.

[26] Neff, L. A., & Karney, B. R. (2005). To know you is to love you: The implications of global adoration and specific accuracy for marital relationships. *Journal of Personality & Social Psychology,* 88(3), 480-498.

[27] Neff & Karney, *op. cit.* p. 480.

[28] Whiffen, V. E. (2005), The role of partner characteristics in attachment insecurity and depressive symptoms. *Personal Relationships,* 12(3), 407-424.

[29] Pollock, A. D., Die, A. H., & Marriott, R. G. (2001). Relationship of communication style to egalitarian marital role expectations. *Journal of Social Psychology,* 130(5), 619-624.

[30] Flora, C. (2005). Mirror mirror: seeing yourself as others see you. *Psychology Today, 38*(3), 52-58.

[31] Flora, *op. cit.* p. 55.

[32] Tim Bevan (Producers), & Stephen Frears (Directors). (2000). *High Fidelity* [Motion Picture]. USA:

[33] Flora, *op. cit.,* p. 56.

[34] Elkind, D. (1967). Egocentrism in adolescence. *Child Development, 38*(4), 1025-1035.

[35] Flora, *op. cit.* p. 59.

[36] *Ibid.*

[37] Downs, K. J. (2003). Family commitment role perceptions, social support, and mutual children in remarriage: A test of uncertainty reduction theory. *Journal of Divorce & Remarriage, 40*(1/2), 35-54.

[38] Dreikurs, R. (1967). *Psychodynamics, Psychotherapy, and Counseling.* Chicago: Alfred Adler Institute.

[39] Mast, M. S. (2005). Interpersonal Hierarchy Expectation: Introduction of a New Construct. *Journal of Personality Assessment, 84*(3), 287-296.

[40] Dreikurs, *loc. cit.*

[41] Brown, J. D., Dutton, K. A., & Cook, K. E. (2001). From the top down: Self-esteem and self-evaluation. *Cognition and Emotion, 15*(5), 615-631.

[42] Brown, Dutton, & Cook, *op. cit.* pg. 623.

[43] Brown, Dutton & Cook, *op. cit.* pg. 625.

[44] Beauregard, K. S., & Dunning, D. (2001). Defining self-worth: Trait self-esteem moderates the use of self-serving trait definitions in social judgment. *Motivation and Emotion, 25*(2), 135-159.

[45] Beauregard & Dunning, *op. cit.* p. 159.

[46] Haley, J. (1973). Uncommon Therapy: The psychiatric techniques of Milton H. Erickson. New York, NY: W.W. Norton & Co.

[47] Eckstein, D. (2004). The "A's" and "H's" of healthy and unhealthy relationships: Three relationship renewal activities. *Family Journal, 12*(4), 414-419.

[48] Eckstein, D., & Cooke, P. (2005). The seven methods of encouragement for couples. Family Journal, 13(3), 342-351.

[49] Eckstein, D., & Cohen, L. (1998). The couple's relationship satisfaction inventory (CRSI): 21 points to help enhance and build a winning relationship. *Family Journal, 6*(2), 155-159.

[50] Cron, E. A. (2002). Couple Rating Scale: Clarifying Problem Areas. *Family Journal, 8*(3), 302-305.

[51] Lessin, A., Lessin, J., Eckstein, D., Kaufman, J. (2005) Five easy of assessing relationship satisfaction. Family Journal, in press.

[52] Eckstein, D. (2003). A F.A.M.I.L.Y. Approach to Self-Care: Creating A Healthy Balance. *Family Journal, 9*(3), 327-337.

[53] Sarnoff, D.P., Sarnoff, P. (2005). Assessing Interactive Creativity in Couples. *Family Journal, 13*(1), 83-87.

[54] Mansager, E., & Eckstein, D. (2002). The transformative experience questionnaire (TEQ): Spirituality in a couple context. *Family Journal, 10*(2), 227-234.

[55] Eckstein, D., Welch, D. V., & Gamber, V. (2001). The process of early recollection reflection (PERR) for couples and families. *Family Journal, 9*(2), 203-210.

[56] Eckstein, D. (2002). The #1 priority questionnaire (#1 PQ) for couples and families. Family Journal, 10(4), 439.

[57] Eckstein, D., Ford, R.M. (1999). The role of temperament in understanding couple's personality preferences. *Family Journal*, 7(3), 298-299.

[58] Eckstein, D. (2002). The Couple's Enneagram Questionnaire (CEQ). *Family Journal* 10(1), 101-109.

[59] Eckstein, D. (2002). The Pet Relationship Impact Inventory. *Family Journal*, 8(2), 192-199.

[60] Kortman, S. A., & Eckstein, D. (2004). Winnie-the-Pooh: A "Honey-Jar" for me and for You. *Family Journal, 12*(1), 67-78.

[61] Eckstein, D., & Shapiro, S. (2004). The guiding self-ideal questionnaire (GSIQ): 12 personality relationship implications. *Family Journal, 12*(3), 292-312.

[62] Eckstein, D., & Morrison, J. (1999). Exploring different expression of love. *Family Journal,* 7(1), 75-77.

[63] Eckstein, D., Leventhal, M., Bentley, S., & Kelley, S. A. (1999). Relationships as a "Three-legged sack race". *Family Journal, 7*(4), 399-406.

[64] Eckstein, D., & Axford, D. J. (1999). Loving and being loved: Commitment implications. *Family Journal, 7*(2), 185-187.

[65] Eckstein, D. (2001). The Couple's Gender-Based Communication Questionnaire. *Family Journal*, 9(1), 62-75.

[66] Eckstein, D., (1993). Games Married Couples Play: Two Theoretical Perspectives. *Family Journal*, 1(2), 173-176.

[67] Eckstein, D., & Grassa, L., (2005). For Couples and Families: The Non-Violent Relationship Questionnaire (NVRQ). *Family Journal*, 13(2), 205-212.

[68] Eckstein, D. (1997). Styles of conflict management. *Family Journal, 5*(4), 240-244.

[69] Eckstein, D., & Jones, J. D. (1998). Thirty-three suggestions for relationship renewal. *Family Journal*, 6(4), 334-337.

[70] Eckstein, D. (1994). Force-field analysis as an aid in decision-making by couples. *Family Journal, 2*(4), 371-373.

[71] Eckstein, D. (2006) Planned renegotiation: A preventative model for marriage and family counseling. Relationship Repair. Victoria, BC: Trafford.

Biographies

Fern Clemmer, Ph.D., grew up in Odessa, Texas. She raised four children and has seven grandchildren. She now teaches Ed. Counseling at the University of Texas of the Permian Basin, serves as Counselor at St. Mary's Central Catholic School in Odessa, TX, as well as Therapist for Andrews Rape Crisis Center.

Armando Fierro received his BA with honors from the University of Texas of the Permian Basin.

Section 19:

Relationships as a "Three-Legged Sack Race"

Daniel Eckstein, Marilyn Leventhal, Sherry Benttey, and Sharon A. Kelley

The authors introduce the three-legged sack race as a metaphor for three contrasting ways of describing a couple's relationship. The interdependent model has the inside two legs of the couple attached and the outside two legs independent. Enmeshed, or overly dependent couples have all four legs in the sack (no individuation). Conversely, independent couples have all four legs out of the sack (detached). After having an individual self-assess his or her behaviors characterizing each of these styles, the authors present some sample responses based on interviews with 55 adults. Attachment theory is then discussed. The article concludes with implications and applications to one's own relationship and identifying a next-steps action plan.

The relationship between couples could be described metaphorically as a three-legged sack race. There has been a traditional country fair contest in which two individuals standing side by side have their inside legs tied together and placed in a burlap sack. They then have to coordinate running together as the two joined legs attempt to run in tandem. Both outside legs remain free of the sack, however, symbolizing that the healthy relationship has a balance of independence and interdependence.

Two classic imbalances occur in family systems theory: One is the concept of too much dependence (no individuation), which often is defined as enmeshment. The authors describe this as having all four legs in the sack. The other extreme imbalance is independence, no contact, all four legs out of the sack, to continue the metaphor. The authors seek to more fully concretize this concept with some actual behavioral examples of the three types. You and your partner will be invited to consider current and/or past relationships and to give behavioral descriptions for the following three typologies in our metaphor.

Some representative responses taken from interviews will be presented. This will be followed by a brief theoretical discussion on attachment theory. Specific suggestions for achieving a better balance between independence, dependence, and interdependence will then be identified. Next, you will be invited to share your responses with your partner as well as to compare your comments. Implications/ applications and next-steps will conclude your self-assessment and the proposed dialogue with your partner about your relationship.

You and (if possible) your partner are invited to respond individually to the following questions. Afterward, you can compare your examples and discuss your different responses with each other.

Activity 27: Your Assessment of Your Relationship

1. With respect to your current relationship, how would you describe your attachment?
2. Relate behavioral examples of what you consider to be examples of independent behaviors in your present relationship (all four legs out of the sack).
3. Cite examples of dependent or enmeshed behaviors from your present relationship (all four legs in the sack).
4. Cite examples of dependent or enmeshed behaviors from your present relationship (all four legs in the sack).
5. Cite examples of interdependent relationship activities (each person having two legs in and two legs out of the sack).
6. Cite examples of independent, dependent, and interdependent behaviors from your past relationships, friends, or family members.
7. Describe your level of satisfaction with the balance of independent, dependent, and interdependent behaviors in your present relationship.
8. What do you predict your partner would say as to your as well as his or her level of satisfaction with the balance of the above three behaviors?

Attachment Theory

What follows is a brief statement of some highlights of attachment theory. A more extensive review of that topic is provided in other articles (Lopez; [1] McCarthy, Brack, & Brack; [2] Pistole [3]).

Simpson, Rholes, and Nelligan[4] observe that a growing number of researchers have begun to explore how different attachment styles influence what transpires within adult relationships. Much of this research has been guided by Bowlby's[5,6,7] attachment theory.

Ainsworth, Blehar, Waters, and Wall[8] identified three primary infant attachment behaviors. Children involved in secure relationships use their caregivers as a base of security to regulate feelings of distress and anxiety. Children involved in avoidant relationships neither actively seek support from the caregiver nor use the caregiver to regulate and dissipate negative affect when it arises. Children involved in anxious or ambivalent relationships make inconsistent, conflicted, and ambivalent attempts to derive emotional support from their caregivers, actions that seem to reflect an underlying sense of uncertainty about the caregiver's availability and supportiveness.

According to attachment theory, the relationships an individual has during infancy, childhood, and adolescence relate to decisions one later makes in adult relationships. Such mental models are thought to become stable and trait-like over time. Early relationships are thus presumed to exert long-term impact on subsequent adult relationships.

Ainsworth[9] noted that adults who possess a secure attachment style tend to develop mental models of themselves as being valued and worthy of others' concern, support, and affection. Significant others are described as being accessible, reliable, trustworthy, and well-intentioned. Secure individuals report that they develop closeness with others easily, feel comfortable depending on others and having others depend on them, and rarely are concerned about being abandoned or others becoming extremely close to them Their romantic relationships, in turn, tend to be characterized by more frequent positive affect, by higher levels of trust, commitment, satisfaction, and interdependence, and by happy, positive, and trusting styles of love.[10]

Adults who manifest an anxious or ambivalent style tend to harbor mental models of themselves as being misunderstood unconfident, and under-appreciated, and of significant others as being undependable and either unwilling or unable to pledge themselves to committed, long-term relationships They report that others are reluctant to get as close as they prefer. They frequently worry that their partners do not truly love them or will abandon them, and often desire to become extremely close to their partners.

Finally, those who have an avoidant style perceive themselves as being aloof, emotionally distant, and skeptical, and significant others as being unreliable or overly eager to make long-term commitments to relationships. Avoidant individuals indicate that they are uncomfortable being close to others and find it difficult to completely trust and depend on others.

Attachment Theory and Divorce

According to Thweatt,[11] a specific pattern of distress presents itself when attachment bonds are disrupted. Such distress occurs in four phases: denial, protest, despair, and detachment. This pattern of responses has been used to explain the paradoxical situation in which the divorce-petitioning spouse becomes distressed over the potential loss of the spouse The attachment bond provides a necessary sense of psychological security and personal identity even when commitment to the relationship is ending. That is because commitment is different from attachment.

Attachment can persist even though there is a loss of love and a reduced commitment to the spouse and the relationship. Commitment is different from attachment Commitment is described as a sense of being irrevocably invested in a relationship and of having feelings that cannot be easily withdrawn and placed elsewhere. It is related to the spouses' sense of marital relationship quality and satisfaction. Conversely attachment involves the symbolic bonds between two people emerging because of shared beliefs, values, meaning, and identity. Such a shared reality of symbolic interdependence develops overtime as a result of an exchange of confirming or disconfirming information in their conversation with each other. This shared meaning provides individuals security and identity. When reduction in commitment to the marriage occurs as a result of decreases in marital quality and satisfaction or increases in attractions that are alternatives to marriage, both spouses will likely experience distress because attachment bonds are threatened. Even though the marriage may be in trouble, spouses may cling to it in a desperate attempt to preserve the symbolic, jointly created property of their world view.

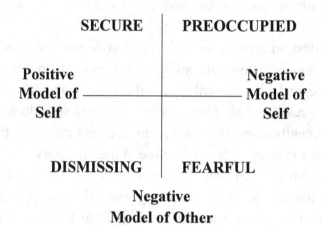

Figure 1. Four-Category Model of Adult Attachment
Source: Bartholomew (1997).

The Four-Category Model of Adult Attachment

Bartholomew[12] conceptualizes four prototypic attachment patterns which are defined in terms of the intersection of two underlying dimensions—how positive to negative models of the self are and how positive to negative models of hypothetical others are (Figure 1). She stated that the self-model dimension is associated with the degree of emotional dependence on others for self-validation. Thus, a positive self-model reflects an internalized sense of self-worth that is not dependent on ongoing external validation, and a negative self-model is associated with anxiety regarding acceptance and rejection in close relationships. The other-model dimension reflects expectations of others' availability and supportiveness. Positive other-models thus facilitate actively seeking out intimacy and support in close relationships, and negative other-models lead to avoidance of intimacy.

Individuals, who are characterized by a positive image of the self and positive images of others, generally received consistently responsive caretaking in childhood. Such a secure typology is thus high on both autonomy and intimacy, and such individuals are comfortable using others as a source of support when needed.

Preoccupied individuals are characterized by a negative self-model and a positive model of others. Inconsistent parenting, particularly if accompanied by messages of parental devotion, may lead children to conclude that they are to blame for any lack of love from caretakers. Preoccupied individuals are obsessed with their attachment needs and actively seek to have those needs fulfilled in their close relationships. The result is an overly dependent style in which personal validation is sought through gaining others' acceptance and approval.

The Association between Adult Attachment and Couple Violence

Roberts and Nolles[13] have made a significant contribution to attachment theory by showing its corresponding relationship to couple violence. They suggest that the association between attachment and couple violence can be explained by the dysfunctional communication patterns that are linked with insecure attachment and that create an environment in which couple violence is more likely to occur. One of the most useful contributions of attachment theory is its ability to explain the apparent contradiction between violence and intimacy.

Attachment can be adequately represented in terms of two underlying dimensions. These dimensions reflect the degree to which an individual feels uncomfortable in close romantic relationships (*discomfort with closeness*) and the degree to which he or she fears abandonment from romantic partners (*anxiety over abandonment*). High discomfort with closeness involves a belief that attachment figures are untrustworthy and cannot be relied upon to provide assistance in times of need. In contrast, high anxiety over abandonment involves a belief that one is "unlovable" and unworthy of help from attachment figures in times of need.

Another common way of viewing attachment has been by way of four discrete categories: preoccupied, fearful-avoidant, dismissing-avoidant, and secure. These four categories are easily conceptualized in terms of the two underlying dimensions of attachment. Fearful and dismissing individuals report more discomfort with closeness, whereas preoccupied and fearful individuals report higher levels of anxiety of abandonment.[14]

The relevance of attachment in the development of couple violence is indicated by several findings. First, many victims of violence in dating relationships interpret their abuse as a sign of love. Second, the first occurrence of violence tends to coincide with periods of transition from one level of intimacy to another. In dating relationships, violence is most likely to occur for the first time following the couple becoming seriously involved. Third, a large number of violent people are not violent outside of the marital relationship. This finding is particularly true for females. If attachment insecurities are seen to underlie women's use of violence, that helps to explain why women are far less likely to be violent in the public domain, where attachment insecurities do not arise relative to the private domain. Retzinger[15,16] has proposed a model of marital conflict in which threatened bonds result in the emotional reaction of shame, which, if unacknowledged by the partner, leads to rage and violence. Thus, there is some support in the literature for an association between attachment (particularly of abandonment) and couple violence.

Couple Violence, Attachment, and Communication Patterns

Roberts and Nolles[17] note that one important way in which insecure attachment may lead to an increased risk of couple violence is through the development of dysfunctional communication. Adult attachment is often linked with the manner in which individuals express their emotions and the level of intimacy in their romantic relationships. Discomfort with closeness is primarily associated with a lack of emotional involvement in relationships and a strong tendency to deny negative affect They also believe that levels of marital conflict are related to attachment, with conflict levels consistently being related to anxiety over abandonment and less consistently to discomfort with closeness. Attachment is concerned with the availability or attachment figures, and conflict can be seen as a threat to a partner's availability. Conflict may offer the opportunity for increased intimacy between partners through the sharing of their beliefs and feelings, and the airing of their grievances. Therefore, conflict may represent a highly anxiety-provoking situation for individuals who are anxious over abandonment and for those who are uncomfortable with closeness.

If conflict does represent a highly threatening situation for those who are anxious over abandonment, then those individuals have three options. First they can integrate with their abandoning partners by simply submitting to their partners' wishes. Second, they can attempt to prevent a partner's abandonment by dominating partners through the use of hostility and exaggerated displays of anger and coercion. Finally, they can avoid the possible abandonment by withdrawing from the conflict, essentially fleeing from the unpleasantness that conflict brings with it, and denying its very existence. Couple violence is positively linked to high levels of withdrawal from conflict. Thus couples in violent relationships suffer from communication deficits that are at least heightened during marital interaction. Also, they tend to withdraw from conflict and to express heightened levels of hostility and anger during conflict interactions.

Implications/Applications Pertaining to Your Relationship

Describe some of your conclusions relating the theory of attachments to your own relationship.

Suggestions for Creating a Better Balance in Your Relationship

Here are some suggestions that our interview sample made for creating a proper three-legged sack race balance between independence, dependence, and inter-dependence in relationships:

- Effective communication: Communicate! Communicate! Communicate!
- Compromise
- Respect

- Trust
- Unconditional love. Being non-judgmental
- Being there for the other person
- A good balance of dependence and independence
- Give and take
- Seek each other's advice. You do not necessarily have to take it but know that their opinion is important. One should not make important decisions without the other one.
- Have at least one meal together every day
- "Dance" together! Do things together: hiking, dancing, bowling, something!
- Do things together and do things separately. Make sure there's a happy medium
- Be there for the other person . . . emotionally, spiritually and physically
- The old cliché: Never go to bed angry at each other
- Don't bring your garbage from your outer leg into the sack

Next Steps

Identify two to three specific behaviors in which you would like to further balance your own relationship.

Summarize what you have learned or relearned about yourself, your partner, and your relationship based on the author's three-legged sack race relationship metaphor.

* * * * * * *

"We function most powerfully when we are giving love. The world has led us to believe that our well-being is dependent on other people loving us. But this is the kind of upside-down thinking that has caused so many of our problems. The truth is that our well-being is dependent on our giving love. It is not about what comes back; it is about what goes out." Alan Cohen (2009). *Bits and Pieces.* Lawrence Reagan Communications: Chicago, Ill., p. 1.

Endnotes

[1] Lopez, F. (1995). Attachment theory as an integrative framework for family counseling. *The Family Journal, 3.*

[2] McCarthy, C, Brack, G., & Brack. C. (1996). Relationship of cognitive appraisals and attachment to emotional events within the family of origin. *The Family Journal. 4.*

[3] Pistole, C. (1996). After love: Attachment styles and grief themes. *The Family Journal, 4.*

[4] Simpson, R., Rholes, W., & Nelligan, J. (1992). Support seeking and support giving within couples in an anxiety-provoking situation: The role of attachment styles. *American Psychological Association, 62.*434-446.

5 Bowlby, J. (1969). *Attachment and loss: Volume 1. Attachment*. New York: Basic Books.

6 Bowlby, J. (1973). Attachment and loss: Volume 2. Separation: Anxiety and anger. New York: Basic Books.

7 Bowlby. J. (1980). Attachment and loss: Volume 3. Loss: Sadness and depression. New York: Basic Books.

8 Ainsworth, M., Blehar, M. Waters, E., & Wall, S. (1978). Patterns of attachment. Hillsdale, NJ: Erlbaum.

9 Ainsworth, M. (1985). Attachments across the life span. *Bulletin of the New York Academy of Medicine. 61*, 792-812.

10 Hendrick, C., & Hendrick, S. S. (1989). Research on love: Docs it measure up? *Journal of Personality and Social Psychology 56*, 784-794.

11 Thweatt, R.W. (1980) Divorce: Crisis intervention guided by attachment theory. *American Journal of Psychotherapy, 34*, 240-245

12 Bartholomew, K. (1997). Adult attachment processes: Individual and couple perspectives. *British Journal of* Medical Psychology, 70, 249-263.

13 Roberts, N., & Nolles, P. (1998). *The associations between adult attachment and couple violence in attachment* theory and close relationships. New York: Guilford Press.

14 Roberts & Nolles, *loc. cit.*

15 Retzinger, S. M. (1991a). Shame, anger, and conflict: Case study of emotional violence. *Journal of Family* Violence, 6, 37-60.

16 Retzinger, S. M. (1991b). Violent emotions: Shame and rage in marital quarrels. Newbury Park, CA: Sage.

17 Roberts & Nolles, *loc. cit.*

Biographies

Sherry Bentley received a BSW degree from the University of Calgary, Alberta, in Canada. She is currently a medical social worker with past experience in correctional, educational, and state social services. She has a Master's Degree in counseling psychology from Ottawa University. She is interested in art therapy and working with children.

Sharon A. Kelley spent 12 years in the banking industry and received her Master's degree in clinical mental health from Ottawa University.

Marilyn Leventhal received a BA. from Hunter College, New York. She is currently a graduate student at Ottawa University pursuing a degree in counseling psychology with a marriage and family specialization. She is a former elementary school teacher with 14 years of experience, and has taught art and Spanish to both children and adults. She is also a realtor, professional artist, and has presented numerous workshops on the art of meditation.

Section 20:

A Dozen Commitment Considerations for Couples

Amy Manning Kirk, Daniel Eckstein, Sheryl A. Serres, and Sallie Helms

Commitment is one of the most frequently cited descriptors of relationships. For example, "I'm in a committed relationship" is often one way adolescents and adults describe their partnerships. "(S)he was just not committed to our relationship" is also a frequently stated reason why a person ends a relationship.

Commitment means different things to different people. One common mistake individuals in relationships make is assuming that their own personal conceptions of commitment are universally felt by their romantic partners. When romantic partners do not live up to these commitment notions, the result can be a sense of betrayal or abandonment between partners.

Adlerian counselor Roy Kern[1] uses the term "immaculate perception" to describe the concept that each of us has our own computer programs, to use a modern metaphor, on many relationship concepts. Love, money, family, gender identity, and religion are but some of the important "programs" we have created growing up.

The problem for many couples is in the assumption that one's own personal meaning or computer program is the same as his or her partners. Certainly shared core values are essential in relationship satisfaction. However, one can feel the other is not committed when it simply means that a partner has a different "program" or perception of the relationship.

The purpose of this article is in providing an opportunity for each of you to interview your romantic partner, to learn more specifically just what is in your personal data bank regarding commitment in your relationship. While we acknowledge that your commitment is not static or never changing, the authors have devised the "Couples Commitment Interview" (CCI) to help you learn more about your conception of commitment and your partners' conceptions of commitment at this point in your relationship.

Outline of the Article

The article will be organized as follows. First you and your partner will be invited to interview each other on twelve specific ways to identify your own personal meanings of the concept of commitment. The authors will then provide some representative research relative to commitment. You as a couple will then be asked to discuss what you have learned about each others' views of commitment.

Pre-Interview Recommendations

Ideally, you and your partner will complete this interview together. If this is not possible, you can, of course, write your own responses and/or discuss it with another person if that is desired.

Before you begin your interview with each other, it is good to remind yourselves of the profoundly simple concept of transactional analysis (i.e. "I'm OK—you're OK").[2] With respect to this interview, that means that basic respect for each of your points of view is desirable.

Other less desirable ways of approaching this interview could be: "I'm OK—you're not OK." That is, your own superior "my answers are THE RIGHT answers" approach to the interview. In such a case you will most probably dismiss your partners wrong responses. Conversely, an "I'm not OK; You're OK" low self-esteem approach will result in elevating your partner's responses as being better than your own comments. And the most discouraging attitude is an "I'm not OK; you're not OK" approach where you both are wrong about your responses.[3,4]

One basic communication skill you are encouraged to follow is that from time-to-time you do listening checks with each other. That simply means that you summarize your partner's satisfaction with what he or she has just said prior to you making your own reply to the particular CCI content. A few suggested times for listening checks will be noted in the interview.

It is your choice on whether to interview your partner on all twelve items, or to take one question with both of you answering it. If you take the later approach it is recommended that you rotate who responds first to each item.

Activity 28: The Couples' Commitment Interview (CCI)

1. What are three general strengths your partner brings to the relationship? What are three assets you feel you bring to the relationship?
2. With respect to the specific topic of commitment, what do you most want to understand about your partner in this discussion?
3. What do you most want your partner to understand about you as you talk about your respective perspectives on the concept of commitment? (listening check)
4. What were some early messages you remember about the concept of commitment when you were growing up?
5. With respect to previous relationships, cite specific examples of both high and low commitment.

---

6. In other areas of your life besides your current relationship, cite some specific examples of when your sense of commitment was strong? Contrast that with times when you did not feel as committed. (listening check)
7. How do you define commitment in your own marriage/relationship?
8. hat do you think the concept of commitment means to your partner?
9. When in your relationship was your commitment highest and when was it lowest? (listening check)
10. With regard to your present relationship to whom or to what do you feel most committed (i.e. spouse, God? children? your principles?)
11. With respect to your present couple's commitment, please complete these sentences . .
    a. I want . . . .
    b. I need to . . . .
    c. I have to . . .
12. In reviewing your responses to the preceding three sentence stems, which of these responses is most important to your commitment in your relationship? (listening check)

Defining Commitment

In An episode of *Grey's Anatomy* (November 2, 2006), a patient said to George, an intern, after devastating news about his wife's pregnancy—(and subsequent news of her unfaithfulness), "You have to decide in a relationship, are you ham or eggs? You know, the chicken contributes to the meal, but the pig is committed to it."[5]

In much of the commitment dialogue, the concept has been framed in terms of relationship permanency.[6] However, many also think of commitment in terms of positive affect toward their spouses[7,8,9] or in terms of moral or structural constraints.[10] Next, we detail some representative definitions of commitment.

Commitment as Permanency

Traditionally, commitment has been framed in terms of permanency, in which guaranteed relationship-preserving behavior is implied.[11] Such commitment is said to be a result of attraction and constraints.[12] It is most noteworthy because of its pragmatic value in making relationships stable and successful. Implications of this commitment are similar to the implications of marriage vows, in which spouses *promise* to unconditionally love and honor each other. Understanding commitment in this way means committed partners will clearly and consistently act in ways that indicate they will continue in their relationships. For example, it has been suggested that committed partners do not contemplate alternative partners.[13]

Empirical studies suggest that this construct of commitment varies little in relationships.[14,15] In the context of marriage, most all couples will say they are highly committed to the permanency of their marriage and marriage-preserving behavior, unless they view their marriage as being very troubled.[16,17] Because this commitment varies little from couple-to-couple, it has symbolic value; however, with little variation, it is also difficult to assess the importance of this conception of commitment to relationship satisfaction or maintenance over time.[18]

A Three-Part Phenomena?

Social psychologists have typically defined commitment in terms of constraints or attractions and rewards.[19] In this context, commitment is said to be relevant to feelings of *wanting, needing* and *having* to be in a relationship.[20,21] These feelings are said to be distinct, with each having separate causes and consequences.[22]

Commitment based upon attraction in a relationship is called *personal commitment.*[23] Personal commitment is rooted in prior attractions and rewards and can manifest itself in attraction to one's partner, attraction to one's relationship (i.e. relationship satisfaction), or attraction to one's identity as a couple.[24] When couples think of their commitment, they most commonly think of it in terms of attraction.[25,26] This form of commitment tends to keep relationships successful and satisfying over time.[27] However, many have suggested that the only commitment relevant to long-term relationship stability (especially in the context of marriage) is that which implies moral constraints.[28,29]

Constraining commitment relevant to needing to be in a relationship is called *moral* commitment;[30] and define moral commitment as "the sense that one is morally obligated to continue a relationship."[31] They suggest that there are three dimensions of moral commitment.

First, there is moral commitment to the relationship itself, which encompasses the idea that a relationship *should* last throughout life. This dimension is reflected in many wedding affirmations that include such life oriented vows as "as long as we both shall live." Second, there is a dimension of moral commitment in which a person feels obligated to a particular person. The final dimension of moral commitment reflects a desire to be generally consistent; that is, to finish what one has begun. Stanley[32] calls this *metacommitment* and suggests that it is related to dedication.

Another form of constraining commitment is *structural* commitment. Structural commitment is a function of partners' ideas about the social or legal pressures they would encounter should they leave the relationship.[33] Structural commitment is also relevant to perceived alternatives one would have, should the relationship be terminated. Perceived alternatives can be alternative partners or alternative lifestyles (i.e. being single).[34] This type of commitment is not salient to relationship quality or stability unless personal and moral commitment diminishes.[35] Partners also do not give much thought to this type of commitment, unless other forms of commitment are low.[36]

Commitment, Spirituality, and Religion

Bregman[37] asserts that definitions of spirituality have made a journey from early definitions that intersected with religion to today's current mystical definitions. Loosely speaking, it appears that spirituality can be whatever it means for you. For many, however, spirituality is expressed through religious beliefs which often have important implications for commitment.

Beliefs about spirituality and religion appear to greatly affect many aspects of couple and family functioning and decision-making. Traditionally, being a couple meant being a *married couple.* Indeed, many marriages still take place in churches, temples, synagogues or places of worship. Marriage ceremonies often include a reading of portions of sacred writings such as the *Bible*, the *Torah*, or the *Koran,* and when making vows to one another, such couples feel they are making a commitment to each other and to their God as well.

Indeed, many married couples report that a practice of engaging in religious activities together provides a source of strength for their relationship. Lambert and Dollahite found that "religiosity acts as a safe container for marital conflict in which conflict is prevented, resolved, and overcome." [38] Five themes emerge in their study that highlighted specific ways couples' religiosity provided a source of support for their relationship. First, the couples reported a *shared sacred vision and purpose* that tends to reduce stress and prepare them to deal with conflict when it occurs. Secondly, *relational virtues* such as selflessness and unconditional love were inspired by their religious beliefs. Third, *scriptural teachings* provided the couple with a source of guidance and a model for dealing with conflict. Fourth, *religious attendance* in houses of worship often brought an awareness of the triviality of current disagreements and helped the couple forgive and move past the disagreement. Finally, *couple prayer* supported the relationship because it lessened anger and served to open communication.

Hunler and Gencoz[39] conclude along with other researchers that religiousness is related to marital satisfaction. Some of the reported studies suggest that religiousness was associated with lower divorce rates, decreased tendency to talk of divorce, and decreased hostile emotions. Their study, conducted with a Turkish sample, support previous findings that religiousness was positively related to marital satisfaction, but did not support previous findings that religiousness is related to marital problem-solving. They speculate that this discrepancy may be due to how certain religions conduct their practices. For example, when religious practices are engaged in *together* as a couple, it may support a problem solving component to marital satisfaction. When religious activities are practiced *individually* or as same sex activities (men worship with men, women worship with women), their role in problem solving was not observed. Regardless, they find that religiousness is still related to marital satisfaction, but they suggest "religiousness, particularly shared religious activities and beliefs intensify marital satisfaction. Moreover, these shared activities and beliefs seem to be helpful in the course of conflict resolution." [40] It is important to point out that positive benefits in some studies were experienced when couples shared the same religious beliefs. If couples do not agree on such important values, it can be a source of conflict. Therefore, it would seem important for individuals and couples to determine their own spiritual and religious beliefs and to whom or what they are actually committed.

For cohabiting couples, there may be a sense of "trying out" the relationship before committing to marriage. Therefore, some couples see cohabitating as a step to determine whether or not they want to commit. However, some suggest[41] that cohabitation undermines the relationship from the start, as it is unlikely that persons will give wholeheartedly to a relationship that has a built-in out-clause. Similarly, LeFrancois[42] concludes that cohabitation typically has negative effects on relationships and on subsequent marriages. Crabb suggests that selfishness is the real problem in relationships and advised partners to consider unselfishly serving the other which is consistent with many religious ideologies. He asserts, "Self-centered living is the real culprit in marriages with problems. Other-centered living is the answer."[43]

Because spirituality is central to commitment, it is important for couples to consider what role spirituality and religion will play in their relationship as a couple. For example, couples should consider how their individual and collective ideas guide their commitment in the relationship, how much responsibility they feel to each other, to their own value systems, or to a higher power to make the relationship work, and whether their individual or collective ideas about spirituality offer any support or sense of comfort and help for the difficulties in the relationship?

Commitment and Adversity

Finally, commitment can also be molded by circumstances which are external to romantic relationship, such as adversity. Examples of adversity include the loss of a partner's job, the death of a parent, or a parent's divorce. The literature suggests that commitment and adversity are intimately linked, and that commitment is not fully realized until adversity occurs. Empirical evidence does suggest that adversity shapes commitment when values regarding commitment entail adversity before adversity occurs. [44]

Commitment and Work in Relationships

Of growing importance in the commitment literature is the idea that commitment is potentially critical relationship capital that can foster success in relationships over time.[45] The literature suggests that commitment can encourage the creation and maintenance of positive conditions in relationships[46] that affect relationship stability and quality. For example, committed couples may develop effective communication skills over time, and these communication skills could foster relationship quality. We illustrate how commitment can be an importan source of relationship quality below in

Figure 1: Model of Relationship Quality

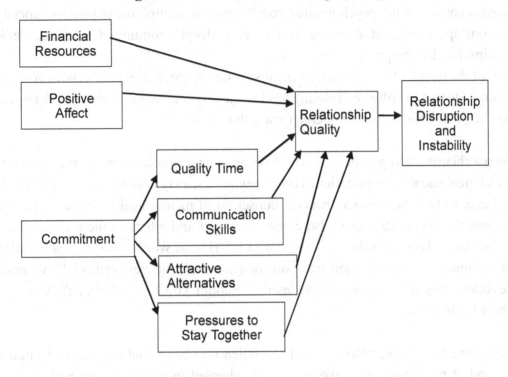

(Adapted from Manning, 2005).

We should note, that while it seems logical that committed couples will affect relationship conditions in positive ways, it is also possible that commitment's importance in affecting relationship conditions may vary from couple-to-couple, with no clear, universal importance to all couples Empirical findings thus far indicate that commitment's influence on relationship conditions is based upon partners' subjective views of commitment; and in fact, those couples who may work harder because of their commitment are oftentimes in troubled relationships.[47]

Because this article suggests an interview and dialog between you and your partner, next we discuss the importance of language in relationships, relative to conceptions of commitment.

The Importance of Language to Commitment

In his book, *The Saturated Self*[48] as well as in other writings, Gergen[49,50,51] asserts that human beings rely heavily on psychological language to make sense of themselves and others. Such language is built into relationship patterns. In other words, "A love affair would not be a love affair without the language of emotions."[52] (Gergen, 1991, p. 227)

Gergen notes that the psychological vocabulary that compliments the romanticist view of relationships is "essential to the formation of deeply committed relations, dedicated friendships, and life purposes."[53]

One of the reasons the present CCI begins by noting three strengths in both your partner and yourself is that too often counseling has been a deficient, *what is wrong with you and me* couples' approach. For example, Gergen notes that:

As psychiatrists and psychologists try to explain undesirable behavior, they generate a technical vocabulary of deficit. This language is slowly disseminated to the public at large, so that they too can become conscious of mental-health issues. As people acquire the vocabulary, they also come to see self and others in these terms. They judge themselves and others as superior or inferior, as worthy or not of admiration or commitment. (How much can you trust an addictive personality? How much devotion does a manic-depressive merit?; Should you hire a bulimic?; Can you cherish a hysteric?).[54]

According to Gergen, "Most of us have fallen heir to romanticist ways of talking and acting, and at the same time have been well-schooled in the principles and practices of modernism."[55] The advent of the technological and informational overload of the twenty-first century, however, has ushered in the postmodern era of the "saturated self"—an era in which "our range of social participation is expanding exponentially . . . in a world in which we no longer experience a secure sense of self."[56]

The narrative of Gergen's book ultimately concerns itself with "problems in intimacy, commitment, and coherent family life," as well as implications for social movements and possibilities of "self-renewal—that is, the prospects for the culture holding fast to its traditional views of self and forms of relatedness".[57] He proposes concepts of relational realities by inviting such contemplations as:

One ponders, "How should I live my life?" and considers . . . "needs for loving relationships," "hopes for children'" [and perhaps "commitment to my marriage?"] . . . Such contemplations are commonplace. Yet consider some contrasting possibilities. How often do we ask, for example, "I wonder what my family will do with its life?" "What will my community do this month?" or "How will my marriage fare today?[58]

Gender—A View from Both Sides

Regarding ethically reflexive scholarship and approaches to therapy, Gergen has observed that the "feminist critiques of the past two decades have established a powerful and sophisticated precedent."[59] Gender sensitive approaches to research and practice[60, 61, 62] have sought "a more balanced repertoire for both genders."[63]

More recently, Chethik revisited gender based research, with a twist. He interviewed approximately 360 married American men "of all ages, classes, religions, and ethnic backgrounds" [64] to ask why, given the social upheaval of the early 1960s, including a sharp increase in incidence of sex before marriage, number of cohabitations, divorces, and out-of-wedlock births, is marriage not obsolete for men. Chethik's interviews of married men revealed that although marriage is no longer culturally necessary, it is something men still want.

Opposing this finding, other research has found that young men who were interviewed in a focus group setting associated concern regarding the potential of financial loss with marriage. Also, they feared that their future wives might want to have children before they were ready for that commitment. Thus, young men indicate that "cohabitation without marriage provides all the desirable benefits of companionship without the potential risks of growing up."[65]

Other research that sought to examine the association between attitudes regarding self-sacrifice and marital outcomes among married couples[66] suggests that men associate long-term commitment with a greater willingness to sacrifice than do women. The authors speculated that this discrepancy might be rooted in women's socialization; perhaps women are socialized to sacrifice, regardless of commitment.

Implications for you as a couple stem from the researchers' conclusion that "true commitment leads to genuine acts of giving between partners." [67] You are encouraged to "engage in meaningful sacrifices as a way to make more visible the ongoing love and commitment between partners." Such behaviors emphasize the "positive effect when one's behavior stands out because it reflects the putting aside of one's own agenda for the good of the partner or the relationship."[68]

Now it is time to reflect on your interview as well as some of your reactions to the material that has been presented regarding conceptions of commitment. Here are some self-reflective questions for you to write for a personal activity. After engaging in this activity, pleasediscuss your responses with your partner.

Activity 29: Integration of Your Interviews

1. What were some of the key concepts that impacted you after reading the literature review?
2. What were some ways the material relates to your own concepts of commitment?
3. In what ways do you feel the literature relates to your partner's views on commitment?
4. As you reflect on your interview, please write a brief summary of what you consider some of the most important things that your partner stated.
5. What were some of the most important things you related to in the process?
6. In what ways do you feel you and your partner are "on the same page" with your perspectives on the meaning of commitment in your relationship?
7. In what ways do you feel you are not aligned in your perspectives of what commitment means in your relationship?

After the two of you discuss your respective answers to these questions, discuss what the possible implications of your discussion might be. For example, what action steps do you feel are appropriate? Do you have a greater understanding of your respective beliefs? You also may want to discuss some of your responses with a trusted counselor, spiritual leader, and/or valued friend.

Summary

The purpose of this article has been to focus upon conceptions of commitment in your relationships. The authors have developed the CCI as a structured way to help you as partners discuss what commitment means to each of you. Salient literature on the topic has also been presented. Future integration steps for you as a couple conclude the article.

Endnotes

1 Kern, R. (2006). Personal Communication.
2 Bern, E. (1964). *Games People Play*. New York: Grove Press.
3 Ainsworth, M. (1985). "Attachments Across the Life Span." *Bulletin of the New York Academy of Medicine*, 61, 792-812.
4 Eckstein, D. (1993). "Games Married Couples Play: Two Theoretical Perspectives." *The Family Journal.* 1,3, 173-176.
5 Rhimes, Shonda. (2006). Grey's Anatomy (Television series). Los Angeles: ABC.
6 Stanley, S. M., Whitton, S. W., Sadberry, S. L., Clements, M. L., & Markman, H. J. (2006). "Sacrifice as a Predictor of Marital Outcomes." *Family Process*, 45(3), 289-303.

[7] *Johnson, Michael P., John P. Caughlin, and Ted L. Huston. (1999). "The Tripartite Nature of Marital Commitment: Personal, Moral, and Structural Reasons to Stay Married." Journal of Marriage and the Family, 61, 160-177.*

[8] Manning, Amy. (2005). *Constructing Resilient Marriages: A Panel Study of Marriages Under Pressure*. Unpublished doctoral dissertation, Louisiana State University, Baton Rouge, Louisiana

[9] Stanley, Scott M. and Howard J. Markman. (1992). "Assessing Commitment in Personal Relationships." Journal of Marriage and the Family, 54, 595-608.

[10] Johnson, Caughlin, & Huston, *loc. cit.*

[11] Leik, Robert K. and Sheila A. Leik. (1977). "Transition to Interpersonal Commitment." In Robert L. Hamblin and John H. Kunkel (Editors), *Behavioral Theory in Sociology: Essays in Honor of George C. Homans*. New Brunswick, N.J. Transaction Books. Pgs. 299-322.

[12] *Johnson, Dennis J. and Caryl E. Rusbult. (1989). "Resisting Temptation: Devaluation of Alternative Partners as a Means of Maintaining Commitment in Close Relationships." Journal of Personality and Social Psychology 57: 967-980.*

[13] Leik & Leik, *loc. cit.*

[14] *Dean, David G. and G.B. Spainer. (1974). "Commitment: An Overlooked Variable in Marital Adjustment?" Sociological Focus 7: 113-118.*

[15] Manning, *loc. cit.*

[16] Dean & Spainer, *loc. cit.*

[17] Manning, *loc. cit.*

[18] Manning, *loc. cit.*

[19] Surra, Catherine A. and Christine R. Gray. (2000). "A Typology of Processes of Commitment to Marriage: Why Do Partners Commit to Problematic Relationships?" 253-280.

[20] Becker, Howard S. (1960). "Notes on the Concept of Commitment." *American Journal of Sociology*, 66, 32-40.

[21] Dean & Spainer, *loc. cit.*

[22] Johnson, Caughlin, & Huston, *loc. cit.*

[23] Johnson, Caughlin, & Huston, *loc. cit.*

[24] Johnson, Caughlin, & Huston, *loc. cit. p. 162*

[25] Johnson, Caughlin, & Huston, *loc. cit.*

[26] Stanley & Markman, *loc. cit.*

[27] Manning, *loc. cit.*

[28] Doherty, William J. (2001). Take Back Your Marriage: Sticking Together in a World That Pulls Us Apart. New York. The Guilford Press.

[29] Stanley, Scott M. (1998). *The Heart of Commitment: Compelling Research that Reveals* The Secrets of a Lifelong, Intimate Marriage. Nashville: Thomas Nelson Publishers.

[30] Johnson, Caughlin, & Huston, *loc. cit.*

[31] Johnson, Caughlin, & Huston, *loc. cit. p. 161.*

[32] Stanley, *loc. cit.*

[33] Johnson, Caughlin, & Huston, *loc. cit.*

[34] Manning, *loc. cit.*

[35] Johnson, Caughlin, & Huston, *loc. cit.*

[36] Manning, *loc. cit.*

[37] Bregman, L. (2006). "Spirituality: A glowing and Useful Term in Search of a Meaning." Omega: Journal of Death and Dying, 53 (1-2), 5-26.

[38] Lambert, N. M. & Dollahite, D. C., (2006). "How Religiosity Helps Couples Prevent, Resolve, and Overcome Marital Conflict." *Family Relations, 55,* 442. Retrieved November 17, 2006, from http://www.blackwell-synergy.com/doi/full/10.1111/j.1741-3729.2006.00413.x

[39] Hunler, O. S. & Gencoz, T. (2005). "The Effect of Religiousness on Marital Satisfaction: Testing the Mediator Role of Marital Problem Solving Between Religiousness and Marital Satisfaction Relationship." *Contemporary Family Therapy, 27*(1), 123-136. Retrieved on November 17, 2006 from http://web.ebscohost.com/ehost/pdf?vid=8&hid=4&sid=aa3ff998-256b-4773- a0b4-da3749454dc1%40sessionmgr103

[40] Hunter & Gencoz, *loc. cit, p. 126.*

[41] Stanley, *loc. cit.*

[42] LeFrancois, G. R. (1999). *The Lifespan,* (6th ed.). Belmont, CA: Wadsworth Publishing Company.

[43] Crabb, L. (1991). *Men and women: Enjoying the difference.* Grand Rapids, MI: Zondervan Publishing House, p. 116.

[44] *Lydon, John E. and Mark P. Zanna. (1990). "Commitment in the Face of Adversity: A Value-Affirmation Approach." Journal of Personality and Social Psychology,* 58,6, 1040-1047.

[45] Manning, *loc. cit.*

[46] Johnson, Caughlin, & Huston, *loc. cit.*

[47] Manning, *loc. cit.*

[48] Gergen, K. J. (1991). The Saturated Self: Dilemmas of Identity in Contemporary Life. New York: Basic Books.

[49] Gergen, K. J. (1985, March). "The Social Constructionist Movement in Modern Psychology." *American Psychologist*, 40(3), 266-275.

[50] Gergen, K. J. (1999). *An Invitation to Social Construction.* Thousand Oaks, CA: Sage Publications.

[51] Gergen, K. J. (2001, October). "Psychological Science in a Postmodern Context." *American Psychologist*, 56(10), 803-813.

[52] Gergen (1991), *loc. cit., p.227*

[53] Gergen (1991), *loc. cit., p. 6.*

[54] Gergen (1991), *loc. cit., p. 15.*

[55] Gergen (1991), *loc. cit. p. 230.*

[56] Gergen (1991), *loc. cit., p. 16.*

[57] Gergen (1991), *loc. cit., p. 17.*

[58] Gergen (1991), *loc. cit., p. 239.*

[59] Gergen (1991), *loc. cit., p. 809.*

[60] Bernard, J. (1982). *The Future of Marriage*. New Haven: Yale University Press.

[61] Gilligan, C. (1982). *In a Different Voice*. Boston: Harvard University Press.

[62] Miller, J. B. (1988). "Connections, Disconnections, and Violations." *Work in Progress*, No. 33. Wellesley, MA: Stone Center Working Paper Series.

[63] Hoffman, L. (1990, March). "Constructing Realities: An Art of Lenses." *Family Process*, 29(1), p. 7.

[64] Chethik, N. (2006). *Voice male: What Husbands Really Think About Their Marriages, Their Wives, Sex, Housework, and Commitment*. New York: Simon & Schuster, p. 2.

[65] Stanley, *loc. cit., p. 1.*

[66] Stanley, et al. (2006), *loc. cit.*

[67] Stanley, et al. (2006), *loc. cit., p. 302.*

[68] Stanley, et al. (2006), *loc. cit., p. 302.*

Biographies

Amy Manning Kirk, Ph.D. *(A Dozen Commitment Considerations for Couples,* with Daniel Eckstein, Sheryl Serres, and Sallie Helms); *(Lemons or Lemonade?: Commitment as a Predictor for Hour Couples Cope with Adversity)* is an assistant professor in the Department of Sociology at Sam Houston State University, Huntsville, Texas. Her primary research interest concerns commitment as a source of marital quality over time. She has been married for eight years and lives in Kingwood, Texas with her husband, Brett, and their three children.

Sallie Helms is a Licensed Marriage and Family Therapist and a doctoral student in the Department of Counselor Education, Sam Houston State University.

Sheryl A. Serres, Ph.D., is a Clinical Professor in the Department of Educational Counseling and Leadership at Sam Houston State University, a Licensed Professional Counselor and an approved LPC Supervisor."

Section 21:

The "Staying Together in Needy Times" (STINT) Couple's Questionnaire

Daniel Eckstein and Phil Ginsburg

Introduction

This article was conceived thanks to the first author who had been working with a couple. After seeing the wife individually a few times, it was clear she felt the relationship had come to an end. She asked if both she and her husband could join me for a session to make her decision very clear to him in a caring and supportive place such as a counseling session.

And so we met. We shared some of the most painful moments (personally for me as well) because the woman was clearly out the door (or more precisely, he was to go out the door), but he came with her to see me in the hopes of saving the marriage.

It's an art as a counselor to have compassion for the vulnerable man who is crying and hopes the marriage can be put back together, when the man doesn't realize that, to use a Southern phrase, "That dog won't hunt."

In one hour, his wife and I managed to help him hear that repairing the marriage was not an option. To his credit, instead of the often seen response of anger and outrage which simply masks the deeper hurt underneath, he went to the hurt instead.

I felt compassion for him all day.

The next day, he came by my office alone.

He said that he finally understood the reality of the situation, and made the decision to detach emotionally and physically. He also said that he and his wife had a very practical conversation about their finances. One important part of the discussion was that if he moved out there would be both no second parent for the children, (ages two and four), but any extra holidays would be out because of the added expenses for additional housing and another car. There are two bedrooms with separate entrances and baths in their home. He was pragmatically proposing they stay under the same roof but go their separate ways in regards to each being free to pursue other relationships.

He also introduced me to an article published in *The Sun, a* London-based paper, "Staying Together in Needy Times." With the downturn in the economy and the many job layoffs, this seemed like a creative idea.

Divorce is one of the most difficult circumstances that an individual and members of the family system can experience. The process of separation can be extremely painful, regardless of the financial conditions that exist for the family. However, for those who are economically challenged, the logistics can be more even more daunting than for those more financially well off. During current economic conditions, many couples who may have made the decision to divorce have been faced with the cold hard reality that the state of their finances may alter their own lifestyle and that of their children even more adversely than may have been the case in a different economic climate.

Divorce lawyers say many couples are delaying the decision to dissolve marriages and are staying in unpleasant situations for fear of being on their own at a time of economic uncertainty. Others are being forced to live together after the divorce is final for financial convenience (Levitz, 2009). Selling a home and splitting assets during a recession can, in many cases, be next to impossible. When the housing market is in a decline, it may be wise to try and retain the asset and sell when the market is more favorable.

If economic circumstances do force couples to live together for a period of time after a divorce, there are many issues to consider. The decisions that people make regarding the details of remaining together even though a divorce has occurred can have a significant impact on the feasibility of the arrangement for the couple themselves and their children. A checklist might be helpful as a discussion point to ensure that there are few surprises that could exacerbate an already difficult situation.

In this article we initially looked at the literature; we then created a "Staying Together in Needy Times (STINT) checklist which might be helpful to you as a couple if you are considering such a way of staying together even when you move apart emotionally.

The article is organized as follows: There is a brief literature overview on the impact of the current challenging economy on relationships. We also provide a checklist in the hope that each of you will complete it alone and then discuss it together. The implications for your relationship are included in the summary of the article.

Literature Regarding the Implications of the
Economic Downturn for Couples

The original source for this title and questionnaire came from an article published in the Feb. 3, 2009 *Sun* magazine. (http://www.thesun.co.uk/sol/ homepage/woman/ article2198045. ece). The authors have not seen this exact phrase used in any other literature.

In one case study, a man moved out but came back two weeks later because he simply could not afford another housing expense. Here is some of their dialogue:

Paula says: "Paul told me he wanted a divorce and moved out. But two weeks later, he came back Not to try again—but because he could not afford to pay the mortgage and rent. "The prospect of having the house repossessed terrified us both. So we agreed to stay put and hope for the best. We do not talk so we do not argue. If we sell the house now we will owe the bank money. And I cannot buy a house on my own without a deposit." Paula now sleeps on an improvised bed downstairs while Paul stays in the master bedroom

Paul says: "We spent a lot on the house to sell it for a profit. Then the credit crunch hit. And now we are in negative equity. Something had to give. My main priority now is keeping a roof over my family's head. Selling now would cost us money. We are trapped. When the economy improves we will sell. Until then we are reliving the worst bits of our relationship every day."

Michels (2008) also focuses on the critical issue regarding what is most often a couple's largest asset, their house, and how this choice influences divorce or separation decisions. As home prices decrease, couples may initially attempt to sell their house even at a reduced price. Often the home is too big for one or the other to live in alone. So more and more couples are taking a pragmatic approach based on economic necessity by finding creative ways of living under the same roof but also being emotionally detached. "Do we eat together?" or "Do we share holidays together with our children?" are but two of the practical issues that you in a couple must negotiate in such situations.

Not all homes have decreased in value. For example, as of Feb. 10, 2010, Les Christie (2010) lists the top ten U.S. cities that have experienced the highest home value increases contrasted with the bottom the communities where homes have decreased in value. Although Naples, Florida was at the highest level of increase in 2006 at 84% over market value when the CNN survey was first conducted, it's now down to 29% below market value. Atlantic City, New Jersey, is now the most overvalued metro area in the nation. At 30.2% over fair market, it is the only city in the dangerous 30%-plus category. Almost at that cutoff is Wenatchee, Washington, at 28.9%. The third most overpriced area is Ocean City (New Jersey). Longview (Washington), Honolulu (Hawaii), Asheville (North Carolina), Portland (Oregon), Bellingham (Washington), Corvallis (Washington), and Salem (Oregon) complete the ten most over-valued U.S. housing markets.

The most undervalued market is Las Vegas, where homes sell for 41.4% below fair market, followed by Vero Beach, Florida (-39.8%), Merced, California (-37.7%), and Cape Coral, Florida (-36.8%)

Articles by Boheim and Ermisch, Rainer and Smith, and Becker, Landes, and Michael extend the pioneering study of the economics of marital instability by Becker, Landes, and Michael (1977) who found that couples with less property wealth would be expected to have smaller gains from marriage and consequently higher levels of divorce.

Boheim and Ermisch (2001) studied approximately 10,000 persons from the British Household Pane Study. They found the annual dissolution rate to be 3.34%. Women who were younger at the start of their partnership were most likely to end their relationship. They also found that partners of the same ethnic background had a one% lower divorce rate but surprisingly people of the same religious beliefs had a slightly higher separation rate.

Changes in economic situation is a prime cause of ending relationships. For example, women who feel they are better off than a year ago are much less likely to separate than women who believe they are worse off than a year before. Boheim and Ermisch summarize their research as follows:

Changes in a couple's economic circumstances affect the probability that a partnership dissolves . . . unexpected improvements in finances substantially reduce the risk of dissolution . . . Conditional on employment, higher women's earnings increase the risk of dissolution and higher men's earnings reduce it . . . Partnership dissolution *increases* with the number of children . . . The odds of dissolution are more than double for cohabiting couples compared with married ones. (p.207)

Rainer and Smith (2008) also focus on the economic implications of housing shocks and partner dissolution in the UK. They note that: "Couples separate when the benefits of divorcing and possible remarrying outweigh the benefits from staying married . . . The decision of owner-occupier couples to split-up is particularly responsive to unexpected decreases in home prices, and these negative shocks significantly increase the probability of marital breakdown" (p. 1). Younger couples with low income, high mortgage debt, and dependent children are most at risk as home values decrease. Thus, downturns in the housing market often are often associated with family (in)stability.

The shock of devalued home prices and also a lower income might also reduce the probability of dissolution as struggling couples chose not to divorce or even to physically separate because they have less equity in their property to share. There simply often is not enough money to buy or rent two separate homes. Rainer and Smith conclude their research by suggesting that: "Well-designed micro policies that support families with low income and high debt (e.g., mortgage interest deductibility, . . . tax rebates) may be the key to reducing the degree to which couples are affected by money lost on their homes" (p. 14-15).

Becker, Landes, and Michael (1977) also provide a useful economic way of conceptualizing the economic impact on marital instability. With respect to couples who are reluctant to separate, the authors provide the following advice, "Dissolution is a response, however, to *new* information, favorable as well as unfavorable. Moreover, the freedom to dissolve reduces the impact of unfavorable information, and thereby reduces the incentive to delay marriage or otherwise search more in order to avoid a mismatch" (p. 1151-1152).

The ability for a couple to reframe the stigma of failure because of the decision to emotionally separate was well illustrated by a colleague of the first author. Although he was president of his state's marriage and family association, he was going through his third divorce. He related the following helpful reframe from his own counselor.

"I wish we could have worked it out," he stated to his therapist.

"It sounds like you worked it out," was the insightful counselor reply.

C. The STINT Relationship Checklist

The following checklist has been developed by the co-authors. It is meant to be a starting point in your own discussion of what is negotiable and what is not, relative to the possibility of or decision to stay together under one roof while moving apart emotionally.

On each item there is a scale from a 1-10. Scores of 1-3 are meant to be absolutely NOT negotiable items; 4-7 maybe; and 8-10 indicate a favorable probability that such an issue can be favorable negotiated. A place for describing and/or elaborating on your reason for choosing a given number is also provided.

It is suggested that each of you independently complete the questionnaire. You can then meet together and compare what is negotiable and what is not. If only one of you is available or if the two of you would like to discuss your responses with a counselor or trusted spiritual advisor, that is an option too. Basic respect dictates that one or the other of you not try to coerce the other to "come over to your way of thinking" on a particular item.

The following checklist is meant to provide a starting point for discussing what would be negotiable and what would be negotiable for each of you should you choose to stay together in a home and yet emotionally detach. There are 11 major topics; on each item check one or more of the boxes to indicate your belief of who would be responsible.

Put the letter **M** for **me**; **Y** for **You** and **U** for **us** together in a manner to be worked out by mutual agreement.

In the box labeled **Negotiable**, give a rating from a 1-10 on how negotiable this particular item might be for you. Scores of 1-3 are meant to be absolutely NOT negotiable items; 4-7 maybe, and 8-10 indicates a favorable probability such an issue can be favorable negotiated. A place for describing and/or elaborating on your reason for choosing a given number is also provided.

Activity 30: The STINT—Relationship Checklist
(Developed by Phil Ginsburg and Daniel Eckstein)

Topic	Me	You	Us	Negotiable	Discussion
1. **Economics/finances** A. House payments Taxes and insurance					
B. Car payments					

C. Utilities
      Communications:
      internet, phone, etc.					

D. Food E. Life/medical insurance F. Clothing (adults and children)					

G. Entertainment
      restaurants, movies, DVD
      movies, DVD rentals,
      kids' activities, cable					

H. Education
    private school tuition
    uniforms
    regular education expenses
    (art projects, field trips,
    sports uniforms and
    equipment				

2. Spiritual
  A. Attend religious
    Service together				

B. Attend together as a family;				
C. different house of worship;				
3. Sleeping arrangements A. same bedroom				
B. separate bedrooms				
4. Dating A. OK to date				
B. Not OK to date				
C. Discuss who, what, where				
D. No discussion				
5. Holidays A. Where to spend them				
B. What side of family				
C. Who attends what holidays and family events				
6. Friends and family A. Who gets the friends				
B. Attendance at Parties and other functions				
7. Daily Routines				

A. Child
    Transportation
    Schools, doctor's
    Appointments,
    extracurricular
    activities, lessons,				

8. Public Appearance A. Present as still together B. Clear that we have separate lives					
9. Agreement not to Disparage each other kids, family, friends					
10. Intimacy A. Sexual intimacy allowed B. Never					
C. Occasionally					
11. Property division/ Responsibilities When physical					

D. Application to You as a Couple

After you have completed the checklist and discussed it with each other and/or with a counselor or spiritual advisor, together write a summary of what each of you are making as agreements for the present moment. Such agreements need to be flexible and subject to change, of course, but hopefully not by one of you unilaterally changing the rules and the agreements when it suits you personally.

1. Here are the areas in which we have an agreement:
2. Here are the areas that we are still discussing that are not in agreement at the moment but still remain "in play" for future discussions.
3. These are the non-negotiable items which constitute a violation of our agreements.

E. Summary

Although the focus of their article is on an actual divorce, there are several activities that you might find helpful even if you are simply emotionally separating. They include: the timeline; a family map and family planning guide; how each of you will relate your own separation story; your agreements and related legal issues; some ways each of you might want to grieve the loss; and a balance sheet for each of you to access your relationship gains and losses.

In the present article, we have attempted to provide a structured checklist that can assist you as a couple in separating but still staying in the same house due to economic circumstances.

The checklist is meant to help identify specific topics for you to consider in such a decision. It also assists in identifying what is negotiable or not for each of you in the separation.

References

Becker, G. Landes, E. and Michael, R. (1977). An economic analysis of marital instability, *Journal of Political Economy*, 85, 1141-1187.

Boheim, Rene, and Ermish, John. (2001), Partnership dissolution in the UK—the role of economic circumstances, *Oxford Bulletin of Economics and statistics*, 63,3, 197-208.

Cogan, Judy. (February 3, 2009). Staying Together in Needy Times, *The Sun. Retrieved from* http://thesun.co.uk/sol/homepage/woman/article218045. ece#ixzz0fh ece#ixzz0fhwFfd9X

Levitz, J. (2009, July 13). What God Has Joined Together, Recession Makes Hard to Put Asunder. *Wall Street Journal—Eastern Edition*, pp. A1-A6. Retrieved from Academic Search Complete database.

Chapter V:
Role Communication Style

Section 22:

The Couple's Gender-Based Questionnaire (CGQ): Thirty-Three Relationship Considerations

Daniel Eckstein, Pat Love, Kristen J. Aycock and V. Van Wiesner III

Since 1993, the first author has written a quarterly column in *The Family Journal* called "For Couples." It features interviews and questionnaires that couples can complete and discuss together for relationship renewal. All columns have been organized according to the following four ways Jay Haley[1] suggests in systematically accessing couples relationships, those being: personality differences, role perceptions, communication skills, and problem-solving methods. Eckstein and Goldman [2] originally published a gender-related couples' communication; the present article is an update on the gender-related research that has occurred since then.

The present article introduces the Couples Gender-Based Questionnaire (CGQ) which has been developed by the authors. The purpose is for couples to explore role perceptions based on some research involving gender differences. Although no individual man or women will fit all the generalizations, an understanding of basic gender differences can help better create an awareness of some different ways of experiencing and of being in the world.

Process

A gender-based questionnaire established on current research appears in Appendix A. There are a total of 33 items. The instructions for completion are to individually read each stem, then answer the statement with an *M* if it is more characteristic of males, an *F* if it is more characteristic of females, and a *B* if the statement is equally true of both males and females. In Appendix B, the reference is cited after each statement in parentheses along with the answers.

After the participants have individually answered the items, they compare their responses to those of their partner. By discussion and consensus, the partner must come up with an agreed-upon best answer to each item. Making an item fit one of the other partners is not the goal of the activity, no is a superiority-inferior implication due to one or the other having more right answers. Rather, an understanding of some basic gender differences that may or not be true of either participant personally is helpful in understanding and respecting basic gender-based differences. After the questionnaire has been taken individually and then discussed and agreed (or agreed to disagree on an item), participants read the brief theory input, followed by a presentation of the actual answers. The items are then scored and the implications of the relationship are discussed.

Review of Literature

It is important to note that in this article, gender-based differences are based on normative male-female statistics. Any individual man or woman may not fit a particular gender generalization, but from the classic "men are from Mars" and "women are from Venus" metaphor introduced by Gray[3] to the contemporary research-based work of Love and Stosny,[4] there are nonetheless some gender-based generalizations that can be made. Before exploring a more formal representative literature review, there is a lighter side to the battle of the sexes.

Gender Differences

Love[5] identifies important gender differences affecting relationships. Men have an instinct to provide and to protect. Males hone their survival skills by competing, ordering, directing, confronting, doing, bragging, and threatening. When a man cannot provide and protect, he usually feels inadequate and shameful.

Conversely, women have an instinct to tend and to befriend. When in conflict, females usually have feelings of stress, upset, and fear. For women, connecting via talking activates pleasure centers in the female brain. Sharing relationship information gives a dopamine and oxycontin rush. Oxycontin is a chemical that facilitates bonding and pleasurable feelings. Females experience an oxytocin rush from gazing, positive emotional interaction, kissing, and having an orgasm.[6] Physiologically, when oxytocin and dopamine are high, loving circuits are activated, but at the same time caution and aversion circuits are shut off. Such hormone surges make the female brain more sensitive to emotional nuances. When a woman can connect, she feels fear; that in turn makes her want to move closer to her partner or to someone else. Conversely, when a man feels shame, he usually wants to move away.

During stress, oxytocin is released in both men and women. With this in mind, people should connect with each other during stressful situations. As previously noted, this is largely true for women. In men, however, the concurrent release of androgens blocks oxycontin's effects, resulting in the activation of the fight-or-flight stress response. As mothers have been the primary caretakers for children throughout our evolutionary history, it is adaptive for women to connect with their children when danger presents; this allows mothers to protect their children.[7]

Humans' biological underpinnings have implications for communication styles. When women encounter relationship stress, they are more likely to seek social support. This social support is often in the form of their partners. Because men do not feel the effects of oxytocin during stress, in relationships they are more likely to withdraw rather than to seek connection with their partners.

Compassion for each other's vulnerabilities is a major antidote to the temptations of infidelity. Basic cooperation requires respect for differences in gender roles. Actual physical contact alleviates fear and pain. According to Love,[8] the number-one cause for divorce and/or separation is disconnection. The number-one cause of disconnection is resentment, and the number-one cause of resentment is withdrawal of interest. Four primary ways of loving a man include:

1. Accepting that the partner provides the meaning in a man's life.
2. Understanding his dread of failure as a provider, protector, lover, and parent.
3. Connecting more through routine, fun activities, touch, and sex.
4. Avoiding control.

The most effective ways of connecting with a man include sex, touch, activity, appreciation, and routine—honor his routine. Men need about three times more of this than women. The four best ways for loving a woman include:

1. Appreciating her importance to you.
2. Making an effort to understand her.
3. Avoiding controlling; protecting is fine.
4. Understanding her fears of harm, your anger, and of deprivation.

The best ways for connecting with a woman include routinely making contact with her, opening the heart to her, connecting, and keeping thoughts and actions positive.[9]

Chemistry is mainly a function of your DNA. It has more to do with your metabolism than your personality or values. The chemical bath your brain enjoys during infatuation is a powerful regulator of fear and shame . . . This sharp reduction of the influence of fear and shame is why, when infatuated, you feel so confident and proud while doing things that you might otherwise find fear-involving or shameful. One reason that affairs rarely turn into viable relationships where they break up marriages is that the chemical relief from fear and shame is short-lived. (The divorce rate for affair partners who marry is 80 percent!) Once the narcotic effects of infatuation wear off, the woman is likely to feel more insecure and the man more ashamed of himself than ever.[10]

Here are activities that cause depletion in one's insulation from infidelity:

child involvement in too many activities (research shows that involving children in more than two activities per a week can put undue stress upon the child as well as upon the family);

over-involvement with work;

consumer spending;

addiction to intensity;

ignoring family and friends;

ignoring enriching activities;

spiritual neglect;

and lack of physical exercise, sex, or romance.[11]

Women are more likely than men to make suggestions in the form of a question.[12] When conversing, men do not often interrupt other men but men interrupt women more often than women interrupt men.[13] Women are more likely to talk about health matters or children and least about politics, religion, or finances, whereas men are more likely to talk about work or sports and least likely to talk about their bodies.[14]

Gender differences in patient-doctor communication were found in a study of six Western European countries researching 1,906 general practitioners and 2,812 patients. Female doctors show more affective behavior, such as empathy, partnership building, emotional support, and reassurances. They also were found to encourage patients' input through the use of concern and partnership statements. Male doctors were likely to give more interpretations and paraphrases.

Information appeared to be given more by female than male doctors, and female general practitioners were better at (therapeutic) listening and counseling. Male doctors were more likely to give more instructions, advisements, and suggestions for patient behavior, and they were more verbally dominant and imposing during the visit.

The nonverbal behavior also differed between doctors' genders; female doctors were likely to give more in the direction of the patient, to use more back-channel (or listeners') responses, and to smile and nod more often. Female doctors offered more options and had more time to negotiate treatment possibilities, both with male and female patients.[15]

Burleson found gender differences relative to relationship support and conflict management. He found that "females rated ego support skill, conflict management skill, and comforting skill as significantly more important than did males, whereas males rated narrative and persuasion skills as significantly more important than did females."[16]

Weisfeld and Stack[17] researched gender differences in 40 happily married U.S. couples. Although these couples showed no significant sex differences in marital satisfaction or in verbal statements regarding commitment, sex differences in the following nonverbal behaviors became apparent: smiling, laughing, and average length of look at spouse. The wives looked significantly longer, as if listening attentively, and husbands used shorter glances at wives, suggesting a monitoring function.

Gottman[18] concluded that distressed married couples often engage in negative cascades—patterns of reciprocal criticism and punishment that escalate until one partner is forced to withdraw. It is usually the husband who withdraws. It is the husband who experiences a stronger physiological stress pattern when the couple fights (even though the husband's face might not show a matching emotional expression of distress, and Gottman speculates that husbands might withdraw in order to reduce the physiological burden of stress). Maccoby proposes that most men are inhibited from launching a full-scale aggressive attack against a female. Whatever the cause or causes, men show higher heart rate, respiration rate, and autonomic arousal in general than their wives do when couples are arguing, and these physiological measures of arousal are lowered when husbands turn away or leave the scene of an argument. It is the ratio of positive to negative affect expressed that is the key predictor of satisfaction in marriage [19] Pasupathi et al. argue that gender differences in communication styles may be both normal and expected, and that efforts to produce an androgynous matched set of communicators may not help couples in the long run.

Michaud and Warner[20] and Baskow and Rubenfeld[21] present studies of gender differences in "troubles talk" that allegedly provide support for the different cultures thesis, that being that men and women communicate in such different ways that they should be regarded as members of different communication cultures or speech communities. However, MacGeorge confronts that suggestion by presenting both their own and three other studies suggesting that men and women provide and respond to supportive messages ("trouble talks") in ways that are much more similar than different. They suggest that the different cultures thesis is a myth that should be discarded.

Lesbian, Gay, Bisexual, and Transgender (LGBT) Relationships

Thus far, this article has focused on a heterosexual dyad because the majority of individuals describe themselves as heterosexual and, therefore, represents the bulk of clients presenting for counseling. Nevertheless, lesbians and gay males seek counseling at higher rates than heterosexuals.[22] Although there are certainly some differences between heterosexual and nonheterosexual relationships, a preponderance of research suggests that more similarities than differences exist.[23, 24, 25, 26] LGBT couples experience many of the same difficulties with communication and understanding as heterosexual couples. One factor unique to LGBT relationships is stress related to heterosexism. A common misconception of heterosexual counselors is that these social stressors lessen the quality of LGBT relationships. In fact, gay and lesbian partners share similar levels of relationship satisfaction as heterosexual partners.[27] Nevertheless, heterosexism adds a dimension to therapy with LGBT couples.

The CGQ can prove helpful to LGBT couples because biology and socialization affect all humans regardless of sexual orientation. For those in the LGBT, it is important to realize that throughout life, males and females receive societal messages informing them of gender-appropriate roles. For example, females may receive positive reinforcement for caretaking behaviors, whereas males may receive positive reinforcement for aggressive behavior. Despite these messages, some individuals, regardless of sexual orientation, fall in the outer ranges of what society identifies as normal gender-typed behavior. LGBT individuals may fall outside of the average range more often than heterosexuals.

The CGQ can be modified for LGBT couples during the processing phase to gain a better understanding of societal messages of gender-appropriate roles that correspond to or diverge from each partners' experiences of their gender definitions. This can be a useful tool for raising awareness of areas in which heterosexist views may affect each partner's views of himself or herself in a relationship. Additionally, it will highlight areas of resilience where the couples have coped positively with discriminatory societal messages. It is important to note that this can also be applied to work with heterosexual couples, as not all questions apply to each and every person of the specified gender and it is important to understand ho couples approach such differences.

Activity 31: The Couples' Gender-Based (CGB) Questionnaire

1. _____ have an instinct to provide and protect.
2. _____ have an instinct to bend and to befriend.
3. The _____ brain has outstanding verbal agility and the ability to connect deeply in friendships.
4. Contact lowers fear in _____.
5. When a _____ feels shame, he/she wants to move away.
6. In _____, conflict creates a feeling of stress, upset, and fear.
7. Listening with both sides of the brain makes _____ better at multitasking.
8. _____ have a larger area of the brain for navigation skills.
9. _____ are better at focusing on a specific task.
10. _____ have more sensitive hearing especially in the range where language exists.
11. Effective communication for _____ involves understanding motivation.
12. During marital conflict, _____'s heart rate and blood pressure will rise significantly more than _____'s.
13. Feeling needed motivates and empowers _____.
14. Advice-giving responses to stressful situations often leave _____ feeling unsupported.
15. For _____, sudden changes in the environment lead to an emotional response.
16. Connection reduces fear and shame for _____.
17. On a typical day _____ speaks 6,000-8,000 words.
18. Constructive communication is related to marital satisfaction in _____.
19. _____ hone their survival skills by competing, ordering, and directing.
20. The best ways to connect with a _____ includes sex, touch, activity, appreciation, and honoring their routine.
21. Stress hormone cortical blocks oxycontin's action in the ___ brain.

22. Warm partner contact is related to lower blood pressure in _____.
23. During marital conflict, _____'s heart rate and blood pressure significantly rises.
24. Because more brain area is devoted to spatial relations, _____ are better able to parallel park successfully on the first try.
25. When under stress, the hormone androgen reduces oxycontin's action in the _____ brain.
26. Gazing, positive emotional interaction, kissing, and orgasms create a _____ dopamine and oxytocin rush.
27. Being able to step into your partner's shoes when they're in distress increases relationship satisfaction for _____.
28. When oxytocin and dopamine are high, loving circuits are activated and caution and aversion circuits are shut off in _____.
29. When a _____ cannot provide and protect, there is a feeling of inadequate and of shame.
30. To love a _____, connect through routine, fun activities, touch, and sex.
31. The number one cause for divorce and/or separation is disconnection for _____
32. Feeling needed motivates and empowers _____.
33. The deepest form of intimacy is beyond words for _____.

Questionnaire Answers

In the spirit of equity, the 33 items of the CGB include 11 each for males and females.

1. Males[28]
2. Females[29]
3. Females[30]
4. Both[31]
5. Males[32]
6. Females[33]
7. Females[34]
8. Males[35]
9. Males[36]
10. Females[37]
11. Both[38]
12. Females[39]
13. Males[40]
14. Females[41]

15. Both[42]
16. Both[43]
17. Female[44]
18. Both[45]
19. Males[46]
20. Males[47]
21. Females[48]
22. Both[49]
23. Females[50]
24. Males[51]
25. Males[52]
26. Females[53]
27. Both[54]
28. Females[55]
29. Males[56]
30. Males[57]
31. Both[58]
32. Males[59]
33. Both[60] (Love, 2007)

Endnotes

[1] Haley, J. (1986). *Uncommon therapy.* New York: Norton.

[2] Eckstein, D., & Goldman, A. (2001). The couples gender-based communication questionnaire. *The Family Journal, 9,* 62-74.

[3] Gray, J. (1992). *Men are from Mars, women are from Venus.* New York: HarperCollins.

[4] Love, P., & Stosny, S. (2007). *How to improve your marriage without talking about it.* New York: Random House.

[5] Love, P. (2007, July). *Research advances on the biology and chemistry of attraction.* Program presented at Sam Houston State University, Huntsville, TX.

[6] *Loc. cit.* pp.1-2.

[7] Taylor, S. E. (2002). *The tending instinct.* New York: Times Books.

[8] Love, 2007, *Ibid.*

[9] *Loc. cit.* pp. 3-6.

[10] *Loc. cit.* p. 89

[11] Love & Stosny, 2007. *Ibid.*

[12] Simkins-Bullock, J., & Wildman, B. (1991). An investigation into the relationship between gender and language. *Sex Roles, 24,* 149-160.

[13] Coates, J. (1986). *Women, men and language.* New York: Longman.

[14] Walsh, A., & Walsh, G. (1993). *Viva la difference: A celebration of the sexes.* Buffalo, NY: Prometheus.

[15] Brink-Muinen, A. v. d., Dulmen, S. v, Messerli-Rohrbach, V., & Bensing, J. (2002). Do gender-dyads have different communication patterns? A comparative study in Western-European general practices. *Parent Education and Counseling, 48,* 253-264.

[16] Burleson, B. (2003). The experience and effects of emotional support. *Personal Relationships, 10,* p. 6.

[17] Weisfeld, C., & Stack, M. (2002). When I look into your eyes: An ethological analysis of gender differences in married couples' non-verbal behaviors. *Psychology, Evolution & Gender,* 4.2, 125-147

[18] Gottman, J. M. (1994). *What predicts divorce?* Englewood Cliffs, NJ: Erlbaum.

[19] Pasupathi, M., Carstensen, L. L., Levenson, R. W., & Gottman, J. M. (1999). Responsive listening in long-married couples: A psycholinguistic perspective, *Journal of Nonviolent Behavior, 23(2),* 173-193.

[20] Michaud, S. L., & Warner, R. M. (1997). Gender differences in self-reported response to trouble talk. *Sex Roles, 37,* 527-540.

[21] Baskow, S. A., & Rubenfeld, K. (2003). Troubles talk: Effects of gender and gender typing. *Sex Roles, 48,* 183-187.

[22] Jones, M. A., & Gabriel, M. A. (1999). Utilization of psychotherapy by lesbians, gay men, and bisexuals: Findings from a nationwide survey. *American Journal of Orthopsychiatry, 69,* 209-219.

[23] Alderson, K. G. (2004). A phenomenological investigation of same-sex marriage. *The Canadian Journal of Human Sexuality, 13,* 107-122.

[24] Gottman, J. M., Levenson, R. W., Gross, J., Frederickson, B. L., McCoy, K., Rosenthal, L., et al. (2003). Correlates of gay and lesbian couples' relationship satisfaction and relationship dissolution. *Journal of Homosexuality, 45(1),* 23-43.

[25] Kurdek, L. A. (2005). What do we know about gay and lesbian couples? *Current Directions in Psychological Science, 14,* 25 1-254.

[26] Kurdek, L. A., & Schmitt, J. P. (1986). Relationship quality of partners in heterosexual married, heterosexual cohabitating, and gay and lesbian relationships. *Journal of Personality and Social Psychology, 51,*711-720.

[27] *Loc. cit.*

[28] Love & Stoney, 2007. *Ibid.*

[29] *Loc. cit,.*

[30] *Loc. cit.*

[31] *Loc. cit.*

[32] Love, 2007. *Ibid.*

[33] *Loc. cit.*

[34] Lyle, B., & Lyle, J. (2006). *Couples communication.* Victoria, BC: Trafford.

[35] *Loc. cit.*

[36] *Loc. cit.*

[37] *Loc. cit.*

[38] Gonzaga, G. C., Campos, B., & Bradbury, T. (2007). Similarity, convergence, and relationship satisfaction in dating and married couples. *Journal of Personality and Social Psychology, 91,* 34-48.

[39] Kiecolt-Glaser, J. K., & Newton, T. L. (2001). Marriage and health: His and hers. *Psychological Bulletin, 127,* 472-503.

[40] Gray, 1992. *Ibid.*

[41] *Loc. cit.*

[42] Gonzega, et al., 2007. *Ibid.*

[43] Grewen, K. M., Anderson, B. J., Girdler, S. S., & Light, K. C. (2003). Warm partner contact is related to lower cardiovascular reactivity. *Journal of Human Stress, 29,* 123-130.

[44] Lyle & Lyle, 2006. *Ibid.*

[45] Christensen, A., Eldridge, K., & Catta-Preta, A. B. (2006). Cross-cultural consistency of the demand/withdrawal interaction pattern in couples. *Journal of Marriage and Family, 68,* 1029-1044.

[46] Love, 2007. *Ibid.*

[47] *Loc. cit.*

[48] *Loc. cit.*

[49] Gonzega, et al. 2007. *Ibid.*

[50] Christensen, et al. 2006. *Ibid.*

[51] Lyle & Lyle, 20006. *Ibid.*

[52] Taylor, 2002. *Ibid.*

[53] Love, 2007. *Ibid.*

[54] Gonzega, et al., 2007. *Ibid.*

[55] Love, 2007. *Ibid.*

[56] *Loc. cit.*

[57] *Loc. cit.*

[58] *Loc. cit.*

[59] Gray, 1992. *Ibid.*

[60] Love, 2007. *Ibid.*

Biographies

Kristen Aycock is in the Department of Counseling and Psychological Services at Georgia State University.

Pat Love is a licensed marriage and family therapist and approved supervisor of Pat Love & Associates.

V. Van Wiesner, III is in the Department of Educational Leadership and Counseling, Sam Houston State University, Texas.

Section 23:

The Non-Violent Relationship Questionnaire (NVRQ)

Daniel Eckstein and Lucy La Grassa

Activity 32: Non-Violent Relationship Questionnaire Instructions

With respect to *your perception* of your current relationship on a 1-10 scale, 1 being *very low* agreement and 10 being *very high* agreement, with each of the following statements. (On the parenting questions (4, 12, and 20) if you have no children, write N/A (Not Apply) in the box).

Scale of Agreement

1-----   2-----   3-----   4-----   5-----   6-----   7-----   8-----   9-----   10
Very low   *Very high*

Non-Violent Relationship Questionnaire

Your score 1-10	Please provide a score for each question
	1. I feel comfortable expressing myself to my partner
	2. We listen to each other without judging each other
	3. I accept responsibility for my own behavior including any past use of violence in our relationship
	4. I share parental responsibilities with my partner (if applicable)
	5. I believe we have a fair distribution of work in the home
	6. We collaboratively make major financial decisions
	7. We seek mutually satisfying solutions to conflict
	8. I am confident that my partner will support me emotionally and not abandon me when I am in need.

Non-Violent Relationship Questionnaire (continued)

1-10	Please provide a score for each question
	9. I am able to do things that are of interest to me in our relationship
	10. We are emotionally supportive of each other
	11. I admit when I am wrong to my partner
	12. I am a positive role model for my children (if applicable)
	13. We make most of our decisions collaboratively
	14. We ensure that both of us benefit from financial arrangements
	15. We understand that change is an essential aspect of our relationship
	16. My partner would never intentionally hurt me by what he or she says or does
	17. I feel safe taking risks on my own initiative without fear of reprisal from my partner
	18. We value each other's opinion
	19. I believe I communicate openly and truthfully
	20. I actively seek advice/feedback on how to be a better parent (i.e. attending parent study groups, reading relevant books, watching educational programs etc.)
	21. We both share responsibility for our relationship
	22. We respect each other's "veto power" on important financial commitments
	23. We are willing to negotiate and compromise with each other
	24. I am confident my partner tells me the truth

The Dynamics of Non-Violent Relationships (NVR)

A non-violent relationship is based on the belief and that you and your partner are different but equals on all levels. You treat your partner as an equal emotionally, physically, psychologically and intellectually. This means that you treat each other with the understanding that your partner's emotional well-being and expression is different than yours and is as important as your own; your partner's physical well-being and expression is different than yours and is as important as your own; your partner's psychological well-being and expression is different than yours and is as important as your own; your partner's intellectual well-being and expression is different than yours and is as important as your own.

You and your partner do not think you are better or superior to the other—just different and you respect and honor those differences. You do not desire to dominate or control your partner or to get your way in the relationship at the expense of your partner. You do not desire to manipulate or deceive your partner to serve yourself. Most importantly, you don't try to get away with anything because you know that everything you do affects your partner—even if it is not overt.

Having the freedom to be who you are while considering your partner's feelings, well-being and expression is turnkey to the success of the relationship. The premise of the relationship is not based on loving your partner for what your partner can do for you—but loving your partner for who they are and honoring how they are without trying to change him/her to suit your own likes and dislikes. This removes any strife in a relationship and replaces it with acceptance.

In order to have a non-violent relationship you need to do away with all self-importance or selfishness and replace these things with equal respect for yourself and your partner; equal appreciation for your interests and your partner's interests; and accepting responsibility for considering equally what matters to you and your partner without putting yourself first.

When you choose to have a partnership, you choose to move from being egocentric to concentric.

Non-Violent Communication (NVC)

Marshall Roseberg[1] has written an excellent book called *Non-violent Communication: A Language of Life*. Lucy Leu[2] has added a *Nonviolent Communication Companion* Workbook which is meant to supplement Roseberg's book. It is formatted to be used both by couples or by groups of couples who want to both commit and to practice skill-building activities based on the theory of non-violent communication (NVC).

According to Roseberg, "NVC is founded on language and communication skills that strengthen our ability to remain human, even under trying conditions . . . NVC has been. NVC guides us in reframing how we express ourselves and hear others. Instead of being habitual, automatic reactions, our words become conscious responses based firmly on an awareness of what we are perceiving, feeling and wanting. We are able to express ourselves with honesty and clarity, while simultaneously paying others a respectful and emphatic attention. As NVC replaces our old patterns of defending, withdrawing, or attacking in the face of judgment and criticism, we come to perceive ourselves and others, as well as our intentions and relationships, in a new light. Resistance, defensiveness, and violent reactions are minimized. When we focus on clarifying what is being observed inevitably blossoms when we stay true to the principles and process of NVC."[3]

Four Components of the NVC Process

Here are the four components of NVC:

1. *observation*
2. *feeling*
3. *needs*
4. *requests*

Roseberg defines them as follows: "First, we *observe* what is actually happening in a situation; what we are observing others saying or doing that is either enriching or not enriching our life . . . simply say what people are doing that we either like or don't like. Next we *state* how we feel when we observe this action: are we hurt, scared, joyful, amused, irritated, etc? And thirdly, we say what *needs* of ours are connected to the feelings we have identified . . . The fourth component addresses what we are wanting from the other person {*requests*} that would enrich our lives and make life more wonderful for us" [4] (authors italics)

Concentric Non-Violent Relationships

Here is a visual way that the authors conceptualize a "Concentric Non-Violent Relationship

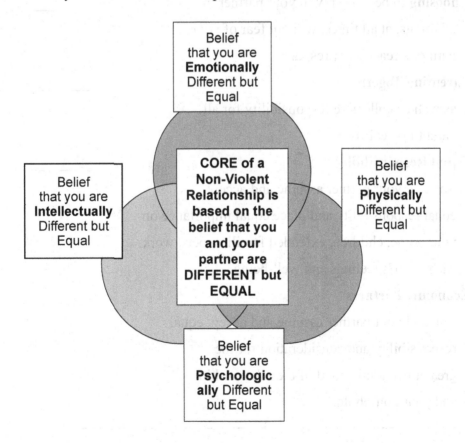

Activity 33:

Predication of Your Non-Violent Relationship Scores (NVRS)

Here is a description of the eight variables that are identified by the authors in the NVCQ.

Variable	Predict Your Score (3-30 for each)
A. Non-Threatening No fear of your partner at any time or about anything. No intimidation in the relationship.	_____
B. Respect Acknowledging, accepting, appreciating, and treating your partner as your equal	_____
C. Choosing to be honest with your partner in all things, at all times, without fear of your partner's reaction or response	_____
D. Parenting Together as well as collective responsibility for all parenting decisions	_____
E. Equal Responsibility You and your partner assume and accept equal responsibility and place equal importance on your home, children, extended families, pets, work, each other's feelings and well-being	_____
F. Economic Partners You and your partner assume and accept equal responsibility and consideration for the greater economic good of the relationship and your household.	_____

G. Fairness   _____

You and your partner appreciate and esteem that
you are emotionally, physically, psychologically
and intellectually different but equal. You can openly
discuss and come to an agreement of what is fair without
pressuring, manipulating or forcing your partner
to agree with you or to do what you would like.

H. Trust   _____

You can trust your partner to support you
emotionally, physically, psychologically and intellectually
at all times. You are not afraid that your partner will
abandon you or hurt you. You are confident that
your partner considers your well-being and your feelings
as much as his/her own.

Given the above theory relative to non-violent relationships, now predict whether you feel your score will be low (3-11) medium (12-21) or high (22-30) for each of the following eight (A-H) variables

Scoring

Transfer your scores from the Non-Violent Relationship Questionnaire (NVRQ) to the boxes below.

Your Score

A Non-Threatening		B Respect	C Honesty	D Parenting Together, if applicable	E Equal Respon-sibility	F Economic Partners	G Fairness	H Trust	
		2	3	4	5	6	7	8	
9		10	11	12	13	14	15	16	
17		18	19	20	21	22	23	24	

Your Subtotal

A Non-Threatening		B Respect	C Honesty	D Parenting Together, if applicable	E Equal Respon-sibility	F Economic Partners	G Fairness	H Trust	

YOUR GRAND TOTAL (sum of A-H)	

Your Score:

24-96	= Low
97-169	= Medium
170-240	= High

For those of you who found that **"D—Parenting Together"** *does not apply, please add 30 points to your score to give you an accurate score.*

Charting Your Non-Violent Relationship Sub-Scores

In the graph below plot your sub-scores on each of the eight variables for both you (+) and for your partner (*).

High								
30								
25								
20								
15								
10								
5								
1								
0								
Low	A	B	C	D	E	F	G	H

Non-Threatening	Respect	Honesty	Parenting Together, if Applicable	Equal Responsibility	Economic Partners	Fairness	Trust

Implications Of Your Non-Violent Relationship Scores (NVRS)

1. Consider your *highest* two scores on the chart. Cite (an) example(s) that illustrates each variable.
2. Now do the same process for your *lowest* two scores.
3. Write one-two paragraphs *in your own* words that address such issues as:
   a. How did your predicted scores compare to your actual scores?
   b. In what ways do you agree with your scores?
   c. In what ways do you disagree?
   d. Now compare your scores to your partner's scores for each variable.
   e. Practice active listening to each of your respective profiles. Neither of your scores is "better" or "more right" than the other.
   f. Practice a non-violent respectful relationship by "agreeing to disagree". You may also want to discuss your scores with a counselor if that seems warranted.

Additional Suggestions for Non-Violent Couple's Communication

1. **Communication that Blocks Compassion**
   Here are five specific ways that couples often block compassionate communication. Roseberg[5] calls them "Life alienating communication"

   a. **Moralistic Judgments**
      This implies "wrongness" or "badness" when our partner doesn't act in harmony with our own values. Blame, insults, put-downs, labels, criticism, comparisons, and diagnoses are all forms of such "moral superiority" judgments.

   b. **Making Comparisons**
      Comparisons generally involve some type of "one-up: (superiority) "one-down" (inferiority) self-elevating or self-deprecating judgment relative to our partner and or others.

   c. **Denial of responsibility**
      This involves using language that implies a lack of choice. Examples include "you made me feel guilty "or "I have to" . . .

   d. **Other Forms of Life-Alienating Communication**
      According to Roseberg:

      > Communicating our desires as demands is another form of language that blocks compassion. A demand explicitly or implicitly threatens listeners with blame or punishment if they fail to comply. Life-alienating communication is also associated with the concept that certain actions merit reward while others merit punishment. This thinking is expressed by the word *deserve* . . . It assumes *badness* on the part of people who behave in certain ways, and calls for punishment to make them repent and change their behavior. Most of us grew up speaking a language that encourages us to label, compare, demand, and pronounce judgments rather than to be aware of what we are feeling and needing . . . These views stress our innate evil and deficiency, and a need for education to control our inherently undesirable nature. Life-alienating communication both stems from and supports hierarchical or domination societies . . . The more people are trained to think in terms of moralistic judgments that imply wrongness and badness, the more they are being trained to look outside themselves—to outside authorities—for the definition of what constitutes right, wrong, good and bad. When we are in contact with our feelings and needs, we humans no longer make good slaves and underlings.[6]

   e. **Requests Versus Demands**

Rosenberg asserts that requests are received as demands when others believe they will be blamed or punished if they do not comply when people hear us make a demand, they see only two options: submission or rebellion. Either way, the person requesting is perceived as coercive, and the listener's capacity to respond compassionately to request is diminished.[7]

This involves communicating to your partner, what we would like to request of each other to enrich each of our lives. We try to avoid vague, abstract, or ambiguous phrasing, and remember to use positive action language by starting what we are requesting rather than what we are not. When we speak, the clearer we are about what we want back, the more likely we are to get it . . . Requests are received as demands when listeners believe that they will be blamed or punished if they do not comply. We can help others trust that we are requesting not demanding by indicating our desire for them to comply only if they can do so willingly. The objective of NVC is not to change people and their behavior in order to get our way; it is to establish relationships based in honesty and empathy that will eventually fulfill everyone's needs.[8]

2. "Giraffe and Jackal Language"

In the companion NVC workbook, Leu notes that the NVC Communication Model is popularly known as *Giraffe Language*. She writes that:

Marshall picked the giraffe, the land animal with the largest heart, as a symbol for NVC, a language that inspires compassion and joyful relationships . . . . Like NVC, the giraffe's height affords a long view into the distance and provides a heightened awareness of future possibilities and the consequences of our thoughts, words and actions. As a language that stresses the expression of feelings and needs, NVC invites vulnerability and transforms it into strength. The long neck of the giraffe reminds us of this important quality of vulnerability . . . Marshall uses a jackal puppet to represent that part of ourselves that thinks, speaks, or acts in ways that disconnect us from our awareness of our own feelings and needs, as well as the feelings and needs of others . . .

A jackal is simply a giraffe with a language problem. As a friend, the jackal gives us the message that we are unlikely to get our needs met if we continue as we are. The jackal reminds us to take our time and find the giraffe way to hear and think before we speak. The NVC practice is to recognize and befriend our 'jackals' by welcoming them into awareness and allowing them to lead us to our feelings and needs. . . . The NVC practice is to recognize and befriend our 'jackals' by welcoming them into awareness and allowing them to lead us to our feelings and needs[9].

Discuss and write a game-plan on how you are your partner might have a more improved non-violent respectful relationship. Write it below; select a review date for the two of you to examine your success in making these changes. Please include some short-term elements—those things that you can both work on right as well as some long-term elements—those things that will take some time to develop and transform in your relationship. *These are short-term and long-term commitments that you will be making to yourself, each other and the relationship.*

Game-Plan for Improving Our Non-Violent, Respectful Relationship

SHORT-TERM GAME-PLAN *(2 months-1 year)*	LONG-TERM GAME-PLAN *(1 year and beyond)*

Summary

When two people choose to become partners they are ideally choosing to grow from being egocentric to concentric. This fundamental shift needs to take place by both partners in order to build a foundation for a non-violent relationship.

Both partners openly acknowledge, accept, appreciate and esteem that they are different from each other but that they are equals in every way—emotionally, physically, psychologically and intellectually.

There are eight building blocks that each partner needs to work on to establish and maintain a non-violent relationship. These include: non-threatening behavior, respect, honesty, responsible parenting (if applicable), shared responsibility, economic partnership, fairness, trust.

It is up to each partner to participate, equally, in building these eight pillars in the relationship. Sharing this responsibility equally removes any strife from the relationship and creates a free and safe environment for each partner to grow. Equality is the core of non-violent relationships wherein both partners live without fear or intimidation. Nurturing each other helps you, your partner and the relationship to grow in harmony and love.

Arun Gandhi is the grandson of India legendary M.K. Gandhi. His parents sent him at age 13 to study with Gandhi due to his own challenge with his anger at slurs as an adolescent in apartheid South Africa. He writes that:

> One of the many things I learned from grandfather is to understand the depth and
> breadth of nonviolence, and to acknowledge that we are all violent and that we need

to bring about a qualitative change in our attitudes. We often don't acknowledge our violence because we are ignorant about it.

We assume we are not violent because our vision of violence is one of fighting, killing, beating, and wars—the type of things that average individuals don't do . . .

Grandfather always vociferously stressed the need for nonviolence in communication . . . Unless, as grandfather would say, 'we become the change we wish to see in the world,' no change will ever take place.

We are . . . [usually] waiting for the other person to change first. Nonviolence is not a strategy that can be used today and discarded tomorrow, nor is it something that makes you meek or a pushover. Nonviolence is about inculcating positive attitudes to replace the negative attitudes that dominate us. Everything that we do is conditioned by selfish motives—what is in it for me—and even more so in an overwhelmingly materialistic society that thrives on rugged individualism.[10]

Gandhi eloquently confronts the larger community issues involved through practicing a non-violent philosophy. *Ahismsa* is the Hindu term that also characterized the philosophy and practice of civil rights leader Martin Luther King Jr. Gandhi further states that, "None of these negative concepts is conducive to building a homogeneous family, community, society, or nation. It is not important that we come together in a moment of crisis and show our patriotism by flying the flag; it is not enough that we become a superpower by building an arsenal that can destroy this earth several times over; it is not enough that we subjugate the rest of the world through our military might, because peace can not be built on the foundations of fear.

Nonviolence means allowing the positive within you to emerge. Be dominated by love, respect, understanding, appreciation, compassion and concern for others rather than the self-centered and selfish, greedy, hateful, prejudiced, suspicious and aggressive attitudes that usually dominate our thinking. We often hear people say: "This world is ruthless and if you want to survive you must become ruthless, too."

I humbly disagree with this contention. This world is what we have made of it. If it is ruthless today it is because we have made it ruthless by our attitudes. If we change ourselves we can change the world, and changing ourselves begins with changing our language and methods of communication"[11]

Information from these recommended on-line sources have been adapted into this article.
www.cybergrrl.com
www.ccsf.edu
www.smartmarriages.com

Endnotes

[1] Roseberg, Marshall. (2003) Non-Violent Communication: A Language of Compassion. Encinitas, California. Public Dancer Press.

[2] Leu, Lucy (2003) Non-Violent Communication Companion Workbook. Encinitas, California.

[3] Roseburg, *loc. cit. pp. 5-6.*

[4] Roseburg, *loc. cit. p. 6.*

[5] Roseberg, *loc. cit.*

[6] Roseberg, *loc. cit. pp. 22-23*

[7] Roseberg, *loc. cit. p. 79*

[8] Roseberg, *loc. cit. p. 85*

[9] Leu, *loc. cit. p. xi-xii*

[10] Roseburg, *loc cit. p. xvi*

[11] Roseberg, *loc. cit. p. xviii*

Biographies

Lucy La Grassa is the managing partner of Formidable Technologies Inc., the licensed distributor of FORscene, the leader in web 2.0 video editing technology for the broadcast, film and new media industries. Lucy was the former partner in La Grassa Chin-Loy Communications, a media, marketing and public relations firm that focused on diversity in the global marketplace. She is a journalism graduate from Ryerson University and lives in Toronto, Canada.

Ms. La Grassa is also a partner in La Grassa Chin-Loy Communications, an international public relations agency specializing in diversity marketing and publicity for people, products and places. Lucy La Grassa is also a communications consultant and team leader with Charger Consulting Corporation where she provides expertise in comprehensive program design and training to meet social and cultural communications needs. She is renowned for her work in issue identification and issue management.

Section 24:

A Linguistic "Asking, Promising, Asserting, and Declaring" Couples' Communication Activity

Daniel Eckstein, Torrey Byles, and Sherri Bennett

The following activity will help partners identify and define four basic "requesting, promising, asserting, and declaring" linguistic couples' communication acts. A couple's assessment and an application activity based on the four communication acts are presented as a method of improving relationships. Fernando Flores[1, 2, 3, 4, 5] originally developed what he calls a "linguistic communication model" in his native country of Chile. The present article applies his communication model to couples.

There are four sections to the proposed activity. You will first be asked to reflect on your global assessment regarding your respective perceptions of the effectives of your communication with one another. We will then offer a brief overview and some illustrations of some of Flores' writings on listening and communication skills. Four specific communication acts will then be presented. Lastly, you will be invited to apply that model to some specific communications between the two of you.

Activity 34: Assessing Your Communication as a Couple
Individually each of you writes down your responses
to the following five prompters.

1. On a scale of 1-10, one being low and ten being high, rate your overall opinion relative to your communication together.
2. Cite some behavioral examples of how you chose that particular number. In other words, what would someone outside of your relationship observe about the two of you that led to your number selection?
3. Cite a specific example of what you feel is strength relative to how you two communicate.
4. Relate a constricting example relative to something that you feel is a re-occurring *challenge* to your effectiveness of communicating at a an optimal level together.
5. Discuss your respective responses to these requests

Note that the very act of you being willing to engage in a conversation about how you communicate is a positive sign in and of itself. Please practice basic respect, listening and responding skills by first acknowledging that neither of you in fact has the *right* or the *wrong* answers. Summarize your partner's responses to his or her satisfaction first before making your own comments.

The Current State of Listening

Flores[6] believes that listening to a companion requires more than just hearing and understanding the words enunciated. It also requires determining what he or she just assumes and therefore leaves unsaid. Effective relationship listening also requires attentiveness to such other dimensions as: the expressive aspect; facial expressions; gestures; and tone of speech. The Native American koan of "if you want to understand my world walk in mile in my moccasins" describes the importance of putting yourself in your partner's shoes.

Without these skills, listening becomes just another matter of recording. It is not responsive, and listening in its strongest, best sense should always be guided by the endeavor of responding to the speaker. Listening is not about receiving information; rather, listening can best be described in relationships as the process of establishing rapport between the two of you.

When you as a couple speak, you are in fact creating an action. When you make a promise or an offer, you are actually acting. Thus, Flores asserts that "speaking is acting."[7]

The way we make assertions about domains of concern, including shared concerns that you as a couple may have, opens up or closes down future possibilities for action between you two. This is one kind of action, i.e., opening up or closing down possibilities for future action through the kinds of assertions being made in your relationship. In making requests and promises to each other, the very action of speaking itself has created a new situation (of commitment) between you and your partner

This new situation is a change to what the situation between you two was before the promise was made. Thus, making a promise is an action. The relationship between you, where one has just made a promise to another, is now different. The very act of verbalizing a promise changes the relationship. The speaking was an action that changes the circumstances. For example, there are now are expectations regarding the promise being fulfilled that now exist.

Assertions, requests, and promises are all examples of linguistic actions. The very act of verbalizing them changes your relationship. Listening is also action in that even if it's *inside one's head only* and not vocally; you are still linguistically making assessments and assertions.

Linguistic Games

Flores has adapted the work of Austrian philosopher Ludwig Wittgenstein by creating what he calls *linguistic games*. He defines those as a recurrently used structure which articulates conversational actions. It is a specific way for coordinating action . . . Linguistic games are stable aggregates of conversational actions that we use recurrently. They have become institutionalized structure of conversations, established ways for dealing recurrently with concerns . . . Many times even without being aware of it, we act in language following an already established and institutionalized way of doing so: we follow a social practice, or, as we say, participant in a linguistic game.[8]

Multi-cultural Implications

Flores cites what he calls the *universal mating dance* which paradoxically has very different rules and regulations to it depending on one's own particular culture. For example, he notes that "The way we organize the conversations in which a man and a woman are mutually seduced has been different at different times in history and is different in different societies today. When we perform the mating dance, however, we are normally performing through certain linguistic games."[9]

Not being aware of this phenomenon often leads to misunderstanding between couples who have been raised with different expectations in these basic courting rituals. What may be a normal action in one culture is considered an insult in another.

Five Rules of Linguistic Communication

Flores[10] asserts there are the five following rules to the game of linguistic communication.[11]

1. The point of the game—the purpose or payoff to use Adler's[12] term.
2. The existential rules—the entities for action and the kinds of activities that will be involved.
3. The rules for action—what couples must, can, and cannot do
4. The rules for strategy—the couples' historical past history or wisdom relative to the original point of the game.
5. The rules for settling disputes. Strategies for settling both expected and unexpected disagreements.

Completing Exchange Conversations

Flores further elaborates on the overall purpose of any communication action as being to *exchange conversations*. He writes that

We human beings are thrown to a future. That means, we cannot avoid having a future and caring about it. We call *having concerns* caring about the future. A concern always involves caring about the future. Even when we becoming concerned about a past event, we are making an assessment about how that even could affect our possibilities for the future. The way we take care of our concerns is by taking action. Our actions can make the future different; they can alter our possibilities ahead.[13]

Flores proposes that a primary purpose of a couple's communication is the *completion of exchange conversations* for resolving the concerns each person in a relationship has. To do this each person in the relationship must both exchange promises also to declare their satisfaction when the promises have been fulfilled. Each partner is then free to make, accept, or decline an agreement of exchange.

Four basic daily couple's communication exchanges—requesting, promising, asserting, and declaring—are the four basic ways in which couples go about these exchange conversations, to use Flores' term. The four communication acts are defined and illustrated below.

A Linguistic Model of Relationship Communication

Flores[14] adapted the work of British linguists Austin and Searle in espousing the following four basic communication activities or *speech acts* that couples use.

1. We *request* that our companion do certain things.
    "Please pick up the kids at school at 3 pm.
    "Please help me by drying the dishes.
2. We *promise* our spouse that we will do things or we refuse (promise *not)* to do them.
    "I'll meet you Friday for lunch."
    "I am not willing to pick up your laundry again this week."
3. We *assert* that certain things are either true or false.
    "There are five critical factors relative to our buying a new car."
    "It is not true that I am interested in being with anyone else beside you."
4. Couples use their authenticity to *declare* things to be valid or invalid for themselves and their partner.
    "I am very interested in going to visit your family on our vacation this
    "That purchase is not a financial option for us right now."

The four key communication questions from such a basic *requesting, promising, asserting and declaring* model for you to consider in your relationship can be summarized as consisting of:

1. Did one of us *request* or *demand* something of the other?
2. Did one of us *promise (or refuse)* something of the other?

3. What did either of us *assert* to be true or false?

4. Did either of us *declare* or *define* something (i.e. did we commit ourselves to a new direction, definition, attitude, purchase, or other situation involving our relationship together)

Conversations for Action

The following two figures provide a visual representation of the linguistic act of (a) making a *request* or of (b) making an *offer*.

Figure 1 illustrates a *request loop* while figure 2 illustrates a similar *offer loop*.

Figure 1, Request Loop

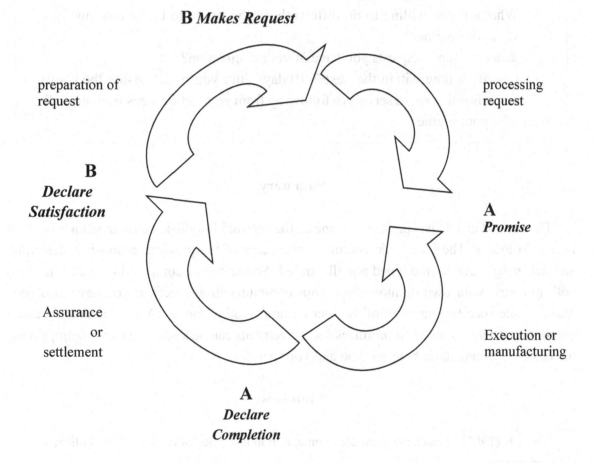

B *Makes Request*

preparation of request

processing request

B
Declare
Satisfaction

A
Promise

Assurance
or
settlement

Execution or
manufacturing

A
Declare
Completion

A = Performer
B = Partner

Adopted from Flores, F. unpublished manuscript presented in workshops by Business in Designs Associates, Inc., Emeryville, CA.

Activity 35: Examples of Your Own Four Communication Methods

Reply to the following items first on your own; then discuss your responses and hear his or hers to you.

1. What are some specific examples of each of these communication acts that have occurred in the past week or two in your relationship?
   requesting, promising, asserting
2. Identify a communication exchange that you felt went particularly well between the two of you.
3. Contrast that with a communication that did not go as well.
4. In your opinion, what are some of the factors which distinguish the successful vs. the challenging communication between you?
5. What are you willing to do differently in the future to better communicate with your partner?
6. What are some requests you have of your companion?
7. Identify a time within the next 7-10 days after you're discussing the above responses that could serve as a follow-up from your action steps from this talk with your partner.

Summary

The present article has presented some of the seminal linguistic communication work of Fernando Flores. The four basic communication acts of "requesting, promising, asserting, and declaring' have been defined and illustrated. You and your companion have been asked both to assess your own opinion about your communication together; you have also been asked to site specific examples of the four communication modes. An understanding and a commitment for making clear promises and agreements can be a positive factor in improving the basic communication between you and your partner.

Endnotes

[1] Flores, F. (1982) Management and communication in the office of the future, unpublished monograph.
[2] Flores, F. and Wenograd, L. (1987). Understanding Cognition. Reading, Ma. Addison Wesley.
[3] Flores, (1991) "Conversations for action". Business Design Associates, Emeryville, Ca.
[4] Flores, F. (1997). "The Impact of Information Technology on Business", Association for computing machinery, San Jose, California, March 4.

5   Solomon, R. and Flores, F. (2003). Building Trust in Relationships. New York: Oxford.

6   Flores, *loc. cit.* (1997).

7   Flores, *op. cit,* p. 5, (1991).

8   Flores, *op. cit.* p. 5-6 (1982).

9   Flores, *op. cit.* p. 6 (1997).

10 Flores, *loc. cit.* (1997).

11 Eckstein, D. (1994) "Games Married Couples Play: Two Theoretical Perspectives," *The Family Journal* April, Vol. 1, 2, #2, 173-176.

12 Adler, A. (1958). *What Life Should Mean to You.* (A. Porter, Ed). New York: Prestige. (Original work published 1931).

13 Flores, *op. cit.* p. 8 (1991).

14 Flores, *loc. cit.* (1982-1987)

Biographies

Sherri Bennett has her Master's in Counseling from University of Texas-Permian Basin, Odessa, Texas.

Torrey Byles is an economic anthropologist who, for 20 years, has helped shape the use of electronic commerce, messaging and transactional systems for business and organizational effectiveness. Currently residing in Ashland, Oregon, he is working on projects dealing with collective intelligence, social finance, and community economics.

Section 25:

A Couple's Advance Directives Interview using the Five Wishes Questionnaire

Daniel Eckstein and Bill Mullener

In a New York Times article entitled: "Why Do We Avoid Advance Directives?" Paula Span (2009) explores resistance from individuals and couples as they complete what is commonly known as living wills. She notes that a 2006 Pew Research Center study found that only 29 % of the people surveyed had a living will. The study indicated that public attitudes on these and many other end-of-life issues are unchanged from 1990, despite advances in lifesaving technology, the aging of the population, and the controversy associated with the Terri Schiavo case. Although most Americans believe it should be up to the individual to ultimately determine end-of-life decisions, rather than the government or medical professionals, like medical, too few actually make any provisions to make their own personal wishes known.

The Pew Research Center's survey also found that while overall attitudes are largely stable, people are increasingly thinking about and planning for their own medical treatment in the event of a terminal illness or incapacitating medical condition. Public awareness of living wills, already widespread in 1990, is now virtually universal. People reporting they have a living will has more than doubled from just 12% in 1990 to 29% today. 69% who are married say they have had a conversation with their husband or wife about their spouse's wishes for end-of-life medical care; only 51% reported doing so in 1990 (Bryant, 2009)

The purpose of this article to provide couples an opportunity to individually consider and then to interview each other regarding their personal wishes. The article will be organized as follows: there will a brief overview of some of the issues and organizations addressing advanced directives. A portion of the *Five Wishes* questionnaire will be presented to complete and discuss with each other. A sample case study will then be presented.

In a Harris Interactive study, Laura Byrne (2009) reported 55% Americans report having no will or medical directives. The study also indicated significant cultural differences. For example, only 33% of African Americans and 25% of Hispanics reported having any type of advance directives.

Advance directives are also known as living wills. These are formal legal documents specifically authorized by State laws that allow patients to continue their personal autonomy by providing instructions for care in case they become incapacitated and cannot make decisions. An advance directive may also be one form of a durable power of attorney in some states. Check with each legal mandates for state or country laws before assuming such documents will be recognized.

A durable power of attorney is also known as a health care proxy. This document allows the patient to designate a surrogate, a person who will make treatment decisions for the patient if the patient becomes too incapacitated to make such decisions. (Bryant, 2009)

The agency for Healthcare Research and Quality (AHRQ) has published a pamphlet citing research relative to patient wishes for care at the end of life (*Kass-Bartelmes & Hughes, 2009*). *They report* that many patients have not participated in effective advance care planning. Although The Patient Self-Determination Act guarantees patients the right to accept or refuse treatment and to complete advance medical directives, AHRQ research reveals that:

Less than 50 % of the severely or terminally ill patients studied had an advance directive in their medical record.

Only 12 % of patients with an advance directive had received input from their physician in its development.

Between 65 and 76 % of physicians whose patients had an advance directive were not aware that their patients had the directive.

Physicians were only about 65% accurate in predicting patient preferences and tended to make errors of under treatment, even after reviewing the patient's advance directive.

Aging with Dignity and *Five Wishes*

Aging with Dignity is a national non-profit organization with a mission to affirm and safeguard the human dignity of individuals as they age and to promote better care for those near the end of life. The work of Mother Teresa of Calcutta served as the inspirational foundation of Aging with Dignity.

Aging with Dignity founder Jim Towey served as Mother Teresa's friend and legal counsel for 12 years and was a full-time volunteer in her home for people with AIDS. It was her care and concern for all people's medical, emotional and spiritual needs which provided the inspiration in 1997 for *Five Wishes*. Called by some: "the living will with a heart and soul," *Five Wishes* today meets the legal requirements in 40 states . . . The document is available in 23 languages and in Braille. (Aging with Dignity, 2009).

Five Wishes Couple Interview

Here is a chance to personalize this for you as a couple. What follows is an interview you both are encouraged to complete with each other. If your partner is not available you can complete this on your own. Also consider writing your own answers in the *Five Wishes* format available from the web-page below. The *Five Wishes* document itself is both an advance directive and conversation starter/structure. http://www.agingwithdignity.org/ forms/5wishes.

pdf is the read only address. Check there for the complete document including additional written directives which are necessary to make the document legal in all but ten U.S. states. There is additional information on their web-site for complete directions.

The following interview has been summarized from the *Five Wishes* document by permission of the publisher. Each of you is invited to interview each other relative to personal preferences. If your partner is not willing or able to complete an interview, consider completing the document and letting your family, friends, spiritual mentor and/or your counselor. That is one concrete way of making your own personal wishes known to them.

Basic respect for your partner's wishes means you listen and respect his or her wishes rather than imposing your own beliefs and opinions. While it is important for the two of you to discuss each of your own preferences, existentially each of you has your own personal requests that are best respected in your partnership.

Activity 36: Five Wishes Questionnaire

Here are the five questions for the two of you to discuss:

1. **The person I choose** to make health care decisions when I can't make them for myself is:
   a.   First choice
   b.   second choice if the first is not available

The following two conditions must both be met for your designated health care agent (or comparable term in some states) to be legally recognized to make health care decisions on your behalf. The two conditions include:

   a.   Your attending or treating doctor finds you are no longer able to make your own health care decisions, AND
   b.   Another health care professional agrees such an assessment is true.

Here are some additional considerations relative to your choices:

While your spouse or other family member may be your first choice, they may be too emotionally involved to make the best choices on your care.

You may also want someone who is geographically close to your primary residence. While the *Five Wishes* form itself has specific directives for a designated health care agent, for your interview with each other, discuss if each of you would like such an individual to make such decisions as: medical care or services like tests, medicine, and/or surgery; admission to an assisted living facility or other residential care; any life saving or life-ending procedures; approve release of medical records; donate any organs or tissues as allowed by law; be allowed access to financial records; and/or to apply for any public or private insurance programs that might be available. Be sure this person first knows your wishes and also agrees to follow them. If you change your mind on your written form you can simply write "REVOKED."

2. **My wish for the kind of medical care I want or do not want is:**
   Here are some of the kinds of directives you want to let your designated health care agent know: what to do when you're in pain; issues of your doctors doing anything to facilitate your death; and food, drink and comfort issues should they be necessary.

   Discuss with your partner your desires relative to life-support issues, including such medical issues as: tube feeding, CPR, major surgery, blood transfusions, dialysis; antibiotics; and/or related medical interventions that might keep you alive.
   Discuss with your partner any spiritual, religious, and/or personal beliefs you have on this matter.
   You may wish to purchase a "do not resuscitate" bracelet if that is your wish.
   Some specific conditions for which you want to provide specific written instructions include issues when you are: close to death, in a coma and not expected to recover; permanent brain damage and not expected to recover; and any other condition under which you would not want to be kept alive.

3. **My wish for how comfortable I want to be is:**
   Discuss with your partner your wishes relative to your care including such issues as: when you are in pain, if you show signs of depression or nausea; any favorite music you would like played; religious readings or poems you would like read if you are near death; and any specific spiritual or religious persons you would like to be present with you if possible.

4. **My wish for how I wish people to treat me**
   Some examples include: you desire to have other people with you; having your hand held and talked to even when you do not appear to be conscious; having prayers and/or members of your faith with you; pictures of loved ones in your room; and dying at home if that is possible.

5. **My wish for what I want my loved ones to know is:**
   Some topics to discuss here would include: forgiveness from and to others; requesting your family to respect your wishes even if they don't agree with you; encouraging your family to seek counseling for grief; issues of burial or cremation; where you would like to be buried; who best knows your funeral wishes; any particular requests of a memorial service; and any other wishes you may have such as organ donation.

Your Own Summary

Write a summary paragraph or two relative to some of the key points of each of your interviews. Also consider going to where each of you will be able to complete the official form which is what will be recognized in many states.

Conclusion

The *Five Wishes* is one of the most widely used methods for communicating one's advanced directives. The purpose of the present article has been to encourage both individual consideration and then an interview between you and your partner regarding each of your advanced directives desires. You might want to discuss these issues with other family members, with trusted spiritual leaders, and/or with a counselor. It is important that you respect each other's wishes. It is also suggested that from time to time the five wishes be revisited and updated as appropriate.

Bibliography

"Aging with Dignity," (2009), retrieved from http://www.agingwithdignity.org/forms/5wishes.pdf, Nov.15

Bryne, L. (2009) *Strong Public Support for Right to Die,* http://people-press.org/report/ 266/strong-public-support-for-right-to-die, Nov. 2, 2009

Kass-Bartelmes, B.,& Hughes, R. (2009). Advance Care Planning Preferences for Care at the End of Life, Issue 12, retrieved from http://www.ahrq.gov/ research/ endliferia/endria.htm, Nov. 2, 2009

Span, Paula, (2009). *Why Do We Avoid Advance Directives?* The New York Times, Oct 27, 2009

Chapter VI:
Problem-Solving Strategies

Section 26:

Thirty-Three Suggestions for Relationship Renewal

Daniel Eckstein and John E. Jones

Conflict is an inevitable part of any marriage. Successful couples do not necessarily have fewer problems; rather, they have greater problem-solving strategies. The present article lists 33 strategies couples can use in the renewal of their relationships. Although these can be used with third-party counselors, they can also be done with only the two partners.

The major consideration in interpersonal conflict situations is, "How can we make a better deal with each other?" The primary purpose of negotiation is a new agreement between you. This goal may be markedly different in the beginning, however. Your initial motivation may be to punish each other or to defend yourself from being caught or accused. Many couples simply want to avoid the conflict altogether, because they view confrontation as a dirty word.

Conflict strongly tends to feed on itself when it is not confronted. Because the term confrontation is often controversial, a definition is in order. Confrontation requires you to pay attention to something that you think is important. It does not mean having a shoot-out or screaming at each other. It does not mean pinning the blame tail on the donkey. It does not mean all-out war. It does not mean making the other person lose face. It does not imply a hostile, unpleasant, recriminating, tension-producing experience. It can in fact be a healing, freeing-up exchange in which you both come to understand yourself and your partner better. You can then better agree on how to get along in the future. It can be a time of forgiveness—both of yourself and of your partner. It can release pent-up energy in order to make it available for accomplishing goals.

When (And When Not) to Intervene

Here is a checklist for deciding if it is timely to use some of the following 33 renewal strategies together.

1. *Readiness.* Are you capable of working through the situation effectively?
2. *Commitment.* Are you willing to do what it takes to improve the relationship?
3. *Influenceability.* Will you be open and responsive to each other's needs and points of view?
4. *Accessibility,* Can you make contact and commit to follow-up with each other?

Logistics for the Exchange

1. These interventions need to take place on neutral ground. Privacy, a lack of interruptions, and no turf dominance are clear requirements. Obviously, having children, friends, or others around will adversely affect the interaction.

2. The initial session should not last more than 90 minutes. This can be a pressure situation, and there is a need to limit the amount of time that the parties in the conflict will talk with each other. If possible, schedule several times together to explore different suggestions.

A Potpourri of Methods

What follows are 33 different ways to help prime the pump in assisting you to explore and improve your relationship.

1. *Fantasy*. Each of you tells the other what you imagine about the other.

2. *Force-field analysis*. Each of you makes a chart of the opposing forces in the situation, those pushing toward change and those resisting (saying, "No," saying, "Yes").[1]

3. *I assume that you know*. Each of you takes turns testing whether the other knows something that the speaker assumes that he or she knows.

4. *Instruments*. Each of you shares with the other scores on self-assessment instruments to build understanding (i.e., Couples Relationship Satisfaction Inventory [CRSI] or Styles of Conflict Resolution).[2] [3]

5. *I-you-we*. Each of you takes a turn making three statements: One begins with *I*, one with *you*, and one with *we*.

6. *Lists*. Each of you makes good news/bad news behavior lists for what you have seen of the other in the last X amount of time. Then take turns on the bad news lists, paraphrasing, until you achieve a sense of closure. You may cash in a chip off the good news list at any time.

7. *More/less/right amount*. Each of you makes the following requests: What I need more of from you, what I need less of from you, and what I am getting the right amount of from you.

8. *Nonverbal communication*. This may involve pushing/shoving, eye-contact encounter, sculpting a pose together, and so forth. The important aspect is the nonverbal nature of the activity.

9. *Fears, ogres*. Each of you shares your worst-case scenarios for the relationship if the conflict is not managed more effectively.

10. *Hopes, dreams*. Each of you shares your best-case scenarios, the dream-come-true, if your relationship went to a higher level of mutual enjoyment.

11. *Paraphrasing.* Each of you repeats in your own words what the other person is saying.

12. *Planned renegotiation.* Each of you agrees to talk at the earliest sign of difficulty, when you feel pinched (threatened) by the other.

13. *Predictions.* Each of you attempts to predict the other's response to this activity: "In the next few minutes, I would guess that you would . . ."

14. *Puzzlements.* Each of you makes the statement, "What puzzles me about you is . . ."

15. *Ratings.* Each of you rates the other on a 10-point scale for any mutually agreed on dimensions (i.e., trust, commitments, loyalty, etc.). Discuss your ratings and the reasons for your respective numbers.

16. *Reflection of feeling.* Each of you feeds back the emotion that the other is experiencing and/or expressing.

17. *Resentment/appreciation/request.* Each of you discusses what you resent about the other, explores the characteristic of the other that is simultaneously being admired, and then makes a request of the other.

18. *Role clarification.* Each of you identifies and discusses your marital expectations of the other.

19. *Role reversal.* Each of you plays the other for a few minutes as a form of feedback. Tell each other how well each of you did as the other partner.

20. *Secrets,* Each of you share data that could seriously jeopardize the relationship.

21. *Self-disclosure.* Each of you tells the other important facts about yourself. See if you can be creative and relate something to your partner that he or she may never have heard you say before.

22. *Solicitation.* Each of you attempts to enroll the other in some project, idea, or strategy.

23. *Tell me more.* Each of you interviews the other for a set period of time, repeatedly making the request, "Tell me more." Then, change roles of interviewer/sharer.

24. *Testing consensus.* Each of you summarizes next-step action planning, observing within the other nonverbal and verbal indicators of commitments to the solution.

25. *Think/feel.* Each of you takes an mm making statements that begin with, "Right now, I'm thinking . . ." and "Right now, I'm feeling . . ."

26. *Three bags full.* Each of you creates graded feedback lists: (a) What is easy for me to tell you about you, (b) what is uncomfortable for me to tell you about you, and (c) what I wish I didn't have to say to you about you.

27. *Three yeses.* Each of you interviews the other until each of you gets an answer of "yes" three times in a row.

28. *Time-out.* Either of you can suggest taking a break for things to cool off at any time.

29. *What/how questions.* Each of you interviews the other, using only questions that begin with what and how.

30. *The time I knew I was in love with you.* Each of you relates to the other again, although you may have said it countless times, the moment/event that convinced you of love for each other. See if you can recall something different or relate it somewhat differently than before.

31. *Metaphor exchange.* Create a metaphor for each other as well as the for relationship. For example, "Our relationship is like a comfortable set of slippers,"

32. *Early recollections.* Each of you shares two or three formative early memories from your childhood. Together, discuss how the memories may be played out or reenacted in the marriage now.

33. *Share peak experiences and times alone and/or together when magic happened.*

A Tribute to John Jones, by Daniel Eckstein

My first mentoring experience with John was as an intern in the year long Laboratory Education Intern Program (LEIP) sponsored by University Associates. As part of that training I attended an organization development workshop. Here is the critical incident involving John as the workshop dean.

I was in a sub-group, and we were to create a pictorial representation of our ideal organization. Our group created what in retrospect I can only describe as quite a "funky" way out there design just perfect for Southern California in the 70s. When each of the other sub-groups came by to visit our creation, John asked us to tell the group about it. We had undulating lines if there is actually such a word. How can one truly explain in limited words such a masterful creative product?

Well, I was doing my best, but not too well I must admit. John interrupted my comments with a "don't pay any attention to Dan,—he's just a horse's ass anyway." I bit my tongue and we went on to another group's explanation. The workshop itself was designed so there was actually an OD consulting team chosen by us to oversee the workshop process, and there was a format so that if we had an issue we could call an evening meeting to address it. I put my name on the list to process the above mentioned incident.

That night at dinner some of the other workshop participants asked me if I had my last will and testament in order. John Jones was a very big man in every sense of the word. One does not mess with Texas or with John Jones.

After dinner our whole workshop community squeezed into a meeting room set up for what was planned to be only six or seven stragglers to view such encounters. All

50 participants were there. With our OD consulting group sitting like the jurists in a trial, I was invited to make an opening statement.

"It felt bad being called a horse's ass," I somewhat meekly said to John. "Oh, that was just some misguided humor," he replied. "That's it then—game over" I said At least I thought it was over. John rose from the chair where he was seated. He walked across the room in my direction. "Hail Mary full of grace," I believe I uttered to myself . . . and I'm not even Catholic.

John was now standing directly in front of me. "I'm a goner" I thought. Instead John reached out his hand to me and said: "Dan, it took a big man to put your name on that list; it took a bigger man to step away from your hurt and anger in an instant." That's Big John for you. During the next decade I became a senior consultant with his co-founded consulting group. We later did workshops and wrote some things together. For one of his last workshops, he came from San Diego to Phoenix to present, as my guest.

I miss you John; you taught me so much about workshops, about writing, and even more about living in joy. Thanks for so many precious memories.

Drs. Daniel Eckstein, Phyliss Cooke, and John Jones

Endnotes

1   Eckstein, D. (1994). Force-field analysis as an aid in decision making by couples. *The Family Journal, 2,* 371-372.

2   Eckstein, D., & Cohen, L. (1998). The Couple's Relationship Satisfaction Inventory (CRSI): 21 Points to Help Enhance and Build a Winning Relationship. *The Family Journal, 6,*155-158.

[3] Eckstein, D. (1998). Styles of conflict resolution. *The Family Journal. 6(3)*, 240-243.

Biography

John E. Jones, Ph.D. was a past president of Organizational Universe Systems. He was best known for his work on experience-based training and the *University Associates Annual Handbook* series book series. He was also a former high school teacher and guidance counselor. He taught in counselor education at the University of Iowa for 8 years and consulted for more than 30 years in school systems in the United States and Canada. Dr. Jones published a wide array of materials that are used by staff-development professionals throughout public schools and higher education.

Section 27:

Into The Woods: Introducing the Couple's Metaphoric Interview Matrices

Sarah Eckstein, Jennifer Straub, Nicole Russo, and Daniel Eckstein

A human's ability to speak is one of the defining characteristics of our species. We are able to communicate our needs, tell witty jokes, comfort each other in times of hardship, and to compile words in such a beautiful manner that just listening brings tears to your eyes. Beyond mere words, however, lie metaphors. One's ability to empathize with Romeo as he finds his poisoned loved one is enhanced exponentially due to the images that arise from his graceful use of wordplay in the following passage from Shakespeare:

> Death, that hath suck'd the honey of thy breath,
> Hath had no power yet upon thy beauty:
> Thou art not conquer'd; beauty's ensign yet
> Is crimson in thy lips and in thy cheeks,
> And death's pale flag is not advance`d there.
> (*Romeo and Juliet*, Act 5, Scene 3)

The potential for genuine expression of one's inner experience can be enhanced through the use of complex message expression in metaphorical manners. As Romeo demonstrated above, this can be used for the excitement of poignant emotions in a theatrical production, but also, this can be practiced by couples in everyday life as they use metaphors to enhance mutual understanding.

Our article begins with an introduction to the use of metaphors in interpersonal relationships, followed by its inspiration, Steven Sondheim's Broadway musical *Into the Woods* (1987). Six specific types of metaphors will then be identified. Hopefully you as a couple may gain knowledge regarding creative value of metaphors. You will also be offered an opportunity to complete an inventory of your own personal arsenal of metaphors that you have compiled throughout your interpersonal relationships in life.

Literature Review of Couples' Use of Metaphors

Relationship metaphors are often used within the media and are usually remembered long after watching the movie. They work as visual synopses because they are remembered for their story content and emotional influence (Sijill, 2011). Two noteworthy examples for the coauthors include the following two classic films *Annie Hall* (1977) and *When Harry Met Sally . . .* (1989), in which relationship metaphors are used.

In the Woody Allen movie, *Annie Hall* exemplifies metaphors within an interpersonal relationship. The movie involves Alvy Singer and Annie Hall. In the course of the film, they both fall in love but later leave one another. Alvy Singer describes their relationship as "A relationship, I think, is like a shark. You know? It has to constantly move forward or it dies. And I think what we got on our hands is a dead shark." (*Annie Hall*, 1977). The metaphor of a dead shark is a striking way to describe the end of a relationship. A similar way of viewing the end of a relationship could also be expressed as: "by the end of our 'discussion,' she was Muhammad Ali moving off the ropes and I was George Foreman in the eighth round—all the punches thrown and about to receive a knockout blow" (Richardson, 2009).

In the movie *When Harry Met Sally . . .*, two young intellectuals meet when sharing a car ride from the University of Chicago to New York City after graduation. Five years later, they meet again on a plane flight. Both times, they discuss why men and women cannot be friends and, upon the arrival of their destination, they go their separate ways. Eventually, they meet again and decide they are, in fact, friends. They eventually fall in love and marry. This is the scene when Harry realizes he loves Sally (Ephron & Reiner, 1989):

Harry: I've been doing a lot of thinking, and the thing is, I love you.
Sally: What?
Harry: I love you.
Sally: How do you expect me to respond to this?
Harry: How about, you love me too.
Sally: How about, I'm leaving.

Many of us can identify with this situation—being taken by surprise by what our partner is feeling or saying. There are often different perspectives of how each partner views the nature of the relationship. As the examples from *Annie Hall* and *When Harry Met Sally . . .* demonstrate, a metaphor is a figure of speech implying one idea is comparable to another (Nystul, 2006). Metaphors occur within our daily conversations particularly when expressing emotions (Kopp & Eckstein, 2004). "We are at the crossroads," "I cannot live without her," and "We were made for each other" are three metaphors that are often used by individuals to describe their romantic relationship. They express something that is difficult or impossible to literally describe. In general, they serve to enumerate problems and in turn make them controllable. A great deal of information and emotion is communicated with the use of one word or a phrase.

According to Eckstein and Sarnoff (2007), relationships can be described by using the following four metaphors: the As and Hs of Relationships; Relationship as a Three-legged Sack Race; Walls and Windows; and Cracking the Shell. The As and Hs of Relationships refer simply to the construct of the letters. The A indicates that one partner is relying heavily on the other. Eventually the lines collapse due to the continuous pressure, which results in the termination of the relationship. The H indicates two strong independent partners that have a linking equal strength connection.

The three-legged sack race illustrates a couple's type of attachment style. Does each partner have one leg in and one leg out indicating a mutually supported/depended relationship or are all four legs out indicating disengagement? The inside two legs in the sack and the outside two legs that are separate are a suggested ideal balance of consecutiveness and independence.

Walls and windows mean just that—a joint wall is formed against the problem by you and your partner and the window provides the opening to reestablish the trust between the two of you. Putting a wall between you and another relationship and/or between you and an addiction are two examples.

Cracking the shell refers to carrying baggage from past relationships into your present relationship. Men might become defensive by not allowing true intimacy into their hearts. Over generalizing from a past relationship to a present one has often been characterized with the single metaphoric image of baggage.

Within the context of a relationship, metaphors are often used to describe love, a problem, or to clarify our roles within the relationship. Using a metaphor to describe love can be done in several ways: as a journey, a physical force, a nutrient, unity, as heat, as a sport, and as a disease (Baxter, 2003). Our basic understanding of each partner's role within the relationship originates from our worldviews—how we see and understand the world around us.

The factors that influence our worldview are often family, culture, and society. We first learn how to view and understand our environment from our parents who teach us the social norms and behaviors that are accepted or not accepted by our society. These behaviors can be associated into metaphors pertaining to our adult relationships, such as "men are the breadwinners" and "women are the caretakers." As we grow older, our values and beliefs are impacted by our society, especially during the teenage years, and follow us into adulthood. Within all of our relationships, we attempt to define and clarify our roles. Role clarification involves each of us identifying our expectations associated with our partner, such as the traditional view of the husband being the monetary provider or the wife being the caretaker of the children.

In a recent couples counseling session, coauthor Daniel Eckstein confronted a man who had decided it was his job description to solve his wife's stated comment that "I'm not happy here on Saba." His role perception was that when she stated a problem, it was his job to fix it. The wife smiled and admitted that she was in fact "a bit of a princess and that she also felt it was 'his job' to fix her problems." Her stated problem had magically been shifted onto him. Both of them, during their more than 40 years of marriage, had mutually accepted this as how each of them behaved in the relationship. A metaphoric image was also used to make the teaching point. If one comes along and sees a baby chicken struggling to open the egg in which it is encased and decides to help the chick by opening the egg for it, that animal will in fact die because the pectoral muscles necessary were not developed. So, too, psychological muscles are not developed when one partner does for the other what he or she can and needs to do for optimal self-worth.

Understanding and using metaphors within your relationship can assist you in building your concept of your marriage, working through marital problems and exploring central themes within the relationship (Withrow, n.d). Metaphors have the potential solutions to your problems (Kopp, 1995). Metaphors can assist you as a couple in understanding the impact, which your relationship problems have on your marriage and family. They can assist you in changing your unhealthy interaction to a healthier one. Linking a metaphor to the problem within your relationship such as "it's a two way street" can assist you in understanding and processing your relational and family dynamics. These factors include the individual freedom and belonging, self and system, vulnerability and self-protection, harmony and discord, and the influence of their family of origin (Withrow, n.d.). Addressing these areas within your relationship can assist you in building a solid foundation and connection with your partner.

Into the Woods

Steven Sondheim and cowriter Jack Lapine's Tony Award winning 1987 Broadway musical *Into the Woods*, brilliantly takes the audience through a metaphoric journey. The musical production uses familiar Brothers Grimm fairy tales to parallel life's quests, wishes, and challenges of finding happiness, love, and coping with fear and the unknowns—the woods of life (Humphrys, n.d.). The musical production is divided by the unfolding of the story lines that take place stage left, stage right, and center stage. Metaphorically, for the purposes of this article, the opening scene represents the relationship between couples. Each of you has your own personal story from your family of origin.

A narrator begins the first scene of Act I by outlining the characters' stories and their quests and wishes. The first half of the play figuratively represents stage left and stage right where each individual story is told. The childless Baker and his wife, who are the catalysts of the story, want to reverse the curse placed upon them so that they can have a child (Abernathy, 2004). Cinderella is introduced as a fair maiden who wishes to go to the ball (Humphrys, n.d.). Jack, from Jack in the Beanstalk, is introduced as a sad young lad who wishes his cow would produce milk. Little Red Riding Hood makes a trip to visit her sick grandmother and survives a wolf attack (Humphrys, n.d.). A witch who stole Rapunzel from the Baker's parents a long time ago escapes from being trapped in the cottage next door to the Baker's house. The witch told the Baker and his wife that if they bring four ingredients to her, she would make a potion to undo the spell. The four ingredients are (a) a cow as white as milk, (b) a cape as red as blood, (c) hair as yellow as corn, and (d) a slipper as pure as gold (Flatow, n.d.). These ingredients signify your needs and wants of finding a partner, developing a relationship, and sharing your life. Each character enters the woods to begin his or her journey in pursuit of finding happiness with a partner.

Center stage represents where two individuals meet to share his or her fairy tale or family-of-origin story. The humor of the production and the symbolic hell that breaks loose occurs when each fairy tale character crosses over into the story line of the other characters in the woods at center stage. Through the turbulent transition between Act I and Act II, the characters become inter—twined and each story becomes blended as part of this exploration.

A similar blending process occurs for many couples. The path into the woods is filled with twists and turns, illustrating the relationship dilemmas that each character had to face to fulfill his or her wishes (Flatow, n.d.). Through the relational expedition, couples begin a crossing-over process marked by discovery and collaboration (Baxter, 2003). The dating process is a type of convergence that occurs in the woods where you enter the world of your partner and where your partner enters your world. You and your partner begin to explore each other's stories as they were prior to meeting. The characters in your life such as family members, cousins, friends, and in-laws become part of the overall blending process.

The seemingly living happily ever after is interrupted during Act II when each character encounters a new relationship crisis. Couples encounter on-going moments, challenges, and situations that require adjustment to maintain a healthy balanced working relationship. Change and discovery occur along the relational trip at times in which detours or alternative paths must be flexibly taken (Baxter, 2003). The process of joining your partner at center stage represents the grand finale where the characters have created their united story.

The audience is encouraged to appreciate that there are three parts in a relationship, "you, me, and it" (Baxter, 2003) or acts at stage left, stage right, and center stage. These acts reflect your relational choices embedded in a rotating interconnected wheel of your metaphoric self-image in your relationship, your image of others, and approach to life. Not only does each of you walk from one part of life's stage into the other story line of your partner's but also, ideally, the two of you combine your stories into a united grand finale.

We now invite you to commence your journey into the woods. Prior to completing your own matrix, please reference the graphic demonstration of the six-specific categories of metaphors as suggested by Kopp and Eckstein (2004). As you review the categories, begin to think about your own metaphoric images (e.g., self-image, relational images, and life situation images).

Six Categories of Metaphors

There are six specific types of metaphors that are grouped into the following categories: (a) metaphors representing one's understanding of one's own self-image without the context of their relationship; (b) one's image of self within the context of their relationships; (c) one's understanding of self and situations; (d) one's image of others; (e) one's image of life situations; and (f) one's understanding of self and their interactions with others (Kopp & Eckstein, 2004). In order to clarify how to use the matrix, there is an introduction to each of the six categories of metaphors which you yourself will be creating in your own matrix:

Category 1: My self-image, regardless of relationship context *I see myself as* . . . Possible examples for a Category 1 metaphor could be:

> I see myself as a chess piece trying to figure out my next move. I see myself as a ball waiting for someone to catch me.
>
> I see myself as a rock that is strong and independent.
>
> I see myself as a hammer and keep beating myself up.
>
> I see myself as an endless mirror with so many roles to fulfill. I see myself as a sand dollar with hidden treasures.
>
> I see myself as a seed starving for water, light, and fertilization.
>
> "I see myself as the world's most dangerous predator. Everything about me invites you in. My voice, my face, even my smell. As if I would need any of that. As if you could outrun me. As if you could fight me off" (Edward Cullen, Twilight).

Category 2: My self-image within the context of our relationship *I am like a* . . . Possible examples for a Category 2 metaphor could be:

> I am like a Facebook member, signing in and out whenever it is convenient for me and sometimes making private information too public.
>
> I am like grass that insists on growing through the tiny cracks allowed by hard cement even though growing in the lawn with all the other grass would be much less challenging.

Category 3: My self-image regarding a problem in our relationship *With respect to ___ I see myself as* . . . The following excerpt from *When Harry Met Sally* personifies the third type of metaphor:

> Harry Burns: There are two kinds of women: high maintenance and low maintenance.
>
> Sally Albright: Which one am I?
>
> Harry Burns: You're the worst kind; you're high maintenance but you think you're low maintenance.
>
> Sally Albright: I don't see that.
>
> Harry Burns: You don't see that? Waiter, I'll begin with a house salad, but I don't want the regular dressing. I'll have the balsamic vinegar and oil, but on the side. And then the salmon with the mustard sauce, but I want the mustard sauce on the side. "On the side" is a very big thing for you.
>
> Sally Albright: Well, I just want it the way I want it.
>
> Harry Burns: I know; high maintenance. (Ephron & Reiner, *When Harry Met Sally . . .*)

This demonstrates how your self-view can differ greatly from how your partner views you and consequentially, misunderstandings can occur. In this case, Sally Albright's metaphor could possibly say "With respect to my level of high or low maintenance I see myself as a sure-footed mountain goat expertly choosing which rocks to spring from and which rocks to dismiss on my bounding journey through the hills." If Harry were to create a Category 3 metaphor for Sally he might quite divergently state that "With respect to her level of high or low maintenance I see Sally as a member of a jury, always needing mountains of evidence to inform her judgment about things being completely right or wrong." In completing the forthcoming matrix, notice how your point of view might differ from those of other significant people in your life. Have these differences in perspective ever caused suffering in your relationships?

Category 4. My image of this person *My parent/role model/partner is like* . . . Possible examples for a Category 4 metaphor could be:

> My partner is like an express train that blows by many stops. My partner is like a green giant always there looking over and protecting me.
>
> My mother is like a momma bear.
>
> My grandfather is like a wise old owl that provides that is full of insight and wisdom.

Category 5. My image of a general life situation (work, injury, retirement) impacting our relationship. *With respect to our life situation is like* . . . Possible examples for a Category 5 metaphor could be:

> With respect to motherhood, it's like a roller coaster with thrilling and scary ups, down, twists, and turns.
>
> With respect to work, it's like a ladder because I'm climbing to the top.
>
> With respect to true love, it is like a good pair of socks, it takes two, and they've gotta match (Richardson, 2009).
>
> With respect to family dinners, they are like landscapes a thousand acres per human heart; they erode but endure all weathers (Richardson, 2009).
>
> With respect to relationships, don't smother each other and let the sunlight in.
>
> With respect to illness, it's like a wave, you just have to ride it out.

Category 6: My image of our relationship *I consider our relationship to be like* . . . Possible examples for a Category 6 metaphor could be:

> I consider it to be like a machine that needs routine maintenance (Baxter, 2003).
>
> I consider it to be like a computer that needs periodic upgrades.
>
> I consider it to be like a taming a lion where I am trying to constantly control others around me.
>
> I consider it to be like a symphony where each instrument is vital to create the harmony.
>
> I consider it to be like a war where you win and lose battles. I consider it to be like an adventure with each new trip is an opportunity to discover new feelings and experiences.
>
> I consider it to be like the four seasons where each transition requires change to adjust to the weather.

The six types of relationship metaphors can be presented visually in the following chart, *Six Slices of a Metaphor Relationship Pie*, created by coauthor Nicole Russo (Figure 1).

Six Slices of a Relationship Metaphoric Pie

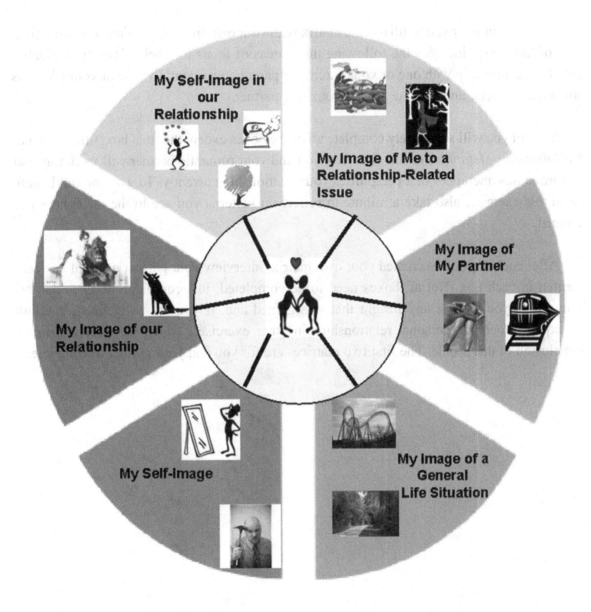

Adopted from Richard Kopp and Daniel Eckstein,
Using early memory metaphors and client-generated metaphors in Adlerian therapy.
Journal of Individual Psychology, 60(2), 163-174

Activity 37:

Instructions for Completing the Couple's Metaphor
Interview Matrix (CMIM)

Now it is time for you to fill out the matrix with your own life information. The horizontal axis of the matrix includes the following three areas of focus for each of you individually: (a) your relationship with one of your parents or parent equivalent; (b) one of your previous romantic partners; and (c) your current romantic partner.

Each of you will **separately** complete all of the boxes except the final box, titled *Couples Collaborative Metaphor*. In this final box you and your romantic partner will work together to form a new metaphor that personifies your relationship currently. To gain the full benefit from this exercise, also take a minute to reflect on patterns you see in the metaphors you created.

After each of you has created your own matrix, interview your partner on what has been written in each box. Not all boxes need to be completed, just complete the ones that are relevant to you. Notice any insight that was gained and, if you are so inclined, continue to explore your interpersonal relationships in other exercises, which we reference in the conclusion of this article. The first two matrices are for you and your partner to complete.

Couple Metaphor Interview Matrix (CMIM), Partner A

My personal self-image in life, regardless of our relationship:
I see myself as . . .

	My mom, dad, or parental figure	One of my previous romantic partners	Our current relationship
My self-image within the context of our relationship: **I am like a . . .**			
My self-image regarding a problem in our relationship: **With respect to ____ I see myself as . . .**			
My image of this person: **My parent/role model/ partner is like . . .**			
My image of a general life situation (work, injury, retirement) impacting our relationship: **With respect to _____ our life situation is like . . .**			
My image of our relationship: **I consider our relationship to be like . . .**			

Couples Collaborated Metaphor:
Our relationship is like . . .

Couple Metaphor Interview Matrix (CMIM), Partner B

My personal self-image in life, regardless of our relationship: **I see myself as . . .**			

	My mom, dad, or parental figure	**One of my previous romantic partners**	**My current romantic partner**
My self-image within the context of our relationship: **I am like a . . .**			
My self-image regarding a problem in our relationship: **With respect to ____ I see myself as . . .**			
My image of this person: **My parent/role model/ partner is like . . .**			
My image of a general life situation (work, injury, retirement) impacting our relationship: **With respect to _____ our life situation is like . . .**			
My image of our relationship: **I consider our relationship to be like . . .**			

Couples Collaborated Metaphor: **Our relationship is like . . .**			

Conclusion

Now that you and your partner have woven the metaphorical tapestry together, take a moment to reflect on patterns you noticed, emotions which were aroused, and thoughts that passed through your mind during this activity. Did you and your partner match with your metaphors of one another? Were there any surprises? What did you learn from this exercise?

Couples who completed this matrix report that they achieved greater awareness of their priorities in terms of what they value in a partner. They became more grateful for the positivity they re-experienced through this creative outlet, and more appreciative that they are no longer in a relationship with a previous partner who treated them more like target practice and less like a precious jewel. Some participants noticed trends in how easily they feel extreme emotions for others such as love and hate. The implications of these trends can therapeutically guide relationship goals for our future.

Not only was this activity designed to stimulate your ideas regarding your past relationships, it was also aimed at guiding you and your partner in a creative collaborative process. What were you and your partner's reactions to creating the final new metaphor together? What facilitates team work? We hope that through this process you will have gained insight into your relational patterns and have further expanded upon your ability to work together with others.

If you are interested in completing other insight-driven activities such as this, here are five additional "for couples" *Family Journal* columns focusing on personal and partner role perceptions: Kirk, Eckstein, Serres, and Helms (2007); Eckstein, Clement, and Fierro (2006); Eckstein and Morrison (2000); Eckstein and Axford (2000); and Eckstein, Levanthal, Bentley, and Kelley (2000).

We hope that through the work you have completed in this process, you have been able to genuinely access your emotions and cognitions regarding some of the significant relationships you have experienced in your life so far. As you continue to walk through the metaphorical woods of life, we encourage you to remember the lessons imparted upon you by the characters of Steven Sondheim's musical: Relationships include compromise, adaptability, patience, and of course love.

Summary

The purpose of this article has been to introduce six specific ways that your relationship can be expressed in metaphoric form. The authors have created the CMIM as a visual way of briefly describing each of your own metaphors. An integrative activity of creating a new metaphoric way of describing your current partnership concludes the activity.

References

Abernathy, J. (2004). Into the woods. Retrieved from http:// www.sondheim.com/ works/ into_the_woods/

Baxter, L. A. (2003). Relationship metaphors. Retrieved from http:// culturopoiesis.blogspot. com /2007/06/relationship-metaphors-by-leslie-baxter.html

Eckstein, D., & Axford, D. (2000). Loving and being loved: Commitment implications. The Family Journal: Counseling and Therapy for Couples and Families, 7, 185-186.

Eckstein, D., Clement, F., & Fierro, A. (2006). The role of image exchange with couples. The Family Journal: Counseling and Therapy for Couples and Families, 14, 71-76.

Eckstein, D., Levanthal, M., Bentley, S., & Kelley, S. (2000).

Relationships as a three-legged sack race. Family Journal: Counseling and Therapy for Couples and Families, 7, 399-405.

Eckstein, D., & Morrison, J. (2000). Exploring different 'expressions' of love. The Family Journal: Counseling and Therapy for Couples and Families, 7, 75-76.

Eckstein, D., & Sarnoff, D. (2007). Four Adlerian metaphors applied to couples counseling. Journal of Individual Psychology, 63, 322-338.

Ephron, N. (Producer). & Reiner, R. (Director). (1989). When Harry met Sally. [Motion Picture]. United States: MGM.

Flatow, S. (n.d.). Synopsis: Into the woods. Retrieved from http:// musicals.net/cgi-bin/ synopsis?sn=41&show=Into the Woods

Godfrey, W. (Producer) & Hardwicke, C. (Director). (2008). Twilight. [Motion picture]. United States: Summit Entertainment.

Humphrys, C. (n.d.). Into the woods. Retrieved from http://www.into-the-woods.co.uk /about_ch.htm

Joffe, C. H., Rollins, J., (Producer), & Allen, W. (Director). (1977). Annie Hall [Motion Picture]. United States: MGM.

Kirk, A., Eckstein, D., Serres, S., & Helms (2007). A dozen relationship commitment considerations. Family Journal: Counseling and Therapy for Couples and Families, 15, 3, 271-276.

Kopp, R., & Eckstien, D. (2004). Using early memory metaphors and client-generated metaphors in Adlerian therapy. Journal of Individual Psychology, 60, 163-174.

Kopp, R. R. (1995). Metaphor therapy: Using client-generated metaphors in psychotherapy. New York, NY: Brunner/Mazel.

Nystul, M. S. (2006). Introduction to counseling: An art and science perspective (3rd ed.). Boston, MA: Pearson.

Richardson, D. (2009). Be a genius with metaphors, thousands of witty metaphors, analogies and smiles. Retrieved from http://www.metaphorsandsimiles.com/relationships/metaphors-analogies-similes.

Shakespeare, W. (2011). Shakespeare navigators. Retrieved from http://www.shakespeare-navigators.com/romeo/T53.html

Sijill, J. (2011). Cinematic storytelling: Using dynamic metaphors in your screenplay. Retrieved from http://www.movieoutline.com/ articles/cinematic-storytelling-using-dynamic-metaphors-in-your-screenplay.html.

Withrow, R. L. (n.d.). The use of metaphor in counseling couples. Article 25. Retrieved from http://www.counseling.org/Resources/ Library/VISTAS/vistas05/Vistas05.art25.pdf

Xamual.com (2009, October 27). 10 metaphors for love. Retrieved from http://www.xamuel.com/10-metaphors-for-love/

Biographies

Nicole Russo recently graduated with her Master's degree in Mental Health Counseling from Capella University. She served as a student ambassador and hosted a twittering event discussing single parenthood and higher education. She has co-authored two articles in The Family Journal: Counseling & Therapy for Couples and families. Ms. Russo volunteers as a psychosocial counselor and volunteers with various organizations in the community. She worked as a case manager serving dual diagnosed homeless individuals and veterans.

Jennifer Straub, MS received her CACREP-Accredited Master of Science Degree in Mental Health Counseling from Capella University in Minneapolis, Minnesota in 2011. She will be eligible for licensure in Pennsylvania as a LPC upon completion of clinical supervision. She is currently a protective services worker at the Northumberland County Area Agency on Aging in Pennsylvania. Her professional work history includes working with a diverse population that includes children, adults and senior citizens in a variety of settings. She has co-authored two journal articles in The Family Journal: Counseling & Therapy for Couples and Families.

Section 28:

Walls and Windows:
Closing and Opening Behaviors for Couples and Families

Daniel Eckstein

This was inspired when the author read an article by a couple therapist named Sylvia Shellenberger & Sandra Hoffman.[1] They described this useful suggestion as being originally suggested by Glass & Wright.[2]

Here is a synopsis of the case described. A minister and his wife sought couple's counseling. In the early sessions the wife accused the husband of having an affair with the church secretary, something he vehemently denied. One day however, the phone rang at their home—the husband answered it. A few minutes later the wife intended to make a call. Innocently she picked up the receiver in another room. She overheard her husband and the secretary discussing their relationship. This confirmed her suspicions about the affair that she had all along.

Confronted in therapy with the truth the husband tearfully acknowledged the lie he had been living. To her credit the woman rather than just leaving the home immediately or having him leave, committed to a problem-solving strategy with the couple's counselor.

Over several sessions they worked on repairing their torn relationship. They both decided that they would stay together and that his relationship with the church secretary would end.

It is at this part the counselor suggested the *walls and windows* intervention. The wall being created was between the couple themselves and the church secretary. To demonstrate their commitment and alignment on the issue they decided to as a couple meet with the secretary to show their resolve in erecting a wall between them and the woman. That concretely translated to the woman leaving her position—it also included the couple going together to the Board of Deacons and acknowledging the affair and in asking and receiving their forgiveness.

The windows aspect of the intervention involved the gradual opening and the re-establishment of the shattered trust that had occurred between them. "Opening windows" became a metaphor of the re-opening of their hearts to one another during subsequent counseling sessions with the therapist.

Your Personal Application

Now you are invited to apply the concept to your marital and/or family relationship. This process is best done individually and then shared and discussed with your partner and/or family.

1. Begin by taking an *intrapersonal*, within yourself ("you to you"); approach—for example, what has been you successful previous history on the concept of *walls*

(boundaries) that you have set between you and someone or something (i.e.—addictive behavior).

   a.   Cite examples of when and how you *successfully* created a needed *wall*.

   b.   Cite examples of walls that needed to be set that weren't. What were the challenges and resistances that interfered?

2. Now focus on your past personal interpersonal history between you and your partner and/or family.

   a.   Cite examples of when and how you *successfully* created a needed *wall*.

   b.   Cite examples of walls that needed to be set that weren't. What were the challenges and resistances that interfered?

3. Lastly consider your *present* relationship now.

   a.   Cite examples of when and how you *successfully* created a needed *wall*.

   b.   Cite examples of "walls that needed to be set that weren't. What were the challenges and resistances that interfered?

4. Discuss how walls and windows can be applied to you now.

5. Develop an action plan, a series of beginning, intermediate, and long-range strategies to utilize the concept of walls (closing) and of windows (openings) to your relationship.

Endnotes

[1] Shellenberger. S., & Hoffman, S. "Creating a Safe Emotional Environment in Systematic Couples Therapy." Sarasota, FL: Innovations In Clinical Practice 17, pp. 65-84.

[2] Glass, S.R., & Wright, T. C. "Reconstructing marriages after the trauma of infidelity." In Clinical Handbook of Marriage & Couple Intervention. London: John Wiley & Sons. (1997): 471-507.

Section 29:

The Angry, The Angier and The Angriest Relationships

Robert Willhite and Daniel Eckstein

Introduction

This article focuses on anger in relationships. It begins with a series of incomplete sentences for you as a couple (and/or family) to complete individually and then with each other. Two additional anger inventories created by R. Willhite will follow. A third section will explore a brief overview of the theory of the emotion of anger in our closest interpersonal relationships. You as a couple and/or family will then be invited to apply the principles to your system. Because of the high correlation of anger and violent behavior and other hurtful interpersonal relationship consequences, you may also want to discuss your responses with a marriage and family counselor.

The Anger Inventories—*Incomplete Sentences*

Begin this exercise by completing your responses to the following incomplete sentences. Your responses and those of your partner and/or other family members are best shared with each other and/or later with a family counselor if appropriate.

Activity 38: The Anger Worksheet

1. When I was younger, anger meant....
2. I know my parents were fighting when....
3. When I got angry....
4. My parents' messages about my anger were....
5. When my mother was angry, she....
6. When my father was angry, he....
7. When my mother was angry, I felt...
8. When my father was angry, I felt...
9. When I was angry, I felt....
10. How did you assume your current mate or significant other would act if angry?
11. Did you get fooled? How?
12. Was there a family member who known as the "angry member"?
13. How did your brothers and sisters express anger?

---

14. When you were a child and you disappointed your parents (or equivalent), how did they respond?
15. When you were a child and you argued with your parents (or equivalent), how did they respond?
16. When you were a child and you went against their advice, how did they respond?
17. Were there healthy correction, empathy, love, encouragement and support from your (step) parents (or equivalent)?

The open-ended statements allow further focus on revelations made when completing The Anger Scale. The questions require individuals not only to identify their angry behavior and that of their family but also to formulate opinions about that behavior.

Activity 39: The Aggression Barometer

The inventory's 10 questions probe the perceptions of explosive, intimidating, abuse anger. It can help pinpoint three or four trouble spots—those areas in which anger is especially problematic.

Rate both yourself (m=me) as well as your perception of your partner (p=partner). If you are doing this as a family, put the first letter of each member of the family in the place you feel is best represented in the following table. Your choices are **not a problem**, **a rare occurrence**, or **a real problem**.

My temper flashes readily.   I got angry and "lost it."
My anger scares others.   My anger controls others.
Criticism infuriates me.   I intimidate with my anger.
When I am under the influence my anger is out of control.
I am physically abuse when I get angry.
Legal authorities have been called when I get angry.
When angered, I am verbally abusive.

The Anger Expression Inventory (The Anger Scale)

Using *The Anger Expression Inventory*, you should first evaluate parents' (or primary caregivers') anger reactions, and then compare those reactions with your own. This helps you understand the role of modeling relative to your own and your partners (plus family members, if appropriate) characteristic methods of coping with anger. Since modeling and imitation are core ways of learning, here is an activity for exploring your family-of-origin anger issues.

Activity 40: The Anger Expression Inventory

Father, Step-father or Equivalent	*Mother, Step-mother, or Equivalent*
Physical Violence	Throw Things
Raise Fists	Threaten Verbally
Explore	Yell
Throw Tantrum	Argue
Make Cutting, Sarcastic Remarks	Get Drunk
Name Call	Bitch
Stay Angry for Days	Have Hurt Feelings
Lecture	Cry
Walk Out	Have a Cold Attitude
Be Sullen	Be Sulky
Diversion	Projection
Withdrawal	Repression

Anger Theory

Here are some quotes about anger.[1]

"People who fly into a rage always make a bad landing."

Will Rogers

"Anger is a weed; hate is the tree."

Saint Augustine

"Anger makes a rich man hated and a poor man scorned."

Thomas Fuller

"It is easy to fly into a passion-anybody can do that-but to be angry with the right person to the right extent and at the right time and with the right object and in the right way—that is not easy, and it is not everyone who can do it."

Aristotle, 4th century B.C.

"Nothing on earth consumes a man more quickly than the passion of resentment."

Nietzsche, Ecce Homo, 1888

"Your temper is like a fire. It gets very destructive when it gets out of control."

Author unknown

Defining Anger

In the *Family Game of Anger* Willhite and Cole[2] note the word *anger* comes from the a Middle English work meaning *grief*. It also derives from Latin and Greek words meaning *to choke off or to strangle*. Rather than deal appropriately with our angry feelings, we often choke them off or stuff them.

Willhite & Cole identify the following essential features of anger.

1. Anger is (almost) universal.
    Everyone gets angry; at least, everyone who's normal.
2. Anger is an appropriate emotion.
    There's nothing wrong with angry feelings. It's how we display those feelings and deal with them that often becomes a problem.
3. According to Gestalt theory, anger is a reaction to unfulfilled expectations. Anger says, "I want." According to Adlerian theory, the intensity of the anger depends upon what the anger person wants—and how badly. Adler said that, "In every individual we see that feelings have grown and developed in a direction and to a level that were essential to the attainment of her personal goal."[3] Adler also observed that "Anger . . . is the veritable epitome of the striving for power and dominance."[4]
4. Anger does not exist in an emotional vacuum.
    Behind the anger is another emotion such as hurt, sadness, or disappointment.
    Anger is almost always accompanied by another feeling or feelings, which we disguise.
5. Anger is expressed in many ways for many purposes.
    Anger feels different to you than it feels to someone else.

    We don't lose our anger; rather we choose to throw it away in a purposeful manner.

    Keene creates a personification of anger by speaking of it in the first person by saying:

    Anger, keep you safe by keeping your full strength available to you in a situation of danger . . . I defend the boundaries . . . you need to survive. I keep one person from being swallowed up by another and thus preserve the duality, which is necessary for love. If you doubt that I am the companion of love, remember the ecstasy of the reconciliation that comes after fighting. If you can't fight, you can't love.[5]

Keene's description helps reveal that anger serves many functions, positive as well as negative. Whether the outcome of anger is good or bad depends on whether or not it is expressed in responsible words and actions.

Powell believes hiding our anger is dishonest. "We . . . defend our dishonesty on the grounds that (telling the truth) might hurt others; and having rationalized our phoniness into nobility, we settle for superficial relationships." [6] So the attempt to hide our anger affects us even more powerfully than the anger itself.

6. Anger responses are learned.

Anger may be a primary emotion, but the way we handle it is modeled on someone else's behavior.

Willhite and Cole observe, "Anger is an emotion expressed in behavior that means 'I won't accept that.' My anger says more about me, therefore, than it says about you. It can be functional only when I take responsibility for it."[7]

Such a definition holds us responsible and accountable for our behavior. But too often, we prefer to blame others for our anger. So often we hear, "See what you made me do?" "You make me so angry" or "You know I get mad when you—." In these situations we blame our anger on someone or something else rather than admitting that we created our own anger.

7. Anger responses can be altered.

We may not believe it at first, but we can change the way we respond to our anger.

For example, Albert Ellis[8] notes this example . . . you are standing on a street corner when someone bumps you from behind. Angrily you turn around to confront your perceived attacker. It is only then that you notice the person who bumped you is blind. Ellis then asks, "What happed to your anger then? Did the person 'make' you made?" He contends it was not the person but your perception in which you chose and optimistically can 'un-chose' anger based on a reappraisal of the situation.

The Rule of Behavior Change

If one party is required to change more than the other, something Willhite and Cole[9] call "The Rule of Behavior Change" goes into effect. This means if one person changes significantly in a relationship, the other person has to do something changeable to accommodate the new behavior. Three adjustment options are available:

1. The partner adapts to the new behavior by creating new behaviors;
2. The partner tries to bankrupt his or her mate back into the old behavior; not because the behavior is functional, but because it's familiar and the dynamics are understood; or,
3. The partner gets out.

Anger, Fear, Hurt, Frustration

The following figure indicates the pathological progression of rage.

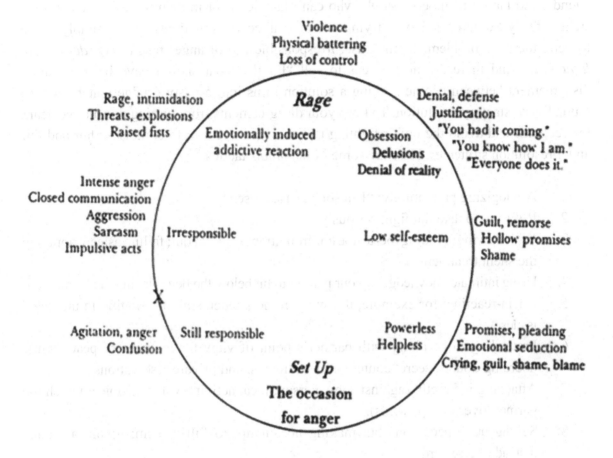

In Willhite & Cole, p. 35. Used by permission.

Misusing Power and Control

Alfred Adler suggested the purposive-ness nature of anger and of all emotions. He observed that children of deaf parents who wanted to demonstrate their anger did not yell or scream; rather the gestures of anger in front of the parent(s). Power and control (Adler called tears *water power*) are frequent payoffs for anger. Some of the negative impacts in relationships include: using intimidation; using coercion and threats; using physical violence; using emotional abuse; minimizing, denying and blaming; using isolation; sexual abuse; and gender-based assumptions.

In contrast if mutual respect and dignity are values and behaviors of the couple or family, the above list will be characterized by: non-threatening behavior; negotiation and fairness; nonviolence; showing respect; honesty and accountability; trust and support; sexual respect; and gender-neutral assumptions.

Anger and Responsible Behavior

Because there are no actual written rules to govern the private contests between lovers, friends, and family members, people who can't handle anger in themselves or others often fight unfairly. Sometimes they're trying to win at all costs; sometimes they're simply trying to deny there's a problem. In any case, irresponsible use of anger results in a *destructive fight style*. And there are no referees to call "Foul!" What should have been a mature disagreement between people seeking a solution turns into a nasty grudge match with no mutually satisfactory resolution. To keep your disagreements from turning destructive, learn to recognize and avoid the unfair fighting tactics. It is important to contrast unfair and fair anger resolution strategies. Here are some of the *unfair* tactics.

1. Apologizing prematurely: "I'm sorry; case closed."
2. Refusing to take the fight seriously.
3. Withdrawing; evading toe-to-toe confrontation; walkout out; falling asleep; applying the silent treatment.
4. Using intimate knowledge of your partner to hit below the belt; playing the Humiliator.
5. Chain-reacting; for example, throwing in the kitchen sink or bringing in unrelated issues.
6. Pretending to go along with partner's point of view for momentary peace while hoarding doubts, secret contempt, resentments, and private reservations.
7. Attaching indirectly (against some person, idea, activity, value or object which the partner loves or represents).
8. Setting up expectations but making no attempt to fulfill them; giving a rebuke instead of a reward.
9. Offering character analysis—explaining the other person's feelings.
10. Playing the "gimme" game—demanding more; nothing is ever enough.
11. Withholding—affection, approval, recognition, material things, privileges, anything that would give pleasure to, or make life easier for, the partner.
12. Undermining—deliberately arousing or intensifying emotional insecurity, anxiety or depression, keeping the partner on edge, threatening disaster.
13. Being a Benedict Arnold—not only failing to defend the partner, but encouraging attacks from outsiders.

Adapted from E. L. Shostrom, and D. Montgomery[10]

Contrast the above list with the more *fair* anger resolution tactics such as:

1. When you feel angry, say so. You're entitled to get angry. Learn to speak up.

2. Fighting between loved ones is natural. Don't be ashamed of fighting with your mate, children, or friends.

3. Do not run away from the angry feelings of your partner, child, or friend. They are entitle to their feelings. Respect their anger and do not smile or laugh at them.

4. Keep listening. Use active listening techniques: paraphrase what the other person says, check to be certain you understand what he or she is thinking and feeling.

5. Be sure you're fighting for a legitimate issue or position. Attach the problem, not the person.

6. Avoid putting down your partner. The resulting resentment makes his or her more defensive and harder to reach.

7. Learn to recognize when you or your partner is merely letting off steam. Don't create fights when your partner is letting off steam. It's not meant for you.

8. Don't collect injuries, injustices, or grievances.

9. Don't hit below the belt or throw back information given in trust. Don't bring up pass mistakes.

10. Don't handicap your fighting form. Don't try to solve problems when you've been drinking or are feeling tired, sleepy, hungry, or unstable.

11. Resolve to be mature enough to admit you're wrong, even though it's painful and embarrassing. It is necessary for personal growth.

Dealing with Anger

According to Jones & Banet[11] anger is the first emotion human beings experience and the last one we learn to manage effectively. As early as four months of age, the human infant's vague feelings of distress differentiate into recognizable anger; for many of us, a lifetime is spent in denying, suppressing, displacing, or avoiding this troublesome emotional experience. Because anger usually occurs within an interpersonal context, it is a frequent challenge for couples and families.

They note that "Anger happens when we perceive an external event (object or person) as threatening or when we experience the frustration of unmet expectations. Although anger seems to be a response to something outside of us, it most often is an intrapersonal event: we make ourselves angry. But because anger is so unpleasant and human being are so adept at projection, we usually attempt to locate the source of our anger outside ourselves with statements such as 'You make me angry,' 'You have irritating habits,' 'You bother me.'"[12] Jones and Banet created the following developmental cycle: threat, assumptions, power assessment, anger.

Anger and Threat

The cycle begins with some perceived threat. "When we perceive an external event as threatening to our physical or psychological well-being, a cycle of internal movements is initiated. As the perception is formed, assumptions are made internally about the possible danger of the threat. The assumption is then checked against our perceived power of dealing with the threat. If we conclude that the threat is not very great or that we are powerful enough to confront it successfully, a calm unflustered response can occur. But if we conclude that the threat is dangerous or that we are powerless to handle it, anger emerges in an effort to destroy or reduce the person threat and to protect our assumed impotency."[13]

Resentment and Expectations

From a Gestalt theoretical perspective, anger is resentment, an experience accompanying a demand or expectation that has not been made explicit. Unanswered demands or unmet expectations are frustrating; they become another kind of threat, which trips off the anger cycle within us.

Maladaptive Expressions of Anger

A frequent way of expressing anger is to turn it inward, against ourselves as guilt and guild frequently produces feelings of depression, incompetence, helplessness, and ultimately, self-destruction.

Expression of anger can lead to violence; turning it inward produces depression. Displacement is ultimately ineffective and can damage innocent third parties. Repeated failure to close the anger cycle can produce a hostile, cynical, negative view of reality. And even though anger usually occurs in an interpersonal context, it is not an interpersonal event, but self-generated. We make ourselves angry, and there is no one else who can honestly be blamed. Suffering the anger often seems to be only alternative. [14]

Displacement is another way of coping with anger. The boss yells at you at work; you yell at your spouse. He or she criticizes the kids; they kick the dog.

Dealing with Personal Anger

Here are five specific suggestions from Jones and Banet for dealing with your anger toward your spouse and/or other family members.

1. *Owning anger.* Acknowledging anger and claiming it as our own behavior is a helpful first step. It increases self-awareness and prevents unwarranted blaming of others. Turning blame and attribution into "I" statements locates the anger where it actually is—inside us. This procedure can help develop a sense of personal power.

2. *Calibrating the response.* Anger is not an all-or-nothing experience. It ranges from relatively mild reactions such as "I disagree," "I don't like that," and "I'm irritated," to intense reactions such as "I'm furious," "I'm enraged," and "I feel like hitting you." Learning to differentiate between levels of anger helps us to assess accurately our capacity for dealing with it.

3. *Diagnosing the threat.* As yourself "What is frightening about the perceived threat? What do I stand to lose?" Anger often happens because we quickly assume that the situation is dangerous—so quickly that we frequently do not why the stimulus is threatening. Diagnosing the threat frequently reveals that it is simply a difference in values or opinion.

4. *Sharing the perceived threat* is a way to make the internal anger cycle a public or interpersonal event. It diffuses the intensity of feeling and clarifies our perceptions. It permits us to receive feedback and consensual validation. It empower you by paradoxically being willing to be vulnerable.

5. *Forgiveness* involves letting go of the anger and canceling the charges against the other—and ourselves. Forgiving and forgetting cleans the slate and is a way of opening yourself to future transactions Forgiveness is a magnanimous gesture that increases personal power. In the Bible Peter asked Christ how many times he should forgive "Seven time seventy" was the reply to indicate how important forgiveness is.

Dealing with Another's Anger

Remember the idea that while anger often appears to be interpersonal, one literally creates anger from the "inside out." So, while family members who are mad at you often make you the target and blame you for their anger, it is important to place the "ownership" of the anger on the sender. That is not to deny that your behavior is not to be explored; rather, the authors are simply encouraging an "intrapersonal—I make myself angry" vs. an interpersonal "you make me angry" approach. Here are some specific recommendations that Jones and Banet[15] offer for anger directed *toward you.*

1. *Affirm the other's feelings.* To *affirm* another's anger is to acknowledge that you are receiving it and to express a willingness to respond. To *disallow* another's anger usually heightens its intensity.

2. *Acknowledge your own defensiveness.* Let the other person know what you are feeling. Acknowledge that your own tenseness may lead to miscommunication and distortion. Develop an awareness of the impact of received anger on your body.

3. *Clarify and diagnose.* Give and request specific feedback. Distinguish between wants and needs. Check expectations. Discover together who own what in the situation. What interpersonal needs and wants are out on the table, the resolution of anger becomes more probable.

4. *Renegotiate the relationship.* Plan together how similar situations will be dealt with in the future. Contracting to practice new behavior may help eliminate the sources of friction. Acknowledge regret and exchange apologies if that is warranted. Agree on a third-party mediator or counselor to help if possible.

Anger Resolution Strategies

Utilizing responsible fight rules may not be all you need to keep cool in a confrontation. For instance, you still need to control your feelings so they don't get control of you instead. Talk to yourself about your feelings. Identify what they are—or what you'd like them to be—with statements like these: "I do feel furious" or "I can feel at ease." If you monitor your feelings this way, you're less likely to get carried away by them. You can further curb your anger by making practical suggestions to yourself by *affirmations*. These statements *affirm* your ability to handle the confrontation and yourself effectively. Willhite has listed some examples below along with the *stages of provocation* during which they are appropriate. He contends that provocation process through four stages. The first stage of provocation is *preparation* (you know something upsetting is about to happen). The second is *confrontation* (it happens). The third is *coping* (you deal with your reactions to what's happening). The fourth is *self-reward* (you reward yourself for staying cool). Here are the stages and some affirmations to make in each of them.

Preparation

1. What is it I have to do?
2. I can work out a plan to handle this problem.
3. I can manage this situation. I know how to regulate my temper.
4. If I find myself getting upset, I'll know what to do.
5. Time to take a deep breath. I will feel comfortable, relaxes, and at ease.
6. This might be a test situation, but I believe in myself.

Confrontation

1. Stay calm, just continue to relax.
2. As long as I keep my cool, I'm in control here.
3. Don't get all bent out of shape, just think of what needs to be done.
4. I don't need to prove myself.

5. There's no point in getting made.
6. I'm not going to let this person get to me.
7. I won't assume the worst or jump to conclusions. I'll look for the positives.
8. It's really too bad this person is acting this way.
9. A person who is this irritable must be awfully unhappy.
10. If I start to get mad, I'll just be banging my head against the wall. I might as well relax.
11. There's no need to doubt myself. What someone else says doesn't matter.

Coping

1. My muscles are starting to feel tight. Time to relax and slow things down.
2. Getting upset won't help.
3. It's just not worth getting so angry.
4. I'll let the other person act like a fool.
5. It's reasonable to get annoyed, but I'll keep the lid on.
6. Time to take a deep breath
7. My anger is a signal for what I need to do. Time to talk to myself.
8. I'll try a cooperative approach. Maybe we're both right.
9. He'd probably like me to get really angry. Well, I'm going to disappoint him.
10. I can't expect people to act the way I want them to.
11. The only actions I control are my own.

Self-Reward

1. It worked.
2. That wasn't as hard as I thought.
3. I could have gotten a lot more upset than I did.
4. I didn't let my ego get the better of me.
5. I'm doing better at this all the time.
6. I actually got through that without getting angry.
7. Overreacting isn't necessary

Seven Steps to Responsible Anger Behavior

Anger is a powerful force. Ungoverned, it can destroy relationships and even lives. It is also unavoidable. All of us get angry; our family members, friends, and intimate partners get angry with us. We cannot avoid anger. But we can avoid acting irresponsibly when we're angry or when others are angry with us. This great and inevitable human force is ours to control. Willhite proposes the following seven steps to responsible anger are a summary of my beliefs:

1. Sometimes (perhaps more often than we care to recognize), becoming angry is a result of doubting ourselves or feeling threatened by another person. It's always important to remember you're a worthy individual endowed with many good qualities.

2. Getting angry may result from overreacting to a particular situation. Sometimes we take things personally without cause. However, even when someone is directly offensive toward us, we can control and contain our anger by recognizing the other person's provocation. In reacting to insults, we become distracted and caught up in unnecessary combat. By focusing on issues and working on self-control, we can avoid being bailed into a quarrel.

3. We often get angry because it's the one thing we've always done in a certain kind of circumstance. As we learn alternative ways of reacting to annoying situations, we are less inclined to react with anger.

4. Controlling anger requires an ability to recognize the signs of anger arousal. As we become more and more sharply attuned to internal signs of tension and upset, we achieve greater ability to short-circuit the anger process. By learning to relax more easily and effectively, we can improve our skill in regulating anger.

5. We can use anger to our advantage. It can be useful in alerting us to upset and to the need for implementing effective action.

6. Anger is often a control issue. If things are getting out of hand or not going our way, we want to seize control. Recognizing and managing our anger is a powerful position. One way to take charge of a situation is to remain calm when the other party would expect or want us to be upset.

7. Sometimes we're angry because we've spent more time being problem-conscious than accomplishment-conscious. We often forget or dismiss the good things we \ do but don't allow ourselves mistakes and failings.

Next Steps

Using the information gained by sharing your personal responses to the inventories, reading the theory, plus any other resources you have relative to an understanding about anger, you are now invited to create an individual and/or joint "anger resolution" game plan—that may include individual/couple/family counseling.

a. My personal game plan _____

b. What I *wish* my partner/family members would do _____

c. What we agree to do as a couple or family _____

Endnotes

[1] McLellan, V. (2006). The complete book of wacky wit. Carol Spring, Ill.: Tyndale House.

[2] Willhite, R.G., & Cole, M.L. (1993) *The Family Game of Anger.* Mountain Home, AR: Keyes Publishing.

[3] Adler, A. (1957) *Understanding Human Behavior.* Pg. 43. Fausett, Premier.

[4] Adler, Pg. 210, *Loc.cit.*

[5] Keene, S. (1979) *To A Dancing God.* New York: Harper & Row.

[6] Powell, J. (1969). *Why am I afraid to tell you who I am?* Pg. 88. San Mateo, IL: Argus Communications

[7] Willhite, & Cole, Pg 6, *loc. cit.*

[8] Ellis, A. (1970) "Humanism, Values, Rationality." *Journal of Individual Psychology,26,* 37-38.

[9] Willhite & Cole, *loc. cit.*

[10] Shostrom, E.L., & Montgomery, D. (1990) *The Manipulators.* Abringdon.

[11] Jones, J., & Banet, A. (1976) "Dealing with Anger" *The Annual Handbook for Group Facilitators.* San Diego: University Associates.

[12] Jones & Banet, Pg. 111, *loc cit.*

[13] Jones & Banet, Pg. 111, *loc cit.*

[14] Jones & Banet, Pg. 112, *loc cit.*

[15] Jones & Banet, *loc cit.*

Biography

Robert Willhite, Ph.D., is currently retired and on the faculty of the Adler Graduate School of Minnesota in Hopkins. For the past 35 years he has been active in the application of Adlerian theory and practice in the form of teaching and private practice on the local and national level. He has written three books focusing on early recollection analysis, dream analysis, and the family game of anger.

Section 30:

Four Couples' Sleep Satisfaction Interviews: Recommendations for Improving your nights together and Eleven Suggested Couples' Activities for Relieving Sleep-Related Challenges

Miller "Rocky" Garrison and Daniel Eckstein

Introduction: How Big is the Problem?

Sleeping with someone may be more intimate than having sex with him or her. When sleep is disrupted, there are often dire consequences for our daytime functioning, mood, memory, relational abilities, and our intimate functioning. After 17 to 19 hours without sleep, performance by sleep-deprived individuals on some tests of cognitive and motor abilities was more impaired than in individuals with a blood alcohol concentration of 0.05%.[1] The purpose of this article is to introduce different types of insomnia and sleep-related breathing disorders. Methods for detecting and treating them within the couple relationship will also be presented.

The article will be organized as follows: following a brief introduction, you the couple will be invited to explore your own past sleep history. You will then interview each other. That will be following by additional information and some specific suggestions for your consideration. You as a couple will be asked to discuss answers to some questions based on the material as a closing activity.

Research Studies Relative to both Sleep and Sleep Deprivation

Because humans spend one third of their lives sleeping, the impact of sleep disruption, both personally and on relationships, is significant. A March 16, 2008, broadcast on the CBS television program *60 minutes* entitled "The Science of Sleep"[2] presented some important research regarding the vital role sleep plays in all animals. Mathew Walker, director of the Sleep and Neuroimaging Lab at the University of California, Berkeley, notes that many research studies conducted with rats dating back to the 1980s found that when they were kept awake indefinitely, they in fact started dying. Adequate sleep for humans is being shown as an important contributor to learning and memory. Adequate sleep can actually enhance memory retention, for example.

Conversely, lack of sleep has been shown to impair your ability to think fast. Driving drowsy is one of the riskiest of all behaviors related to sleep disturbances. "Micro-sleep," the term for the split second lapses, is all that is necessary to drive off the road. And investigations into such recent disasters as the Exxon Valdez oil spill, Chernobyl, the Three Mile Island disaster and the 2003 Staten Island ferry crash all involved human error correlated with sleep deprivation.

Additional research reported in the *60 minutes* program found similar neurological brain functions characterized as a "hyperactive brain response," in which the amygdala in the brain that signals danger and the frontal lobe controlling rational thought and decision-making, to be similar in sleep deprived individuals as is found in individuals having psychiatric disorders. A related study by Van Cauter,[3] at the University of Chicago School of Medicine, found a pre-diabetic state which could lead to type-two diabetes in people getting only 4-6 hours of sleep a night, after just six nights. Leptin in their brains also registered they were hungry even when the individuals thought they had recently eaten. Researchers hypothesized this could, in fact, be a new contributing factor to the rise in obesity. Additional health problems normally associated with the aging process are also being linked to lack of sleep, notes David Dinges of the University of Pennsylvania.

Activity 41: Sleep Satisfaction Life-line Interview

Directions:

In the following activity each of you is invited to individually create your own profile. You will then interview each other regarding each of your responses.

Begin by each of you taking a piece of paper and drawing a horizontal line across the center of the page. Make hash marks depicting your birth on the left margin and your current age on the right margin. You can lump several years together if you prefer. The horizontal line represents the 50% level of your overall satisfaction with your sleeping history at various times in your life.

Now graph your highs and lows at various times of your life. You can draw a symbol or write one or two words to illustrate the reason for your "'Dow-Jones' Sleep average" across your life span.

Below your drawing, respond to the following instructions:

1. As a child, what do you remember relative to the issue of sleep regarding your parent(s) or primary care giver?
   a. For example, if both parents (or step-parent(s) were present, did they sleep together in the same bed?
   b. What do you remember them telling you and what do you remember of your own experience relative to their sleeping experiences?
   c. If you had a single parent for a period of time, where there others who slept in your house? How was that for you?
   d. If you were in an institution such as foster care or an orphanage, where did the adults sleep? How was that for you?

2. On a scale of 1-10, one being low and ten being high, rate your own level of satisfaction early sleep related experience from ages 1-3. If you have no memory this far back what were you told about your early years of sleeping? Write a sentence or two explaining your numerical rating.

3. Do the same processes for ages 4-7—relate any re-occurring dreams and/or nightmares for each age group also?

4. Rate sleeps satisfaction for ages 8-10—are sure and explain your rating.

5. Do the same thing for ages 9-12; and then every five years up to your present age.

6. With respect to your first nine years of life, respond to the following questions:

7. a. Did you sleep in a bed alone some or all of those years? How was that for you? For example, was your bed comfortable? Was your environment quite or noisy? Did you feel safe?

   b. Did you sleep with others in the same bed part or all of the time? If so, how was that for you?

   c. Since much childhood abuse takes place at night in beds, contemplate any childhood abuse you either witnessed to others and/or to yourself.

   d. What decisions and/or overall impressions do you remember making as a young child up to about age seven relative to sleep?

8. In reviewing ages 10-12, how would you characterize this time in your life? Did you have slumber parties or sleepovers at others' homes? If so, how was that for you?

9. List significant sleep related experiences for when you were 13-20.

10. Do the same thing for young adult years (21-30); middle adulthood (30-40) and for each subsequent decade up to your present life as appropriate.

11. Throughout your entire life up until your present partner, note your experiences of sleeping with others.

12. Write 2-3 sentences summarizing your overall level of satisfaction sleeping with your present partner.

13. Each of you now interviews each other on your respective sleep related histories.

14. Now take some time alone to reflect on your own sleep story—what are some of the major themes that emerged?

15. What are some of the highlights of your partners sleep related experiences?

16. Together the two of you summary the current implications for your relationship right now based on your respective sleep histories.

One nationwide survey of sleep habits[4] found that on most nights, 61% of the respondents reported sleeping with a significant other, 31% reported sleeping alone, 12% reported sleeping

THE COUPLE'S MATCH BOOK

most nights with their pet, and 5% reported sleeping with their child(ren). When asked if their own or their partner's sleep disorders have caused significant or moderate problems in their relationship, 8% agreed. When asked if being too sleepy has affected their intimate relationships, 19% said yes.

Respondents were statistically divided into groups based on their answers to a wide range of questions about their sleep habits. There were five groups identified by this process. That included two good sleeper groups (*healthy, Lively Larks* and *sleep savvy seniors*) comprising 48% of the sample and three poor sleeper groups (*dragging duos, sleepless and missin the kissin,* and *over-worked, over-weight, and over caffeinated*) making up the remaining 52% of the sample.

The *dragging duos* segment made up 20% of the respondents. These people generally worked long hours (55% reported working over 40 hours per week, compared to 42% of the rest of the sample), got less sleep than they needed to function at their best (41% compared to 23%), and reported that their partners had at least one symptom of insomnia (92% compared to 76%). Fifteen percent of respondents were *sleepless and missin the kissin.* The people in this segment were more likely to be women (74% compared to 51% overall), more likely to have a medical condition (84% compared to 61%), and often experienced depression and/ or anxiety. These people said that either their own or their partner's sleep disorder caused significant or moderate problems with their relationship (25% compared to 8%) and/or that being too sleepy had affected their intimate relationships (42% compared to 19%).

Of those respondents who were married or living with someone, 77% reported that their partner experienced at least one symptom of a sleep problem or disorder in the past year.[5] Snoring was the most common complaint (67%), followed by frequent body movements or twitches (34%) and pauses in breathing (19%). A similar number of these married or cohabiting respondents (76%) reported that their partner had at least one symptom of insomnia within the past year. Awakening feeling still sleepy was the most common (56%), followed by awakening too early with difficulty getting back to sleep (46%), waking during the night (38%), and difficulty falling asleep (37%). Nineteen percent of these respondents reported that their intimate relationship was affected because of being too sleepy, and 33% reported that either their own or their partner's sleep disorders caused problems with the relationship.[6]

Activity 42:

Discuss with your partner which relationship metaphors best describe each of you:

1. healthy, lively larks
2. sleep savvy seniors
3. dragging duos
4. sleepless and missin' the kissin'
5. over-worked, over-weight and over caffeinated

The Stages of Sleep

Although the average sleep duration for adults is between seven and nine hours per night, there are some short sleepers who only need four or five hours of sleep a night and some long sleepers requiring nine or ten hours to feel rested through the day. When the electrical activity of the brain is measured during sleep, stages of sleep are identified. Stage one is a drowsy, relaxed state between waking and sleeping. After a few minutes, stage two emerges—it is when we actually turn of" to our surroundings. This stage of sleep typically lasts between 30 and 45 minutes in the first sleep cycle of the night. Stages three and four are collectively called slow wave or NREM sleep. Breathing, heart rate, and blood pressure are all at their lowest level and very slow brain wave patterns, named delta waves, are evident. These stages last about 45 minutes in the first sleep cycle of the night.

The first sleep cycle is followed by a few minutes in stage two before moving to rapid eye movement (REM) sleep. REM sleep is associated with dreams; the brain is as active as it is when awake, and the body is active. During a sound night's sleep, a person progresses from stage one to stage four and then REM sleep in about 90 minutes. A good sleeper will move through four to six of these 90-minute cycles during the night, spending about 5% of the night in stage one, 50% in stage two, 20 % in slow wave sleep, and 25 % in REM sleep.[7]

Sleep Regulation

Sleep changes every night. The following two interacting regulatory processes have been identified in determining timing of sleep and waking, those being the *circadian process* and the *homeostatic process*.[8]

The Circadian Process

Research has identified several biological and behavioral functions that vary on a *circadian* (meaning about a day) cycle.[9] These include our body temperature, heart rate, muscle strength, a variety of hormonal secretions, and our daily alternation in sleeping and wakefulness. If there are no external timing cues, our clock creates a rhythm that varies slightly from 24 hours.[10] Body temperature is lowest in the early morning and begins to increase just before sunrise. It continues to climb until mid-afternoon, when there is a short decrease before rising again until about 6:00 pm, the daily peak. Each person has a circadian clock for activity level, alertness, and sleepiness.

Since some partners are morning people and others are night people, each reaches optimum levels of functioning at different times of the day. Changes in temperature and wakefulness occur regardless of how well each slept the night before. Even when there has been sleep deprivation, a person will feel variations in energy level and alertness according to the circadian cycle. One of the most concrete challenges of having different time clocks relates to when each person would be most receptive to intimacies. One of the challenges for many is that when one is "coming down" there other is just "getting up" relative to the specific issue of sexual arousal.

Most people have experienced drastic changes in their circadian clocks by traveling across several time zones. The strongest environmental signal for setting the circadian clock is light. Here are two web sites featuring a test so each of you can find out more about your personal circadian rhythm: The first is the circadian rhythm test which can be taken for no cost at: http://www.apollolight.com/ apps/circ_assess_survey.html.[11] The second is the daily rhythm test, which is also free at: http://www.bbc.co.uk/science/humanbody/sleep/crt/.[12]

Circadian Clocks

Discuss with your partner your circadian clocks. What is your preferred sleep schedule? Your partner's? Are you larks or owls? Have there been challenges in each of your desires for sexual intimacy? How easy is it for you to adapt to jet lag? Do you like to sleep warm or cold, with the window open or shut?

The Homeostatic Process

Sleep loss can result in a greater tendency for each of you sleeping more; such sleep also lasts longer following a period of sleep deprivation. Recovery sleep is deeper and more restorative than normal sleep.[13] It is called deeper because your vigilance levels are higher, there is more confusion upon awakening, and there are other variations in the non-REM portions of sleep. It is called more restorative because the lost sleep is not recovered minute for minute during recovery sleep. No ratio of lost sleep to recovery sleep required has been identified. Getting less sleep than you need creates progressive increases in sleep debt until the debt is eventually paid off.

Sleep Disorders: What Can Go Wrong?

The American Academy of Sleep Medicine[14] describes all currently recognized sleep and arousal disorders using the most current and sound scientific information. This list of sleep disorders is divided into the following eight categories:

1. Insomnias (difficulty initiating sleep, maintaining sleep, or waking up too early, or sleep that is chronically non-restorative or poor in quality)
2. Sleep-related breathing disorders (disordered breathing during sleep)
3. Hypersomnias of central origin not due to a circadian rhythm sleep disorder, sleep-related breathing disorder, or other cause of disturbed nocturnal sleep (inability to stay awake and alert during the major waking episodes of the day)

4. Circadian rhythm sleep disorders (alterations or misalignment between the timing of an individual's daily rhythm of sleep propensity and the 24 hour social and physical environments)

5. Parasomnias (undesirable physical events or experiences that occur during entry into sleep, within sleep, or during arousals from sleep)

6. Sleep related movement disorders (relatively simple and usually stereotyped movements that disturb sleep)

7. Isolated symptoms, apparently normal variants, and unresolved issues

8. Other sleep disorders

This article focuses on the first two categories, because they are the most common sleep disorders and are most likely to be present in your relationship.

Insomnia

This category of sleep disorder is the one most couples encounter. Difficulties getting to sleep, staying asleep, awakening too early and/or awakening still sleepy are clearly disturbances of sleep. Insomnia can impact a relationship in two ways. First, one of the two has disturbed sleep, which then disrupts the partner's sleep. A partner who is not sleeping well frequently provokes disturbed sleep in the other partner. Second, the daytime difficulties associated with disturbed sleep will impact the other partner as well as the sufferer himself or herself. Irritability, fatigue, low motivation, and memory impairments create relational challenges, which both partners must address. Included here are disturbances of sleep in which there is the perception of poor quality sleep even when the sleep period is normal. The general criteria for insomnia include a disturbance of sleep and daytime impairments occurring despite adequate opportunity for sleep.

How to Treat Sleep Disorders

Naiman[15] advocates the following seven ways for treating sleep disorders:

1. Rest practices—these include such activities as: meditation, prayer, self-hypnosis, neurofeedback, yoga, deep breathing exercises, journaling, expressive arts, and light reading. A yoga technique known as Yoga Nidra ("yogic sleep") is also helpful.

2. The 4-7-8 Breath; in either a sitting up or lying down position, begin by placing the tip of your tongue against the bridge of your upper teeth. Throughout the process you'll be exhaling through your nose with a whooshing sound through your mouth. Naiman describes the actual process as follows: "a. exhale completely through your mouth. b. Close your mouth and inhale quietly through your nose to the count of 4.

c. Hold your breath to the count of 7. d. Exhale completely through your mouth to a count of 8." [16]

3. That constitutes one complete cycle; complete it again three more times always using the 4-7-8 ratio; do this 2-3 times every day.

4. Ride what Naiman calls the "rhythms of rest" by calibrating your circadian rhythms with exposure to morning light, taking rest breaks during the day, and enjoying a daily 20-minute midday nap.

5. Keep your body sleep-friendly by minimizing your caffeine and alcohol intake, avoiding counterfeit "booster" energies, and by getting regular cardiovascular exercise.

6. Create a sleep sanctuary by keeping your bedroom cool, dark, quite, making sure you feel safe and getting your clock away from your head and bed.

7. Use the nighttime as sleep medicine by simulating dusk through dimming your lights and/or using "blue-light blockers," products that selectively filter out the blue wavelengths of light that suppress melatonin production. Also use the evening for writing, gentle yoga, warm baths, and intimacy with yourself and your partner. Over the counter melatonin supplements can also be helpful for some people.

8. Minimize nighttime wakefulness by keeping daytime activities out of your bed, going to your bed itself only when sleepy (or for other couples intimacy). If you are unable to sleep get out of bed until you do feel sleepy.

Cognitive behavior therapy (CBT) has also proven to be of assistance in treating sleep related challenges. Counselors and other help care professionals can be of assistance. Ellen Michaud's *Sleep to be sexy, smart and slim*[17] describes that process in more detail. Gregg Jacobs[18] is a psychiatrist at Harvard. A description of CBT with sleep disorders can be found on-line.[19]

Sleep Related Breathing Disorders

Apnea means absence of breathing; hypopnea means partial breathing. An episode of sleep apnea can last anywhere from 10 seconds to 2 or 3 minutes. This ends with awakening momentarily, perhaps thrashing around, gasping for air, and falling back to sleep. You or your partner may or may not regain consciousness or recall the awakenings, but one's sleep architecture is modified. After returning to sleep, another apnea episode usually begins again soon. Difficulties in breathing during sleep are divided into 2 broad categories: obstructive sleep apnea, where there is an obstruction in the airway making it difficult to breathe, and central sleep apnea, where breathing is decreased or absent because of central nervous system or cardiac dysfunction. Obstructive sleep apnea is far more common than central sleep apnea.

Obstructive Sleep Apnea, Screening, Detection, and Treatments

In obstructive sleep apnea, there are repeated episodes of apnea or hyperpnoea. These last at least 10 seconds and are usually between 10 and 30 seconds. Occasionally an episode will persist for a minute or longer. These episodes generally occur during stage one, two, and REM sleep rather than in stage three or four. Snoring between apneas is typically reported by partners, as well as episodes of gasping, choking and frequent movements that disrupt sleep. Obstructive sleep apnea usually occurs in association with fat buildup or loss of muscle tone with aging. These changes allow the windpipe to collapse during breathing when muscles relax during sleep. The person's effort to inhale air creates suction that collapses the windpipe or the soft palate.

Unintentional sleep episodes during wakefulness, daytime sleepiness, restless sleep, fatigue, and insomnia are common. Persons with obstructive sleep apnea usually wake up gasping, choking, or short of breath. Partners generally report loud snoring and/or interruptions of breathing during the person's sleep. A polysomnographic sleep study must find 5 or more apneas or hypopneas per hour of sleep and evidence of breathing effort.

Estimates of prevalence vary greatly depending on how an apnea or hypopnea is defined. When there are five or more apneas per hour of sleep and excessive daytime impairment, the prevalence is estimated to be four percent in men and two percent in women. Prevalence increases with age and weight. Menopause is a risk factor for this disorder for women. Smoking appears to increase the risk. There are some inherited traits that increase risk, and family patterns, such as overeating, may also increase risk for obstructive sleep apnea.

If you have sleep apnea, there may or may not be an awareness of awakening during the night; however there will most probably be excessive daytime sleepiness and fatigue. If your partner has sleep apnea, you will most likely be aware of their breathing interruptions during sleep and/or loud snoring. Many couples who were unable to sleep together in the same room have been helped significantly by having sleep apnea machines. Not only do they assist in better breathing, one very positive side effect is that they also reduce disturbing snoring as well. Screening tests are available on the web. On-line Sleep Apnea screening test[20] and also features the sleep apnea screening tool.[21] A thorough evaluation by a physician specializing in sleep disorders is essential for diagnosis and treatment.

If you believe you or your partner has sleep apnea, there are several things you can do while waiting for your appointment with a sleep physician. Alcohol, nicotine, and sleeping pills are likely to make sleep apnea worse. Losing weight may help and it is likely to be a part of the treatment plan after you see the sleep doctor. You can elevate your head with pillows or by sleeping in a recliner. Sleep is sometimes improved if you avoid sleeping on your back. You may respond well to various breathing strips products, while others of you may do well with dental devices. Continuous positive airway pressure (CPAP) is the most widely used treatment. A mask, which delivers air at slightly above room pressure, is placed over the nose before going to sleep. This keeps the airway open so breathing and sleep is improved.

Summary

Sleep disorders are one of the most under-diagnosed disorders and therefore can be one of the greatest sources of stress in relationships. The present article has presented four suggested activities couples can do relative to insomnia and sleep related breathing disorders. The ability of each partner to have less interrupted sleep and more quality sleep at night can make the days much healthier and happier for both.

Endnotes

[1] Williamson, A. M., & Feyer, A. M. (2000). Moderate sleep deprivation produces impairments in cognitive and motor performance equivalent to legally prescribed levels of alcohol intoxication. *Occupational and Environmental Medicine, 57,* 649-655.

[2] "The science of sleep," (2008), *60 Minutes,* March 16 broadcast. Retrieved March 30, 2008, from www.cbsnews.com/stories/2008/03/14/60minutes.

[3] *Ibid.*

[4] National Sleep Foundation. (2005). *Sleep segments.* www.sleepfoundation.org.

[5] *Ibid*

[6] *Ibid*

[7] Sleep Research Society. (2005). *SRS Basics of Sleep Guide.* Westchester, Illinois: author.

[8] *Ibid*

[9] *Ibid*

[10] Lavie, P. (2001). Sleep-wake as a biological rhythm. *Annual Review of Psychology, 52,* 277-303.

[11] Circadian rhythm test, (2008). Retrieved March 30, 2008, from http://www.apollolight.com/apps/circ_assess_survey.html.

[12] Daily rhythm test, (2008). Retrieved March 30, 2008, from http://www.bbc.co.uk/science/humanbody/sleep/crt/.

[13] Benington, J. H. (2006). Sleep homeostasis and the function of sleep. *Sleep, 23,* 959-966.

[14] American Academy of Sleep Medicine. (2005). International classification of sleeps disorders (2nd ed.): Diagnostic and coding manual. Westchester, IL: author.

[15] Naiman, R. (2008). Night mind: making darkness our friend again. *Psychotherapy Networker.* March, April, 33-37.

[16] *Ibid,*. p. 37.

[17] Michaud, Ellen. (2008). *Sleep to be sexy, smart, and slim.* Pleasantville, NY: Readers Digest.

[18] Jacobs, G. D. (1998). *Say Good Night To Insomnia.* New York: Owl Books.

[19] Jacobs Gregg. (2008). Cognitive behavior therapy and pharmacotherapy for insomnia, retrieved from http://archinte.ama-assn.org/cgi/content/abstract/164/17/1888, June 30.

[20] On Line Sleep Apnea screening test. (2008). Retrieved March 31, 2008, from http://www.sleep-tests.co.uk/.

Biography

Rocky Garrison, Ph.D.(*Four Couples' Sleep Satisfaction Interviews: Recommendations for Improving Your Nights Together)* is in private practice in Portland, Oregon and teaches and supervises at the Pacific University School of Professional Psychology.

Section 31:

"Six-Thinking Hats" Problem Solving Model to Couples Counseling

Daniel Eckstein, Chi-Sing Li and Yu-Fen Lin

The purpose of this article is to demonstrate the application of Ed De Bono's Six—thinking Hats[1] problem solving method to an actual couple. The problem solving technique was applied to a multi-culture related case study involving a husband from Hong Kong and a wife from Taiwan. They both currently reside in the South Eastern U.S. The Six Hats (6-H) will be defined and illustrated.[2] What follows is a brief overview of the key features of Ed De Bono's 6-H. More in-depth information can be found in De Bono[3] as well as the following web page: www.edwdebono.com.

The **white** hat covers facts, figures, information needs, and gaps. "I think we need some white hat thinking at this point," means, "Let's drop the arguments and proposals, and look at the data base." **Red** hat thinking covers intuition, feelings and emotions. The red hat allows the thinker to put forward an intuition without any need to justify it. The **black** hat is the hat of judgment and caution. It is used to point out why a suggestion does not fit the facts, the available experience, the system in use, or the policy that is being followed. The **yellow** hat focuses on the positive optimistic aspects of the situation. The **green** hat is the "thinking outside the box" creative hat. It explores new possibilities alternatives, and new concepts.

The **blue** hat is a hat for thinking about thinking. The parallel metaphor for blue hat thinking is that it is like the conductor of the orchestra. This hat is for process control. It is a final reflection on the other five hats that have been both over and under-utilized in the problem solving exploration.

De Bono's metaphor of various hats is an apt one as it indicates a structural sorting out of the problem-solving process by wearing one hat and in that mode limiting the focus to that respective focus. When used with couples, they and the interviewer first put on a hat. They then jointly explore the situation from that perspective exclusively, and together they then "remove" the one hat and then put on another problem solving focus hat.

From the classic Gestalt empty-chair technique perspective, it is the equivalent of structurally moving from one *chair* by being that respective polarity and then changing the focus when moving back to the other. The only difference is that in De Bono's model there are six hats rather than two empty chairs.

Case Study

All three authors have utilized the six thinking hats (6-H) problem solving method in their graduate counseling supervision classes. The following case study involved the first author interviewing the husband/wife, second and third authors respectively. The brainstorming

6-H application focused on the long term consideration for the education and the future development of their 6-month old daughter Annabelle corresponding with the implications to their own career relative to those decisions. From a multi-cultural perspective, the discussion involved issues residing in the U.S. Hong Kong and/or Taiwan.

White Hat

The first part of the interview consisted of creating an informational paragraph relative to the cultural background of the couple. Here is a synopsis of their respective cultural history. Some data is available; some information on the couple is missing or will be added by them for future research).

Chi-Sing Li was born in Hong Kong; he was the youngest of five siblings. After finishing his high school in Hong Kong, Chi-Sing studied in the U.S. Having completed his bachelor degree, he returned to Hong Kong to be a secondary school teacher for 6 years.

During this time, he got married and had two children. He came back to the U.S. and completed his master and doctoral degrees in Counseling. He worked as a therapist/consultant of Employee Assistant Programs for over ten years. He is a Licensed Professional Counselor Supervisor and a Licensed Marriage and Family Therapist Supervisor in the State of Texas. Chi-Sing is currently an assistant professor in Sam Houston State University where he married his current wife Yu-Fen.

Yu-Fen was born in Taiwan. She is the fifth of six siblings. After completing her BA and her master of Divinity in Taiwan, she too obtained her student visa and completed a master degree in Counseling in the U.S. She then returned to Taiwan and worked in a bible college and a seminary in Taiwan for eight years. She is currently in the U.S. for her doctoral study. They now have a six-month-old baby named Annabelle.

The next white hat focus consisted of the citizenship issues of each partner. Chi-Sing Li is both a citizen of Hong Kong and a U.S. permanent resident. Chi-Sing will be eligible for U.S. citizenship in two more years. Yu-Fen is a citizen of Taiwan and an international student in the U.S. By virtue of being born in U.S., Annabelle is a citizen of U.S. Because of her parents' citizenships, she is eligible to apply citizenship in both China and Taiwan.

Additional white hat data are that Chi-Sing's two children currently reside in Hong Kong. He also has a sister and brother in the U.S. and a nephew in Thailand. The rest of the families reside in Hong Kong. Yu-Fen's family currently resides in Taiwan.

Her previous theological seminary has a teaching position for her when she finishes her doctoral degree. Chi-Sing could teach in Taiwan because he knows the language and he has already several years of teaching experiences in the U.S. Should they choose to stay in the U.S. for the education of Annabelle, they both can be involved in the university teaching and/or private practice. Chi-Sing speaks Cantonese, Mandarin, and English and Yu-Fen speaks Taiwanese, Mandarin, and English. This means they can reside in Taiwan or Hong Kong or

U.S. If Annabelle is going to grow up in an English speaking environment, the parents hope that a part of her education will be learning Cantonese, Taiwanese, and Mandarin.

Red Hat (feeling)

Both of them were asked to share their respective feelings towards the various options. Chi-Sing began by acknowledging that since he has been away from Hong Kong for the past twenty years, he does not have yearning for home. Yu-fen interjected that Hong Kong was more a distanced memory for him; he agreed with that assessment. Other than the fact that Chi-Sing's children and some of his family are there, he has no interest of going back there with his new family.

He described Taiwan as a "new place." He said, "I have never worked there before. I'm not sure about the cultural adjustment and whether I can fit in or not. And while I am worried, I am willing to try."

He described Texas as "my comfort zone. It's not that I necessarily like it the best but it's where I feel most comfortable." When other U.S. places that are new to both Chi-Sing and Yu-fen like California or Canada, were raised as other "new us as a family together," Chi-Sing replied that both his age (50) and uncertainty around job opportunities overall led to a tendency to experience more anxiety and worry as primary emotions.

Yu-Fen responded by noting that with respect to the family moving to Hong Kong, she did not consider that as an option at all. In regards to Taiwan, she said, "I have more passion to go back there to contribute, and I think Chi-Sing can contribute a great deal there too." Regarding California or Canada, she said, "I love this option because I know that I would enjoy the multicultural environment there, and I think it's good for Annabelle to grow up in that kind of environment."

With respect to their interpersonal relationship, Yu-Fen stated that during this discussion when Chi-Sing used the phrase "give up your career" while she initially said nothing at the time, later in the session, she expressed a feeling of unfairness that the language implied that she solely would be the one to give up her career, and she wanted to ask the same question relative to "him giving up his career to follow mine."

[**Interviewer note:** It's an important consideration that while we are chronologically focusing solely on the data of each respective hat, sometimes in an interview, even when a "respective hat" has been completed, there is often a spontaneous revisiting of a previous hat. Depending upon one's personal loose/rigid interviewing boundaries, the counselor can either choose to park or hold that thought. The other option is being consistent with De Bono's *only wear one hat at a time*. The interviewer should acknowledge that one hat has been taken off and another one put on.]

With respect to the above "give up your career" content, the red hat feelings of unfairness that Yu-Fen expressed later in the session itself was an emotion that she was initially less aware of at the moment. Another benefit of the various hats is that even though the red feeling hat has in fact been taken off by the couple, the very process of systematically identifying feelings led to her later becoming more aware of those feelings and expressing them at that time. Chi-Sing's new feeling based on Yu-Fen's reaction was confusion. The interviewer's intervention was to ask of Yu-Fen "How can Chi-Sing rephrase his statement to be less inflammatory to you?" She responded, "Instead of using the phrase 'give up your career', I would prefer to hear that 'have you considered other career options'?"

Black Hat (the downside of each possibility)

Both agreed that the major downsides of Hong Kong are Yu-Fen not speaking Cantonese, the twenty years that Chi-Sing has been away, and the unstable political uncertainty of Hong Kong which is now a part of communist China. Both Yu-Fen and Chi-Sing agreed the downside of Taiwan is the future education of their daughter Annabelle. Terms such as spoon-fed, rote-memory and dogmatic were some negatives they identified. Both Hong Kong and Taiwan have a serious pollution problem due to the dense population. The downside of the current location of TX is that they both are minorities. There is no Asian community within a 50 mile radius. They have to drive an hour and half to be able to purchase the foods that are part of their Asian diet. There also is a strong prevailing conservative environment, which often discourages diverse perspectives.

With respect to possible relocation to California or Canada, the issues of age and job instability were identified. The interviewer noted that in the future more "white hat information" would be needed in for this to be a more seriously considered options.

Yellow Hat (optimism)

The major hope of either Hong Kong or Taiwan is that they are physically close to Chi-Sing's children. Regarding the hope of Taiwan, they both will get support from Yu-Fen's family and friends. Yu-Fen has a position waiting for her in the seminary; she has a strong desire to influence Taiwan's next generation by integrating theology and counseling. The value of Asian family thinking is another strength of a possible relocation to the Far East. Annabelle would be much more likely to speak many Asian languages.

Both California and Canada were viewed as more multicultural than their current location. If they were to visit with their family in Asian, it is closer and easier.

Chi-Sing said that he feels most comfortable in Texas, and they just recently bought a new home. The low cost of living in Texas in contrast to places like California was also noted as another positive.

The other future optimism is that within the next two years, they should both have a Ph.D. and a counselor license that expands their practitioner/university teaching options wherever they may be. These may increase the joint income, which would help to pay for Annabelle college education. When they were looking at hopes, they both were in agreement that Annabelle may get a better education in the U.S.

Green Hat (creative thinking outside the box)

The interviewer noted that full-time online teaching appointment with such universities as Capella, Walden, or the University of Phoenix makes it possible for them to choose any location for the most desirable education of Annabelle.

The couple also acknowledged that from a Gestalt polarity perspective, it is not limited to having to select just one location. In fact, many husband/wife PhDs have often worked in two geographic locations. Even if one is in the U.S and the other in the Far East, it is only ten hours flight distance away. If they both are in university teaching appointments, they also would have extended Christmas breaks. It was also noted that there is greater flexibility for university teachings with between semester and other holiday breaks.

Blue Hat (process versus content)

The couple began their overall review of the preceding five hats by noting an increase hopefulness and optimism of the various alternatives that had emerged during the discussion. They also stated that they had gained more understanding of each other. They liked that while there was a formal structure regarding each specific hat's function, the interview itself was fluid and flexible enough to accommodate the natural unfolding of the conversation. Another major "Ah-ha" was the importance of nature and a nurturing environment no matter where they go relative to Annabelle's future education.

With respect to the process intervention question, "Which hat(s) were over-utilized and which hat(s) were under-utilized in our session?" Yu-Fen reported that even after the session had ended, Chi-Sing stated, "Now I feel more hopeful regard to our future planning."

"It encouraged me to hear that from him," Yu-Fen quoted. Yu-Fen appreciated that the "blue hat process oriented intervention" refocused the strong feelings that surfaced in the interview, even though the red feeling hat had already been taken off. Overall, Yu-Fen felt each hat was balanced in respective focus in the overall interview.

Chi-Sing stated that although more time had been spent with the white hat, the activity was overall helpful. The specific benefit of the red hat feeling polarity also enriched their communication from his perspective. The green/creative hat seemed to be under-utilized, and further exploration could help expand their options.

Summary

One of the major benefits of this particular case study involves the growing phenomenon of a couple's joining together and forming a new family unit coming from different cultural backgrounds. In this specific case, the "yours" and "mine" cultures of Taiwan and Hong Kong are now coupled with a current "ours" US culture. Future implication of both these and other cultures is the primary purpose of the interview. We have utilized the Six-thinking Hats problem-solving method in a variety of individual, couples and counseling supervision activities. We like to use the Gestalt empty-chair metaphor relative to the benefit of focusing exclusively in the moment on one specific polarity. The only difference is that instead of two empty chairs in the De Bono model, there are in fact six different hats to "put on one at a time."

In this specific couple's interview, there was more white hat" data gathering thinking than usual introduced by me as the interviewer simply because of the unique multi-cultural/citizenship issues relating to the U.S., Hong Kong, and Taiwan cultural heritages of the couple. In this interview I was impressed by the many listening checks coupled with lots of summarizing and paraphrasing each couple did with one another throughout the session.

One major core shared value that emerged from our talk was the Asian value of family. My own observation to the couple in our final summary was how that value was reflected even in the "presenting problem" being explored.

"The very decision that your focus was on your daughter's education five years from now reflects both long-term strategic planning. Also the primary focus was on the education of your child five years from now and not simply on how you two together can blend your own careers with each other," I commented.

"An important Asian value is that we want our children to have a better world than us," they both agreed in response.

In using the Six-thinking hats with couples, one of the major benefits is that both the couple and the interviewer work *collaboratively* as a team focusing jointly together on each respective hat. For example, in another couple interview, they appreciated that in their own previous problem-solving attempts the wife tended to be the overly optimistic yellow hat, while the husband tended to be the overly negative black hat. Collaborating together as a team helps minimize such polarized entrenched positions between couples.

Another benefit of the model is that it provides a shared ongoing nomenclature problem-solving perspective. "We need more *hat thinking*; we also are too focused on *hat thinking* are representative couple's comments reflecting the ongoing value of an ongoing blue hat process-oriented perspective to relationship problem solving skills.

Endnotes

[1] De Bono, Edward. (1999). *Six thinking hats.* New York: Little, Brown and Company.

[2] Jensen, D., Feland, J., Bowe, M., & Self, B. (2006). A 6-Hats Based Team Formation Strategy: Development and Comparison with an MBTI Based Approach. Retrieved 9/7/2006. from http://www.usafa.af.mil/df/dfem/research_info/ed_research/6hats.pdf

[3] De Bono, E. & Msn.com. http://www.edwdebono.com/

Section 32:

Combining Socratic Questions
With the
ADAPT Problem-Solving Model:
Implications for Couples' Conflict Resolution

Al Milliren, Mary Milliren and Daniel Eckstein

Problem solving for conflict resolution is a difficult activity that can complicate almost any relationship. No matter how well intentioned, conflict resolution often becomes a major stumbling block for couples. Al Milliren and Wes Wingett[1] have identified an Adlerian-oriented approach, respectfully curious inquiry (RCI), for use by counselors that is heavily focused on Socratic questioning. Daniel Eckstein, Phyliss Cooke, and John Jones[2] created a developmental problem-solving model called *ADAPT*. The purpose of this article is to combine Socratic questions with the ADAPT model to produce a unique conflict resolution method for couples.

In her book, *Encounter in the Classroom*, Elizabeth Hunter[3] states there should that any innovation involves the three dimensions *structure*, *content*, and *process*. Structure consists of those elements providing for organization such as schedules, physical environments, plans, or models. Structure creates a focus or provides for a discipline in taking a desired action. In this instance, we have the ADAPT model developed by Eckstein et al.[4] ADAPT is a five-step developmental structure, which can assist couples in systematically organizing the problem-solving process. The acronym stands for

      A—analyze the gap,
      D—develop resources,
      A—align goals,
      P—plan interventions, and
      T—track implementation.

In analyzing the gap, the relationship challenge is defined as best as the couple can in their own words. This is followed by a determination of the resources available to solve the problem. Goal alignment focused on the need for both partners to be on the same page as much as possible. If that is not possible, the couples need to take the time to either get aligned and/or paradoxically to agree to disagree. Once the goal is defined, it is essential to begin to plan for appropriate activities allowing for goal attainment. Finally, follow-up is essential as a means for tracking the implementation of the solution.

Content consists of the subject matter. In this instance, the content would include the thoughts and feelings each member of a couple experience as they work at resolving an issue in the relationship. The demand would be for honesty and openness about one's thoughts and feelings. Problem solving is a process that should lead to success with one another where feelings of win-win take precedence. If the solution arrived at is at the expense of one of the partners, then, in the long run, neither wins.

What is often overlooked is the human interaction or process dimension of an activity. The overall objective is problem solving. Behaviors and attitudes by either partner that either elevate or denigrate oneself or the other tend to be negatively correlated with effective problem solving. Putdowns, such as blaming, criticism, contempt, denial, interruptions, and stonewalling have to be avoided. What destroys most problem-solving activities is a vertical relationship, where one person acts superior to the other, masquerading as if it is egalitarian.

Milliren and Wingett,[5] while engaged in identifying the therapeutic style of Alfred Adler, developed a conversational approach that they call RCI. They advocate for the extensive use of RCI in both exploring and solving problems with another person. The process of RCI includes the following seven dimensions:

F = *Focusing* on what it is the person wants and arrives at mutually agreed on goals.
L = *Listening* attentively, empathetically, and reflectively.
A = *Assessing* strengths, resilience, and social interest.
V = *Validating* resources and "characteristics" in a manner that encourages growth.
O = *Engaging* in the *humor* that abounds in the ironies of social living.
R = *Replacing* information gathering (factophilia) with appropriate clarification, creative intuition, imaginative empathy, and stochastic questions
S = *Socratic dialoguing* (What? Who? Where? When? How?)

Socratic dialogue serves as the *key* element of the process. Although the discussion is centered on the asking of numerous questions, it is a dialogue between equals. There is an air of open mindedness that seeks to understand the other person's reasoning. The question, "Why?" is never asked because this only serves to create defensiveness. The assumption in a Socratic dialogue is that there is no one right answer but that everyone can contribute to an increased understanding of the problem. Conflict resolution is approached as a cooperative activity in search of a better solution where two heads are genuinely perceived as being better than one.

An Adapt Scenario

Mark and D'Arcy are a young couple that are both enjoying their second marriage. Mark, 41, has two boys, ages 16 and 13, from his previous marriage who visit on an irregular basis because of sports' schedules. D'Arcy, 25, has a daughter who is 8 ½ and, while living with the couple on a regular basis, visits her father every other weekend. Mark and D'Arcy have talked about having additional children because they both dreamed of having fairly large families at one time. They have not reached any conclusion about whether or not to have more children although D'Arcy is now thinking about getting pregnant. She would like to have Mark's support in this decision but has also contemplated going off the pill "just to see what would happen." They have decided to set aside some time to talk about "family matters." In this abbreviated ADAPT dialogue, the Socratic questions are set in italics to make them easier to identify.

D'Arcy: We haven't talked for a while about our family and having children. Since the kids are all going to be gone this weekend, can we set some time to talk?

Mark: Sure. That would be great. I've been thinking about that too.

D'Arcy: Let's go out to dinner and then come back here to talk. Would Friday or Saturday be better?

Mark: Let's do Saturday. I'm usually pretty wiped by Friday night.

D'Arcy: Saturday it is! I'll take care of reservations. Where shall we go?

Mark: How does Luigi's sound?

D'Arcy: Perfect! Consider it done. Thanks Mark.

Analyze the Gap

Anxiety might generally be described as the "gap" between the real and the ideal. This step focuses on stating the problem and then identifying how it is now as opposed to how they would like it to be. Each of the partners helps the other to describe these two elements—the real and the ideal. The sole purpose is to identify the gap—if any. If there is a gap between the partners, then some resolution needs to be obtained. Otherwise, the goal is to move the perceptions of real and ideal into congruence.

D'Arcy: *So, what have you been thinking about our family?*

Mark: Well, I know you really would like to have a bigger family and I always thought I wanted that too. But lately, I rather like the fact that, just like this weekend, we really need some time just to ourselves. *What's your thinking?*

D'Arcy: I really like our time together too. It seems like we're always dealing with visitation and negotiating schedules. Steve keeps changing the weekends he gets Dakota and your boys are getting older. They have their friends and sports and right now they just don't seem to enjoy coming as much.

Mark: I know. I feel bad that sometimes they seem to just not want to be with us anymore.

D'Arcy: Yeah, it bothers me too. *What do you think is going on with that?*

Mark: I don't think it's us so much. Like last month, they had all the tournaments on the weekend so there was just no time.

D'Arcy: *What have they said about it?*

Mark: I don't know. We talked about their schedules and stuff . . . but I don't know if they miss coming or not.

D'Arcy: *Well, Dakota misses them coming. Just the other day she was asking why the boys* don't come as much. And we sure didn't have much time with them over the holidays and such. And then I started thinking it would be nice to have a child of our own. *What do you think about that possibility?*

Mark: *I was doodling the other day and I got to thinking that I'd have about 7 more years of* supporting the boys, through college and all. With Dakota, there'll be about 12 more years. If we had another child now, it would be about 20 more years. With all our expenses, we never have any money for ourselves. So, right now, 20 years seems like a long time to keep doing without. I'd be over 60 by then. I don't mind the kids having all that but I'd like to do some things while we are still young enough to do them. *Is that something you've ever thought about?*[6]

D'Arcy: *Actually*, I want that too. I love our time together with just us. And we haven't done much of that since before we got married. Yet, I really want a family that is just "ours." When the boys don't come and Dakota's with her father, I really miss doing family things. I know we always talked about having a big family and that is really important to me. I guess this is "the gap." We have to decide what is more important.

Develop Resources

At this point, there is brainstorming. For each partner, the question is focused on moving from where each is now to where they would like to be as a couple. How did they solve problems like this in the past? What resources did they employ? What skills, attitudes, activities, and so on were needed?

Mark: When I think about it, I really would like to get out from under the extra expenses as soon as we can.

D'Arcy: I've thought about that aspect, too. Sometimes, I feel so selfish for wanting to do things just with you.

Mark: Yeah, I love the kids but I get tired of it being about them all the time.

D'Arcy: So, it sounds like it's all coming down to money and timing.

Mark: Speaking of which. When's the last time your ex sent a support check?

D'Arcy: Well, not for quite a while. But he's had some hard times. I just don't know how much we can count on him nor when. He does take good care of Dakota while she's there and he did buy her a new winter coat this year.

Mark: Well, I would say that financially we are doing about the best as we can. I can't see that we could add the expense of another child. I am tired of struggling to make ends meet.

D'Arcy: Yeah. When the boys are here, they use the extra bedroom and I don't want them to feel they don't have a place here. And Dakota is pretty used to having her own room. I don't think it would work out so great to have her sharing that room with a new baby. Which means we'd probably have to add on to the house? I know we can't afford to buy a new place.

Mark: Well, I've been doing pretty well this year. The boss said I should be getting a good bonus check as well as a pay increase next quarter. That should help some. Maybe I could talk to the boys about helping me finish the basement. Maybe make them a space of their own. There's already a bath down there with a shower.

D'Arcy: *So, where are we now about all this?*

Mark: Well, we kinda got the space problems figured out and we'll have more income. *What do you think?*

D'Arcy: I understand all the financial and other things we've been discussing. But there is such a big part of me that wants to have another child. I was hoping you'd be all for it, too. I've really been thinking about going off the pill and just see what happens.

Mark: Whoa! *Would you really do that without talking with me first? Do we both really want this?*

Align Goals

Is this what we really want? Do we agree that this is of value to both of us? The partners need to find common ground and, in the process, identify what is keeping them, if anything, from being fully behind the outcome they seem to want.

D'Arcy: I would never do that without telling you first. That wouldn't be fair. But it doesn't seem fair either to have to give up a dream we had about having a big family.

Mark: Well, it has been my dream too. I hate to give up on it without trying to figure out a way to make it happen. *How can we come to some sort of agreement about this?*

D'Arcy: Do we agree that we still want to have a bigger family?

Mark: I'm thinking so, but not if we wait too long.

Planning the Intervention Strategy

Once agreement is reached on the outcome, it is important to brainstorm all the various options for getting there. This first step should be completed without evaluation of any of the options. The second step is to look at the options to see which ones make sense. What is important here is to identify what the situation requires to achieve the desired outcome? Finally, a plan should be formed. When decisions are made that have no implementation plan, the forward movement all but disappears.

D'Arcy: So let's make a list of what we have to do here . . . We have to talk to the boys.

Mark: We need to draw a plan for remodeling the basement. (Pause) And a timeline for when we are going to do what. Oh yeah, and we need to make sure what my bonus and pay increase will be.

D'Arcy: Maybe we could set a date for going off the pill . . .

Mark: And a date for "if not pregnant by . . ."

D'Arcy: We'll need to discuss all this with Dakota too. Is there anyone else we could talk about this with to get another perspective?

Mark: It probably would be good to do that. Let's evaluate each of these and prioritize them. Then let's see who we might discuss it with.

D'Arcy: Should we get a calendar and figure out our target dates?

Mark: Let's add in some dates as *checkpoints* to see how we're doing along the way.

Track Implementation

Mark and D'Arcy have a plan and seem to be well on their way to implementation. They wisely added some dates to their calendar for checking on their progress. Too often, good implementation plans fall apart because there is no plan for follow-up. By tracking the implementation, they can see if they are still on the same page or if they need to analyze the gap again.

Some Additional Socratic Questions to Use in the Adapt Dialogue

In a moment, we are going to ask you to engage in an ADAPT dialogue. Your first step will be to identify a problem that is impacting your relationship. In this section, however, we will list some of the more powerful Socratic questions you might elect to use in your conversation. The purpose of your interview is to dialogue together and not engage in debating an issue

---

Activity 43: Analyze the Gap

How well are we doing with _____?
What is it we want?
How is this situation now?
How would we like it to be?
What are our differences of opinion about _____?
Are there points on which we agree?
What are they?

Activity 44: Develop Resources

What are some of the things we already have that allow us to do _____?
When we solved a problem similar to this in the past, what did we do?
What kind of attitude did we incorporate as we looked to solve this problem?
What were some of the specific skills we used?
What activities did we undertake?

Activity 45: Align Goals

How do we know that we both really want this?
In what ways do we both really value this?
What do we have to do to get on the same page about this?
What stops each of us from being fully behind this outcome?

Activity 46: Planning the Intervention Strategy: Go to BED

What are some things we need to do from here? (**B**rainstorm without evaluation.)
Which of these are possibilities?
Which ones make the most sense in terms of what the situation requires? (**E**valuate each of the options.)
What will we need to do to proceed?
What other resources will be needed?
What might we want to consult with someone else about?
What might some of the first steps be?
And, where do we want to begin? (**D**evelop a plan for getting on with it.)

Activity 47: Track Implementation

When should we revisit this question/situation to evaluate how we are doing?
How will we know when we have achieved our solution?

Your Personal Adapt Process

Identify a problem that is affecting your relationship. You are now asked to follow the "suggested outline" below. The process may seem a bit stilted but do not let that get in your way. It is important that you engage in the dialogue if you wish to arrive at a successful solution. It is suggested that one partner interview the other in all the analyze the gap questions; then reverse the process and the partner being interviewed in the first part now be the interviewer in same section questions too. In the next section, both partners interview each other; we suggest you reverse the order of who goes first or second after each round. Here is the suggested interview sequence using the ADAPT developmental model.

A—Analyze the Gap

Define in your own words, as best you can, your assessment of our relationship challenge?

Follow each of your Socratic questions with what might be labeled as an "empathetic response" (ER) or a "listening check" (LC). ERs focus of reflecting the other person's feelings about the subject, that is, "What I hear you saying is____," "You appear to be feeling ____," or "So, you feel ____." LCs offer a summary of the other person's point of view, that is, "Is that correct? If not, clarify my understanding for me if possible please," "I'm wondering if you are saying ____," or "So, from where you sit ____."

Shift your focus on your partner's perspective of the problem (the "real") by now addressing his or her vision of the problem being resolved successfully (the "ideal"). What would it look like, feel like, sound like, and/or even smell life for you if this problem were solved? How could it help our relationship? Follow with ER and LC statements.

How would I, your partner, or someone else important to you know the problem has been solved? What specific changes would be evident? Again, follow with ER and LC statements.

Is there anything else you feel is important to discuss relative to the gap between what is happening now on this issue and what you hope will happen in the future?

Conclude analyze the gap section with an overall summary statement of what you understand to be the key points your partner has brought out in this interview—only after you have done so to your partners' satisfaction then change roles and have the interviewer become the focus of the Socratic questions.

D—Develop Resources

The purpose of this section is to determine what resources are available to solve the problem. Such resources could include financial, emotional, spiritual, technical, and other forms of support available to help solve the problem.

Think of a time in our relationship when either or both of us have successfully resolved a problem? Describe the issue itself and how it came to be resolved in a specific detail as is possible. If no example for the relationship is identified, have your partner relate a time when he or she successfully resolved a dilemma. Follow-up with ER and LC statements.

What top three to five strengths, virtues, skills, and/or abilities did either or both of us exhibit in this successful endeavor? List these and respond with ER and LC statements.

How any of the above-mentioned positive attributes might be successfully used in our current challenge?

Give an overall summary statement of what you feel are the key points being made by your partner in the developing resources section. Change roles after you have been successful in summarizing your partner's responses to his or her satisfaction.

A—Align Goals

In this section, you are to shift the focus from the actual solution to your relationship challenge (a "task" approach) to a more process-oriented exploration. Just as the wheels of a car need to be balanced and in alignment, so do both of you need to be "on the same page." ERs and LCs are essential here. Remember the ultimate goal of the interview is for problem solving. Blaming, criticizing, and disagreeing are symptoms of an "I'm better and superior" or "I'm worse and inferior" basic ego position that usually sabotages relationship problem solving success.

Now that we have discussed our own perspectives on these issues, let's talk about the areas in which you feel we have basic agreement? (ER and LC) In which areas are we in disagreement? (ER and LC) How can we get "on the same page" relative to our mutual goals? (ER and LC) How might we paradoxically "agree to disagree" as another way of aligning our intentions? (ER and LC) Summarize your partners key points for all of the align goals section before reversing roles.

Note: Your success in this phase of the ADAPT developmental problem-solving model will be significantly reduced unless you can mutually agree either that you are aligned or you respectfully "agree to disagree" at this checkpoint in the model. Although the tendency might be just to "go ahead anyway" with the next sections, we urge you to agree or to "agree to disagree" on your goal alignment before moving on in the interview process.

P—Planning Interventions

In this phase, your goal is to begin to identify specific interventions that might be used. One partner should begin by providing an overall summary statement of key points in the suggestions made by the other partner. Be sure to incorporate ERs and LCs. Then, change roles.

T—Track Implementation

This is the time when you decide how you can monitor your progress, reevaluate your approach, and/or return back[7] to the intervention section with another strategy. Use ERs and LCs throughout this process.

Summary

The article has presented the union of Socratic questions with the ADAPT problem-solving developmental model applied to couples' confronting a relationship challenge. Authors' Note: Correspondence concerning this article should be addressed to Daniel Eckstein, Medical Psychology, Saba University School of Medicine, Saba, National Caribbean, Netherlands e-mail: danielgeckstein@yahoo.com

Biography

Al Milliren, Ed.D., N.C.C., B.C.P.C., is currently in private practice and although semi-retired, Al works with his partner, Nancy Campbell, M.S., LPC, doing counseling and coaching at their practice, A*S*K, in Jonestown, TX. Al has had almost 50 years experience either working as a counselor or preparing counselors for positions in schools, community agencies, or private practice. He earned his B.S. in Business Administration and M.A. in Guidance and Counseling from Bradley University in Peoria, IL. His doctorate (1972) was in the area of educational psychology and counseling from the University of Illinois at Urbana-Champaign.

Al holds Diplomates in the North American Society of Adlerian Psychology and the American Psychotherapy Association. He has been an active member in and officer of the North American Society of Adlerian Psychology. Al is a Nationally Certified Counselor and is Board Certified in Professional Counseling. He has been a junior high school counselor and teacher, an elementary school counselor, and a professor at Illinois State University, the University of Texas of the Permian Basin, Governors State University, the Adler School of Professional Psychology, and Columbia University in SC. In addition to working in the public schools, he has served as a counselor and consultant in private practice and community agencies.

Dr. Milliren is a national and international speaker/workshop presenter and has authored or co-authored several books and numerous articles on Adlerian Psychology and related topics. He recently completed a unique book on encouragement with colleagues Julia Yang and Mark Blagen, *The Psychology of Courage.* Al's current work is with Anger Management, a brief and time-limited approach that is focused on assisting clients in exploring their basic life convictions and beliefs. In so doing, these individuals are better positioned to make more effective decisions for meeting the demands of life.

Mary Milliren, MS is a former elementary school counselor and special education consultant in the Midland-Odessa area in Texas. Prior to that, she worked with students with learning and behavioral dysfunctions in both Charleston, South Carolina, and Ottawa, Illinois. She earned her bachelor's degree in special education and her master's degree in counselor education from Illinois State University. She has a particular emphasis on developing practical strategies for enhancing positive learning/behavior outcomes. She is currently developing curriculum for elementary schools focused on social interest and social responsibility

Endnotes

[1] Milliren, A., & Wingett, W. (2005). *In the style of Alfred Adler.* Unpublished manuscript.

[2] Eckstein, D., Cooke, P., & Jones, J. (2004). *The ADAPT problem solving process.* Unpublished manuscript.

[3] Hunter, E. (1972). *Encounter in the classroom: New ways of teaching.* New York: Holt, Rinehart & Winston.

[4] Eckstein et al. (2004), *loc. cit.*

[5] Milliren & Wingett (2005), *loc. cit.*

[6] Eckstein et al. (2004), *loc. cit.*

[7] Milliren, A., & Wingett, W. (2004) *Conversations in the style of Alfred Adler: RCI/TE.* Unpublished workshop handout. West Texas Institute for Adlerian Studies, Odessa, TX.

Section 33:

Forgiveness: Another Relationship "F Word"—A Couple's Dialogue

Daniel Eckstein, Mark Sperber, and Shannon McRae

One of the most frequent quotes on the importance of forgiveness was from the poet Alexander Pope who said "To err is human; to forgive divine." Theologian Reinhold Niebuhr said "We are saved by the final form of love which is forgiveness." And Bryant McGill suggests "There is no love without forgiveness, and there is no forgiveness without love" (Thinkexist.com, n.d.). A global non-denominational group also created an International Forgiveness Day that was first celebrated August 3, 2008 was also held on August 2, 2009 (Forgivenessalliance, n.d).

Knutson, Enright, and Garbers (2008) provide an excellent overview to the developmental pathway of forgiveness as contrasted with condoning, excusing, or forgetting what happened to someone. Instead, forgiveness is a response to unfairness of resentment or anger toward an offender and the restoration of more positive feelings, thoughts, and behaviors toward that person (Enright, 2001; Worthington, 2001).

The relationship of anger to forgiveness is also an important consideration. Although expressing anger can aid short term catharsis, this can be counterproductive unless the anger is reduced or eliminated by such a process as forgiveness. Depression and anxiety often continues or even increases if anger is not addressed in relationships (Enright & Fitzgibbons, 2000).

Forgiving one's partner does not mean justice is not sought or that a solution based on mutual respect and valuing of both oneself and of one's partner is not pursued. Seeking justice is much more favorable than revenge or get-even tactics. Because anger has negative physiological implications such as elevated blood pressure and increased heartbeat, it is in one's own self-interest to forgive his or her partner.

Although there are some examples where forgiveness is an instant onetime event, more likely it is a process that has a higher probability of lasting success if it occurs over 12 weeks or more (Baskin & Enright, 2004).

In the spirit of a long-term developmental process, the authors have devised a series of reflective questions that are designed to aid an individual's growth in forgiveness, especially in the context of a committed relationship. One of the major shifts is toward a problem-solving stance versus blame or punishment. It is recommended that the following reflections first be considered personally rather than discussed with one's partner. Indeed, because the act of forgiveness is a more internal process, it is possible that your partner may neither be aware of nor even informed of such actions. And if your overriding motivation in forgiving your partner is based on self-elevating moral superiority, then very likely a prideful boasting to your partner by a "how magnanimous of me to be willing to forgive your despicable behavior" attitude will simple create a different set of relationship issues. Forgiveness experiences can also be enhanced by discussing and processing your relationship in the presence of a trusted counselor and/or spiritual confidant.

What follows will be a blending of introspective relationship-formatted questions coupled with relevant research plus some specific forgiveness strategies. Because this activity involves a combination of content and discussions, activities for you and your partner will be in another font throughout the article.

Activity 48: Exploring Forgiveness

A. Exploring your past history on the concept of forgiveness
   1. What are some of your earliest memories relative to the concept of forgiveness?
   2. What do you remember regarding any religious, spiritual, or educational concepts or suggestions about forgiveness?
   3. Consider an actual incident involving someone else who modeled the essence of forgiveness. What was the context of the incident? What did the person say or do? How did you know forgiveness had occurred? How did this event affect you personally?

B. Exploring your own personal history with forgiveness before your current significant relationship
   1. Now remember examples of when you forgave someone else. Answer the questions from A3.
   2. Rate yourself on a 1-10 scale, 1 being low and 10 being high, on your own overall satisfaction with your ability to forgive others.
      Your rating:
      Explain what that rating means to you:
   3. Shift your focus to the issue of remembering one or more examples of when you successfully forgave someone else. Consider the same reflecting questions as in A3.
   4. Rate yourself on a 1-10 scale on your own satisfaction of forgiving others as you were growing up.
      Your rating:
      Description of your rating:

C. Focusing on your current relationship
 1. Rate yourself on you forging your partner
   Your rating:
   Description:
 2. Rate your satisfaction of your partner forgiving you.
   Your rating:
   Description:
 3. Cite one or more specific examples of when you felt forgiveness occurred between you as a couple.
 4. Contemplate incidents for which you still harbor resentment or anger.
 5. Identify similar issues you believe your partner may have toward you.

Spiritual Forgiveness

A sense of humor is often good medicine in spiritual matters of forgiveness as the poet Robert Frost demonstrates with ""Forgive me, O Lord, my little jokes on Thee and I'll forgive Thy great big one on me." In a similar vein, Emo Phillips writes "When I was a kid I used to pray every night for a new bicycle. Then I realized that the Lord doesn't work that way so I stole one and asked Him to forgive me"(Wisdom Quotes, n.d.).

On a more serious note, forgiveness is a major theme of most religious texts. In the *Koran*, it is written: "He who forgiveth, and is reconciled unto his enemy, shall receive his reward from God." And the *Bhagavad Gita* stresses that "Splendor, forgiveness, fortitude, cleanliness, absence of malice, and absence of pride; these are the qualities of those endowed with divine virtues, O Arjuna" (World of Quotes.com, n.d.).

One of the most frequently quoted verses of scripture (*Bible*) in the Christian world is from Matthew 18:21-22: "Then Peter came to Jesus and asked, 'Lord, how many times shall I forgive my brother when he sins against me? Up to seven times?' Jesus answered, 'I tell you, not seven times, but seventy-seven times.'" (*New England Bible*, n.d.).

No stranger to both public humiliation and to forgiveness, former U.S. First Lady and current U.S. Secretary of State Hillary Rodham Clinton adds her own p.s. to that verse by wryly noting: "In the Bible, it says they asked Jesus how many times you should forgive, and he said 70 times 7. Well, I want you all to know that I'm keeping a chart" (Wisdom Quotes. com, n.d.).

In an essay on the concept of forgiveness in Judaism, Rabbi David Rosen notes that: "The theme of God's forgiveness for man's sins is recurrent in Talmudic and Midrashic literature and reappears in later rabbinic writings and the synagogue liturgy . . . the *Talmud* states, 'He who sins and regrets his act is at once forgiven' (Hag. 5a; Ber. 12b) and the *Midrash* states, 'Says the Holy One, even if they (your sins) should reach to Heaven, if you repent I will forgive'

(Pes. Rab. 44:185a. Ps. 835). The Tosefta even gives a statistical figure to the matter, basing itself on Exodus 34:6-7 and says that God's quality of forgiveness is five hundred fold that of His wrath (Tosef., Sot. 4:1)" (Rosen, David, n.d.). In one national U.S. survey, 1,379 members of different religious groups were sent a questionnaire relative to the role forgiveness has played in their own religious study groups. A total of 61% said their respective religious group had helped them to forgive someone, 71% said they had experienced healings of relationships as a result of their group, and 43% said they had worked on improving a broken relationship in recent months. They frequently cited having *emotional capitol* and *spiritual capitol* as a consequence of such spiritual classes on forgiveness (Wuthnow, 2000, 2009).

The Religious Society of Friends, an organization more familiarly known as Quakers, was founded in England by George Fox, in 1624. Here is a list of those convictions regarding relationships within the spirit of Quakerism:

1. Recognizing that God is in everyone.
2. Affirming the Spirit in oneself and others.
3. Creating space for the Light; fostering and preserving opportunities congenial to the Spirit.
4. Living with simplicity, avoiding materialism or mere conventionality.
5. Defusing tensions with the help of the Spirit; striving to deal openly and lovingly with others when conflicts arise.
6. Seeking alternatives to violence in words and actions.
7. Listening for the truth in the words of others.
8. Speaking the truth as discerning it with cordiality, kindness, and love.
9. Avoiding gossip, breaking confidences, or the disparagement of others.
10. Resisting temptations to falsehood, coercion, and abuse.
11. Avoiding behavior that supports social ranking (Comfort, 2007).

Couples can always follow the "Quaker Way" by bearing in mind what the Quakers have used for over 300 years. William Penn was a Quaker, as was Isaac Pennington. From a Quaker perspective, you and your copartner should recognize that God is in you both. This is especially important even when the two of you are in disagreement with one other. Some sample comments to make to one another include:

"How did you feel when I _____?"
"What could I have done differently?"
"What way could we better come to agreement in the future?"
"I apologize for being insensitive."

Any of these short sentences can open doors for quiet friendly communication together and certainly in communion with God, who is ever present from the Quaker perspective.

The recommendation in this section is that the two of you interview each other on the religious/spiritual relationship in each of your early lives and in your relationship right now. Even though you may well have discussed such matters many times in the past, practice interviewing your partner to review and/or to revise such discussion. Below are some sample questions for each of you to ask one another. Again, if your partner is unwilling or unavailable to dialogue with you, consider your own responses and consider relating them to a friend and/or trusted person such as a counselor, teacher, coach, or spiritual leader.

Activity 49: Dialogue on Religious and Spiritual Relationships

1. Begin with a discussion regarding both your own family of origin's beliefs (or not) in a Higher Power. What were they and in what are some concrete examples of how you personally have (a) accepted, (b) rejected, and/or (c) modified those beliefs.

2. Now focus specially on the relationship of forgiveness and both your past and current religious/spiritual beliefs. For example, what are some of the teachings you recall from sacred texts? Alternatively, what are some examples that inspire you toward forgiveness? Are there specific rituals, ceremonies, or other ways in which forgiveness is to be sought of God or a Higher Power than you?

3. Have you ever prayed, meditated, or whatever forms your own belief system suggests to God and asked forgiveness? If so, what has been your experience in asking for such forgiveness? In what ways do you feel you have been both successful and unsuccessful in asking and in receiving what you felt was spiritually related forgiveness?

Self-Forgiveness

Some representative quotes on the value of self-forgiveness include William Shakespeare's "Do as the heavens have done, forget your evil; with them forgive yourself." Mahatma Gandhi said: "The weak can never forgive. Forgiveness is the attribute of the strong;" Mohandas Gandhi wrote that: "Forgiveness is choosing to love. It is the first skill of self-giving love." And Martin Luther King, Jr. said it this way: "We must develop and maintain the capacity to forgive. He who is devoid of the power to forgive is devoid of the power to love. There is some good in the worst of us and some evil in the best of us. When we discover this, we are less prone to hate our enemies" (Wisdom Quotes.com, n.d.).

Canadian researchers Eaton, Struthers, Shomrony, and Santelli (2007) found that an individual's own self-esteem was a determining factor in the ability to forgive. Those with defensive or fragile self-esteem focused on and responded to parts of the apology confirming the harm done by the transgressor, rather than the transgressor's remorse. There was therefore less forgiveness and more avoidance and revenge than when the transgressor does not apologize. Those with secure self-esteem and those with defensive self-esteem were the least forgiving and also the most vengeful and avoidant after receiving an apology. Their findings suggest that apologies may not have their intended effect when offered to individuals with defensive self-esteem.

Philosopher Eckhart Tollee (2005) suggests: "The moment you forgive you have reclaimed your power from the mind. Non-forgiveness is the very nature of the mind, just as the mind-made false self, the ego, cannot survive without strife and conflict, and the mind cannot truly forgive. Only you can" (p. 33).

Candice Pert (2007) describes the neurobiology of forgiveness and why it is in your own self-interest for you to forgive both your companion and everyone else for that matter. Holding onto grudges has been shown to be associated with high blood pressure and lower back pain.

Benefits of forgiveness is in removing blockages to peptides and releasing opiate receptors. The frontal cortex is where we find a high density for possibilities of pleasure. One of the physiological benefits of prayer and/or meditation is that it increases the blood flow of nutrients and takes out toxic waste especially from the prefrontal cortex. And in contrast to medications that affect the whole body, meditation is more localized to be of maximum benefit in what Pert calls "pumping up your frontal cortex" much as muscles are pumped up in physical exercise. Greater openness for synchronicity and receptivity to pure tone and sound are further benefits to slowing down one's breathing which occurs in a more quite relaxed state (Pert, 2007). The following is an experiential activity to involve the mind/body in the forgiveness process.

Activity 50: Experiential Activity

1. In this activity, there will be both an interpersonal and an intra-personal focus. You and your partner are again encouraged to interview each other in a similar format as described in activity I above. Be sure and ask for and to self-disclose specific positive examples of when self-forgiveness was successful as well as challenges or perceived failures for you.

2. Because one of the most challenging aspects of forgiveness is toward oneself, there will also be an introspective part of this process. The content and the process may be explored in the presence of your partner or some other trusted persons of trust. They can also be contemplated alone and later shared with such individuals.

---

3. What follows is a combination of personal and professional practices of the first author. For maximum benefit from the activities, get yourself in a more quiet and/or relaxed state than usual. Some strategies to achieve a relaxed environment include putting on soothing music, a walk in nature, personal prayer or meditation, t'ai chi, yoga, or running. These examples involve physiologically moving from the sympathetic to the parasympathetic central nervous system. Activating the parasympathetic nervous system is the optimal state for healing the wounds of forgiveness and provides a context that is more conducive to forgiveness.

4. The simple act of being more mindful of your breathing is also useful. For example, simply breathe in through your nose to the count of three, hold your breath to the count of three, and then exhale to the count of three. If you are so inclined, you can also repeat the widely recognized mantra "Om"; or consider saying "re" on the in breath and "laxe" on the out breath.

5. Most of us breathe in only to the upper part of our chest. So the next step is to practice what the Buddhists call mindfulness by consciously moving you're in breath in the direction of your lower abdomen. You or a counselor can help anchor or ground that experience by also repeating the words "deeper" and "slower" to further assist in becoming more still and more quite.

6. Another suggestion is on the in breathe to say "compassion and peace" to yourself and on the out breath "happiness and joy."

7. These are simply some of the various ways to slow down your thoughts and to be more available for the physiological process of helping create new neurological pathways that are part of the change process moving from self forgiveness to self-appreciation. The activities help prepare you for the healing process.

8. When you feel you are in a more relaxed state, begin by simply saying to yourself . . . ." I forgive myself for . . . . Complete that sentence and then simply repeat or have someone else repeat the "I forgive myself for . . . ." stem for 5-10 min.

9. Now imagine your favorite color. Let it fill you and surround you. Say to yourself "I love to forgive myself and others" for as long as it takes you to feel genuine conviction of the truthfulness of such an affirmation. Put your focus as much as possible on what the Eastern tradition calls the "third eye," the spot between your two eyes, raised slightly up a bit. It is the symbol on the back of the U.S. dollar bill.

10. Deepen your affirmations with such additional comments as "I forgive myself and others consciously and I will hide nothing from myself in this experience."

11. Allow your own creative process and/or your own spiritual tradition to further guide you at this point. Consider adding something like "And what I seek for me I seek for everyone" as part of your consideration of others in your own journey.

12. When you feel complete, simply end the process as you began it by again following your breathing in and out coupled with a feeling of gratitude for such a time of reflection and of healing.

13. Take 15-20 minutes to integrate your experience by again stretching, walking, and/or reflecting quietly on your experience.

14. Next commit your experience to actual paper or computer by writing down both your acts of forgiveness and what you appreciate about yourself. Acknowledge to yourself some of your good qualities including your willingness to forgive.

15. If you feel that forgiveness is still lacking, imagine writing that person's or your own name in your own heart and say things like "I love you—I forgive you—I want the very best for you."

These are examples of how to facilitate your own self-forgiveness. You may also want to and/or be required by others such as legal authorities to make some type of restitution for the harm you have done to others. Such actions are beyond the scope of this particular article but are a part of the overall implication of the impact of your behavior on others.

Forgiveness Theory

Antjie Krog (2008) of the University of Western Cape in South Africa reflects on the critical role forgiveness has played in racial reconciliation in that country. In the introduction to his Nobel Prize speech, Wole Soyinka (1976) noted that some Africans seemed able to forgive and reconcile enmity after much suffering and injustice because of the following world view:

There is a deep lesson for the world in the black races' capacity to forgive, one which, I often think, has much to do with the ethical precepts which spring from their world view and authentic religions, none which is ever totally eradicated by the accretions of foreign faiths and their implicit ethnocentrism. (Bell, 2002, p. 87)

There is a difference between forgiveness (letting go, personally, of resentment and the past) and reconciliation (mutual commitment to an improved ethical future). In describing how these two concepts were demonstrated in Rwanda, Staub, Pearlman, Gubin, and Hagengimana (2005) defined forgiveness as presenting a change in the harmed party, while reconciliation was a change in both parties.

Because the definition of forgiving usually includes the development of a more positive attitude toward the other, reconciliation and forgiveness are clearly connected. We define reconciliation as mutual acceptance by members of formerly hostile groups of each other. Such acceptance includes positive attitudes and also positive actions that express them, as circumstances allow and require (Krog, 2008, p. 355; Staub, Pearlman, Gubin, and Hagengimana, 2005).

There is a bigger world perspective of interconnectedness or what is called *ubuntu* that is part of such a South African philosophy. According to Krog,

> Interconnected forgiveness says: 'I forgive you so that you can change/heal here on earth, then I can start on my interconnected path toward healing.' The effort is towards achieving full personhood on earth. This means that forgiveness can never be without the next step: reconciliation and reconciliation cannot take place without it fundamentally changing the life of one that forgave as well as the forgiven one. Although it allows for the perpetrator to ask for forgiveness (and in fact prefers the perpetrator's quest for forgiveness to be the beginning of the process), it also allows for the possibility of the victim to move towards wholeness without the perpetrator asking for forgiveness—in other words, the victim may forgive without even being asked and thus the power towards wholeness stays firmly in the hands of the victim. After the act of forgiveness, however, the perpetrator must change. (2008, p. 357)

Writing from the Netherlands, Karremans and Van Lange (2008) researched the link between forgiveness and cognitive interdependence, the mental state characterized by pluralistic representations of the self-in-relationship. They found that forgiveness was associated with a greater perceived overlap between "Other in the Self scale" and greater use of first-person plural pronouns (we, us, our, and ours) in open-ended descriptions of their relationships.

Relationships can differ importantly in the way partners see themselves as two independent persons or in the way they view the relationship as a collective unit in which there is a high level of interdependence. Aron, Aron, and Smollan (1992) found that relationship closeness for an important part exists to the extent that individuals think as if the partner is included in the self (i.e., inclusion of another in the self). Agnew, Van Lange, Rusbult, and Langston (1998) argued that people in relationships see themselves more as part of a "pluralistic self-and-partner collective" (p. 939) to the extent that, over time, they become more committed to the relationship partner. Their research demonstrated that strong commitment to a relationship partner is associated with greater spontaneous use of plural pronouns (we, us, our)when describing the relationship. Commitment was also positively associated with cognitive interdependence toward the relationship partner.

Karremans and Van Lange (2008) propose that "unlike commitment, the psychological state of forgiveness (and unforgiveness) results directly from a specific interaction within the relationship in which a person felt offended or hurt by the relationship partner. When the person is somehow reminded of this incident . . . level of forgiveness regarding the offense may—at least temporarily—overrule the influence of relationship commitment on cognitive interdependence . . . level of forgiveness regarding a specific offense influences cognitive interdependence, above and beyond the effect of relationship commitment . . . a person who has not forgiven the offender may cognitively distance him—or herself from the other, resulting in relatively low levels of cognitive interdependence, while a person who has forgiven the offender will display relatively high levels of cognitive interdependence" (p. 77-78).

In describing how a sense of "we" versus "I" is important in relationships, Karremans and Van Lange (2008) conclude their research on the relationship benefits of forgiveness as follows:

Forgiveness helps individuals to feel part of the relationship again, as indicated by a greater perceived overlap of circles representing self and partner and a greater use of plural pronoun use in descriptions of their relationship.

Forgiveness seems especially important to understanding the immediate and concrete consequences of specific social interactions on identity processes in relationships." (p. 86)

Forgiveness Recommendations

Affirmations are one specific way to anchor the reality of forgiveness both mentally and physically. Pert (2007) suggests that such affirmations are best prefaced with an "I know . . ." statement involving passion and conviction. "I know forgiving myself and others for errors in the past allows me to heal." is one example. Another is "I choose to enjoy the pleasure of giving and of receiving pleasure without guilt."

According to Worthington (2006), forgiveness is in essence a character issue, and to forgive, a person has to learn to become a forgiving person. Learning to become a forgiving person is integral for each of you as you learn to both value and cultivate the relationship. It is an ongoing process not a onetime action.

Although Worthington (2001) believes that an important component of forgiveness is decision, his emphasis is on the importance of emotional replacement. He has created the acronym of REACH in describing forgiveness. The developmental steps are as follows:

Recall the hurt;
Empathize with the perpetrator;
Give the altruistic gift of forgiveness;
Publicly commit to forgiveness; and
Hold onto forgiveness.

Worthington also presents four "Ds" of reconciliation: Decide whether to reconcile, Discuss reconciliation, Detoxify the relationship, and develop Devotion to each other.

Empathy is the cornerstone of both forgiveness and reconciliation. The restoration of trust is the chief challenge of reconciliation and this requires both parties to be trustworthy.

Discussion involves intentional and explicit conversation about the transgression. Empathy is also important at this stage too. "Empathy is just as crucial for seeking forgiveness as for giving it . . . the strongest predictor of unwillingness to seek forgiveness was inability or unwillingness to empathize with others" (Worthington, 2001, p. 183).

A recent study by Burnette, Davis, Green, Worthington, and Bradfield (2009) examined the role of attachment theory to forgiveness outcomes. A key finding was that those defined as having anxious attachments were higher in rumination and concurrently were lower in forgiveness according to the scales. In addition, those who were defined as insecure were lower in empathy and also had lower forgiveness scores. The results indicate a relationship between attachment styles and typical strategies of responding to a transgression. The implication for clinical practice is the emphasis on assessment of patterns of response to transgression to aid growth in forgiveness. Furthermore, a clinician would do well to pay attention to attachment issues as couples attempt to work through forgiveness and reconciliation of marital transgressions.

Forgiveness Checklist

What follows is a checklist, originally developed by Enright (2001), Enright and Fitzgibbons (2000), and then modified in a computer-based survey by Knutson, Enright, and Garber (2008, p. 199).

Below is the rank-ordered developmental sequence of 82 participants who identified specific acts of forgiveness in their own lives. It can help you be more concrete in your own forgiveness with your partner.

Descriptors of Forgiveness

> Admitted to myself that my partner hurt me.
> I became aware of my anger.
> Admitted to myself that I felt shamed or humiliated by what he or she did.
> Lost my energy by staying resentful.
> Thought over and over about what happened.
> Compared my unfortunate state with my partner's more fortunate state.
> Realized that I may have been permanently changed by the offense.
> Thought of people in general, not just my partner, as bad or selfish.
> I realized that my old ways of handling this problem were not working.
> Willing to consider forgiveness as an option.

Committed to forgive him or her.

I thought of my partner in broader and more positive terms.

Stepping inside his or her shows to experience what that felt like.

I developed compassion for him or her.

I tried to bear the pain so that I don't pass it on to others.

Tried to do something nice for him or her.

I found a new positive meaning to the suffering I endured.

Realized that I needed to be forgiven for my own past mistakes.

Realized that I can get support from others as I forgive.

I developed a new purpose in life as a result of this experience.

(Adapted from Knutson, Enright, & Garbers, 2008.)

The movie *Smoke Signals* is an American Indian produced, directed, and starring cast involving the story of a teenage son confronted with the task of forgiving his father who abandoned him in his youth. The movie won the 1998 Audience Award and the Filmmakers' award at the Sundance Film Festival. Although the context of the quote is about a father and son relationship, the authors propose that the content also applies to you as a couple as well.

How do we forgive our fathers? Maybe in a dream. Do we forgive our father for leaving us too often, or forever, when we were little? Maybe for scaring us with unexpected rage, or making us nervous because there never seemed to be any rage there at all? Do we forgive our fathers for marrying, or not marrying, our mothers? Or divorcing, or not divorcing, our mothers? And shall we forgive them for their excesses of warmth or coldness? Shall we forgive them for pushing, or leaning? For shutting doors or speaking through walls? For never speaking, or never being silent? Do we forgive our fathers in our age, or in theirs? Or in their deaths, saying to them or not saying it. If we forgive our fathers, what is left? (Internet Movie Database, n.d.).

* * * * * * * * *

"A good rule of going through life is to keep the heart a little softer than the head." John Graham, (2000). *Bits and Pieces*. Lawrence Reagan Communications: Chicago, Ill., p. 1.

References

Agnew, C. R., Van Lange, P. A. M., Rusbult, C. E., & Langston, C. A. (1998). Cognitive interdependence: Commitment and the mental representation of close relationships. *Journal of Social and Psychological Psychology*, 74, 939-954.

Aron, A., Aron, E. N., & Smollan, D. (1992). Inclusion of other in the self scale and the structure of interpersonal closeness. *Journal of Social and Psychological Psychology*, 63, 596-612.

Baskin, T. W., & Enright, R. D. (2004). Intervention studies of forgiveness: A meta-analysis. *Journal of Counseling & Development*, 82, 79-90.

Bell, R. H. (2002). *Understanding African philosophy. A cross-cultural approach to classical and contemporary issues in Africa*. New York: Routledge.

Burnette, J. L., Davis, D. E., Green, J. D., Worthington, E. L., Jr., & Bradfield, E. (2009). Insecure attachment and depressive symptoms: The mediating role of rumination, empathy, and forgiveness. *Personality and Individual Differences*, 46, 276-280.

Comfort, W. (2007). The Quakers: *A brief account of their influence on Pennsylvania*. *Mechanicsburg, PA*: Folk Art Publishers.

Eaton, J., Struthers, C., Shomrony, A., & Santelli, A. (2008). When apologies fail: The moderating effect of implicit and explicit self-esteem on apology and forgiveness. *Self and Identity*, 6, 209-222.

Eckhart Tolle, E. (2005). A new earth: Awakening your life's purpose. New York: Plume.

Enright, R. D., & Fitzgibbons, R. P. (2000). *Helping clients forgive: An empirical guide for resolving anger and restoring hope*. Washington, DC: American Psychological Association.

Karremans, J., & Van Lange, P. (2008). The role of forgiveness in shifting from "Me" to "We.". *Self and Identity*, 7, 75-88.

Knutson, J., Enright, R., & Garbers, B. (2008). Validating the developmental pathway of forgiveness. *Journal of Counseling & Development*, 86, 193-200.

Krog, A. (2008). 'This thing called reconciliation . . .' forgiveness as part of an interconnectedness-towards-wholeness. *South African Journal of Philosophy*, 27, 4, 353-366.

Memorable quotes for Smoke Signals. (2009). Retrieved February 17, 2009, from http://www.imdb.com/title/tt012031/quotes

New English Bible. (n.d.) About Christianity. Retrieved February 17, 2009, from http://christianity.about. com/od/whatdoesthebiblesay/a/bibleforgiveness.htm

Pert, C. (2007). *To feel Go(o)d: The science and spirit of bliss*. Boulder, CO

Rosen, Rabbi David. (n.d.) Retrieved February 17, 2009, from rabbidavidrosen. net/doc/Judaism

Sounds True. Retrieved February 17, 2009, http://christianity.about.com/od/ whatdoesthebiblesay/a/bibleforgiveness.htm.

Soyinka, W. (1976). *Myth, literature and the African world*. Cambridge: Cambridge University Press.

Staub, E., Pearlman, L., Gubin, A., & Hagengimana, A. (2005). Healing, reconciliation, forgiving and the prevention of violence after genocide or mass killing: An intervention and its experimental evaluation in Rwanda. *Journal of Social and Clinical Psychology*, 24, 297-334.

ThinkExist.com. (n.d.). Retrieved February 17, 2009, from com/cat_forgiveness.html

Vitz, P. C., & Mango, P. (1997). Kernbergian dynamics and religious aspects of the forgiveness process. *Journal of Psychology and Theology*, 25, 72-80.

Wisdom Quotes. (n.d.). Retrieved February 17, 2009, from 2index.html

World of Quotes.com. (n.d.). Retrieved February 17, 2009 from www.worldofquotes.com/topic/Forgiveness/ 2index.html).

Worldwide Forgiveness Alliance. (n.d.) Retrieved February 17, 2009, from

Worthington, E. L., Jr. (2001). *Five steps to forgiveness: The art and science of forgiving*. New York: Crown Publishers.

Worthington, E. L., Jr. (2006). *Forgiveness and reconciliation: Theory and application*. New York: Rutledge.

Wuthnow, R. (2000). How religious groups promote forgiveness: A national study. *Journal for the Scientific Study of Religion*, 39, 125-139. Retrieved February 19, 2009, from www.jstor.org/pass/1387498

Authors' Note: The authors would like to acknowledge the assistance of Dee Dee Dirk, Meghan Burton, and Andrew Benesh.

Section 34:

Two Couples' Problem Solving Activities:
The One Hour Conference and A 6-Step Dialectical Method

Susan Rosenthal and Daniel Eckstein

For the past twenty years, all "for couples" columns have been organized using Jay Haley's (1980) suggested four considerations for couples' assessment. They include:

1. Understanding and respecting personality differences: Adler (1957/1981) stressed that both inferiority and/or superiority are in fact "two sides of the same coin," to use his metaphor

2. Role perceptions (each of the person's respective job description): "Are they on "the same page?" (Goal alignment, according to Adler)

3. Communication: John Guttmann's classic four horseman of the apocalypse metaphor consists of blame, sarcasm, contempt, and stonewalling as communication barriers. (Gottman and Silver, 1999)

4. Problem solving skills: Couples who stay together have no fewer actual problems. Instead, they stay together because they use problem solving strategies rather than a blame or denial approach to relationship challenges.

The purpose of the following article is to identify two specific activities developed by first author Susan Rosenthal that you as a couple can complete together. The profound simplicity of the first article is that sometimes the very action of committing time together demonstrates specific relationship qualities that are identified in bold print and parentheses.

A. <u>The One Hour Couple Conference</u>—Balancing intimacy and contact; a strengths based approach

This is an activity which can be periodically used for relationship renewal. The specific qualities involved in improving your relationship are listed in parentheses throughout the suggested seven step sequence:

a. Chose a time when you will be free from interruptions (not before bed). Your conversation can have a specific topic, or it can be a general sharing of thoughts and feelings. **(Cooperation)**.

b. Sit or lie back-to-back or side-by-side or in any comfortable position which does not allow you to see each other's face. **(Autonomy)**

c. The first time, flip a coin for who goes first. After that, each of you will take turns going first or second **(Cooperation)**

d. During the first 30 minutes, partner #1 addresses the designated topic and/or shares thoughts and feelings on any subject. Be sure you take the entire 30 minutes, even if some of that time is spent in silence. **(Intimacy)**

e. Partner #2—give your full attention to your speaking partner. **(Intimacy).** Do not interrupt or make any noise or movement which would communicate a reaction of any kind. Such respectful listening allows your partner to speak from the heart **(Autonomy)**

f. After the first half-hour, switch roles between speaker and listener. **(Balance)**. This is a good time to go to the bathroom or change to a more comfortable position. If you go second, there is no obligation to address what was said by your partner. However, if you are using the conference to resolve a specific problem, you can take turns addressing the issue at hand **(Autonomy)**.

g. The partners end their time with an expression of appreciation for the other **(Intimacy)**. After the conference, do not discuss any of the material raised in the conference if doing so will lead to an argument. If you do find yourselves arguing unproductively, stop and schedule another conference the following day to continue the discussion **(Cooperation)**. Outside of conference, keep the focus on what is going well in your relationship, including any positives that came out of the conference **(Intimacy)**.

At the end of your time together, take some time to focus on committing yourselves to speaking with one another. Apart from the actual content of your discussion, the authors have particularly highlighted the following four positive virtues ideally manifested in the act of your commitment to caring enough about your relationship to spend time together:

Be sure and discuss **cooperation**, **autonomy**, **intimacy**, and **balance** in your discussion. Talk about your level of satisfaction with each point and also discuss how you might also refine those factors in your relationship. Using a strengths-based approach, also commit to including **encouragement** as you conclude your conversation. For more practice on the skill of encouragement see Eckstein and Cooke, (2005) and Eckstein(2000).

Couple conference once a week. If you are fighting a lot and there are many problems to resolve, you can schedule conferences more often, but not more than once a day. Confine your arguments to the couple conference until they are resolved **(Cooperation).** If you and your partner are "cooperating" to avoid a conference, then ask yourself if you are really serious about improving your relationship. If you are, then take responsibility for making sure the conference happens. If you are having regular couple conferences, congratulate yourselves for doing the work necessary to build an attuned and cooperative relationship between equals.

B. A 6-step Dialectical Method for Resolving Couple Conflicts

This activity features a more structured problem-solving approach to a specific problem or issue confronting you as a couple. While it is ideally suited for you to complete with your partner, if he or she is unwilling or unable to participate, the activity can be completed alone.

Although the activity is written for you to complete as a couple, it can also be completed and later discussed with a counselor or other trusted person or persons. Each step is meant to be completed by each person independently and then discussed with your partner.

Step 1: The External Conflict

In one sentence, write down what you think the *general* problem is from your perspective.

Step 2: What You Most Want

Write down, in point form, what you found most attractive about your partner when you first met, fell in love, or got married. Take the first (or most important) item on your list and use it to complete the following sentence, "What I most wanted or hoped for from [my partner] was _____."

Is what you most wanted from your partner something that you did not have when you were growing up? For example, if what you most wanted from your partner was to feel secure, did you grow up in chaos? If what you most wanted from your partner was to feel appreciated, did you feel ignored as a child?

As an example, if you wrote "intelligent" on your list, were you hoping for someone who could see beneath the surface to the real you? If you wrote "funny" were you hoping for a happier life?

Step 3: What You Believe About Yourself

As a child, did you believe it was your fault that you did not have what you most wanted? For example if you most wanted to be accepted, but were frequently criticized as a child, did you conclude that it was because you weren't good enough? If you most wanted to be heard, but were frequently disregarded, did you conclude that it was because you weren't important?

Complete the sentence, "Because I didn't have what I most wanted as a child, I thought I was (or wasn't) _____." Again both of you do this independently from one another

Step 4: The Internal Conflict

For many people, what we most fear is related to what we most want. This can create so much conflict inside us that we won't allow ourselves to have what we want. An example would be that Jane fears being vulnerable and wants to feel safe. Jane's partner takes such good care of her that she can finally relax, but she is afraid that if she relaxes something bad will happen. John fears being rejected and works hard to please his partner, who is thoroughly pleased with him. But John fears that if he relaxes his efforts he will make a mistake and then he will be rejected.

Imagine that you could have from your partner what you most want (from step 2), but did not get as a child. Imagine for a moment what that might feel like. Would it be easy to accept or would it create a problem for you? Both partners do this.

Step 5: Unhealthy Collaboration

Write down how you think the conflict inside you might be contributing to the conflict between you and your partner and sabotaging what you most want.

Here is one example: "Because I wasn't taken care of as a child, *I very much want to be taken care of but I feel unworthy* so when [my partner] tries to take care of me, it doesn't feel right, so I criticize her and she backs off leaving me feeling abandoned and not cared for." or "Because I wasn't appreciated as a child, *I most want to be appreciated but I feel inadequate*, so I hide what I'm feeling and thinking and [my partner] gets angry at me for not communicating and I feel like I'm not good enough."

Step 6: Building Healthy Cooperation

If the conflict between you and your partner is being driven by the conflict inside you, then you must resolve your inner conflict first. (You may need the help of an experienced therapist to do this.) Healthy cooperation is built when each partner is primarily focused on resolving his or her inner conflict and secondarily supporting the other partner's efforts to do the same. Write down what you think YOU need to do.

Here is an example of the six step couple problem solving in action: Sam and Mary have been married for seven years and have two small children. Sam works in the family business and Mary stays home with the children. Their conflict began shortly after their marriage and has persisted despite many efforts to resolve it. Sam and Mary feel stuck and wonder how long they can stay married if their conflict is not resolved. In one therapy session, Sam and Mary agreed to try the method with the following results:

Step 1: The External Conflict
Sam: The problem is that Mary expects me to be perfect.
Mary: The problem is that Sam hides things from me.

Step 2: What You Most Want
Sam: What attracted me to Mary was her loyalty. What I most wanted from Mary was that she would be there for me, no matter what.
Mary: What attracted me most were Sam's broad shoulders, his strength. I wanted him to take care of me.

Step 3: What You Most Fear

Sam: When I was a child, I wanted to please my father, but he was always critical. I thought I could never do anything right.

Mary: My mother was an alcoholic and she sent me to school in dirty clothes. I was so ashamed of having nothing. I thought I was some kind of low life.

Step 4: The Internal Conflict

Sam: If Mary were to stand by me no matter what, so that I could reveal all my faults, then I'm afraid she would be so disgusted with me that she would reject me.

Mary: If Sam were completely reliable, then I would have no reason to worry and that's when something bad would happen and we would be out on the street.

Step 5: Unhealthy Collaboration

Sam: When there is a financial problem, like a bill that I haven't paid, I get so scared that Mary will find out and be mad at me that I put it away and forget about it. It's stupid because it's a small thing, but I get really scared and I can't deal with it. Then the bills pile up and I get even more scared to tell her. Of course she eventually finds out and she is furious with me.

Mary: I don't trust Sam to take care of us financially. He hides things and then there's a crisis and we are in trouble. I know it makes him nervous but I have to watch over everything he does.

Step 6: Building Healthy Cooperation

Sam: I know I have to be more honest with Mary. But I'm so ashamed. I hide myself and I hide my mistakes. I can't be honest with her until I can believe that I am a good person and a good provider, even if I do make mistakes.

Mary: I'm angry with Sam for messing up our finances and I have a hard time seeing the things he does well. I'm so afraid of being destitute that I don't trust him to take care of me. It would be easier on both of us if I could appreciate and enjoy what Sam does for me.

Comments

Sam and Mary

As a child, Sam was so badly neglected that he mistakenly concluded that he must be a complete loser. No matter how well he does in life, he fears that he will be exposed as a loser and his wife will leave him. This fear is so powerful that when he makes even a small mistake he panics and banishes the problem from his mind to make it go away. Unfortunately for Sam, the problem deferred is the problem that grows. His (now large) mistake is eventually revealed and Sam gets the angry blast that he was dreading from Mary. Mary's anger re-enforces Sam's belief that he must be a loser so, although he promises not to hide any more problems, he cannot keep his promise. Mary is threatening to leave her husband if this problem is not solved. Mary's rejection is what Sam most fears but also expects, because he doesn't believe that he deserves anything better.

Without realizing what he is doing, Sam has set up a situation that perpetuates his own misery. In essence, he is re-enacting his childhood trauma, using Mary as a stand-in for his rejecting father. Because of his internal conflict (wanting acceptance and believing that he doesn't deserve it) he would be driven to construct a similar conflict with any partner. Sam cannot be honest with Mary until he believes that he is entitled to make mistakes and not be rejected for them. Sam mistakenly believes that Mary will not tolerate his imperfections, when it is really Sam who cannot tolerate them.

As a child, Mary suffered severe physical neglect. She was the hungry, dirty child who was picked on by the other kids. Mary has improved her position in life, obtaining an education and becoming a loving, responsible mother to her children. Despite the occasional financial crises in their family business, Sam has provided reasonably well for Mary and their children. But Mary's memories of how bad it can be cause her to panic whenever there is a financial problem. She fears that at any moment she will be plunged back into the destitution of her childhood. Mary believes this will happen because it is all she deserves. But she thinks that the problem is Sam's "incompetence." Her tension over financial matters and her scrutiny of Sam's activities make him nervous, and feed into his fear that he has to be perfect.

When Sam hides small problems that grow to become large, Mary's security is deeply threatened and she reacts with understandable rage. Sam's avoidance re-enforces her belief that he is incompetent and she will never be secure. Without realizing what she is doing, Mary has set up a situation that perpetuates her own misery. In essence, she is "re-enacting" her childhood trauma, using Sam as a stand-in for her irresponsible mother. Because of her internal conflict (wanting to be taken care of and not believing she deserves this) she would be driven to construct a similar conflict with any partner. Until she feels more deserving of being supported, Mary will be unable to support Sam's efforts to manage the family's finances. Mary mistakenly believes that Sam is incapable of supporting the family, when it is really Mary who feels too undeserving to trust anyone to support her.

Concluding Comments

The 6-step dialectical method for resolving couple conflicts is a non-blaming Adlerian approach, which reveals how you as a couple collaborate to create the problems in your relationships, and how you can collaborate to solve those problems.

The purpose of asking what was most admired about your partner and what was most wanted from your partner, and its relation with what was lacking in childhood (steps 1-3), is to reveal how this particular relationship was created in this particular way to meet each of your unmet needs.

Steps 3-5 reveal how the therapeutic potential of a relationship can be thwarted when each of you retains basic beliefs about yourself which prevents you from getting what your wishes fulfilled.

When you blame each other for frustrating your own desires, conflict between the two of you is inevitable. Because each of you often feels powerless to end the misery, the key to solving the problem is to reveal the existence, origin and purpose of each partner's self-defeating inner conflict.

When emotionally injured individuals come together, they sincerely hope that the love of the other will heal them. If lack of self-love prevents this, they may begin an unhealthy collaboration where they transform their inner conflicts into interpersonal conflicts, confirming their deepest fears. The resulting re-enactment of childhood misery is accompanied by childhood feelings of powerlessness. They can't live with each other but neither can they live apart.

Breaking through this cycle of misery and blame requires making a clear distinction between the past (when we were children with little understanding and few options) and the present (where we have much more power). It is also necessary to conduct a sober re-evaluation of the idealized caretaker and the self-blame that sustains this myth.

When personality is constructed around a self-negative belief (e.g., I am no good), changing this belief will shake a person to the core. But with adult understanding of the past and therapeutic support in the present, we can change what we think about ourselves. With professional therapy and months of difficult and painful work, Sam and Mary were able to reduce their conflicts and increase the amount of healthy cooperation in their lives. Both of them wanted the same thing—to be understood, accepted and loved. When this was revealed and when their own unwitting sabotage was also revealed, the path was cleared for the fundamental changes they were seeking.

All four of Jay Haley's couples assessment tools can also be found in many couples renewal activities are described in Eckstein (2013) Here are15 additional problem solving activates that can be found in previous "for couples" columns.

1. Eckstein, D. (1999). Styles of conflict management. *The Family Journal: Counseling and Therapy for Couples and Families*, 6(3), 239-242.

2. Jones, J., and Eckstein, D. (l999). Thirty-three suggestions for couple's conflict Resolution. *The Family Journal: Counseling and Therapy for Couples* and *Families,*6(4), 334-336.

3. Eckstein, D (1994). Force-field analysis as an aid in decision making for couples. *The Family Journal: Counseling and Therapy for Couples and Families,* 2(4), 371-372.

4. Eckstein, D., Welch, D., & Gamber, V. (2001). The Process of Early Recollection Reflection (PERR) for Couples and Families. *The Family Journal: Counseling and Therapy for Couples and Families*, 9(2), 203-209.

5. Eckstein, D. (2002). Walls and windows: Closing and opening behaviors for couples and families. *The Family Journal: Counseling and therapy for couples and families,* 10(3), 343-344

6. Willhite, R. & Eckstein, D. (2003). The angry, the angrier, and the angriest relationships. *The Family Journal: Counseling and Therapy for Couples and Families,* 11(1), 202-209.

7. Hydock, R. & Eckstein, D. (2006). Help me help you: The 4-factor goal support. system. *The Family Journal: Counseling and Therapy for Couples and Families,* 14(2), 113-118.

8. Garrison, R. & Eckstein, D. (2009). Four couples' sleep satisfaction interviews: Recommendations for improving your nights together. *The Family Journal: Counseling and Therapy for Couples and Families.* 17, 1, 58-63.

9. Eckstein, D., Lee, C., & Lin, Y. (2008). The use of Ed DeBono's 'six-thinking hats problem-solving technique with couples. *The Family Journal: Counseling and therapy for couples and families,* 16, 3, 254-257

10. Milliren, A., Milliren, M. & Eckstein, D. (2007). "Combining Socratic Questions with the "ADAPT" Problem-Solving Model: Implications for Couple's Conflict Resolution, *"The Family Journal: Counseling and Therapy for Couples and Families,* 15,4,415-419.

11. Eckstein, D., Sperber, M., & McRae. (2009). Forgiveness: Another Relationship "F word"—A couple's Dialogue. *The Family Journal: Counseling and Therapy for Couples and Families.* 17, 3, 256-262.

12. Ginsburg, P and Eckstein, D. (2010). The Staying together in needy times (STINT) couples questionnaire, *The Family Journal: Counseling and Therapy for Couples and Families.* 18, 3,310-320.

13. Nelson, J., Li, C., Eckstein, D., Ane, P., & Mullener, W. (2008). Antidotes for infidelity and prescriptions for long lasting relationships: Four couples' activities. *The Family Journal: Counseling and therapy for couples and families,* 16, 375-378.

14. Eckstein, D., Junkins, E. & McBrien, R. (2003). Ha, ha, ha: improving couple and family Healthy Humor Quotient (HHQ). *The Family Journal: Counseling and therapy for couples and families,* 11(3), 301-305.

15. Baute, P., & Eckstein, D. (1993). Rules for a structured separation. *The Family Journal: Counseling and Therapy for Couples and Families,* 2(4), 276.

Biography

Susan Mary Rosenthal, MD (McMaster '74) provides psychotherapy for individuals and couples in Guelph, Ontario. She also teaches psychotherapy courses for Adler Graduate Professional Schools in Toronto.

Section 35:

The Process of Early Recollection Reflection (PERR) for Couples and Families

Daniel Eckstein, Deborah Vogele Welch and Victoria Gamber

The purpose of this article is to offer a specific method for couples and/or family members to consider the implications of a formative personal early recollection (ER) on one's current relationship. The authors have created the "process of early recollection reflection (PERR)" as a systematic way of understanding and then changing or re-writing early experience. This can be a powerful way to change current life behaviors and experiences.

The Process of Early-Recollection Reflection

Instructions: Each individual (you, your partner, or other family member) is encouraged to independently complete this exercise. Later you will be encouraged to discuss your experiences together.

Write down an early memory from as far back in your life as possible. Make sure it is your actual memory and not someone else's. If you're thinking, "I really can't remember anything," try relaxing and ask yourself such questions as:

- Can you remember an early birthday party?
- Can you recall any of your teachers when you were young? Did one or two stand out? Why?
- Did your family take vacations? What do you remember from those vacations?
- Can you remember the day you learned to ride a bike or some other first childhood accomplishment? What happened?
- Can you remember a special holiday, Christmas or Hanukkah—a special present you received?
- What did you do for fun? What did you do at bedtime?[1]

Now write down the memory word for word as you remember it. To help you remember as much of the memory as possible keep asking yourself "and then what happened?" until you have no more memory of the event.

One day I remember: _____

My major feeling(s) was (were): _____ The most vivid aspect of the memory was: _____

The Importance of Early Recollections (ERs)

Early recollections become the lens through which we view all that we perceive. The lens either amplifies or distorts our future experiences in ways that are unconscious.

A family member's early recollections provide valuable clues to his or her lifestyle. The projective nature and the simplicity with which a person will generally disclose an early recollection (ER) make using it a powerful counseling technique. ERs help identify the basic existential conclusions a person has formed about himself or herself, others, and life in general.[2]

Shulman and Mosak[3] have noted that psychologist Alfred Adler was able to gain clinically salient insights from ERs on such issues as the person's basic attitude toward life; hints as to why a particular direction or strategy was adopted; compensatory devices developed to cope with perceived inadequacies; courage or lack thereof; preferred modes of coping; preferred interpersonal transactions; the presence or absence of social interest; and core wants, needs, values, and motivators.

The importance of an individual's selective recall of early childhood events has a specific diagnostic and therapeutic purpose in Adlerian psychology. Early recollections are keys to increasing understanding of the individual. The technique also has potential as a therapeutic tool in family counseling.[4]

According to Adler among the psychological expressions, some of the most revealing are individual memories. "His memories are reminders he carries about with him of his own limits and the meaning of circumstances. There are no chance memories; out of the incalculable number of impressions, which meet an individual, he chooses to remember only those, which he feels, however darkly, to have a bearing on his situation. Thus, the memories represent his story of my life, a story he repeats to himself to warm him or comfort him, to keep him concentrated on his goal, and to prepare him by means of past experience, so that he will meet the future with an already tested style in action".[5]

There are several common elements between Adlerian Individual Psychology and family systems therapy in both theory and clinical applications. According to Carich and Willingham,[6] Adler and later Dreikurs were the original initiators of working with the family system in Vienna in the 1920s. One of these elements is what Adler[7] described as the concept of social interest, which emphasizes social interaction, social influences, and relationships within a social context over time. Becvar and Becvar[8] describe the family as an emotional system, much like the Adlerian concept of social influences and family atmosphere. This emotional system is a universal and transgenerational phenomena.

According to Nims & Drikmeyer[9] "Part of family systems therapy is providing an area for family members generations to meet and dialogue. It is during that dialogue that the emotional process inevitably surfaces. Family members have the opportunity to confront their attitudes and beliefs about each other and as a result hopefully become more self-aware and differentiated. The early recollection approach of using multiple generations is an excellent teaching tool to facilitate this process.

Marcus, Manster, and Spencer [10] note that Adlerian psychologists believe that there are only memories that have purposefully, if not consciously, been remembered over the years because they represent a tightly woven combination of self and experience. Thus, the memories recalled in ERs are important indicators of adult personality and life style.[11] Family and marriage counselors understand ERs as capsule summaries of one's present life philosophy, believing that people remember incidents in their lives that are consistent with the views of their own lives and places in the world.[12]

Shulman and Mosak [13] note the following common thematic topics found in ERs *dethronement* (the birth of younger sibling or another person entering who takes center stage), *surprises, obstacles, affiliation, security, skill tasks dependence, external authority, self-control, status, power, morality, human interactions, new situations, excitement, sexuality, gender, nurturance, confusion, luck, sickness,* and *death*. The second part of the ER, the subject's feeling and identifying what was most vivid about the ER, gives valuable insight into what the person *concluded* about the event, the "and therefore . . ." Shulman & Mosak provide the following list of representative response themes: *observer; problem-solving; compliance or rebellion; a call for help; revenge; suffering; manipulation; seeking excitement; pretense; denial; resolve; competence; social interest; activity; distance-keeping; cooperation; overconfidence; self-aggrandizement; criticism;* and *feeling avoidance*.

Kaplan [14] suggests the following ten questions be answered by family members relative to ERs:

1. Who is present in the recollection?
2. Who is remembered with affection?
3. Who is disliked in the recollection?
4. What problem(s) is (are) confronted in the recollection?
5. What special talent(s) or ability is (are) revealed in the recollection?
6. Is the recollection generally pleasant or unpleasant?
7. What is the client's level of activity in the recollection?
8. What emotion does the client feel and/or show pertaining to the recollection?
9. What does the recollection suggest to you about the client's social interest?
10. What fictional goals(s) is (are) implied in the recollection?

Rather than a person being a "prisoner" of one's ERs, a core Adlerian concept is that ERs can change as a result of such interventions as counseling. For example, Dreikurs [15] writes that:

> *The final proof of the patient's satisfactory reorientation is the change in his basic mistakes, indicated by a change in his early recollections. If a significant improvement has taken place, new incidents are recollected, reported recollections show significant changes, or are in some cases completely forgotten.*

Eckstein [16] empirically demonstrated that ERs do appear to change significantly as a result of long-term therapy. Actual pre/post ER changes help illustrate the dramatic difference in the "feeling tone" of one person's changing ERs.

Pre-Counseling

"My father put me on my sister's two wheeler—I didn't trust him—I was terrified—I screamed at the top of my lungs—I felt I was too young to ride.

Nine Months Later

"My father was trying to teach me to ride a two-wheeler—he was trying to teach me to ride—He then took me off, knowing I was too scared. I should have been more cooperative. Later I went back and pretended I was riding. He wasn't hurting me; I felt I should have "been more cooperative."

As the youngest of four female siblings, this woman had sought counseling with the first author due to her doubt of being successful as a freshman in college. Her positive experiences that first year of college helped her confront her dependency-based self-doubts. Newly discovered self-confidence is reflected in her later memory.

Note that although the same event was remembered, there was a dramatic shift in how the woman attributed much more positive motives to her father plus her own enhanced feelings of self-confidence in her actual life in the second version.

According to Quinn,[17] a change in one's story or script can greatly alter how we see and relate to the world. Our past experiences have etched a given "map" or script into our brains and this affects how we process information. Old scripts become formidable barriers to tear down and replace. To gain new insight these scripts have to be reexamined. Periodically it is important to "reinvent" ourselves so we can create our lives as we choose them to be, rather than being stuck in old cyclical patterns. Enlarging our perspective is difficult. But if we take the time to examine these scripts and re-write them, we become more empowered. Re-writing our scripts or stories gives us a new way to see the world, and more energy for the process of living. It also makes improved present family relationships possibly more positive.

Leman and Carlson [18] believe that "one of the biggest lies people tell themselves is, I can't really change—this is the way I am. While it is true you can't change the basic grain of your wood, there is a great deal you do to change the way you live with that grain. You can reshape that grain by using the A-B-Cs of truth therapy:

- *Accept* the fact that your memories can be lying—at least a little bit.
- *Believe* the truth instead of the lies that are ingrained into your lifestyle.
- *Change* your behavior by using different self-talk."

In a manner similar to the sharing process advocated in article, they do encourage couples to share ERs with each other. Here are some strengths they suggest couples attempt to identify after sharing ERs; concerned about others, decisive, listens well, responsible, takes good care of self, committed to God, enjoys children, puts marriage first, patient, kind, and forgiving.

The Process of Early Recollection Reflection (PERR)

In order to gain more understanding and possibly review or rewrite one's early experiences the authors are suggesting the following process, which has been adapted from the dream work of Corriere and Hart.[19]

The authors propose the following ways of viewing the memory according to role, feeling, or clarity. These concepts are defined as follows:

Role—How active or passive are you in the memory? For example, to use a metaphor from the game of pool, consider the difference between a "cue ball" and an "8 ball" personality. The cue ball is an actor and motivator, making things happen. In contrast the 8-ball personality sits passively on the table waiting to knock into a pocket. So too the issue of role is how active or passive were you in your memory? Are you the starring character or a secondary player, just observing or not even visible in the memory?

Feeling—How much *do you* recall your emotional experience? Can you remember how it felt *then* in your body *right now*? For example, did you feel "a quiver in the belly," "a contraction in your throat," or "a warmth in the heart?"

Clarity—How clear is your memory? How vivid is your recollection of the setting, the people, the landscape, and the dialogue? Do you have a cognitive understanding of what occurred in the experience and why?

Choose to focus on either Role, Feeling, or Clarity for this activity the first time around. You can later go back and work with the other two.

Read your written memory aloud to your partner and/or other family member. As you look at the scale notice where you would place yourself in this memory. Next, in order to re-write or to improve your mastery, your next step is to move up one level using your creative imagination. Your family member/partner may coach you by saying "if it were my experience, I might imagine . . . ." Or "knowing you the way I do, perhaps you might consider _____."

Activity 51:
PERR Process—(Select one of these)

Role

1. Write your role in the Early Recollection (ER). Circle the number that corresponds to your role (1-5).

    a) _____ No Role — You have no role in this memory/experience.

    b) _____ Passive — Your role is that of someone who is present but uninvolved and unresponsive.

    c) _____ Slightly Active — There is some response by you to the events, but for the most part your role does not change the outcome of the memory/experience.

    d) _____ Active — Your activity is obvious in the ER. Your activity has some effect on the outcome of the memory/experience.

    e) _____ Very Active — Your activity is a significant part of the ER and significantly affects the outcome of the memory/ experience.

2. Use your imagination to move up one level in the ER. (For example, if you were at a in your role, how would the ER be different if you were a 3?) Allow yourself to make up a change in the ER with yourself at the higher-level role. Write a few words about your role currently, and then about how you might imagine your role at the higher-level ER.

    _____

    _____

3. How is your role in this ER similar to a role you take in your life now? (Think about your role in work, play, family, relationships, or any area of life.) Is there currently any area of life in which you express more but hold back?

    _____

    _____

Feeling

1. Rate your feelings in the ER. Circle the number that corresponds to your feeling level (1-5).

    a) _____ No Feeling — You have no feeling, your memory is about things or events that remains neutral.

    b) _____ Slight — Your ER evokes some vague or slight feeling in the background.

THE COUPLE'S MATCH BOOK

c) _____ Moderate   Your ER contains some definite feeling that you can describe. But it doesn't influence your memory.

d) _____ Strong   Your ER contain strong feeling that has some influence in your recollection.

e) _____ Complete   Your feeling is intense. You are aware that you are feeling and you allow it to occur fully and completely.

2. Use your imagination to *move up* on level in the ER. (For example, if you were at a 4 in your feeling, how would the ER be different if you were a 5?) Allow yourself to make up a change in the ER with yourself at this higher level of feeling. Write a few words about your current feeling level and the new imagined feeling level. Remember your partner and/or other family members can help coach you on the shift.

_____

_____

How is your feeling in this ER similar to the way you feel (or don't (feel) in any area of your current life now?

_____

_____

Clarity

1. Rate your clarity in the ER. Circle the number that corresponds to your clarity level (1-5).

a) _____ No Clarity   Completely confused. Your recollection pictures are incoherent. Events and feelings have no relationship.

b) _____ Slight   There is much that is unclear or distorted in your recollection. But it does not completely obscure the ER images.

c) _____ Moderate   Your ER is somewhat clear and direct. You have a general idea of what is going on in the scene, even though some elements may be distorted.

d) _____ Strong   Your memory is clear and direct, but you don't necessarily understand why things are happening, the purpose or the meaning.

e) _____ Complete   Your ER is completely clear. Your recollection is clear and direct and you understand why things are happening, it makes sense, there is purpose and meaning.

2. Use your imagination to *move up* one level in the ER. (For example if you were at a 1 in your clarity, how would the ER be different if you were at a 2?) Allow yourself to make

up a change in the ER with yourself at this higher level of clarity. Write a few words about your current level of clarity, and your imagined clarity at the next higher level.

_____

_____

3. How is your clarity in this ER similar to your life *now*? Is there an area of your life where your clarity is similar to the clarity of this ER?

_____

Representative Examples

Here are some actual ERs utilizing the authors' proposed PERR method of exploration.

1. *Role* example—Here is how the second author, Deborah Vogele Welch, used the PERR process working with her role in an (ER) early recollection.

   "My memory is that I was very passive at the age of 6. I remember trying to speak out in my first grade class. I was trying to help my teacher, Mrs. Phillips, by yelling to the other kids to 'be quiet.' My teacher screamed at me. I am humiliated for speaking out. I remember deciding to become quiet and never to again trust speaking in large groups. I rate my role in this ER as a 2, as I slightly remember myself being present, but I was mostly uninvolved and unresponsive during the event. I would have rated myself a 3 (slightly active), if I had tried to change the outcome after the teacher yelled at me. But I didn't, so I was a 2."

   Here is how Deborah used the PERR Process. Years later she journaled about the event, then she used her imagination to move up to a 3 (slightly active) in the memory. Deborah thought it over and decided it would have been possible to take a different role in the experience. She could have told Mrs. Phillips that she felt she had been unfair. She could have decided to continue to voice her thoughts and be slightly active regardless of the incident.

   Deborah realized this event affected her for many years. She acknowledged that she had overcome much of the passivity from her childhood years. But as she moved to the next level in the PERR process, even more benefit emerged. She asked herself, how is the role in the ER similar to a role you take in your life now? A current situation popped into her mind. She suddenly became aware of a current behavior that was more passive than she would like in the midst of some tense company organizational politics. She had told herself up to now that she had no power in the situation so there is no point doing anything. She decided she would take a more proactive stance and speak out about the situation. She re-wrote the story in her imagination, and found herself more powerful in her organization as a result of the PERR process.

2. Here is an actual memory of the third author, Victoria Gamber, to illustrate working with the *feeling* component of the PERR.

"I remember being at a garden party on a bright summer afternoon. I stooped down to observe a tiny creature in the grass in a sparking world. 'Vicki,' I heard my aunt slap out angrily, 'get out of that mud this instant. You're filthy.' Suddenly I remember it felt as if the world had gone gray. There was no sudden storm, no flash of lightning. But suddenly I felt very different, unsafe. There was a sickening feeling in the pit of my stomach. The fear grew into a sense of grave danger. I decided never to share anything that touched me deeply. Perhaps by sharing nothing of myself, I could protect against irrationality and remain safe. The others in my life became my focus and I lost touch with my inner core."

Here is how Victoria used her imagination to move from level where the feeling is strong and intense, but not complete to level 5 where she allows the feeling to emerge fully and completely.

"My throat aches now just remembering the incident. The pain feels overwhelming and part of me wants to retreat, but by staying with it and moving to the center of the fear instead of being overwhelmed I see a picture of my aunt. The feelings shifts into sadness. I'm feeling very sad that my aunt can't experience all the beauty in nature, that she's stuck in the mud." When feeling becomes more complete it doesn't feel so much like I'm threatened by her as I feel compassion for her. It's not about me needing to be safe; it's about her inability to see the beauty in the world. I rate my feeling as a 5 now."

3. Here is an example from author, Deborah Vogele Welch, of working with a client on *clarity* in the early recollection:

Julia says, "I don't understand why things are happening this way at work. I take one step forward and two steps back. I don't seem to be getting anywhere with building our organization." Deborah asked Julia to talk further about what she was experiencing at work. Julia said, "It doesn't make any sense. I feel like I'm doing all the right things, but I always end up overwhelmed and tired. I can't lead well from this state. That style seemed to work when I was an independent agent—but now that I have to lead other managers it's not working." Deborah asked Julia to remember a time she felt this same way when she was much younger. What was the first time Julia ever remembered this same kind of experience. Julia was silent for a full minute. Then she said, "It reminds me of when I was 15. I had my first job doing secretarial work. My boss was a perfectionist. In order to survive I had to be perfect. I made a decision then to work at 150%. It seemed to work for me at the time. I kept the job. But for two years working there I ran around 'frazzled.' I felt very tired and didn't understand why. I never got any promotions or moved up in the company."

Identifying her clarity in the ER it was 4 (strong)—The memory was clear and direct, but she didn't understand why things are happening. She was asked to imagine the memory at a 5. "It's hard to imagine." "Well, just pretend you did know . . . and say whatever comes to mind" Deborah suggested. Julia replied:

"I'm behaving this way because I'm fearful. I'm fearful I will lose my job; fearful I won't be good enough. And because I am so fearful, I am overworking all the time, and losing the opportunities to share meaning-fully with those who could be resources for me to get a promotion at the company."

When invited to contemplate how the memory might apply to her life *now*—if she were to apply that clarity and meaning to her current situation, she said, "I tell myself I don't have time to do any long term visioning, or time to share with those who could help this business develop. But perhaps I could relax a little and take more time."

Activity 52:
Additional ER Reflection Activity

In addition to reflecting on some of the suggested themes identified early [20] and answering some of the ten questions raised by Kaplan,[21] here are some additional reflective questions for your relative to your ER.

1. How did this ER feel to you?
2. Did you like the role you had in this ER?
3. What about the clarity? Are you clear about the ER and your experience or is it confused?
4. Did you feel feelings in this memory?
5. What is this ER trying to tell you about your life now?
6. Does this ER address your future?
7. Imagine *recreating* the memory. How would you change it?
8. Does this ER address your future?

Integrative Activity

First, identify some of the key insights relative to your own ER.

_____

Second, what are some of the key insights relative to your partner or other family member's ER?

_____

Lastly, how do the two memories interact and/or influence you and your partner or family? For example, what are the system's ramifications of these events?

_____

Summary

An understanding of one's self is essential to being an effective partner or family member. Jean Houston[22] believes that:

We have been crippled and threatened in our capacities to experience both inner and outer worlds. We are unable, most of us, to see, touch, taste, smell and hear as well as we once could. Stale habits of perception and the thick, darkened glass of concepts have gotten in the way of our precepts. Similarly, we have cut off from our freedom to be what we really are by the idols we have made of our habits, by society's expectations for us, by social and professional demands that we shape us to their design. Francis Bacon once referred to these as 'the idols of the tribe and of the marketplace,' and they continue to cripple us in varying degrees and in various ways.

She also believes that:

The human psyche, both personal and universal, is a tale of death and resurrection, with rhythms of awakening alternating with rhythms of forgetting and even sleep. While in darkness, we grow and change and prepare for reawakening to new life forms. The present winter of our discontent, with its ontological breakdown of most of the structural givens of the social, moral, political, and psychological orders, is also the cocoon of a different way of living on this earth.[23]

The poet T. S. Elliot said it this way:
Time present and time past
Are both perhaps present in time future
And time future contained in time past.
(Four Quartets: "Burnt Norton")

The power of ERs is that in the culture of the psyche there is apparently no time line. History is present in all its parts, and is there to be recovered and drawn upon as a vast and inexhaustible resource. The present article suggests a specific technique creatively tapping the vast internal healing capacities of an individual who takes the time to explore the relationship of one's past ERs to his or her present relationships.

The authors introduce the PERR as one method of gaining insight and of improving oneself through action-oriented changes. The PERR is an adaptation of a dream related model developed 20 years ago by Corree & Hart in *The Dream Maker*.[24] The potential advantages of the proposed process include the following:

1. The gradual quality (scaling)—moving up just one notch
2. It is usually non-threatening to up it just one level.
3. There is refinement (improvement) to the process
4. The person is active involvement in interpretation because the meaning is internal to the person and therefore has higher "psychological ownership."
5. Concurrently, the person is encouraged to use his or her partner and/or family member as a coach.
6. It is a fairly easy transfer of the theory to actual behavior

Biographies

Dr. Victoria Gamber, a core faculty member in General Psychology at Capella University. She is a licensed psychologist in Colorado and Hawaii. For 25 years she was in private practice on the island of Oahu and in Denver, Colorado.

Dr. Gamber served as Associate Professor of Psychology at Ottawa University where she coordinated the practicum program and as adjunct faculty at University of Hawaii, Hawaii Loa College and the Professional School of Humanistic Studies. She has extensive experience supervising doctoral interns and post-doctoral fellows in Hawaii and Colorado. Dr. Gamber has conducted seminars in the United States and abroad. She is a member of the International Psychosynthesis Network, and the former director of the Focusing Network for the state of Hawaii.

Dr. Gamber received her Ph.D. from the University of Pittsburgh and completed doctoral work in philosophy and education at University of California, Berkeley. Her background in phenomenological psychology was from Duquesne University, Pittsburgh. She has recently published 5 articles in a number of journals and has completed a book for publication on Team Spirit with Dr. Deborah Vogele-Welch.

As core faculty in Capella's clinical psychology program, Dr. Gamber wrote several course syllabi in counseling theories and group practice and she generally teaches the theories courses. She coordinated the Scottsdale Residency Program for the clinical learners.

Deborah Welch, Ph.D. is the author of "Forgiveness at Work: Stories of the Power, Possibility and Practice of Forgiveness in the Workplace." Deborah coaches leaders in colleges, school districts, foundations, corporations and small businesses. She is an innovator in virtual processes for learning across distances. She designed and regularly co-facilitates a yearlong global virtual servant leadership program. She is also a core faculty member at Capella University and since 1999 she has been teaching graduate level courses in the Psychology of Leadership and guiding dissertation work.

Endnotes

1. Leman, K, & Carlson, R. (1989). Unlocking the Secrets of Your Childhood Memories. Nashville, TN: Thomas Nelson

2. Eckstein, D. (1999). Early-recollection skill building workshop. The Journal of Individual Psychology, 55, 4. 437-448.

3. Shulman, B.H., & Mosak, H.H. (1988). Manual for life-style assessment. Muncie, IN: Accelerated Development, Inc.

4. Nims, D. & Dinkmeyer, D. (1995). Early recollections as a communication tool between generations. Individual Psychology, 51, 4, 406-412.

5. Adler, A. (1931). What life should mean to you. Boston: Little, Brown

6. Carich, M.S., & Willingham.W. (1987). The roots of family systems theory in Individual psychology. Individual Psychology, 43, 71-78.

7. Adler. A. (1964). Social interest: A challenge to mankind. New York: Capricorn.

8. Becvar, D. S., & Becvar, R. J. (1993). Family therapy: A systematic integration. Needham Heights, MA: Allyn & Bacon.

9. Nims & Dinkmeyer, loc. cit. p. 409.

10. Marcus, M. B., Manaster, G. J., & Spencer, D. (1999). Client and counselor-trainee early recollection. The Journal of Individual Psychology, 55, 1, 82-87.

11. Ansbacher, H. L., & Ansbacher, R.R. (Eds.) (1956). The individual psychology of Alfred Adler: A systematic presentation in selections from his writings. New York: Harper & Row.

12. Manaster, G. J., & Corsini, R. J. (1993) Individual Psychology: Theory and practice Chicago: Adler School of Professional Psychology.

13. Shuman & Mosak, loc. cit.

14. Kaplan, H. (1985). A method of the interpretation of early32 recollection and dreams. Individual Psychologist, 41, 4, 525-533.

15. Dreikurs, R. (1967). Psychodynamic psychotherapy and counseling. p. 71. Chicago: Alfred Adler Institute.

16. Eckstein, D. (1976). Early recollection changes after counseling: A case study. Journal of Individual Psychology, 32, 212-223.

17. Quinn, R. (1996). Deep change: Discovering the leader within. San Francisco, CA: Jossey-Bass.

18. Leman & Carlson, loc. cit. p. 107

19. Corriere, R. & Hart, J. (1977) The dreammaker: Discovering your breakthrough dreams. New York, NY: Funk & Wagnalls.

20. Shulman & Mosak, loc. cit.

21. Kaplan, loc. cit.

22. Houston, J. (1984), The Search for the Beloved. p. 93 Los Angeles: Jeremy Tarcher

23. Houston, loc. cit. p. 14.

24. Corriere & Hart, loc. cit.

Section 36:

The Relationship Decision Making Box (RDMB): A Questionnaire for Exploring the Decision-making Process

Nate Larsen, Malcolm Gray, and Daniel Eckstein

For the past twenty-one years, this "for couples" column has focused on Jay Haley's (1980) four methods of assessing couples, including:

1. understanding and respecting personality differences;
2. role perceptions;
3. communication, and
4. problem-solving skills

The purpose of the present article is to present a questionnaire for helping access couples' decision making process. Such a focus can be represented as an example of role perceptions While the content of decision making is important for couples to understand, an equally critical and often overlooked consideration is the process by which each partner approaches that decision-making.

Following a brief introduction to the Relationship Decision Making Box (RDMB) questionnaire, each partner will take, score, and then discuss their respective scores. A brief review of some representative research literature will follow. Your next steps application and some additional "for couples" past articles for additional role perception activities will conclude the article.

Introducing the RDMB

For couples, equity in decision making seems to be paramount in today's increasingly individualistic culture and having a format for measuring how this occurs within relationships is the basis for the development of the Relationship Decision Making Box (RDMB). The RDMB is a brief self-evaluative exercise drawn from the primary author's experience in conducting marital therapy at a mid-western, regional mental health clinic

The RDMB produces a quick, immediately accessible snapshot of decision making patterns in relationships. It can be administered as part of an assessment and as part of the treatment in conjoint couple's therapy.

Instructions: Individually, indicate your own opinion based on a scale of 1-10 relative to how much decision making you personally contribute to ten major relationship areas. By indicating your own perceived amount of decisions made, you will also automatically calculate how much you perceive your partner has been in charge of the decision making process for each issue. There will be a total combined score of 100%. With this instrument, decision-making percentages can be noted for individual issues as well as for the relationship as a whole.

Activity 53:
The Relationship Decision Making Box

Name: _____ Date: _____
Years in Present Relationship: _____ Gender: M / F

Below is a sample of major decisions that typically occur on a routine basis within most relationships. For each relationship decision making issue listed below, circle the number that best reflects the amount of decision making you perceive yourself to have compared to your partner. For each issue, the higher the number circled the more decisions you are making in your relationship—the lower the number circled, the less decision making you perceive yourself to have for that issue. (If an issue listed below is presently not a part of your relationship, then use your best judgment in deciding the amount of decision-making you think you would have if it were a part of your relationship.)

Decision Making Issues:

1. Who makes the most decisions regarding how the money is handled within your relationship?
   Money: 1   2   3   4   5   6   7   8   9   10

2. Who makes the most decisions regarding how chores are handled within your relationship?
   Chores: 1   2   3   4   5   6   7   8   9   10

3. Who makes the most decisions regarding how to parent the children in your relationship?
   Parenting: 1   2   3   4   5   6   7   8   9   10

4. Who makes the most decisions regarding social activities in your relationship?
   Social Activities   1   2   3   4   5   6   7   8   9   10

5. Who makes the most decisions regarding problem solving in your relationship?
   Problem Solving: 1   2   3   4   5   6   7   8   9   10

6. Who makes the most decisions regarding religious practices in your relationship?
Religion: 1   2   3   4   5   6   7   8   9   10

7. Who makes the most decisions regarding employment issues in your relationship?
Employment: 1   2   3   4   5   6   7   8   9   10

8. Who makes the most decisions regarding transportation issues in your relationship?
Transportation   1   2   3   4   5   6   7   8   9   10

9. Who makes the most decisions regarding school issues in your relationship?
School: 1   2   3   4   5   6   7   8   9   10

10. Who makes the most decisions regarding how intimacy is handled in your relationship?
Intimacy: 1   2   3   4   5   6   7   8   9   10

Scoring and Interpretation of the R D M B

Name: _____ Date: _____

Years in Present Relationship: _____ Gender: M / F

Things to remember:

A.   Each number corresponds to a percentage. An example would be if 8 is circled regarding a particular issue, then 8 equals 80% which automatically implies that Partner A believes 80% of the input came from that partner and believes that Partner B had 20% input into making decisions.

B.   After each percentage is noted for each issue, then a total percentage can also be achieved by adding all percentages together. For example if a participant circled the following numbers; 5-4-9-7-2-8-4-3-7-2 this would equal 50%-40%-90%-70%-20%-80%-40%-30%-70%-20%. These percentages would then add up totaling 510, which is then divided by 10. The final score is 51% decision making in the relationship.

C.   This instrument is designed to generate:
   1.   A decision-making percentage for each partner regarding each issue.
   2.   A decision-making percentage for each partner regarding the relationship (all ten issues).

D.   Scoring consists of transferring the numbers circled for the ten relationship issues (partner A) to the Relationship Decision Making Box below. For example, if the number 4 was circled for issue # 1 then this is transferred to the score line for the issue directly below, then to the grid line 1-10 with a slash mark for each issue, and then by indicating the percentage below for each issue, which in this case would be 40%. The grid represents both partners. For each issue shade in from the slash mark back to 0 with one color (partner A) and from the slash mark up to 10 for the other (partner B). All ten percentages are then added together and divided by 10 in order to calculate the total percentage of decision-making for partner A, while the remaining percentage represents partner B.

Relationship Decision Making Box (R D M B)

(Score)	1 2 3 4 5 6 7 8 9 10	(Percentages)
	(Place a slash mark on grid below)	
Money	____	____ %
Chores	____	____ %
Parenting	____	____ %
Social Activities	____	____ %
Problem Solving	____	____ %
Religion	____	____ %
Employment	____	____ %
Transportation	____	____ %
School	____	____ %
Intimacy	____	____ %
	Total:	____ %

(Partner A) Total_____% divided by 10 =_____% of decision making

(Partner B) Remainder =_____% of decision making

After each of you completes and scores the questionnaire, discuss the following issues together:

1. What is your overall reaction to your scores? Were there any surprises?
2. What were your areas in which you most agreed?
3. Discuss and make a game plan for how you two might change the distribution of decision-making in one or two specific areas.

Review of Research Relating to a Couple's Decision Making

According to Stritof and Stritof (2012) most couples consider the following decisions to be major items of discussion:

- Where the two of you will live.
- How many children you will have.
- Parenting styles.
- How you will spend and save money.
- The amount of free time you will spend together.
- Household chores.
- Decisions regarding a crisis.
- Future plans.

With respect to the decision making process itself, these authors stress that making decisions should be a shared responsibility. Studies have shown that the unhappiest people in a marriage are often those who have the burden of making decisions alone. In the most successful marriages, decision making is a shared activity . . . Another characteristic of a successful marriage is that both partners are sincerely concerned about the wishes and personal preferences of the other. They are both willing to go more than halfway in reaching mutually satisfying compromises. Decisions or compromises that are made are made willingly instead of grudgingly."(p.2)

In an interview on Pete's "Oprah and Friends" radio program, Klapow(2009) notes that: "Making decisions as a couple is not so much about what you decide on, but rather how you go about the process of making the decision, If you approach each decision with the same game plan, then over time, you will become experts at decision-making." Using a SMART mnemonic, he proposes these five steps to collective decision-making: set, monitor, arrange, recruit and treat. The five steps in more detail are:

1. **Set a specific goal**—the more specific the better
2. **Monitor your discussion**—explore the process of how you are problem-solving
3. **Arrange the situation for success**—Make sure you are not hungry or in a time crunch, so that you can give the issue the deserved time for discussion
4. **Recruit support from one another**—compromise is more probable when a team approach is valued in the discussion
5. **Treat yourselves**—Celebrate successes in a concrete way such as a hug, a special meal, or in some similar ceremony that honors your problem-solving commitment.

Marshack (2000) uses the images of justice and the statue of Liberty to advocate an emerging more equalitarian joint problem solving relationship model. While her model addresses only a heterosexual partnership and is based on certain gender stereotypes, the metaphor is creative nonetheless in a more equalitarian problem-solving relationship decision making process. She says that:

> Lady Liberty represents this principle of the combined talent and energy of an entrepreneurial couple. That is, a woman was chosen to represent America rather than a conquering male warrior, because of the desire to represent our country as welcoming immigrants . . . Lady Liberty is carrying a torch in her hand, not a sword, symbolizing the enlightenment of democracy that shines out to the world. She holds the Declaration of Independence in the other hand as evidence that we are all created equal. On her ankle is a chain that is broken, representing freedom from oppression. Yet the statue is enormous, representing strong and powerful leadership and even domination in the world . . . . Just as Lady Liberty welcomes immigrants, the wife can welcome a variety of options and possible solutions to a problem, weighing those options impartially just as Lady Justice does. Lady Liberty also represents decision making in that she is holding the Declaration of Independence or the law of the land, just as the husband's strength is to get the decision made and follow it with action, as is implied by the sword that Lady Justice holds. In either case, whether it is the husband's or the wife's decision-making strategy, the goal is a fair decision . . .

In one research study, Houlihan and Roger (1990) contrasted ten satisfied and ten self-reported unhappily married couples describing how they make decisions of low, moderate, and high levels of difficulty. Responses were coded as reflecting the use of equity, need-based, situational, or other norms. Results were consistent with previous findings that a state of equity is associated with marital satisfaction but also indicated that multiple norms are used in decision making of both satisfied and dissatisfied couples. Decision difficulty influenced use of both situational and need-based norms. A trend was found for satisfied husbands to make greater use of need-based norms than dissatisfied husbands when decisions were high in difficulty. However, this trend did not apply to wives. Houlihan and Roger's findings appear to support a distinction between equity as a state and equity as a process and as supporting an instrumental utilitarian pragmatic value theory of decision making.

Additional Role Perception Activities

Here are five other suggestions: All "for couple" columns can be found in Eckstein (2013).

1. Eckstein, D., Clement, F., &Fierro, A. (2006). The role of image exchange with couples. *The Family Journal: Counseling and Therapy for Couples and Families*, 14, 71-76.
2. Eckstein, D., & Morrison, J. (2000). Exploring different expressions' of love. *The Family Journal: Counseling and Therapy for Couples and Families*, 7, 75-76.

3. Eckstein, D., &Axford, D. (2000). Loving and being loved: Commitment implications. *The Family Journal: Counseling and Therapy for Couples and Families*, 7, 185-186.

4. Eckstein, D., Levanthal, M., Bentley, S., & Kelley, S. (2000). Relationships as a three-legged sack race. *The Family Journal: Counseling and Therapy for Couples and Families*, 7, 399-405.

5. Kirk, A., Eckstein, D., Serres, S., & Helms. (2007). A dozen relationship commitment considerations. *The Family Journal: Counseling and Therapy for Couples and Families*, 15, 271-276.

Summary

The purpose of the article has been to introduce the Relationship Decision Making Box to you as a couple's problem-solving activity. Additional couple's renewal activities can be found in Gottman and Silver (2000), Olson and Stephens (2001) and Hendrix and Hunt (2003) and Eckstein (2013).

References

Eckstein, D. (2012). *The couples' match book: Activities for lighting, rekindling, or extinguishing the flame.* Bloomington, Indiana: Trafford.

Gottman, J., and Silver, N. (2000). *The seven principles for making marriage work.* New York: Random House

Haley, J. (1980). *Uncommon therapy.* New York: Norton.

Hendrix, H. and Hunt, H. (2003). *Getting the love you want workbook.* New York: Atria

Houlihan, M., Roger, T. (1990). Decision making of satisfied making of satisfied and dissatisfied married couples, *Journal of Social Psychology*, (130 (1), 89-102.

Klapow, J. (2009) The "smart" five step decision making model. Retrieved from http://www. cnn.com/2009/LIVING/personal/01/08/o.making.decisions.couple/, Oct. 30,2012)

Marshack, K. (2000). Couples can balance dynamics of decision-making process, *Vancouver Business Journal*, November 23. Retrieved from (http://www.kmarshack.com/_blog/ Articles_-_Entrepreneurial_Couples/post/ Couples_can_balance_dynamics_of_ decision-making_process/), Oct. 30, 2012.

Olsen, D. and Stephens, D. (2001). *The couple's survival workbook.* Oakland, Ca.: New Harbinger

Stritof, S. and Stritof, B. (2012) *Decisions in marriage*, Retrieved from http://marriage.about. com/od/loveisadecision/a/decisions.htm, Oct. 30, 2012.

Chapter VII:
Closing Comments

Section 37:

Cracking the Shell

Daniel Eckstein

I was fortunate to study cross-cultural appreciation with Dr. Jean Houston for nine months in 1984 while visiting Greece and Egypt as part of our program. During our trip in Egypt, I proposed to Carol de Andrade. We were later married in the ancient temple of Abydos by Jean as we journeyed by boat along the Nile River.

The night before our wedding I wrote the following piece that I read to Carol in front of the other 125 members of our group. Most of us have experienced betrayal in one form or another. Here is an encouraging way of considering the potential benefits that can come for all of us: forgiveness is the key to redeeming our betrayals. Jean Houston believes that:

"This is why betrayal is such a strong theme in all the great religions and myths . . . The only way to be ennobled and to forgive truly is through love. In giving more than one thought one could, one discovers that one has much more still to give. This is the mystery and miracle of love, and it changes the very fabric of reality, the very structure of our lives. When we are able to give forth, to give of ourselves beyond our protective shell and see the other in wonder and astonishment . . . then something evolutionary happens and we and the betrayal are not the same. Then love is restored, revealing the larger consequence and the deeper unfolding" (Houston, p. 117).

I like that quote particularly because of the reference to a protective shell. Here is a very personal example. I use the metaphor of cracking the shell to describe my own armor; I reversed the names Daniel, Jean, and Carol in the story. I am like a turtle, as are many men. We have strong resilient shells on top; and a very tender, vulnerable belly underneath the seemingly impenetrable fortress.

Once upon a time in the land of Id there lived a turtle named Leinad. He had a very hard brown and black shell that covered his black and orange head, tail, paws and feet. He was blessed to be born the first born of two wise turtle priest orators who cared very much for him and his three younger brothers and sisters.

At an early age, Leinad had a profound experience of something much larger than himself. It came to him in the quietness of the night and in the music he heard at sundown and sunrise down by the watering hole. He felt it in the bright yellow sunshine, in the cool green grass, the oozy slick black mud, and in the gentle raindrops cascading off his durable shell. Although he didn't fully grasp the meaning of it all, at age four he went forth and dedicated his life to understanding and serving that Vast Force. "Suffer the little turtles and let them come unto me," he heard in his little head that day.

In the years that followed Leinad went to school with his friends. There he struggled with subjects like reading and writing. He wrote with a different claw than most of his classmates and he often saw the letters in books and on the board backwards and upside down. Thus, he didn't do too well in his studies—besides, there was so much excitement all around the forest he could hardly sit still in those rock desks. He especially cringed when the teacher recited poems like "What are little girl turtles made of? Sugar and spice and everything nice!—and what are little boy turtles made of? Nails and shells and puppy dog tails." He was always in the redbird slow-learner class while most of his friends were in the accelerated bluebird class. Fortunately, there was one time each day they all went outside and played games involving kicking and throwing in the forest. There he felt alive, happy, and important.

Thus, Leinad learned he was strong and could run fast, which is still pretty slow as turtles go you know.

In later years he received more education by being willing to engage in a form of a turtle demolition derby where men got together in an oval pit and smashed into each other's shells. He did this pretty well, but eventually, inevitably, like all his other fellow participants, his shell and paws became dented, bruised, and broken. He was in much pain, but he learned to hide it well inside himself for he also received much praise, plaques, and adoration from others. He even got his picture taken for a turtle bubble-gum card.

But even in his greatest moments of achievement there was still something missing. "There must be more to life than this," he thought. And always he'd crawl, ever so slowly, in pursuit of that vision he had many years earlier.

Along the journey, he was often described as a loner. Keeping to himself helped his discipline and achievement, but there were long nights when he felt that aloneness.

He was fortunate to spend twelve years of partnership with a petite turtle from the southern pond of Calhoun Falls, but one day he realized that something was missing from their life together. "You've never really opened your heart to me," she lamented as they moved to other parts of the forest. Fortunately, they were eventually able to transcend their hurt and rejection to become life-long friends.

So on and on he searched. "It is only a dream," he began to believe, "an impossible dream." One weekend he attended a seminar by a famous orator named Neaj. In it he relearned that it was possible to transcend his body and fly, and the experience rekindled the dreams he'd had for so long of joining tortoises from other distant ponds, as well as other animals like the lion, giraffe, and elephant. He even experienced being a dolphin, a snake, and a mosquito. He learned more that confirmed his early beliefs. "There are Large Forces out there and they are *in you,*" the sage said. This was just great stuff. Then he heard his quiet inner voice say, "Go speak to this wise woman; she will know you, and she will tell you the next step."

She did know him, and she spoke of an extended year-long training school.

It was near a settlement called the "Big Apple, a crowded, noisy place with twice as many turtles. "'What's it called?" he asked. "Can't tell you—it's a mystery," she replied.

He signed up anyway, even though it was a journey across many ponds and streams to get there. It was indeed a wise choice, for he learned marvelous truths that year. He particularly enjoyed an exercise where they all spun around on their shells—the turtle twist he called it. During that year he realized that at times he was not remembering the truth; at other times he was knowing the truth but not obeying it; and in still other moments he was obeying that personal inner truth, but was being fearful of the awesome force and responsibility that came with it.

During the classes he was especially attracted and simultaneously afraid of a particular female. Her name was Lorac, and her piercing eyes were jet black, with the kind of knowing penetration reflecting ancient wisdom. "'I am so excited being in her presence," he thought. But I am also afraid of such a powerful being, for one terrible look of her eye sent lightning bolts capable of utter destruction. He knew that many men feared the power of this and similar turtles, calling them witches, burning many of them in great fires. Their fear was that the force of this female turtle seemed to contain the very essence of life and death itself. "Don't trust her for she'll take you off and have you chopped up and made into a soup," he lamented.

Nonetheless, mustering all his courage, he timidly approached her with the insight, "I just realized why I've avoided you these past months—you cracked my shell open and chopped off my head in another era, but I'm seriously considering risking it again." "Funny, lots of men say that to me," she replied in a friendly way.

And so the dialogue began. In subsequent classes they spoke of such similar interests as writing and running. In fact, in addition to writing her own books, she agreed to help edit his own forthcoming book about male turtle transformation. He invited her to his pond for the annual Tortoise Harathon. She accepted, and they pulled their shells all 26.2 miles of the event—and somewhere along the way they knew they cared for each other very much.

During that week, a female tortoise psychic foretold, "There is a golden ring between you—and your relationship is an essential component for your personal growth. From it shall come a baby girl turtle who will be your spiritual teacher . . . and Lorac will soon move to be with you Leinad." "Nay, nay," both of them protested simultaneously making the sign of the cross. "This is not part of my five-year plan," the two free and independent turtles proudly proclaimed.

But in the days that followed they spent many happy moments crawling, swimming, sunning, sleeping, and other various activities which make turtles squeal in happy, happy delight. Thus, when they were apart, he was exceedingly sad and lonely. Realizing how long he had yearned for such deep, intimate companionship he asked her, "Would you like a date with me?" "'Oh, yes," she replied. "'Okay, put me down for the next 60 New Year's Eves."

In his ecstasy, he also confronted his great fears—deep hurtful beliefs that he had spent many years striving to overcome such as . . . "You never do it right—she'll reject you eventually—she'll break you open." One particular theme he called the Cinderella complex, meaning that he was a desirable turtle for a few hours, but that at 12:00 midnight he would turn into an orange pumpkin. "You've never stayed in a relationship long enough to test your hypothesis," she gently confronted. "'Let's pretend it's a 12:01 right now." She also wrote a poem of a turtle who had a vision of the wise sorcerer who said to the knight, "you will slay no dragons or fight no battles that you will not find in your inner most heart."

Thus, in a very rapid time, they came to love each other very much. So they joined with 140 other turtles for the conclusion of the year-long mystery training. They were shut inside a vast mid-pier, a kind of in-between place of power that seemed to be left behind by former turtles as a sign that they could indeed fly through the sky. During that fateful day, Leinad held a magic stick and felt it vibrate in his left paw, and he realized an even greater respect for the strength and wisdom of Lorac. "Am I becoming too dependent on her for my happiness?"' he once again feared. "And if I truly let her in, will she crush me?"

That night they seemed closer than ever before. It was like an inner wall, a secret hall that had protected Leinad was about to be opened. Indeed no one had even been in that cherished inner temple. A long withheld tear rolled from his eye, "Please do not crack my shell—for, yes, it is my prison, but it also is my fortress," he sobbed. "'And my shell is so hard because my heart is so soft, when the hurt and angry arrows are shot at me I must be able to protect myself. So please don't remove my shell and open that door unless you really want to be there," he pleaded.

"Nay, nay my beautiful, gentle one," she replied. "For in my destruction there is also a healing—you are not just your shell. And, I do believe you can crack open your own shell in such a subtle way that it is still there for functional protection, but there is also a secret exit and entry to and from that will allow you to once again fly with the eagles. And, besides, I need you also," Lorac continued lovingly stroking his vulnerable underbelly. "For I too have many dents from other times. I need you to help me touch and heal the parts of me I cannot reach by myself. Besides, I cannot open that door from the outside; rather the only latch is from within your heart—it is you who must open that door." Then slowly, ever so slowly, the shell was cracked, the protective walls fell down, and the door to the temple of his heart was opened. And so it was that Leinad experienced a relationship at a level previously unknown to him, and it was good, very good.

Several days later they entered into the belly of a great fish and journeyed up the Nile River. There they crawled over many sacred ancient temples. "Are there examples of a god or a goddess being successfully married without one or the other losing their power?" Leinad asked during one of their late night talks. "Well, in the land they call India I heard of two wise turtles called Rama and Sita who went to many distant lands, making passionate love every place they went," she replied. "Truly my kind of gods," the ever reptilian-brained Leinad replied. ne day two other turtle couples invited them to join together in a celebration of transformational union. They too had discovered each other as what they called "twin flames," or lifelong partners, as part of their study with the orator Neaj. Thus, in a sacred temple of Abidos surrounded by loving turtles from many lands, the four of them were raised on a sacrificial stone. Those that witnessed the event that day swore a lightning bolt from heaven pierced their shields and deeply united them and all fellow participants in a moment that melted all separation and linked them together forever in love that day in the ancient land that bonds souls and blends hearts. And the great winged one was seen hovering over them all whispering "'welcome home my brothers and sisters, welcome home."

Carol and I were married thirteen years before we divorced in 1994.

Section 38

Al Ellis: Up Close and Personal

Daniel Eckstein and Debbie Joffe Ellis

Daniel Eckstein's introduction:

One of my most significant professional honors was the privilege of introducing Al Ellis at the December, 2005 Evolution of Psychotherapy conference in Anaheim, California. Prior to the conference itself, I watched Al and his wife Debbie Joffe Ellis together. At age 9, Al was very fragile. I was touched by the tenderness I observed between them. It was obvious Al Ellis had "gone soft." The original "Little Dirty Harry" whose often profanity laced comments sent some people scurrying from his workshops in disgust. It was part of his presentation. And yet, late in life Al was soft and sweet. Debbie was by his side; I got a "contact high" just being in their presence.

I am pleased editor Steve Southern agreed with my request for us to write this personal tribute to Al. The article will be organized as follows: following a classic quote by Carl Rogers, a few of the more current background works summarizing his work will be presented. Personal notes by Al about his love for Debbie and vice versa which were written for a forthcoming relationship book (Eckstein, 2012). A note Debbie wrote a few years after his death and a tribute at his 2007 New York City memorial conclude the article.

Al is forever linked with Fritz Perls and Carl Rogers in the Three approaches to psychotherapy tapes (1986). Volunteer client Gloria is one of the most watched sessions in the history of psychotherapy. A video of Al's session with Gloria can be viewed at http://video.google.nl/videoplay?docid=-7965308202224028422# (retrieved June 16, 2011).

Al's co-presenter in that series Carl Rogers describes the paradox of the personal and its universal resonance this way:

> Somewhere here I want to bring in a learning, which has been most rewarding, because it makes me feel so deeply akin to others. I can word it this way. *What is most personal is most general.* There have been times when in talking with students or staff, or in my writing, I have expressed myself in ways so personal that I have felt I was expressing an attitude which it was probable no one else could understand, because it was so uniquely my own . . . . In these instances, I have almost invariably found that the very feeling which has seemed to me most private, most personal, and hence most incomprehensible by others, has turned out to be an expression for which there is a resonance in many other people. It has led me to believe that what is most personal and unique in each one of us is probably the very element which would, if it were shared or expressed, speak most deeply to others. This has helped me to understand artists and poets as people who have dared to express the unique in themselves" (1961, p.26).

Our goal here is to share an up close and personal person perspective for a relationship based journal in the hopes of sharing how Al not only wrote about happiness in relationships, he also practiced what he preached in his own intimate relationship with Debbie. Additional material on Al's significant contributions to counseling theory can be found in this issue with Phil Ginsberg's book review of Al's autobiography (2012). Other relationship concepts and applications can be found in Ellis (2004), Ellis (2010), and Ellis and Ellis (2011).

What follows is how Debbie describes her love for Al as originally written in 2006 prior to his death.

Debbie Joffe Ellis on Al

It is very hard for me to find words that adequately describe the strength and solidity of the relationship between Al and I—it seems strange that finding apt expression for something so natural and real is difficult to do.

I suppose I have an aversion to limiting greatness and for a force as powerful as our love—words may be inadequate. Well—I'll do the best I can for now . . . .

As Al said, we have tremendous love and respect for one another. Our values and beliefs are, with very few exceptions, the same. Both of us care more about helping others and contributing to others than in material gain.

We both enjoy the funny side of things, and I love Al's humor. I enjoy his cheerfulness—Al essentially has a very happy nature, and I also greatly enjoy his brilliance, his warmth, his compassion and his care towards me and for others.

We truly listen to one another—and if we differ or disagree about anything, which happens only rarely, neither of us is interested in putting the other one down. Neither of us wants to be right in order to make the other one wrong. We really think about how we contributed to the situation, and each of us wholeheartedly works on him/herself and takes responsibility for however we may have contributed to the disagreement.

We don't damn or abuse the other one. Even when we don't like something they said or did. If any effort is required to ease difficulties—each of us wholeheartedly and unquestionably makes that effort. There is a natural rapport and connection between us, a strong attraction that has not lessened over time, and for me—if anything—gets stronger. We both are passionate by nature, with strong willpower, and the ability to commit-to and persist-with anything we put our minds and hearts to.

We enjoy each other. Just being together in the same room—Al doing his work, I doing mine—there is pleasure in just being together. Talking, working, reading, touching, relaxing—or none of the above—we simply love being together. I love looking at Al—enjoying his handsomeness, his beautiful hands and the elegant way they express, his absorption in his writing, the dreamy way he gazes upwards at times whilst he is thinking of the next sentence to write, or the way he holds his pen in his mouth whilst he uses his hands to busily turn pages or reach for notes, and he way he smiles at me.

I love his sweetness, his outrageousness, his daring, his brutal honesty. I would say that I absolutely love the majority of Al's qualities and characteristics. His determination inspires me. Even when he is not feeling too well, he pushes himself to do his work to which he is greatly dedicated. At the Evolution of Psychotherapy Conference, held at Anaheim, California in December, 2005, very few people knew that he was suffering from agonizing back pain. He gave 8 major presentations, and 2 presentations which were spontaneously arranged, presenting brilliantly and receiving heartfelt standing ovations. He never complained about his suffering.

His courage is remarkable. At the time of writing this, there is a brutal situation at the Institute that bears Al's name, with much bad behavior against Al and me. This has been going on since late 2004. To watch how consistently Al practices his philosophy, to see how he endures the situation with dignity and acceptance, whilst still spending hours of his precious time making effort to fight the injustice, is a great privilege.

Another area in which Al's outstanding courage is seen is that of the physical ailments which he copes with stoically and bravely. Nearly 3 years ago he had his large intestine surgically removed due to massive infection there, and now has an ileostomy bag. He is a brittle diabetic, he has painful arthritis, hearing difficulties—but never does he waste time on self-pity or complaint.

Al is a person of such deep humanity, integrity and authenticity. My mind, heart and spirit feel fulfilled when I am with him. Time does not bring complacency—my fulfillment grows deeper and I feel fortunate each day of my life to be with him.

Some people may wonder about our age difference—me in my 40s, Al his early 90s. To me Al is not, has never been, an age. I don't think of him as an older man, or of me as a younger woman. To me he is the vital magnificent man I love. That's it.

Others wonder what it is like to be with someone so famous. Whilst I of course acknowledge his fame, and am in awe of the massive contribution he has made and continues to make to countless people, I don't think to myself—"I am with a famous person". Fame doesn't mean much to me—it's fleeting—can come and go—so what. It is not his fame that excites me—it's the character of the man, and his uplifting and ongoing contributions. But even without these contributions—I'd love him just as much.

I love his humility, his lack of ego, and his way of doing the thing that represents his truth, rather than doing that which will make him more popular. When people attack Al and/ or his views, usually defensively because they don't like the truths Al reveals, Al tolerates their view, but will not change himself just to appease them. Al is THE most honest person I know.

Al is misunderstood by some who wrongly judge his colorful (at times) language and humor, his daring and audacity. Al graciously tolerates these people too.

There are days, at this present time of dispute with the Albert Ellis Institute, where the circumstances are very brutal and difficult. Real concerns abound. And yet we still regularly feel fortunate.

We still have life and the will to keep fighting for justice, and in addition to that, we feel fortunate to be together. Even during the really dark days. We feel grateful for one another. So—hopefully in these words I have revealed some of the aspects that contribute to our unusually strong closeness—

- Love
- Respect
- Shared Values
- Gratitude
- Enjoyment
- Cherishing
- Being

~Debbie Joffe Ellis~

And here is how Al described his relationship with Debbie:

My relationship with my wife and partner, Debbie Joffe, has been the best one of several major relationships that I have had for a number of reasons:

1. Debbie has intrinsic good character and kindheartedness to all living creatures, especially me.
2. She unusually loves toward me and puts my health and interests first and foremost.
3. She keeps in mind and makes my appointments for healthcare, makes sure that I keep them, and accompanies me to my appointments.
4. She aids me in dealing with very difficult people in my life, including hostile people at the Albert Ellis Institute, and helps me refuse to make myself upset about them.
5. She warns me and corrects me when I go too far in my strong language to difficult people and when I excoriate them in press interviews.
6. She nicely and graciously puts up with the impossible demands that I put on her.
7. When important things do not work out right away, she keeps them in mind for the future.
8. She independently and ingeniously gets good ideas for both of us to work at and plans them out with me.
9. She encourages me to do sensible things to help myself but takes care not to plague and push me too hard about them.
10. Debbie also has an unusual, devoted, and helpful character, which very few people have. It makes her quite a strange, beautiful person. We both respect and love each other and expect to keep doing so forever.

~Albert Ellis~

Here is a postscript written by Debbie after Al's death

In May 2006, only weeks after we completed the above chapter, Al succumbed to pneumonia. Doctors did not think he would survive it. They spoke words preparing me for the high probability that Al may not last more than days or weeks.

But Al was determined to survive. To the utter amazement of the medical staff, Al survived for nearly 15 more months. During many of these months, Al remained active. In between continual medical treatments and grueling physical therapy, amidst at least three life-threatening health setbacks, Al would allow students to visit for workshops in which (as he'd done for over 50 years) he would talk, answer questions, and demonstrate his Rational Emotive Behavior Therapy approach with volunteering students. Al allowed journalists to interview him. He would spend time thinking about writing projects and unresolved Institute issues, and dictate various thoughts and letters for me to send out. As time went on, Al's body was becoming weaker and weaker. His organs were not able to keep up with his determination to recover. One of our doctors said that he had never seen a person as courageous as Al, or anyone with such authentic dignity and acceptance throughout the incredible pain and physical suffering which Al was enduring.

I write this postscript just over a year after Al's passing. My feelings are still raw, the pain immense, but I'll write briefly on the topic, which is the focus of this chapter—our relationship.

Throughout the brutal time of Al's increasing health decline, as his energy was waning and he hadn't the strength for any work or activity, the one good thing we had, the *only* good thing, was our love for one another. In the hospital, I was able to get a stretcher put in the room for me to sleep on. And in the rehab center there was a recliner chair I used for that purpose. Not that Al and I were able to sleep much. We were together all day, every day. I'd be present for practically all of Al's medical procedures.

For hours each day I would stroke his head. Often I would gently massage his body. Through the night I'd reach over and we'd hold hands. When his body was not in too much pain I'd lie on his bed with him and we held each other. Each and every day we expressed our gratitude and feelings to each other. For the last few weeks of his life, I was able to take Al back to a home environment.

On Tuesday, July 24, 2007, half an hour after midnight, held in my arms as I kissed him, Al took his last breath. The oft-used expression "The love doesn't die" is totally true for me, as is the immeasurable pain of life without Al's physical presence.

I do my best to keep going each day. To keep doing his work, as he had entrusted me to do. To keep doing my best to not just teach his philosophy, but to live it. To keep his brilliance and spirit alive by sharing his work, wisdom, humor, and story whenever and where-ever I can. To keep experiencing, immersing myself in, and appreciating the profound enormity of our love. Forever:

And here is Daniel Eckstein's tribute to Al:

Presented at a memorial service, Sept. 28, 2007, New York City

I am deeply honored to speak tonight some of my personal tribute to the legacy of Albert Ellis. When I was in graduate school in the '70's he was already a legend in our field. Along with Carl Rogers and Fritz Perls, Al interviewed Gloria, the widely viewed sessions in our history. In his session with Gloria he confronted her faulty logic by reframing her own words of being worried of not being good enough and thus getting stuck with "icky men." Ellis confronted her overgeneralization by noting "we all know some "icky" women who get some splendid men."

I contend that Al was our professions own one of a kind "little dirty Harry." Al's immortal one-liner sound bites were laced with profanity and sexual connotations. Some examples include: "don't 'should' all over yourself;" masturbation is wonderful/mustrubation is horrible."

Thanks to Al when I wanted to curse in my classes I simply attributed the profanity as being from him. He seemed to take delight in sending people running from his audiences in disgust at his "potty mouth."

As the former president of the North American Society for Adlerian society, not only did he honor the contributions of Alfred Adler to his own work, he was a lifetime member of our organization. In contrast to the big ego's who act like they personally invented their own models from scratch, Al consistently acknowledged others who had positively influenced his thoughts.

My personal brief encounter with Al was at the 2005 Evolution of psychotherapy conference. I had the distinct honor of introducing the then 92 year old legend to a crowd exceeding 2,000 therapists. Woody Allen once said, "50% of life is just showing up." I fondly remember in the '90's attending a workshop by Al via satellite that he conducted from his hospital bed. Nothing like a trip to the hospital was going to stop him from keeping his agreements.

At the evolution conference Al wowed us once again. At the end of the program, I simply said the Debbie "I saw a lot of love between the two of you—and Al could not have done what he has been able to at this conference without your help."

I believe that Cupid's arrow won over the heart of Al, the rational lion-hearted legend. I am much honored he wrote a piece about his love for Debbie that will in my own forthcoming relationship rescue book. And the great big smile on his face in his photo with Debbie was simply not something I'd seen in all those past decades of his presentations. I feel such love transcended age and ideology. Here are some of my comments I made in that introduction.

In *On beyond Zebra* (1990) Dr Seuss (Theodor Geisel) wrote

> Said Conrad Cornelius O'Donnell O'Dell, my very young friend who is learning to spell'

The A is for Ape. And the B is for Bear. The C is for Camel the H is for Hare.

After going through the alphabet Dr. Seuss continues "through to A is for Zebra. I know them all well said Conrad Cornelius O'Donnell O'Dell.

So now I know everything anyone knows from beginning to end. From the start to the close.

Because Z is as far as the alphabet goes.

Then he almost fell flat on his face on the floor when I picked up the chalk and drew one letter more. A letter he never dreamed of before!!

And I said, "You can stop if you want with the Z but not me!

In the places I go there are things that I see that I never could spell if I stopped with the Z.

I'm telling you this 'cause you're one of my friends. My alphabet starts where your alphabet ends" (p.63-64).

In like manner Al took us far beyond Z in his own rational emotive alphabet. Most of you can repeat these with me—the A is for activating event; The C is for the consequence; Does A cause C? No no no a thousand times no Al rises up from the grave to proclaim. It's that B—the belief and often it's just so dog gone irrational . . .

So the solution is to bring on the Disputation troops—from that one comes the E—re-energized along with an F for new Feelings." And to his alphabet I add "G" for you Al are truly one of the Giants of our profession.

It's been said "the greatest use of a life is to spend it in a cause that will ultimately outlive it." I am confident that having transcended his own bardos that Al will hear something similar to my own Biblical phrase "well done thy good and faithful REBT master and servant leader."

With the help of my Sam Houston St. Univ. counseling colleagues Gary Hood, I, and Chi-sing Lin, Debbie on the camera, we'll close with two tributes in song to Al. First, from his immortal rational songs there is "perfect rationality"

Sing along with us now

> Some think the world must have a right direction
> And so do I, and so do I
> Some think that with the slightest imperfection
> They can't get by—and so do I
> For if, I have to prove I'm superhuman and better far than people are
> To show I have miraculous acumen—and always rate among the great
>
> Perfect perfect rationality is of course the only thing for me!
> How can I even think of being if I must live fallibly?

Rationality must be a perfect thing for me!!
Rock it with us on the refrain now
Perfect perfect rationality is of course the only thing for me
How can I even think of being I must live fallibly?
Rationality must be a perfect thing for me!!

And if you're willing to stand with us and raise a toast, here are my words to the classic "drink with me" from L'Miserables."

Raise those glasses high now if you will . . .
"Drink with us to days gone by . . . . smile with me in song's Al wrote
Here's to many times he straightened our heads;
Here's to many times he spoke of the bed.
Here's to Al and Debbie too.
Drink with us to days gone by
Al showed how to live and die
Tonight we honor Al who taught us so well
All his life he stressed we make our own hell
Here's to Al and Debbie too
Drink with us to days gone by
All his work we still live by
At this shrine of friendship never say die
Let the wine of Al's work never run dry
Here to Al with all our love.

References

Eckstein, D. (2012). *The couple's match book: Techniques for lighting, rekindling, or extinguishing the flame.* Bloomington, Indiana: Trafford.

Ellis, A. (2004) *Rational emotive behavior therapy—It works for me—It can work for you!* Prometheus Books, New York.

Ellis, A. (2010). *All out! An autobiography.* Prometheus Books, New York.

Ellis, A.(2011) Introduction to rational emotive psychotherapy and counseling session with Gloria, retrieved from http://video.google.nl/videoplay?docid=-7965308202224028422#, June 16.

Ellis, A., & Ellis, D. (2011). *Rational emotive behavior therapy.* (2011) American Psychological Association. Washington DC.

Geisel, T. (1990) *On beyond zebra!.* New York: Random House. 1990

Ginsberg, P. (2012) A book review of Al Ellis' All out. *The Family Journal,* (in press).

Rogers, Carl. (1961). *On becoming a person: A therapist's view of psychotherapy*. London: Constable.

Rogers, C., Perls, F., Ellis, A., & Shostrom, E (1986). *Three approaches to psychotherapy*. Corona del Mar, Ca: Psychological & Educational Films.

Section 39:

A Dozen Reflections on Writing the "For couples" Column in *The Family Journal:* for the Past 18 Years.

Daniel Eckstein

Many of the articles that I have included in this book were originally published in *The Family Journal: Counseling and Therapy for Couples and Families*. I am grateful to Sage publishers for permitting me to use my work here. Writing with others is a relationship in and of itself. Here are 12 things I learned along the way as I reflect back on the completion of this manuscript.

1. "You teach best what you most need to learn" is an apt koan as stated by Richard Bach in *Illusions* (1977). The personal application is that I have been married twice for thirteen years each. I lived with two other women. I describe my relationship voyage as a trip on the Titanic. In the spirit of the song "there must be 50 ways to say good-bye to your lover," I can name 100. Along the way I've worked with couples, I've taught at universities, and I've done my best to help couples renew their relationships. I've been single the past twelve years. I remember what ABC sports used to say in their opening Wide World of Sports montage: "The thrill of victory and the agony of defeat." Hopefully both the joys and pains of relationships help me in having compassion for the couples I've seen in my three-plus decades of private practice.

2. Most of my articles have been written with others. Writing together is another kind of relationship. Will Schutz (1958) uses the three variables of *inclusion, control*, and *openness* is his *FIRO-B* questionnaire. Each of the three has an "expressed from me to you" and a "wanted from you to me" consideration. This translates to working together on an article or the books I've co-authored and involves: *inclusion expressed* ("Would you like to collaborate on an article?" I've asked). *Inclusion wanted* has been when I've been approached at a convention or through e-mail asking me to be part of their project. The control issue is a biggie. My own *expressed control* begins with what topics are even considered. Control issues involving who is a co-author and who is a contributor with thanks, plus the order the names are listed in the article, are other issues. *Wanted control* involves the appreciation of co-authors and editors who urge that something stay or go, the sequence of the article, plus the research and writing of the background material for the column. *Expressed openness* can be illustrated by how much self-disclosure I have made in the columns. There may be some exceptions, but for the most part I have not written in first person.

What I shared in #2 above is the most I've said about myself in those 17 years. It's consistent with Jon's original recommendation that the column address the couple directly. Many times I have stated, "You as a couple" and "your relationship," so that I, as one of the authors, may do my best to establish intimacy by speaking directly to you the couple rather than to my counseling colleagues. *Wanted openness* has been when I've invited co-authors to share their own couple's journey. For example, some articles identified that authors were, in fact, the couple in the article; other times, it seemed more appropriate to simply describe "a couple."

3. I also apply the wisdom of Fernando Flores's four basic communication acts that are described in Eckstein, Byles, and Bennett (2007). In all communications with co-authors I've attempted to:

    a. **"Asking,"** to use the action verb of Flores's model;

    b. **"Promising"** to do my part or in some cases not agreeing to a request for a timetable or content-related decision;

    c. **"Asserting,"** the process of saying the article is too long, it does not flow, or the delicate assertion that a co-author's case study needs to be reduced by half;

    d. **"Declaring,"** saying it's a wrap which is the last stage before that glorious moment when I send the article to the editor.

For prospective collaborators, I would summarize this section in this way: Plato did all his philosophy in dialogue. The dialogue, or in this case, the joint team effort, truly adds a synergistic effect to the final product. There is also a management koan that goes: "If you want to get something done, ask the busiest person to do it." As the point guard on most of these columns, I've organized and put together their ideas. I have found it true that the busiest "I have no time" folks are the very people who meet deadlines and who keep their agreements. Like any relationship these are "high yield" to use the medical students term where I now teach.

4. My experience as a senior consultant with the Pfeiffer and Jones University Associates team was invaluable in helping me learn a variety of what we then called training technologies. Questionnaires are one of my favorites. People love to take and score questionnaires as part of a "who am I?" existential quest. Consistent with my *voyage of the Titanic* relationship metaphor, I illustrate the potent value of questionnaires by describing my experience standing in line at the supermarket check-out. Many rows of candy and magazines are placed for that one last impulse oriented sale. "Seven Questions To See If You Are A Good Lover" is the bold headline on one magazine. "I'm not going to do it—no, I'm not—no way," I say as I reach for the magazine. Alas, once more I score a one or two at the most on a seven point scale, which

once again re-affirms that I'm best as a counselor of couples and not a consumer myself.

5. Re-framing is an invaluable counseling action oriented intervention. My own Adlerian application of the concept is described in Wines, Nelson, and Eckstein. When writing both articles and books early in my career, I re-framed my initial defensiveness at seeing my sentences sliced and diced by the process of "ascribing noble intention" based on the premise that the goal of the editor was the same as mine, which was to make the best possible product possible. That helped me with the Adlerian concept of goal alignment.

6. My Adlerian colleague, Rich Kopp, and I have written about the use of metaphors in counseling I've created and adopted several metaphors in my columns. One of my favorites is "relationships as a three-legged sack race" (Eckstein, Levanthal, Bentley, and Kelley,). The A's and H's of relationships (Eckstein,) used a colleague's letter A, in which the upright bars lean on each other, compared with an H, where they were straight (as opposed to collapsing in the middle from leaning on one another too much). Sharon Kortman was generous in working with me and allowing me to adopt her Winnie-the-Pooh personality typologies to a questionnaire (Kortman and Eckstein). Walls and windows was inspired by a technique I read by a marriage counselor involving both opening doors (windows) while also creating barriers (walls). This case study involved a wife who had been wounded by the husband's infidelity (opening), but who also created a wall between him and his extra-marital lover (closing) behaviors.

    My former Sam Houston State University colleague Jane Nelson created a wonderful metaphor which was included in an invited article for a *Family Journal* theme issue on Infidelity. Our title was *Antidotes for infidelity and Prescriptions for Long-Lasting Relationships* (Nelson, Li, Eckstein, Ane, & Mullener). Musical relationship metaphors were featured in Duffey, Somody, & Eckstein. David Sarnoff and I applied four of my family journal metaphors from the *Family Journal* column in a case study for an Adlerian oriented theme issue of the *Journal of Individual Psychology* on couples counseling).

7. Multi-cultural issues have been important themes for writing colleagues and for me. Chi-Sing Lin is from Hong Kong; his wife, Yu-Fen Li, is from Taiwan. We created a cultural relationship interview matrix (CRIM) (Li, Lin, & Eckstein). We also partnered on the application of Ed deBono's "Six-Thinking Hats" (Eckstein, Li, & Lin).

    Another cross-cultural article applied the Buddhist 8-fold Noble Path to couples (Ginsburg, Eckstein, Lin, Li, & Mullener). Two Hispanic colleagues, from my

Univ. Texas-Permian Basin days, and I collaborated on The Language Relationship Questionnaire (LRQ) (Eckstein, Juarez-Torrez, and Perez-Gabriel.

8.   Mentoring has also been one of my goals. A quote attributed to Adler is "what are the needs of the situation?" Probably 75% of the co-authors have been either graduate students and/or colleagues needing to get published (or perish) in their institutions. Many of the columns came when I went to a conference and added an inspiring presentation. I've had a knack for spotting good ideas and for also saying "just get me your work and I'll add some of my own and package it into the column format."

9.   As for advice to beginning colleagues, I would say that one of the lessons I've learned is to let go of the article. When I was a sportswriter for the Greenville (South Carolina) News while in graduate school at the University of South Carolina, I learned that if the story was in my typewriter (how long ago was that?) and the 12 midnight deadline came for the morning newspaper, there was no story that next morning. While deadlines are not that restrictive for a journal article, my point is that there needs to be a time when you let go of the story and send it out the door. I am saddened as I write remembering a couple of collaborative articles in which the co-author would not look at the final publication because all they saw was what was wrong. Commitment to excellence is a noble virtue. When overused, it means the product is never acceptable.

10. From my consulting days with the military, I learned that many things have three and four letter abbreviations. When we finish a questionnaire, we create an acronym like CRIM, PRI, NEFM (Noble Eight-fold Matrix) and STINT (Staying Together In Needy Times couple's questionnaire). It gives a certain face validity to the instrument.

11. Two gender-related questionnaires are Goldman and Eckstein; and Eckstein, Love, Aycock and Wiesner. As I mentioned above, questionnaires where couples take, score, and profile their results often have high interest. My own style is to get a basic concept/typology from a book and identify the variables. Using the author's descriptors or illustrations I then create questions that are usually answered in a Likert style five point agree-disagree scale. I have a colleague who used the Enneagram extensively in her practice. I got several of the books she suggested for me and created a couple's oriented questionnaire.

12. In all these years of writing, I've never lost the excitement I have when the article arrives all laid out so well by the editors and the staff at Sage. One of the advantages

of a selective memory, because I live more as an optimist than a pessimist, is when, after I finish an article, I hear from a group of students in Saudi Arabia or a US class of sixth graders who share touching letters about the loss of their own pets. These letters bring such tears to my eyes as I type this that I can hardly see the keyboard.

Here is a summary of the four methods of assessment I've adopted from Jay Haley. Chapters have been written in this book on each of the four topics.

a. **Personality differences**. My Adlerian background led me to revise this to "understanding and respecting personality differences."

b. **Role-perceptions**. This is a basic job description of what I consider my role to be in the relationship and what I consider my partner's to be. Goal alignment is the Adlerian term if we are on the same page in such perceptions.

c. **Communication skills** or lack thereof, as the case may be.

d. **Problem-solving skills**. I remember Carl Rogers (yes, in person—Al Ellis too—again demonstrating I'm old as dirt) saying in a workshop that when he researched couples who divorced, when compared with couples who stayed together, there were no less problems in the latter group. What distinguished that group was a commitment to problem-solving however.

In my own clinical practice, during the first session I often have a couple assess themselves on those four variables using Solution-Focused scaling questions.

The final section of this Match book has featured personal relationship stories from individuals and couples. Some have focused on a particular topic; others have been very candid and personal about their own relationship journey. Intimate stories of being beaten in previous relationships have been shared in the hopes that others will profit from those painful experiences. The paradoxical comment by Carl Rogers that "what is most personal is also the most general" is the background wisdom of such intimate relationship stories in that last chapter.

Epilogue

I began this relationship journey by quoting Kahlil Gibran with the contrasting phrase of "so as love crowns you, so too it crucifies you." You have also been introduced to the following four specific ways Jay Haley suggested for assessing your relationship: understanding and respecting personality differences; role perceptions; communication skills; and problem-solving skills. Each of the four topics featured its own chapter.

Within each section there have been several varieties of activities for you either or alone if your partner is not available or ideally for you two together to complete an activity, to read some of the theory behind the activity, and to apply it toward improving your relationship. You have also been encouraged to discuss some of the activities with a trusted spiritual teacher or mental health counselor, social worker, or psychologist.

A final section featured very personal stories by individuals and couples in which they describe both being crowned as well as crucified by love.

The title of the book used the metaphor of matches and flames. The match book was a double entendre to a literal striking of a match as well as the growing popularity of such internet dating sites as *match.com.*

Three developmental relationship phases were also included in the title: the birth of a relationship (lighting the flame); the building and repair of that relationship (rekindling); and finally in some cases the extinguishing of the flame.

To their credit many states now have pre-marital counseling as suggested and sometimes required prior to marriage. Many of the activities in this book are well suited for both the beginning and the maintaining/repairing phase of courtship.

Let me say a few things about the extinguishing aspect of relationships. With more than one marriage in the West now ending in divorce, there is lots of business for marriage and family counselors like myself. Many couples seek therapy when the house is already going up in flames. Sometimes there is time to salvage it; at other times its like was mentioned by Woody Allen and his "what we have here is a dead shark" way of describing his ending relationship with Diane Keaton in the movie Annie Hall.

Here are some considerations for the extinguishing aspect of a relationship.

1. Consider this reframe of what it means to end a relationship. For example, most often it is defined as being a type of failure. There is generally plenty of blame on the other and/or personal shame at personal shortcomings too.

    Many years ago a colleague was going through his third divorce. It was doubly or in this case, triply hurtful and embarrassing because he was in fact the president of his state's marriage and family professional counselors association. To his credit he was in counseling himself.

    "I wish we could have worked it out" he told his therapist.

"It sounds like you worked it out" was the astute reframing reply.

Thus, painful as it often is, separation and/or divorce are still a problem-solving strategy.

2. Here is an intervention that has often been helpful in my own marriage counseling. It involves changing the focus from an interpersonal between you and your partner to an intrapersonal within just you to you about you contemplation. It sounds like this:

    "I'd like to invite you to change from reflecting on what did or did not happen between you and your partner to focusing just on your own inner feelings . . . I'd like you to reflect on the hopes and dreams you had for yourself within your partnership. I'd like you to consider that often on a deeper level beyond the hurt and anger there is a deeply felt sense of grief. The grief relates to the loss of a dream. There were hopes and wishes you had for yourself in the context of this relationship. And now they are ending."

    At that point the intrapersonal anger between the couple is often replaced by silent or sometimes outright sobs of sadness at the shift of focus to grief and loss.

3. The uncoupling stage is often the most dangerous for physical and/or emotional abuse. Almost 40% of the deaths due to violent behavior to women in the US come at the hands of her partner. Breaking of restraining orders with a murder-suicide is one of the tragic ways of literally ending relationships. Since I have used fire related metaphors in the title, I often tell couples that the fire in your fire place warms and heats your home. The fire in the middle of your living room floor burns it down. On a personal level, a year ago a former college football colleague violated a restraining order between him and his estranged wife by going to her home. There he shot her and then completed a murder-suicide. His son escaped alive after also being shot. Fire is often part of the passion of romance; in stages of disintegration, it's too often on the living room floor. Professional therapy, spiritual counseling, feeling the support of family and friends, and even a personal trip just to literally get away from it all are some of the antidotes to the pain of uncoupling.

4. There are several articles on what we've called "the other F word," that being forgiveness. Personal forgiveness and forgiveness of one's partner can go a long way in both healing the wounds and also making it possible to be friends in the future even after the romance has died.

5. Sublimation is a classic defense mechanism that we describe in psychology. For example, the Taj Mahal was built by a king grieving the loss of his beloved queen. I

had a friend who was a professional country western song writer. Each time she broke up she created a blues ballad. I'd call her after not talking for several months.

"How are you doing?" I'd ask.

"I just wrote another great song" she'd reply.

And so it's just about time to extinguish the flame of this couples match book. Throughout the various articles and stories I've attempted to introduce such Eastern concepts as the eight fold path of right action from a Buddhist perspective.

I'm reminded of the Tarot; I had some colleagues who not only were counselors but who also read Tarot cards. About all I know that is relevant here is that at the beginning of the Tarot journey, the person who is starting on the path of the 78 cards representing a metaphoric journey through life is called "the fool." At the end of the path, the person has hopefully gained greater wisdom and insight, thus becoming "the wise fool."

Certainly there are popular songs with "I've been a fool for love" in the lyrics. My hope is that in a small or large measure throughout the journey of this book that you've become a somewhat wiser fool for love. Savor and cherish the crowns of love's joy and happiness, and at the same time, have the courage to endure the pain and sadness of its crucifixion too.

For a flame to be extinguished, there had to have been a fire in the first place. Sometimes it's the memories of the flame that linger long after the passion has ended.

I bid you adieu having just celebrated my 65th birthday; Of those, 40 have been post-doctorate as a licensed counseling psychologist. And 21 of those have now been writing the 'for couples' quarterly column for *The Family Journal*. The idea for this book was birthed and has taken at least the last ten of those years in completion.

As I imagine a big cake complete with 65 burning candles (not the trick ones that don't go out), I take a deep breath, make a wish, and extinguish all those candles.

My birthday wish for you is that somewhere within the pages of this Couples Match book that a word, a phrase, a concept, an activity, an ah-ha, an insight, a right action, renewed compassion, tons of forgiveness, and a laugh or two maybe lightly sprinkled with some tears also have indeed been gifts for you and your relationship.

On behalf of all of us who have combined the many ingredients that have resulted in this Match Book cake, please enjoy and celebrate with us at the completion of this true labor of love.

As we conclude this journey I conclude with this poem by Constantinos Cavafys called *Ithaca*.

When you set out on your journey to Ithaca,
pray that the road is long,
full of adventure, full of knowledge.
The Lestrygonians and the Cyclops,
the angry Poseidon—do not fear them:

You will never find such as these on your path,
if your thoughts remain lofty, if a fine
emotion touches your spirit and your body.
The Lestrygonians and the Cyclops,
the fierce Poseidon you will never encounter,
if you do not carry them within your soul,
if your soul does not set them up before you.

Pray that the road is long.
That the summer mornings are many, when,
with such pleasure, with such joy
you will enter ports seen for the first time;
. . . visit many Egyptian cities,
to learn and learn from scholars.

Always keep Ithaca in your mind.
To arrive there is your ultimate goal.
But do not hurry the voyage at all.
It is better to let it last for many years;
and to anchor at the island when you are old,
rich with all you have gained on the way,
not expecting that Ithaca will offer you riches.

Ithaca has given you the beautiful voyage.
Without her you would have never set out on the road.
She has nothing more to give you.

And if you find her poor, Ithaca has not deceived you.
Wise as you have become, with so much experience,
you must already have understood what Ithacas mean.
    (retrieved from http://www.poetry-chaikhana.com/C/CavafyConsta/Ithaca.htm,
    Dec. 19, 2012)

So, too, in the process of both being crowned as well as crucified in your heart, hopefully we can also celebrate. It has been the journey that is important in our quest for intimacy.

When all is said and done, the path of the heart is truly the only real dance there is. Celebrate, celebrate, and dance to the many moods of the music of love.

Dr. Daniel Eckstein